# Warsaw Boy

# Warsaw Boy

*A Memoir of a Wartime Childhood*

## ANDREW BOROWIEC

*Edited by Colin Smith*

VIKING
*an imprint of*
PENGUIN BOOKS

940.53 (handwritten, top left)

VIKING

Published by the Penguin Group

Penguin Books Ltd, 80 Strand, London WC2R 0RL, England

Penguin Group (USA) Inc., 375 Hudson Street, New York, New York 10014, USA

Penguin Group (Canada), 90 Eglinton Avenue East, Suite 700, Toronto, Ontario, Canada M4P 2Y3
(a division of Pearson Penguin Canada Inc.)

Penguin Ireland, 25 St Stephen's Green, Dublin 2, Ireland (a division of Penguin Books Ltd)

Penguin Group (Australia), 707 Collins Street, Melbourne, Victoria 3008, Australia
(a division of Pearson Australia Group Pty Ltd)

Penguin Books India Pvt Ltd, 11 Community Centre, Panchsheel Park, New Delhi – 110 017, India

Penguin Group (NZ), 67 Apollo Drive, Rosedale, Auckland 0632, New Zealand
(a division of Pearson New Zealand Ltd)

Penguin Books (South Africa) (Pty) Ltd, Block D, Rosebank Office Park,
181 Jan Smuts Avenue, Parktown North, Gauteng 2193, South Africa

Penguin Books Ltd, Registered Offices: 80 Strand, London WC2R 0RL, England

www.penguin.com

First published 2014
001

Set in 12/14.75pt Bembo Book MT Std
Typeset by Jouve (UK), Milton Keynes
Printed in Great Britain by Clays Ltd, St Ives plc

A CIP catalogue record for this book is available from the British Library

Hardback ISBN: 978-0-670-92242-0
Trade Paperback ISBN: 978-0-241-00451-7

www.greenpenguin.co.uk

For all the Warsaw boys – especially
the ones who never grew up

# Contents

17. The Grey Ranks                                     143

18. Training                                           152

19. Summer in the City                                 164

20. A Mixed Beginning                                  176

21. Stalin's Revenge                                   187

22. Massacre                                           192

23. 'The Worst Street Fighting Since Stalingrad'       210

24. Into the Sewers                                    222

25. Joining the Elite Zośka Battalion                  232

26. The Czerniaków Bridgehead                          238

27. Goliath!                                           250

28. Wounded and Captured                               262

29. Stalag XI-A                                        278

30. The Melancholia Patient                            290

31. The Decision                                       302

32. Spring 1945                                        315

    *Afterwards*                                       339

    *Further Reading*                                  363

# List of Illustrations

## *Section One*

## Section Two

Most of the images are from the archives of the Warsaw Uprising Museum and many are the work of photographer Eugeniusz Lokajski, a former Olympic athlete who once held the world record for throwing the javelin. He was killed towards the end of the fighting when a bomb fell on his house. Other pictures are from the author's collection for photos 1–4, 43–5; the United States Holocaust Memorial Museum in Washington DC for photo 7; the Bundesarchiv for photos 16, 30; the AKG Images for photos 32, 40, 41; and the Imperial War Museum, London for photo 39 (IWM 4489).

N

*Baltic Sea*

**LITHUANIA**

Königsberg

**EAST
PRUSSIA**

Katyn

Rastenburg
(Hitler's HQ, 1944)

**USSR**

Berlin

Treblinka

Poznań
(Where the ambulance
trains coincided)

Warsaw

Łódź
(My birthplace)

Lublin

Breslau

Kielce
(Where I spent
my early years)

Belzec
(Concentration camp where
Maków Jews were murdered)

**GERMANY**

Kraków

Oświęcim
(Auschwitz)

Lwów
(Where I started my war)

Maków Podhalański
(Where I lived
with my father)

Przemyśl
(Where I saw
a fugitive shot)

**CZECHOSLOVAKIA**

**AUSTRIA**

**HUNGARY**

**ROMANIA**

German annexed area
German occupied area
Soviet occupied area

| 0 | 100 miles |
| 0 | 150 km |

Poland under Nazi and Soviet occupation,
September 1939 – June 1941

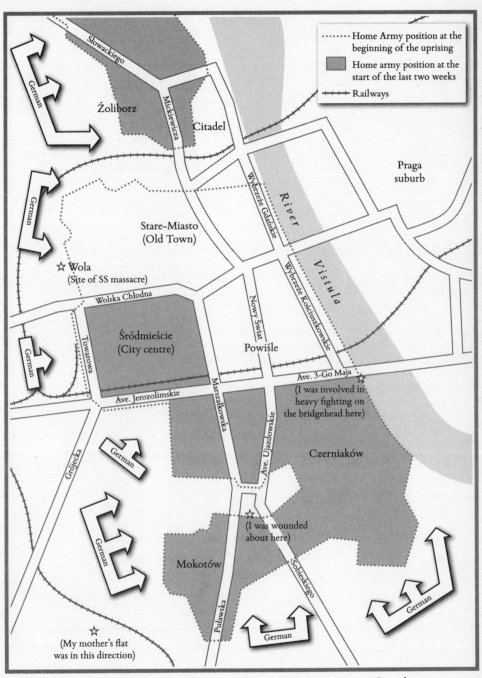

**Legend:**
- ⋯⋯⋯ Home Army position at the beginning of the uprising
- ▓ Home army position at the start of the last two weeks
- ┼┼┼ Railways

Słowackiego

German

Żoliborz

Mickiewicza

Citadel

Praga suburb

Wybrzeże Gdańskie

River

Stare-Miasto (Old Town)

German

Vistula

Wybrzeże Kościuszkowskie

☆ Wola (Site of SS massacre)

Wolska Chłodna

Nowy Świat

Śródmieście (City centre)

Towarowa

German

Powiśle

Ave. 3-Go Maja

☆ (I was involved in heavy fighting on the bridgehead here)

Ave. Jerozolimskie

Marszałkowska

Ave. Ujazdowskie

Czerniaków

Grójecka

German

German

German

☆ (I was wounded about here)

Mokotów

Sobieskiego

German

German

Puławska

☆ (My mother's flat was in this direction)

Positions held during the Warsaw Uprising, 1 August – 2 October 1944

# Author's Note

*Warsaw Boy* was conceived some seventy years ago, when I had just turned sixteen. It was started towards the end of 1944, with notes I pencilled on Red Cross toilet paper while recovering from my wounds in the hospital of a prisoner-of-war camp, in Germany. It was all the captured British medics who were treating me could find for me to write on. As well as my own experiences, these jottings included interviews with other wounded men from the Uprising. My most senior contributor was the lieutenant-colonel who had commanded the northern suburb of Żoliborz and had clung on to the last western stretch of the Vistula that was still in our hands until all hope of rescue from the Russians across the water was lost.

When I arrived in America as a scholarship student, I typed up my notes and filed them away. I intended, one day, to write a full account of my wartime childhood, culminating in its premature coming of age during the Uprising. Somehow these notes survived the constant disruptions that are so often the lot of the career foreign correspondent.

In the early 1970s, I was living in Cyprus when the Hong Kong-based British philanthropist Norman Marsh, whose yacht sometimes anchored off my home near Kyrenia, helped make it possible for me to take some time off journalism and return to my notes.

I chose to write my story in the form of a *very* autobiographical novel in which the fiction was mainly limited to changing a few names. One of the reasons why I approached it this way was because, at that time, memoirs tended to be the prerogative of famous people – newspaper journalists were rarely considered sufficiently well known. The other was because I thought writing my account in the third person might make it easier to bridge the chasm that existed between a middle-aged English-language journalist and the Polish-speaking boy of some thirty years before. When I had reached the point where

I knew I had to stop making changes to my own typewritten script, my wife, Juliet, typed out a final draft of 559 pages – about 140,000 words.

It was never published. Agents and publishers suggested changes I wasn't prepared to make. In the summer of 1974, I very nearly lost the manuscript altogether when we had to temporarily abandon our home in Kyrenia during the Turkish invasion of that year. I put it aside and in between reporting on conflicts in the Middle East and the Balkans – I was last shot at in Croatia, at the age of sixty-three – produced six well-received non-fiction books, including political histories of Yugoslavia and Cyprus. Then, in 2001, the US academic publisher Praeger brought out my *Destroy Warsaw! Hitler's Punishment, Stalin's Revenge*, an historical overview of the Uprising.

Some reviewers – notably the retired-US-officer-turned-historian Robert Forczyk – regretted that I had provided only 'the barest details' of my own experiences during the Uprising. This whetted my appetite to return to an account of the whole story of my war and, from time to time, I tried turning parts of the novel into the memoir I should have written in the first place. Some pages of the original manuscript were missing, but – like many octogenarians, who may not recall all the events that occurred last week – things that happened to me in the 1940s often return with startling clarity. That said, they were usually more memorable.

A couple of years ago, I showed some of these revisions to my friend Colin Smith, a writer and former foreign correspondent on the *Observer*, who, in the words of one reviewer of his work, 'has built an impressive reputation as a military historian'. Colin showed them to Eleo Gordon, Editorial Director at Penguin UK, who liked what she saw and suggested he help me edit my story.

The result is this book.

*Andrew Borowiec*
*Nicosia, November 2013*

# Altengrabow

Bombs had wrecked some of its buildings but the small town's railway tracks ran through the tidied rubble, and the station itself was still functioning. Dead leaves littered the siding we were on. The sky was grey and the air smelled of rain.

'*Los!*' shouted the guard.

It meant 'move' and was a word we would hear a lot.

A man in a French forage cap and 'KG' – for *Kriegsgefangener* (prisoner of war) – stencilled in huge white letters on the back of his greatcoat helped me off the train and into an ambulance. It was already full of bedraggled men. Some of them, like myself, had wounds swathed in dirty paper bandages.

An elderly-looking German holding a French Lebel rifle – booty from 1940, when the Nazis seemed invincible – was the last to get in, slamming the door behind him.

'*Los!*'

The ambulance lurched forward and gathered speed. Through two square windows in the rear door I glimpsed a few trees, the reassuring domesticity of a woman pushing a pram, a male cyclist.

'You're all lucky,' announced our new guard. 'You're going to an international prisoner-of-war camp. Not a concentration camp. You're lucky you're not Jews either.'

A couple of my bandaged companions nodded. The guard's words relaxed us. Unless he was lying through his teeth the nagging uncertainty was over. During our passage in padlocked freight wagons, across Poland's wet flatlands and into Germany, there had been time enough to ponder our fate. Would the Nazis honour the promise they had made in Warsaw to treat us as captured soldiers? It hadn't happened at the beginning of the Uprising when the SS had massa-cred thousands, most of them innocent civilians.

But this guard wasn't SS, just an ordinary Wehrmacht soldier, a bit too old for the uniform he was wearing, which – like his captured rifle – had known better days. And he seemed to want to reassure us that, as long as we behaved, we had nothing to worry about. Some-body offered him a cigarette, the Polish variety, with its dark tobacco that was all you could get during the occupation. The German nod-ded and stuck it into the cuff of his field-grey overcoat.

The ambulance stopped and the guard unlocked the double doors before stepping outside. A group of men in a variety of uniforms appeared and began to help us get out. The first thing I saw was a thick barrier of concertinaed barbed wire, a tower with a searchlight and a row of wooden huts. To my right there was something that looked strangely like a small sports field. I looked again and, yes, that net in the middle could only be for volleyball.

I could walk, but only with a stiff-legged shuffle like an old man's. The left shoe I was wearing on my right leg, just below the bandages, was pinching and painful. Two left shoes were all our nurses had been able to find for me.

Shortly before we surrendered, I had got rid of my jackboots and the Waffen-SS leopard-spotted camouflage smock I had eventually acquired. An enormous stock of these had been looted from a War-saw warehouse and then salvaged when the original recipients had no further use for them. We had worn them with our red and white Pol-ish armbands – just as some of us had painted the same colours around our German helmets – but nobody wanted to risk being captured in them.

'Slowly, slowly and you'll be all right,' said a tall man in halting but serviceable German as he helped me towards one of the huts. My helper was wearing a British battledress with a black cat shoulder badge. (I recognized it from German newsreels and later discovered the cat was the insignia of the 56th (London) Infantry Division.)

Only a couple of my fellow Poles were in uniform; they were older men who had joined the Uprising wearing their carefully pre-served uniforms from 1939. The rest of us had replaced our pilfered camouflage with a bewildering assortment of mismatched civilian clothing collected from the ruins of Warsaw's apartment blocks.

The men in their different uniforms were watching the British medics, for that is what they were, as they helped us in. Among the watchers was a group shod in wooden sabots and speaking French. As I limped past, one of them pointed at me and said to his companions, '*Celui-là, en smoking!*'

And no doubt I was worth a second glance, for above my two left shoes was surely the most incongruous outfit of all: a new and well-fitting satin-lapelled black dinner suit, known in France as *le smoking*. Thus clad, I entered Hitler's Stalag XI-A. All that was missing was a clean shirt, a bow tie and a matching pair of shoes.

This is the story of how I got there.

# 1.   Early Years

*Kielce, central Poland, 1934*

The stables were warm and smelled, not unpleasantly to my six-year-old nostrils, of horse manure. The carriage house next door was even more interesting with its collection of shiny landaus and the smaller yellow carriages used by low-ranking officers. There was the smell of leather, of the liquids used by soldiers to polish the carriages, and the sweat of the soldiers themselves.

My father, Colonel Stanisław Borowiec, was the deputy commander of the 2nd Infantry Division. Only one of the division's regiments was stationed in the town itself. When it paraded down Ulica Sienkiewicza, the town's main street, it was led by a band with a large bass drum mounted on a small cart pulled by a pony. Behind the band marched the infantry, wearing the Verdun pattern steel helmets the French had sold us (along with much else in the way of military equipment). As they passed the reviewing stand they always broke into a goose-step – just like our German neighbours, only better.

'When I grow up, I will be an officer, *n'est-ce pas, Mademoiselle*?'

'You will be what your father tells you to be.'

'But my father is an officer!'

'You'll never be anything until you've learned French. Now silence.'

She always told me to be quiet and to learn French. Other boys didn't have to. But I didn't see much of other boys, anyway. Instead I went for long walks with mademoiselle, who was quite tall for a woman, with blonde hair and narrow feet and hands. Her name was Jadwiga Miączyńska, and after finishing her education in France she had been married to a Polish count. But the marriage was over, and now she was my governess. She was also my father's lover. That had probably always been his intention, but she did her best to keep up appearances.

I listened to her recite French poetry and wrote out French phrases in my copybook. I had to be careful too; she punished me for every mistake and blot by making me copy it all out again, sometimes a hundred times.

But this strictness was confined to her teaching role. She was not a harsh woman. Far from it. 'Mademoiselle' was reserved for the French lessons. Most of the time she liked me to call her 'Mateczka' – meaning 'Little Mother', or perhaps 'Little Mummy', for it is very affectionate – and I was happy to do it. My real mother was Zofia Arct, the daughter of a senior military doctor who had retired with the rank of general. My father was about twenty years her senior and had been married once before. The previous year, when I was five, she had left him for the much taller and much younger Intelligence Corps captain who lived in the apartment above us.

As the 'guilty party' of the divorce, the Court had restricted Zofia's access to me to two visits a month. They were scheduled to take place on the 3rd and the 18th, were not to exceed three hours, and had to take place at my father's home. She was not allowed to take me out without my father's permission, which was never granted.

I found these encounters difficult. Sometimes my mother was a bit tearful. Mostly she smiled and tried to crack jokes with me, but I was a solemn little boy, awkward and stiff, uncertain how to behave. The truth was that I did not know her very well, certainly not as well as I knew my father and Mateczka, and I did not want to offend them by being too friendly.

As things turned out, it soon became impossible for her to keep even the allotted visiting hours because her new husband had been made a defence attaché. She accompanied him on his postings to various European capitals, where he worked from the Polish embassy. There was, however, a plus side to this because, no doubt racked by guilt, she would return with expensive foreign toys: there were clockwork motorboats that moved fast enough in the bathwater to create a miniature wake; solid little German cars that never fell off the table when you played with them because of a clever rubber contraption fitted underneath; and, best of all, metal building sets with which I constructed barracks and fortresses for the tin and lead soldiers that had gradually replaced my cardboard cut-outs.

My soldiers were my pride and joy. I had at least a hundred of them, and they came in various sizes and nationalities. There were British grenadiers in their red tunics, Uhlan cavalry and some white-robed Abyssinian warriors who were presumably inspired by the ones that had defeated the Italians at Adowa, in 1895. (This humiliation was currently being avenged by Mussolini's blackshirts with their aircraft and poison gas.) My favourite were the Polish light lancers who had fought in Napoleon's *Grande Armée* – to be exact, *Le 1er régiment de chevau-légers lanciers polonais de la Garde impériale*. But I never grew tired of playing with any of them. They were the standard, indeed, the much anticipated gift for both Christmas and my name day – the feast day of the Catholic saint after whom you were named and, in Poland, celebrated with an enthusiasm that greatly exceeded the mere happenstance of a birthday.

My father's name day was usually much more exciting than my own. The regimental band would line up outside our windows and play the Radetzky March and other lively military airs. It was almost as good as the formal parade on Constitution Day, in May, and Armistice Day, in November.

Most mornings Colonel Borowiec led a group of officers out riding, usually accompanied by a few prominent civilians. Sometimes there was a lady or two in the party wearing jodhpurs and long shiny boots, no doubt dismaying elderly onlookers by eschewing the long skirts required to ride side-saddle. I remember a soldier groom invariably made a point of helping a boyish countess into the saddle, to her obvious displeasure. The barracks were near the centre of the town but the riders showed no hesitation about trotting down the main street; traffic was sparse and horse-drawn cabs easily outnumbered the occasional automobile.

One day we moved out of the barracks complex, and the comfortable married quarters assigned to Colonel Borowiec, into a quiet apartment some way from the centre of town. A few days before, I had seen my father for the last time in his full dress uniform with sabre and medals as he prepared to take the salute in a senior officer's farewell parade. I did not approve of this move. There would be no more regimental bands playing outside our windows. Worst of all, no more rifles and uniforms.

'Mateczka, will my father wear a civilian suit every day?'

'*Oui, mon chéri.*'

'But why?'

'Because the government doesn't want him in the army any more.'

From scraps of overheard conversation I learned that some of the officers who used to ride with my father would look the other way if they passed him in the street. All this was utterly bewildering for a small boy who was accustomed to his parent being treated with the greatest respect. It was several years before I understood enough of Poland's pre-war politics to be able to piece together the reasons for Colonel Borowiec's premature transfer to the reserves.

It occurred in the spring of 1935, shortly after the death of Marshal Józef Piłsudski. In 1920 the marshal had been the architect of a rare Polish victory over the Russians, when Bolshevik invaders did their best to strangle at birth the independent Poland that had emerged from the post-war ashes of the Czarist Russian and Austro-Hungarian empires. Not surprisingly, Piłsudski became a popular figure. Six years later he came to power as the leader of a military junta that, in the nature of these things, declared itself to be the true guardians of the national flame amidst a sea of corrupt politicians. As dictatorships go, it was a benign one – nothing like what was about to happen with our German neighbours – and leading Polish Jews were among his greatest supporters.

But the army itself was divided between pro- and anti-Piłsudski factions. Officers like my father, who had fought during the 1914–18 war in regular units of the old Austro-Hungarian Army, rather than in the marshal's Polish legions, tended to belong to the latter. When the great man died, the anti-Piłsudski faction thought their moment had come. Some even envisaged a general election and the restoration of parliamentary rule, which would show that Poland was no different from France and Britain and the other democracies of western Europe. But the pro-Piłsudski clan rallied and purged the army of these dangerous elements. My father, who had expected to end his career with the rank of major general commanding a division, was among them.

For a long time he stayed at home, reading his books, playing his violin and piano and speaking to Mateczka in rapid French so that there was little chance I would understand what they were saying. He now had time to take me out for walks and even insisted on holding my hand. Apart from the acute embarrassment this caused, it took me a while to get used to the idea that the large hand enclosing mine was no longer needed to return the respectful salutes of passing soldiers. The colonel was just another anonymous civilian; his uniform with the silver stars on its epaulettes was hanging, mothballed, in a wardrobe.

We no longer enjoyed our own intimate contact with soldiers, inhaling their unique odour of sweat, tobacco, boot polish and the grease they put on their bayonets so that they slid more easily from their scabbards. When they marched through the city centre we were reduced to the spectator status of other mere mortals.

We had obviously come a long way down in the world.

Then my father was given a job to do, and things began to get a little better.

Hitler had been in power for over two years, and it was becoming apparent that Russia might no longer be our major enemy. The main issue with our western neighbour was over the Baltic port of Danzig which, thanks to the League of Nations, had been under de facto Polish control since 1919 as a 'Free City'. The trouble was that most of its inhabitants were German speakers and now appeared to be ardent Nazis, all clamouring in the name of natural justice for their native city to be subsumed into the Reich.

Poland began to prepare for war. Among its priorities were schemes to improve its readiness for aerial warfare, with civil defence and basic flying training, and these schemes provided opportunities for recently retired officers. My father was given an office in a new building outside Kielce's city limits with a chauffeur-driven car, which he also learned to drive himself, to take him to and from it. His duties also took him to various airfields, and sometimes Mateczka and myself were allowed to accompany him. My favourite outing, about an hour's drive away, was a visit to one of the gliding schools he regularly inspected.

It was an exciting spectacle. The launch point was the brow of a hill, and I was usually allowed to get close enough to the cockpit to observe the nervous-looking student pilot clutching the glider's steering bar.

'*Naciagaj!* (Heave!)' Two long lines of sturdy peasants, each holding on to a long rope, started running down the hill.

Then, and it was a matter of exquisite timing, the instructor decided when the ropes were taut enough and shouted, '*Pusc!* (Let go!)'

The small glider, intended to give the student at the controls his first sensation of flying something, was catapulted into the air, only to fall gently into a field a few hundred yards below. Horses were then employed to drag the glider back to the hilltop, where it was prepared for the next flight. I was old enough to find this mixture of horses and flying machines a little incongruous.

'Does one always have to fly a glider before flying a real plane, Papa?'

'In some countries one does.'

'Why?'

'Because it's a cheaper way to learn how to fly. Real planes cost much more money.'

So this was how I learned that we were the kind of country that had to train its pilots the cheap way. I was always trying to assess Poland's worth as a military power, constantly seeking some reassurance that our forces were somewhere near the top of the European military league table along with Germany and Italy. If the available evidence did not match my expectations, I became quite downcast. The horse-drawn machine-gun carriages that rattled over Kielce's cobblestones were bad news. So were horses and wooden gliders. When a cinema newsreel revealed that young Germans were also flying gliders, I was considerably comforted and moved Poland up a few notches.

★

It was about this time that my father decided that Mateczka's private tutoring was no longer enough and, though she would continue to give me French lessons, I should go to school. I was eight years old by now and most children my age already had two years of formal education behind them. But which school? My mother had recently given birth to my half-brother, whom I had not yet met, but my upbringing was that of an only child with a private tutor.

I had been an avid reader from an early age. My father was advised that, if he could afford it, the best thing for me was a local private school. After preliminary tests revealed I was at least a year ahead of my age group, I started in the second grade, where I was the youngest child in the class.

I was outfitted at Baum's, a Jewish clothes shop on Kielce's main street, where the management had put up a large red and black wall poster depicting the grinning skull of a German helmeted death's head hovering over a vulnerable-looking map of Poland. Here I was bought a leather satchel for my schoolbooks, a blue serge uniform and a four-cornered cap with the school badge on the front.

Once inside, the school building smelled mainly of floor polish. New pupils were immediately directed by the caretaker to the cloakroom where we were each allotted a locker. Shoes were removed, put in the locker and replaced by the soft slippers that were stored there. When it was time to go home the process would be reversed. I noticed that the teachers were not required to wear slippers.

For the first year school made little impression on me apart from fostering a nagging sense of injustice because, as well as the homework set by my teachers, I was still required to take French lessons with Mateczka. In class I was usually in the top five for most subjects, but I was a high-spirited child and the teachers sometimes complained to my father about my boisterous behaviour – talking in class, and so on. This would lead to certain consequences at home.

'*Je ne serai jamais méchant à l'école.* I will never be naughty at school.'

I wrote this out hundreds of times in both languages. The long columns of my punishment phrase would remind me of columns of marching soldiers. It was not much consolation.

There were five Jewish children in my class – two girls and three boys. Twice a week a priest in a long black cassock came to give us religious instruction. When this happened the Jewish children would gather up their books to spend the next hour in the recreation room. Like all schools in Poland we had lessons on Saturday mornings, during the Jewish Sabbath. The Jewish children, who all came from the kind of families that were well integrated, attended Saturday lessons as well. But afterwards, they stayed behind for their own prayers and religious instruction from a rabbi.

Pre-war Poland had the largest Jewish community in Europe. At just over three million it was about a tenth of the total population. Some had arrived during the Russian pogroms of the previous century, but many had been in the country for generations. Poland's reputation for granting asylum to persecuted Jewry started in the Middle Ages; by the sixteenth century, scholars were referring to the Jewish culture that blossomed in the Polish-Lithuanian Commonwealth as the *Paradisus Judaeorum*.

Quite early in life I learned to distinguish between three different categories of Jews. There were ultra-Orthodox Hasidim who lived in the crumbling wooden houses of the poorest neighbourhoods where, in summer, the streets stank of open sewers. Adult males were always bearded and, whatever the weather, they wore long black coats. Their wives dressed in voluminous skirts and completely covered their heads in kerchiefs. The women in some sects were rumoured to have shaved their heads so that they were entirely bald, though indoors they were said to wear wigs on special occasions. Boys my age never ventured out without skullcaps and, like their fathers, had some of their hair twisted and curled into the side locks they called *pejsy*. They had a few words of Polish but generally spoke their own language. Most Poles insisted that the Hasidim spoke something called 'Jewish' but it was, of course, the Germanic-rooted Yiddish that was the lingua franca of the Jews throughout central Europe.

Then there were the Jews who dressed normally and seemed to own most of the shops in town, ran the real-estate agencies that helped people find apartments, and arranged almost everything that had to be arranged. Yiddish was probably still their preferred language but their Polish was usually fluent, if sometimes heavily accented.

Finally, there were Jews who were just like everybody else. Some of these would come to our apartment to play bridge with my father. Among them was our doctor. There were, I understood, even Jews who went to church rather than a synagogue. So all these people were Jews? It was confusing. Was it a nationality or a religion? The Jews were asking themselves the same question and demonstrating their conclusions on the street.

The word that dominated their debate was 'Zionism'. I had no idea what it meant, but I saw it everywhere. It was in newspaper head-lines, daubed in huge letters on the walls of Kielce – where at least one third of its citizens were Jewish. Sometimes it would be preceded by the words: 'Down with . . .' This was the work of the socialist General Jewish Labour Bund, who utterly rejected the idea of estab-lishing a Jewish nation state in British Mandate Palestine (even if the British would let them) on the grounds that all European Jewry might be expelled there, whether they wished to go or not. Instead they preached the virtues of assimilation. They had the support of the mainstream Polish left-wing parties – though in some cases some-what tepidly, since the prevailing anti-Semitism did not exactly make it a vote winner.

Opposing them were the militant Zionists of Vladimir Jabotin-sky's Betar movement, who despised any idea of assimilation as a lost cause and wanted to establish a Jewish nation state. They marched through the streets in step, wearing bright blue uniforms, and some-times indulged in fisticuffs with their co-religionists in the Bund. 'Jews to Palestine!' they yelled. The same chant was parroted by the kind of rabidly anti-Semitic Polish nationalists who were in complete agreement with this slogan because they had no wish to assimilate the Jews. As far as the Jabotinskyites in Betar were concerned, this was excellent news. Extreme Catholic Polish nationalists only proved their prescient point. Nowhere were the Jews more assimilated than in Germany, they argued, and look what was already happening there. One way or another, the Nazis would export their doctrine of hate. A pogrom was on the way, insisted the Jabotinskyites, perhaps the biggest pogrom in European Jewry's blood-soaked history, and the only sure way to avoid it was to get to Palestine.

I was a child, blissfully unaware of the pros and cons of Zionism. I was not even sure where Palestine was, though I suspected it was somewhere sunny and overseas. What I did find out was that, if you wanted to cause a rumpus, all you had to do was run along a school corridor yelling at the top of your voice: 'Jews to Palestine!'

My headmaster was understandably careful of his school's reputation as the kind of place where assimilated Jewish parents would be happy to pay the fees, safe in the knowledge that their offspring would not be exposed to the slogans of the street. Obviously there could be no doubt where I had acquired my views. I was, after all, the son of a retired colonel. What could you expect? How was the headmaster to know that my father was by no means always typical of his tribe: his broadly liberal views not only championed the agrarian reformists of the Polish Peasants' Party but were entirely in sympathy with Piłsudski's pro-Jewish platform. Summoned to the school to collect me as soon as possible, he managed to persuade the headmaster that my slogan shouting was a childish prank and certainly not something that had been imbibed at home.

I was reprieved and allowed to remain at the school, though there seems to have been a mutual agreement that a stern punishment was in order. Certainly writing lines was not considered appropriate. When I got home I received three stinging strokes across my bottom from my father's riding crop. As I grew older these beatings became more frequent. I was usually made to receive them lying face down on my bed, though there was none of the bare-buttock flogging popular among the more exclusive British schools of the day.

One Sunday, shortly after my disgrace, I heard the dreaded word 'Palestine' again. I was sipping a hot chocolate in the high-ceilinged salon of a house that felt more like a palace than a home. Entering it with my father, our overcoats were not taken by a maid (as they would have been in our own apartment) but by a liveried footman. We were visiting the wealthy Jewish owner of a furniture factory, a supporter of the Bund.

'Palestine is a mistake,' he told my father. 'Our place is here.'

'Yes, your place is here,' my father agreed. 'But all those who want to stay in this country should become a part of it. You either belong or you don't. And if you don't belong, isn't it better to go where you think you might?'

'It is not always easy to belong,' said our host.

Then they noticed I was listening and switched to German.

My father could also get along in Yiddish. Part of my paternal grandfather's career in the Polish tributary of the Austro-Hungarian postal service had been spent in a small town with a large Jewish population. His two sons, my father and my Uncle Józef, had picked up the language then. My father's service in the Austro-Hungarian Army, where he started as a teenaged cadet, had given him fluent German. He spoke good French, and his Italian was passable. (After being twice wounded on the Russian front, he had ended the First World War in Northern Italy, fighting the Italians and their British allies around Caporetto, in what is now Slovenia.) He could play the violin, pick out a lot of Chopin on the piano, make interesting drawings and carve small heads in soft wood – one was of a bishop – which he fitted on the top of his walking sticks.

He was a cultivated man with a good library, but his formal education had not gone beyond the level required for officer cadet training and he always resented the way his parents had found the money to send his elder brother Józef to university. As a result, my uncle was now a wealthy lawyer living in the eastern city of Lwów, whereas my father was an axed colonel with a job in civil defence. Later in life I began to realize that my father had always been ambivalent about his military career. Once the 1919–20 campaign against the Russian Bolsheviks was over, he had often found peacetime soldiering, in the first sovereign Polish army for over a century, with all its infighting and politicking, a tedious business. Jadwiga Miączyńska, his lover and my French tutor, obviously sympathized.

'Perhaps one day you'll be like your father,' she once suggested.

'You mean an army officer, Mateczka?'

'*Non, mon petit.* An intelligent, talented man.'

Apparently the two did not always go together.

Poland is an old country, but we were living in its latest reincarnation: a flag-conscious, early-twentieth-century nation state midwifed by the Treaty of Versailles, and apparently in need of careful nursing. Every Saturday morning there was a school ceremony where the boys from the senior class gripped all four sides of a large Polish flag while the rest of us arranged ourselves around them and sang a song that included the words: 'We are the future of the nation.'

For the first time in my life I had a friend, a boy from my class who was slightly older than me. On Saturday afternoons, after school, we were allowed to play at each other's homes. Sometimes I went to his house but more often he came to mine, because it was a bit bigger and we were not under the feet of adults. I also had more toys, and my friend liked to play with my lead soldiers. Some boys, of course, lived in much bigger homes and had many more toys. But the only time I was envious was when they had more soldiers.

Then my circle of small friends expanded. Despite some misgivings, my father allowed me to join the junior wing of the school's Boy Scout troop, along with most of the other boys in my class. Poland had the first scouting movement outside the British Empire, and from the beginning its ethos was stridently nationalistic. The Polish scouting oath pledges: 'It is my sincere wish to serve God and Poland with the whole of my life, to offer my willing help to others and to obey the Scout and Guide law.'

In 1910 a Polish language edition of Baden Powell's *Scouting for Boys* was available in Warsaw, two years after it had been published in London and eight years before Poland regained its independence. The founders of the Polish Scouting and Guiding Association, always known by its Polish initials ZHP (*Związek Harcerstwa Polskiego*), never made the slightest pretence that ZHP was merely about clean living and campfire singalongs. By happy coincidence the closest Polish translation of the movement's internationally famous 'Be Prepared' motto is '*Czuwaj*', the watchword of the medieval Polish knights who guarded against Mongol invasion and a word with a certain resonance in the Polish psyche.

For me it was all very exciting; it was the nearest I had yet come to anything vaguely military. Unfortunately, my father did not entirely share my enthusiasm for this British import. His main objection was that I was far too young. Some of its meetings went on way past my bedtime, and I was forbidden to attend them. As a result, I did not learn all the things the others were learning concerning tracking, tying knots and the ability to make a kind of bread over an open fire using only flour and water.

But shortly before the start of the long summer holidays my disappointment was overshadowed by some much more disturbing news. Once the school term was over my father would not have to work any more. We were going to move out of Kielce and live somewhere else.

'But what will you do, Papa?'

'I'll work in the garden, sketch, do my carvings. Perhaps I'll even write something.'

What garden? It seemed to me like the waste of a man's life.

## 2. A Mountain Town

*Maków Podhalański*

'Papa, will there be any soldiers in our new town?'

'No, thank God. But there's a river, and mountains and fresh air. And you will learn to ski.'

There *were* soldiers, four of whom were lieutenant-colonels, but they were all retired, as were the senior civil servants who lived nearby. Maków (we rarely used its full name) is a Carpathian mountain town not far from the Slovak part of what was then the Czechoslovak border. Some kind of hamlet had probably existed in the valley for centuries, but it did not become a town until the railroad first reached it in the 1880s.

Fifty years later, the population was about 3,000 strong of whom perhaps a little over 200 were Jews. There was a central marketplace with a statue of the Madonna, a long main street lined with two-storey houses and, slightly above it all, at the lower end of a pine-covered slope, a pretty cream-coloured church built by locals who had emigrated to America. Dotting the slopes above it were the white-painted peasant cottages of many of its congregation. To the east, built on an incline dominating the river valley, was a hostelry for the exclusive use of vacationing employees of the state railway. Its existence was the only reason why express trains from Warsaw and Kraków deigned a brief halt at our humble country station.

Finding the right house had taken some time and several visits. Accompanied by Mateczka, we drove to the town somewhat jerkily, with my father at the wheel of his car, the chauffeur having been given a couple of days off. We always stayed at the same small Jewish-owned hotel where, for breakfast, I was served coffee mixed

with beaten egg yolk and sugar. I thought it was about the best thing
I had ever tasted.

Otherwise these were tedious expeditions for a small boy. The
choice seemed endless. There were dilapidated houses in what looked
like huge parks, and small uncomfortable houses with small gardens.
Several times we found ourselves driving up to some hut in one of
the clearings above the church.

'I could make something of it,' my father would say.

'*Mais non*,' protested Mateczka. 'There isn't even a place to install
a bathroom!'

Much to her relief he eventually settled on a house with all the
necessary plumbing. The house was so new, it was not yet completed; there were painters and other workmen, sacks of cement in
the garden, and the smell of fresh paint was everywhere. It was a simple,
unpretentious two-storey building with a large basement occupied
by a young caretaker and his wife. At this point the garden had hardly
been planted, but it looked like a good place to play games with Mik,
the red setter puppy my father had recently given me.

The following morning, while my father was busy with the build-
ers, I took Mik for a walk. He was unaccustomed to a lead and eager
to explore, dragging me along after him. We were stopped by a small
boy who was cracking a horsewhip.

'You're a Jew!' the boy shouted.

'I'm not,' I replied, perplexed.

'Then cross yourself to prove it,' he challenged, triumphantly
cracking his whip.

But this was impossible, because I needed both hands for the leash,
and the puppy dragged me onwards before I could think of a reply.

We arrived at the central square, where I saw a peasant cart with a
wicker frame pulled by two horses and moving at a fast clip. On the
front seat, next to the driver, was an altar boy in full regalia periodically ringing a bell. On the back seat sat a cassocked priest. As his
carriage drew level to them almost all the nearby pedestrians dropped
to their knees and crossed themselves. I had never seen anything like
it before and had no idea how to react.

'That was a priest going to see a dying man,' my father explained later.

'But why was the altar boy ringing the bell?'

'Because when a priest goes to the bedside of a sick person he carries the Host with him.'

'Do they do that in big towns too?'

'Yes, but they don't advertise it.'

'Why not?'

'People are too busy; there is too much traffic in the streets. Here, things are different.'

'Should I have knelt like everybody else?'

'One always kneels before Jesus Christ.'

Yet I had never seen my father in church. When I went to Mass with Mateczka on Sundays he never came with us. He said that he listened to the service on the radio, or he communed with God privately. I found it quite confusing. Later I realized his reluctance to attend Mass was probably because the new colonel and his son's handsome governess were already the subject of considerable gossip.

Maków was not without interest to a small boy. Tumbling down its mountain backdrop came the Skawa River, fairly shallow in places but cold even in high summer. Nonetheless, this is where my father taught me to swim. And it is where I fleetingly caught a glimpse of Mateczka's breasts as she changed into one of the daring new two-piece costumes in the secluded, sandy bend we had occupied.

My father began an ambitious programme of clearing the garden, sometimes assisted at his weeding by Mateczka, who always wore long white gloves for the occasion. The heavy work was done by a hired labourer who lunched in the shade of an apple tree on hunks of bread and slices of sausage washed down with a small bottle of vodka. The bottle was corked and, since he was without a corkscrew, he removed it by rhythmically tapping the bottom of the bottle with the heel of his hand until enough of the cork had emerged to pull it out. It was a trick I never tired of watching.

In addition to my toy soldiers I had begun to collect stamps. I was reading more than ever, devouring books from a range of authors, including translations of the westerns written by the German writer

Karl May, one of the most popular writers in Continental Europe. Albert Einstein read his adventure stories of Old Shatterhand and his faithful Apache sidekick, Winnetou. So, apparently, did Adolf Hitler.

Much of my father's military library had ended up in the attic of the new house, along with a trophy Russian rifle, slightly rusted, and a sabre with 'Honour and Country' engraved on its blade. But as far as I was concerned the best items in this treasure trove were the back issues of an illustrated military quarterly with page after page of compelling black and white photographs: shell-pocked landscapes; the recent and not-so-recent dead; determined-looking machine-gun teams; artillerymen with spent shell cases piled around their guns; horse-drawn ambulances; and muddy infantry staring defiantly into the camera from waterlogged trenches.

I suppose it would be safe to say that when I arrived at my new school my reading ability was above average and my knowledge of military affairs unusually precocious. The school itself was a shock. Instead of the elegant parquet flooring, there were rough wooden boards. One was not required to leave one's shoes in the dressing room. Indeed, there were no dressing rooms. The desks were simple and not very comfortable to sit at; some classrooms even had old-fashioned benches.

Nor did I take easily to my classmates. Most were boys from the surrounding villages who spoke with an accent very different to my own. They were poorly dressed and constantly mocked me as some kind of Little Lord Fauntleroy. My only friends were boys from Maków itself. These were the sons of shopkeepers, the stationmaster and the manager of the hotel for railway employees. Unlike their country cousins, they vaguely resembled the children I knew at my private school in Kielce.

'This school is a mistake,' I overheard Mateczka telling my father one evening. 'He cannot continue.'

'When I was a child I went to a similar school,' he said. 'It didn't prevent me from becoming a reasonable human being.'

'You are keeping him here out of sheer selfishness, because you want his company. He could go to one of those Jesuit boarding schools.'

With an adult's understanding I now realize that she was giving my father his cue to reply, 'No, I'm keeping him here because I want the company of his French tutor.' But he simply chose to say, 'He's not going to any boarding school right now.'

Mateczka sighed. My father's choice of school was bound to win the day.

Perhaps she thought that urging him to send me away would increase her prospects of becoming Madame Borowiec in a household where she could hardly be the governess of an absent child. It was not long after the move to Maków that I became aware of a certain aura of wickedness about our household. With her airs, her accent, her hats and gloves and her highly suspect relationship with my father, my beloved Mateczka was the small town's scarlet woman. The oblique remarks and knowing giggles of my contemporaries brought blushes to my cheeks and even reduced me to tears. I would have given anything to be part of a normal household. To be able to roam for hours with the other boys. Not to know that, behind my back, my father was referred to as 'the mad colonel with the red dog'.

At my new school I was considered a difficult child and consigned to an unruly class terrorized by an unbalanced teacher named Chrzan (the Polish word for horseradish). In 1783, some two centuries before most of the rest of Europe, Poland had become the first nation in the world to ban corporal punishment in schools. Horseradish did his best to circumvent this. A tall, stooped figure with puffed-out cheeks and a hawk nose, he had an odd gait and ambled through the crowded corridors cunningly distributing sly pokes and blows with his walking stick.

Classes often began with the kind of irrational orders that recruits in boot camp learn to expect from their instructors.

'Empty all your pockets!' came the command.

Demurely the girls would reveal little more than combs, neatly folded handkerchiefs and perhaps the odd pressed flower. The boys' desks were soon covered with the objects that, by some uncharted magnetic force, attach themselves to the prepubescent male: rusty penknives, dice, tangles of string, used postage stamps in crumpled envelopes and objects that defied immediate identification.

Triumphantly, Horseradish would confiscate everything except combs, pocket money and the rare handkerchief. We all firmly believed that he gave these treasures to his own three children, who were at senior school.

My second year in Maków saw the Munich Agreement, Prime Minister Neville Chamberlain's famous 'peace for our time', with a humiliated Czechoslovakia conceding territory to Germany. Even Poland took advantage by sending its tanks to 'liberate' the 200,000 or so Polish speakers living in the long-disputed Czech-Polish border territory, not all that far away from Maków. It was hardly Poland's finest hour, and Dr Goebbels' propaganda ministry exploited it as proof that Germany was not the only nation that felt it had legitimate grievances about the size of Czechoslovakia.

At school we were all hoping that the Czechs would resist, and there would be a proper war – but, unlike the Poles, the Czechs do not fight for hopeless causes. This explains why Prague's belle époque architecture has outlived its Warsaw equivalent.

At home we had cold war. Mateczka and my father were no longer speaking. When I was old enough to understand I realized that it was because he refused to marry her. In those days, people set such store by marriage. Decadent bohemians living happily in sin risked eternal damnation. At the time I had no idea why they were always shouting at each other. All I knew was that when she eventually packed up her lovely things and left, she was as heartbroken as I was.

This must have been about the beginning of 1939, and she was almost immediately replaced by a woman my father had found by placing classified advertisements in certain newspapers: 'Retired colonel, divorced, seeks live-in governess/housekeeper for his ten-year-old son. Good salary. Sundays off. Must be a woman of good character.'

Ada (short for Władysława) was a bit younger than Mateczka, probably in her late thirties, but not as good looking. Her hair was neither brown nor blonde, but somewhere in between. She was rounder in the face, shorter, a little plumper. Nor did she speak French. Speaking French was an aristocratic accomplishment, and

I suppose her background was lower middle class. But she did speak good German, because her family came from that western part of Poland where it was widely spoken.

Naturally, I did not regard Ada as a fit replacement for Mateczka. Even if her predecessor had not existed, I would have resented Ada's unaccustomed insistence that I return my toy soldiers to barracks and fold my clothes up; these were prissy German obsessions, I told myself, unworthy of a true Pole. But Ada was no more German than I was. Her first language was Polish. Being an intelligent person, she had picked up the language because it was widely spoken in the area where she lived. She was not what Hitler had begun to refer to as *Volksdeutsch*, describing those communities of linguistic and cultural Germans who found themselves marooned by some historical misfortune (usually to do with the 1919 Treaty of Versailles), living outside the present boundaries of the Reich. Czechoslovakia's Sudetenland Germans, now recently gathered to the Fatherland, had been one example. Danzig Germans, still clamouring for their Führer to set them free, were another.

Whenever Berlin launched fresh political or territorial demands against Poland, the matter was formally discussed at school. The authorities appeared to regard it as part of our civic education.

'We will give them nothing. Nothing!' promised Horseradish in one of his patriotic rants.

'Can't we give them anything at all?' one boy, our solitary peacenik, once asked.

'A piece of red-hot iron!' screamed Horseradish. 'That's what we can give them.' And he punctuated each word by caning his desk with his walking stick. 'Red – *thwack!* – hot – *thwack!* – iron – *thwack!*'

By now I had become an altar boy and sang in the church choir. One of several boy sopranos, on two occasions I was even permitted to sing solo. And I had soon memorized all the responses to the Latin Mass. At home, in the privacy of my room, I would recite both roles.

'*Introibo ad altare Dei*,' I would say, doing my best to imitate the deep baritone of our priest.

Then, in my natural treble, came the response, '*Ad Deum qui laeti-ficat iuventutem meam.*'

'The trouble with this household is that they're godless,' I once overheard one of our maids tell a friend. 'It's a wonder that child has any religion at all.'

It was about this time that Poland was celebrating its latest saint and national hero. Pope Pius XI had canonized the seventeenth-century martyr Andrzej Bobola, a Jesuit priest tortured to death by Cossack rebels during their uprising against the Polish-Lithuanian Commonwealth. In June 1938, his remains arrived in Warsaw from Rome, where they had rested since 1923 (ever since the Soviet author-ities had handed them over as a token of their gratitude for recent Vatican aid during a famine). The corpse was said to be in a remark-able state of preservation, adding proof of divine favour and proving a source of amazement, for we altar boys were all well versed in the injuries inflicted on the martyr during his last hours: his body had been whipped bloody then burned with torches; an eye removed; needles pushed under his fingernails; and, finally, his tongue cut out because he insisted on praying out loud for his tormentors' deliver-ance.

All this was very relevant. Spain was in the throes of a merciless civil war, and there were widespread reports of atrocities against its clergy. I read all about it in the *Catholic Guide*. Spanish boys my own age were beaten by the Communists for trying to rescue the Host from a burning church. And priests, Bobola-like, prayed for the for-giveness of the firing squads about to send them to a better world. Fortunately, the godless ones were receiving their just deserts. Photo-graphs in the *Guide* showed priests in a liberated town blessing marching troops and a general kissing a grateful bishop's hand.

'The Communists are losing the war in Spain, *n'est-ce pas, Papa?*'

'They aren't really Communists.'

'But they're against the Church and God, and they're killing priests!'

'It's not that simple. One day you'll understand.'

What was there to understand? Our fellow Catholics were under

attack. The barbarians were at the gate. True, there were some confusing developments. Naturally Russia was giving some assistance to
the Communists. But even more obvious was the support being given
by the Germans and their Italian allies to the side that was protecting
the Church. They had not only sent aircraft and tanks to Franco's
insurgents (there always seemed to be pictures of Heinkel biplane
bombers) but also the men to operate them.

'They're practising for the war they're prepared to start unless
everybody gives them what they want,' said my father.

# 3. The Last Days of Peace

By the spring of 1939, the imminent prospect of war with Germany dominated all our lives. Newspapers, cinema newsreels and radio bulletins rarely spoke of anything else. At my school even the poorest children contributed to the fund to buy a heavy machine gun for a distant regiment we had never seen. Schoolchildren and factory workers in the bigger cities were photographed handing over brand-new tanks and anti-tank guns that had been built with the funds they had raised.

In March, Hitler tore up what remained of the Munich Agreement. The Wehrmacht rolled unopposed into what was left of Czechoslovakia. From the balcony of my room I looked out on to the forested slopes that marked our frontier with what Germany now called the Protectorate of Bohemia and Moravia.

Previously, it had always been assumed that, when the war came, the fighting would be on Poland's western frontier with Germany and would then become even more remote as we pushed the Nazis back towards Berlin. Maków would be a backwater. But I soon realized that the occupation of Czechoslovakia had opened up some interesting possibilities. As well as attacking from the west, the Germans could launch a simultaneous strike across our southern border, if they felt like it. Suddenly we were close to a front line.

Almost every day now there were Polish troop movements through Maków and its surrounding area. Army trains rattled through our little station night and day. Some even stopped there. Sometimes their loads looked a little desperate – I saw freight wagons loaded with peasant horse carts, apparently commandeered for transport – but others did not disappoint. Once, I was delighted to discover an armoured artillery train tucked away on a siding, its locomotive puffing steam and obviously ready to move away at a moment's notice. Partly shrouded by tarpaulins, the barrels of huge guns (to my eyes

big enough for battleships) protruded from steel turrets. A freight
wagon at the end of the train even carried two small tanks. An officer
with a captain's insignia, and wearing a black beret, patrolled the
tracks, stiff backed and proud.

Elated, I rushed home to tell my father what I had seen and found
him carving one of his little wooden heads. Some of them were quite
amusing: a mitred bishop; a Prussian soldier with spiked *Pickelhaube*;
a skullcapped Orthodox Jew; and a Devil, who bore an uncanny
resemblance to its creator.

'An armoured train can really do a lot of damage to the enemy,
*n'est-ce pas, Papa*?'

'But it is also a slave to the railroad tracks. Once the tracks are
destroyed it can't move.'

This brutal logic dismayed me. 'Then why do we have armoured
trains?'

'Because we are the victims of an outdated military doctrine.'

'But why don't they change the doctrine, Papa?'

'Because people in power usually don't like change.'

Doctrine was a word I would hear a lot. It usually happened at week-
ends when I would accompany my father on walks with Mik, now
accustomed to the leash, and we would encounter other retired officers on similar perambulations. Few, if any, were as high ranking as
Colonel Borowiec but all seemed imbued with what, to my ears, was
a far more pleasing notion of Poland's military strength than my
father's gloomy assessment.

'Forty regiments of cavalry,' I once heard him say. 'In this day and
age, it's an aberration.'

Nonetheless, our wall posters assured us of victory. 'Strong!',
'United!', 'Ready!' proclaimed the captions to pictures showing reso-
lute columns of infantry marching beneath a sky carpeted with our
planes. Newspapers were printing long lists of people who had volunteered for suicide squads – they called themselves 'human torpedoes'.

At school Horseradish became increasingly militant. 'We will not
give up a single button of our uniform,' he vowed, quoting the words
of the commander-in-chief.

At the start of the summer, our town got its own garrison. They were a frontier defence force battalion, mostly made up of resentful-looking reservists. Anti-tank guns appeared in the yard of a flour mill. On the fence outside the courthouse a sergeant put up a carefully stencilled sign that declared it to be 'Garrison Headquarters'. Then one of our school's two main buildings was turned into a barracks, and the school year ended early.

The changing of the guard outside the headquarters building took place at six every evening. The new unit would line up opposite the one being relieved, and there was always a lot of saluting, presenting of arms and heel clicking. Sometimes it was carried out by a dismounted cavalry unit, with their spurs jangling and their carbines slung diagonally across their backs, ready to spring into the saddle.

It was exhilarating, and I had a good friend with whom to share my pleasure. He was a summer visitor from the north of the country who shared my passion for things military. Together we assisted at almost every changing of the guard. And if we were really lucky, we might be allowed to make a personal contribution to national defence by washing the soldiers' mess kits. As a token of his appreciation one soldier gave us a loaf of dark army bread. Thrilled, we took it back to my home.

'But who's going to eat it?' demanded the maid, a practical girl.

We each began munching a huge piece. After some perseverance, we had to admit that it wasn't very good. I confided to my friend that hardtack biscuits, which I had sampled in Kielce during my father's last garrison posting, were much better. Unfortunately, soldiers had to be on active service, or at least on manoeuvres, before they were permitted these fighting rations.

My friend seemed to know a lot about girls. I put this down to him living in a city where there were more of them around. He made constant references to them and appeared to be well acquainted with the workings of their most intimate parts. At night, brooding over some of the things he had told me, I felt hot and uncomfortable. My erections troubled me. I was by no means certain that it was supposed to be like this. What if I found myself naked in front of a girl with this thing sticking out? She'd laugh at me.

Much more exciting were the troop movements and the steady progression towards war.

'Looks like you'll soon be going back on full pay, sir,' I overheard the old postman telling my father.

Papa was sitting under an apple tree carving one of his statuettes. His visitor was delivering his monthly pension in cash (cheques were a rare thing in Poland in those days). Banknotes and silver change were counted out, and my father handed back a small tip with the signed receipt. I used to wonder why this important public servant went unarmed on these occasions. After all, his big leather pouch not only contained my father's pension but also the monthly stipends of the other retired officers and civil servants in the area. As a result, almost everybody in Maków seemed to know exactly how much these retirees were getting.

'They can't possibly spend it all,' I once heard the wife of a local tailor say to another woman.

'Are we rich, Papa?'

'I wish we were.'

'But you get much more money than other people, even on half pay!'

'The other people should be getting more money. That's the trouble with the system.'

Criticism of the system made me feel uncomfortable. I felt it smelled of disloyalty, even treason. I was particularly irritated by the attitude of my Uncle Józef, the successful lawyer who was my father's elder brother. Uncle Józef had briefly stayed with us that summer in order to attend the funeral of their father, who had died in a nearby town, aged ninety-one. It was a big affair with an honour guard and a firing party.

My grandfather was one of the last veterans of the failed 1863 uprising against Czarist Russian rule in Poland. For those who survived the fighting, retribution ranged from public execution to Siberian exile. But my grandfather had escaped to territory under Austro-Hungarian control and had managed, eventually, to build a career in that complex empire's post office. He must have been delighted to have a son serving as an officer in the first Polish national army for

125 years – the army that, in 1920, crushed the Bolsheviks and saved central Europe from Russian domination.

After the funeral we all repaired to a restaurant. At my end of the table, the main topic of conversation among the adults was the good fortune that had befallen the woman who had been grandfather's long-time and much younger housekeeper. Apparently, she had not only inherited his house but also a considerable part of his money. I was not paying much attention, for something much more interesting had happened. Four reserve officer cadets had entered. Each of them held his cap in the same position, under his left arm and, bowing slightly, clicked his heels.

'They make robots out of these idiots,' complained my uncle, his napkin tucked into his shirt collar, bits of the meal in his full beard. He enjoyed his food and had put on a great deal of weight since I last saw him.

'They also teach them manners,' snapped my father.

'They should be building better roads instead of playing at marionettes,' said his elder brother, who normally contrived to have the last word.

My father made no comment.

My uncle slept for most of the drive back to Maków, where we bade farewell to him at the station. He was going to Kraków, where he would change trains for an eastbound express back to his home in Lwów.

Before they parted, my father said something to his brother.

I heard him reply, 'Of course, they'd be welcome. I'm sure it would be safer.'

It would be some time before I realized what they were talking about.

Over the next few days events seemed to race along. Men gathered around wall posters announcing the call-up of reservists, checking the cards they carried with them to see if their category had been included. Next came the marvellous news that the start of the new school year, in September, had been indefinitely postponed. Bliss was it to be alive.

Drunken reservists frequently had to fight their way on to trains packed with returning holidaymakers, among them people who no longer felt comfortable away from home and had decided to cut their vacations short. My precocious friend who knew about girls and shared my fascination with things military went down to the station with me to watch these departures. Neither of us could understand why these reservists had drunk so much when they were about to board a train that would take them away to such a fabulous adventure.

Then, one day, my friend was also on a crowded train and I was waving goodbye to him.

When I got back to the house I found my father and Ada, the housekeeper, cleaning their pistols. At the time it was not all that uncommon for women in Poland to own a small-calibre weapon for personal protection. I think Mateczka had one too, though I never saw it. Ada had brought this little automatic handbag gun with her when she left her home in western Poland for her new job. Now it was lying on the kitchen table, alongside her employer's similarly dismembered big army-issue automatic; barrels, unloaded magazines and various other parts were all laid out on an old newspaper, together with cleaning rags. I watched Ada pick up one of these and apply some oil from a small bottle.

'Not too much,' Papa cautioned. 'It'll make it jam.'

When they had finished, my father amazed me by persuading Ada to swap his beautiful service pistol for her smaller gun, which he seemed to think was much more convenient. 'I can stick it in a pocket, and it won't get in the way,' he said.

Shortly after this, I was walking along the street with my father when he introduced himself to a passing captain.

The captain clicked his heels.

'I was wondering if you might be able to help me,' Papa said.

The captain clicked his heels again.

'I'm expecting to be called up any day, but my field uniform was made up five years ago and it doesn't fit me as well as it did. Do you know where I could find a replacement?'

'The machine-gun company's quartermaster may be able to help, sir,' the captain suggested.

My father thanked him, and the captain departed with a final respectful percussion from his footwear.

But the recommended quartermaster was unable to oblige. In the end, Ada volunteered to alter the old uniform, letting the waistband out and moving the buttons of the tunic.

It was completed just in time. A policeman turned up the next day, at dusk, delivering a brief telegram that ordered my father to report for duty at a logistical headquarters in Kraków. There followed a hectic evening of searching for all the bits and pieces of his kit – 'Where are my binoculars?' – writing out various authorizations to enable Ada to take over the running of the household, as well as other dull matters of adult significance quite incomprehensible to a child.

Ada told me to kiss my father goodnight and go to bed, but I refused to do so until I had seen him in his warrior garb again. To humour me, he put on his uniform, holstered his pistol, pulled on his riding boots and led me to my bedroom where he told me to be a good boy, do what Ada told me and kissed me good night.

The next morning he was gone.

# 4. War Breaks Out

*Eastern Poland, September 1939*

A few days after he had been called up, a letter from my father arrived at our house in Maków. It instructed Ada to make sure I had a suitcase packed and was ready to leave the next day for my uncle's home in Lwów, Poland's most easterly major city since 1920 (much to Moscow's dismay). It has a quarrelsome history and a divorcee's list of known names. Today it is Lviv, a city in the western Ukraine. Generations of German speakers have preferred to call it Lemberg, and in English it is normally spelled Lvov (which is the Polish pronunciation, but not the spelling).

Because of the continued build-up of German forces across the Slovak frontier my father considered Lwów a much safer place for me than Maków. A plan to evacuate me had been agreed with his brother at my grandfather's funeral. Ada would remain alone in the house with the dog. No doubt, duty permitting, she could expect sporadic visits from her employer who, the letter explained, would be picking me up personally.

What my father might not have made clear was that Mateczka was re-entering our lives. He would only be taking me as far as the big rail junction at Tarnów, about 100 kilometres from Kraków. She would meet us there and accompany me the other 300 or so kilometres further east to Lwów. She apparently intended to remain with me for the duration of the war which, once the French and the British had joined in, was not expected to last very long. For me it was all marvellous news, with the adventure of going to live in a big city and the company of the woman I loved at least as much as the mother I hardly knew. Without her it might have been a different story. I was rarely comfortable in the presence of my cynical Uncle Józef and his rotund wife, and I found their demonstrations of affection suspect.

I left Maków in a curious hybrid vehicle, normally used by senior Polish railway officials. It had been adapted to run along the tracks of their empires by swapping its factory-fitted wheels for the sort normally found on a locomotive. It had been issued to my father because he was now in charge of all southern Poland's military rail traffic, tasked with overseeing its maintenance and security and generally seeing that the troop trains ran on time. I was, of course, very disappointed in him.

'So you're not going to fight, Papa?'

'There are many ways of fighting.'

'But you're not going to fire your gun?'

'Not very likely. I have another job to do. Not everybody shoots in the army.'

'And will you be there when our soldiers enter Berlin?'

He said it was time to leave, and we made our goodbyes to Ada before going to the station. Our special vehicle and its driver awaited us at a signal stop, just after the platform ended, where it was low enough to get into it. From the outside it looked exactly like any other car, except that no tyres were visible. It was only when I was inside, sitting on the back seat, that I noticed there was an important difference. There was no steering wheel. The driver operated the accelerator, brakes and gears. But the rails did the rest, just like a locomotive.

Being lower on the ground, the car seemed to travel much faster than any steam engine. It whizzed along, startling stationmasters at sleepy country halts into giving hasty salutes, causing work gangs along the track to rest on their picks and shovels and doff their caps, and darting under bridges guarded by curious members of the *Obrona Narodowa*. This was a kind of home guard, with white armbands on their civilian jackets, and armed with antiquated, long-barrelled rifles of a kind I had only ever seen in picture books. My father explained that they were on the lookout for German saboteurs recruited by the Nazis from among Poland's German ethnic minority (the people Hitler called the *Volksdeutsche*). The popular term for these saboteurs, borrowed from the Spanish Civil War, was 'fifth columnists'. And before long, I was to hear much more about them.

We stopped near Kraków, in the sandbagged suburban station where Southern Command's Senior Rail Transport Officer had set up his headquarters. As the strange rail car pulled up, several of my father's staff officers were waiting in line to greet him. I noticed that they were all middle-aged and were dressed in a variety of vintage uniforms, several of which could have done with the kind of attention recently rendered by Ada to the raiment of their commanding officer.

I ate supper with my father and then spent the night at this station, sleeping in a compartment of a carriage that had been shunted on to a siding. I shared it with a boy, the son of another officer, who at his parents' behest was also being evacuated in an easterly direction. Beds had been made up for us on the seats but we were both excited, and it was a long time before we stopped talking about the forthcoming war. It was hard to sleep in that compartment, stuffy on a midsummer night, even with a window partly down. At some point I half woke to the sound of men shouting and doors slamming, but then I drifted back to sleep.

Next morning, my father came to collect me and took me to his quarters for breakfast. I noticed he was unshaven, which was unusual, and he looked tired.

'Did you sleep well?' he asked.

'Yes, Papa. There was some shouting, but I went back to sleep.'

'Ah, you heard it, did you? We had a time bomb go off in the main left luggage office at Tarnów station. I had to rush over there.'

'Did people die?'

'I'm afraid they did. At least fifteen at the last count. And I don't think some of the wounded are going to get better. It could have been even worse. If the Kraków express had come in on time, the main platform would have been crowded. But it was eight minutes late.'

'Do you think the Germans did it? The columns?'

'You mean the fifth columnists?'

'Yes.'

'Well, the police have arrested somebody, and I believe he's at least half German.'

'Will we still be going to Tarnów?' I had visions of my whole wonderful adventure coming to an end.

'Oh yes. It's quite safe now. There are lots of police and soldiers there.'

And so it proved. Tarnów was a large rail junction, and the damage was confined to a small area of the main station building. We met up with Mateczka at the station's crowded restaurant, where we were eventually served lunch while my father told her about the bomb and the latest casualty figure, which put the fatalities at over twenty.

'The police are saying he comes from Bielsko-Biała,' Papa said.

It was a city on the Czech border with a mostly ethnic German population.

'It almost feels as if the war has already started,' said Mateczka, serene as ever in hat and gloves and altogether worthy of the hug and kiss I allowed her.

After I had finished I was encouraged to leave the table and watch a battery of heavy field artillery, each gun pulled by eight horses, being loaded on to a troop train while Mateczka and my father had one of their private conversations. Shortly afterwards, on another track, our eastbound express to Lwów was ready to depart. Through the open window of our compartment my father exchanged a few last words in French with my escort and gave me a pocketful of loose change. I promised to write to him every day, and the train slowly began to move away.

I waved until he was out of sight, pleased to think that, with these German saboteurs around, he might have some real fighting to do.

It was a long journey, though hardly uninteresting for me. I was treated throughout to the sight of what seemed like an interminable cortège of troop trains going in the opposite direction. On some station platforms soldiers who were not yet required to board their transports crowded around steaming field kitchens. The outline of field guns could be discerned under straw-coloured camouflage nets.

Despite the warm late August sunshine, I noticed their crews were wearing new-looking winter uniforms.

At sunset we approached the dark silhouette of Lwów's triple-spired Church of St Elizabeth and came to a halt under the huge glass canopy of the central station. We followed a porter who carried all our bags out to the taxi rank on leather straps attached to his shoulders. Yet more troops filled the station. I was beginning to think ours must be the biggest army in the world. Wall posters warned in large letters: 'Attention! The enemy is listening.' I wondered how? There was so much noise.

Our taxi was slowed by a marching column escorted by men on horseback.

'The 19th is going to the front,' our driver explained.

Then one of the horsemen waved him on, and within a matter of minutes we were at my uncle's house. On arrival I was smothered by what I suspected were theatrical effusions of tenderness from the obese lady of the house while Mateczka, who knew exactly what I was thinking, tried to keep a straight face.

Their home was a big four-storey building practically next door to the old Austro-Hungarian citadel that remained the headquarters for the local military.

'On Sunday you can see the troops march to church,' promised my uncle, who knew what pleased me.

My uncle and his family lived in a spacious wooden-floored apartment that occupied the entire top floor. It was lined with bookshelves and carpeted with expensive rugs. The other floors he let out but, as far as I could work out, he had sole use of the surrounding garden with its fruit trees, pathways, flower beds and lawns. There was a cellar that had been turned into a communal air-raid shelter with chairs and oil lamps. Discreet buckets and chamber pots had been placed in corners, behind screens. House owners who failed to do this could be fined or even imprisoned.

The next day, I heard the air-raid sirens tested for the first time. A runner from the local civil defence command came to check that arrangements had been made to properly black out the windows and that the glass was criss-crossed with tape so that people would not be cut to pieces if it splintered into shards. The runner was not much bigger than myself; he was wearing a Boy Scout's uniform, with a civil defence armband, and carrying a gas mask. Never had I been so envious of someone in all of my almost eleven years.

'Can I be a runner, Mateczka?' I asked after he had left.

'Don't be silly.'

Yet the atmosphere in this city, with its crowds and traffic and its walls plastered with appeals and instructions, brimmed with the promise of endless opportunities for a willing boy. The streets were already full of people in all kinds of uniforms, many of them, like the Boy Scout I had so envied, carrying gas masks in boxes on shoulder straps. Even some women wore khaki overalls with Red Cross armbands. What decent Pole would want to miss out?

'Exhibitionists,' sneered my uncle. 'Everybody suddenly wants to dress like a patriot.'

Mateczka and I were accompanying him during an afternoon walk along a crowded sidewalk. From a little way off, heard but unseen, came the oompahs of a military band.

The Second World War started the next morning, on Friday 1 September. On a more personal note, it opened for us with a first air raid that occurred before Mateczka and I – or, for that matter, anybody else in my uncle's apartment – even knew that hostilities had begun. We had left the house early and were browsing in a bookshop when we heard the air-raid siren.

'I suppose they're testing again,' said the saleswoman, a slight edge to her voice.

'I don't remember an announcement in the newspaper,' somebody said.

Mateczka, who was slightly above it all, as usual, waited while our purchases were wrapped. Meanwhile, the sound of the siren grew louder, more insistent.

She had bought me a popular history by one of my favourite authors, set in the immediate aftermath of the 1914–18 war. *Lwów's Eaglets* was about the famous Polish teenagers who, in the anarchy that followed the break-up of the Austro-Hungarian Empire into its component parts, took on a regiment of Ukrainian riflemen and helped save Lwów for Poland.

It was as we emerged from the bookshop that I saw people looking up and spotted planes going in and out of the cloud cover. Not too high, not too low, and flying in a neat formation, the planes pierced one cloud only to vanish into another one before I had finished counting them. There were some isolated shots and what we would soon come to recognize as the lingering black puffs of smoke left by exploding anti-aircraft shells.

'For God's sake take that child away,' a woman wearing a brown beret shouted at Mateczka as she elbowed her way past us. We thought her very rude. Far from taking cover, most people were swarming on to the street, either to see what was happening or to tell others what they believed had occurred.

'They've hit the airport. Not a single hangar has been left intact.'

'St Elizabeth's Church has gone too.'

'The glass dome at the central station has been shattered to pieces.'

Then the siren sounded the all-clear, and the city's red and cream tramcars started clanking along the streets again.

We got home just in time to listen to Polskie Radio's first wartime communiqué. I remember my surprise at the announcer's calm and measured tones. He sounded no different from any other day.

Apparently there had been air raids on all our major cities, but the announcer failed to make any special mention of Lwów. Apart from a Polish torpedo boat sunk in the Baltic, most of the damage appeared superficial. Our frontiers had been violated in a number of places. However, in at least one case the enemy had been immediately repelled, leaving several destroyed tanks behind.

The man arrested for the Tarnów station bombing was named as Antoni Guzy, a locksmith with a German mother and a Polish father. He told the police he had not done it for money.

The best news item was the stirring defence of the Polish fortress on Danzig's Westerplatte peninsula. About 200 Polish soldiers armed with a few artillery pieces, mortars and heavy machine guns were holding off twenty times that number despite air attacks and support from the heavy guns mounted on Germany's old training cruiser

*Schleswig-Holstein.* If Polish soldiers could do so well against these sorts of odds, it was obvious they would be invincible when evenly matched. Even Uncle Józef found it difficult not to look impressed.

News bulletins now dominated our lives. Much to my relief the only one who was rarely present to hear them was my uncle. He had been given some senior position in one of the citizens' committees; he now wore an armband trimmed with gold and displayed an exclusive pass on the windscreen of his car. But at midday, and shortly before the light supper we ate in the evening, the rest of us all congregated around the radio.

We heard that the Polish government had invoked the Anglo-French guarantees and that France and Britain, which had already mobilized their reserves, had given Hitler an ultimatum: either withdraw from Poland, or we declare war. By the third day, Sunday 3 September, Hitler, as expected, had failed to respond. This meant that France, with its enormous army, and Britain, with its powerful navy and the biggest empire the world had ever seen, were now at war with Germany. If we Poles found it difficult to defeat the Germans by ourselves, it seemed all we had to do was hold the fort and wait for the cavalry to arrive.

'Westerplatte still fights on,' Polskie Radio informed us every morning.

Then, on the seventh day, there was no such announcement. We later learned that our garrison had surrendered. As a mark of their respect, the Germans had allowed its commander to keep his sabre.

In between the news bulletins, which were often boringly repetitive, the radio broadcast its usual fare of concerts and other programmes. These were often interrupted by civil defence announcements on the arrival of enemy aircraft over various parts of the city. Sometimes they were intended for anti-aircraft units and were of a distinctly cryptic nature: 'Ko-Ma arriving; W-R anticipate; chocolate, repeat, chocolate.'

They were almost invariably followed by an authoritative voice breaking into a broadcast with a warning in plain language: 'Attention, attention. This is the commander of the Lwów region. I declare an air-raid alert for the city. Take cover.'

A minute later, sirens would sound and Mateczka would seize a small pre-packed suitcase with one hand, grab hold of me with the other, and together we would run down the four flights of stairs to the cellar.

Once, we had got as far as ground level when we heard a couple of sharp cracks. We looked outside, through the open front door of the house, and saw something that stopped us in our tracks. A soldier was standing in the middle of the street, squeezing off shots at the Luftwaffe with his rifle. Even I – who, like most boys, had an abiding belief in military miracles – knew that his target was hopelessly out of range. Yet after each shot this soldier methodically worked the bolt of his weapon to eject the empty cartridge case, then aimed and fired until he had finished a five-round clip. Suddenly he became aware that we were watching, and to this day I can still recall the look of blank incomprehension on his face. There were probably many more like him.

The raids were not huge, rarely involving more than a dozen or so aircraft. Such small, silvery objects failed to scare. Some raids took place at night, when there was the added adventure of being woken up and going down to the shelter with a coat over my pyjamas. In that first week, nothing dramatic happened in the vicinity of my uncle's house. A few fatalities occurred elsewhere, but in our cellar we could hear only muffled explosions

Nonetheless, most of the tenants did go to the shelter, not only to be on the safe side but because it was also becoming something of a social occasion. Poles and Ukrainians, whose languages are very close, chatted happily together. One of the things they had in common was that they all told similar and highly improbable war stories.

'Our lancers opened their tank hatches and dropped grenades inside.'

'The Germans are afraid of the bayonet. They run like rabbits.'

'Berlin is in ruins. The French, British and our pilots have smashed it to bits. Our planes were the first to arrive.'

'Our cavalry is advancing in East Prussia.'

'The French have broken through the Siegfried Line.'

Then the sirens sounded the all-clear, and we all emerged into the sunshine of a balmy September.

But after a while, even I began to accept that, on the whole, the radio hinted at a different story. The news bulletins repeatedly spoke of 'regrouping' or 'retreating to straighten out the front'.

One evening, there was a young man in my uncle's apartment with a list of all the towns that were now in German hands.

'Will the French come and help us, Mateczka?'

'Of course, the French will come and defeat the Boche.'

Her confidence was comforting. After all, she spoke the language. She was bound to know. It was undeniable that the French, with a bit of help from others, had defeated the Boche in the last war. When it came to fighting they were almost as good as the Poles.

# 5.   The Siege of Lwów

Evening meals were taken in a dining room rendered airless by the blankets used as blackout covers on the windows. Both Mateczka and my large aunt tried to cool themselves with small fans they kept by their plates, flapping themselves like disturbed birds. It was the kind of casual discomfort that frayed tempers. During my uncle's infrequent appearances at table from his civil defence duties, the atmosphere sometimes became even stickier. His contempt for the military and all its works knew no bounds, and he seemed to love to tease me with it.

'So where are those interceptor planes they used to show us at their parades? Where are the radio reflectors that are supposed to tell us where enemy bombers are? How can a nation of thirty-five million, with a million-strong army, collapse so soon? Where are our famous generals?'

'At the front!' I shouted one evening.

Mateczka told me later I was red in the face with fury, and I got the impression she was proud of me. In those days children did not, as a rule, shout at adults. But I think she made an exception as far as Uncle Józef was concerned.

'More likely running away,' he snapped. 'They're all running away.'

'My father is not running away!'

'I'm sure he is. Running away with all the others.'

At this point I was on the verge of tears. I suppose, on my uncle's part, a lot of it had to do with some kind of incurable sibling rivalry. Here was a childless man who needed to bait his younger brother's adoring son, zealous guardian of Polish military honour.

Then, a few days later, my hero himself made an unannounced appearance, accompanied by an aide and a driver. Their car was dusty, and the roof was camouflaged with green foliage. All three looked tired and unshaven.

They wanted food and they wanted the radio news on. The last was not as easy as it should have been, because the Luftwaffe had knocked out Polskie Radio's main long-wave transmitter, so we had to find a local station that was still functioning. When we did come up with a news bulletin it was one of those stereotypical communiqués announcing – always without excitement – tactical withdrawals, as well as the number of enemy planes Polish forces claimed to have shot down.

My father told a different tale of chaos and confusion amidst constant air attacks. Not only were the roads clogged with refugees but so too were his precious railway lines, where evacuation trains filled the tracks. This made it impossible to send troops where they were urgently needed. Senior Polish officers had a high opinion of themselves. It was not quite twenty years since they had saved western Europe from Bolshevik terror by stopping the Russian Bear at the Vistula. But in that war both sides had mostly used cavalry and infantry. In a very short time we would all learn to call this 'blitzkrieg' – lightning war.

'Did you fire your pistol, Papa?'

'Yes, my pet, I did. Several times. I fired to frighten looters and to get people off the road so that we could get back to the front.'

'Couldn't the police do that?'

'Some of them were the police.'

Delighted though I was to see him, his presence was a major shock to all of us. This was the eighth day of the war and here was my father, not advancing on Berlin but deep inside Poland. My whole concept of my country and its strength was beginning to crumble. Could it possibly be that Uncle Józef was right and the army, even my father, were running away? Of course, I did my best to maintain my belief in ultimate victory. The French and the British would attack and our brave soldiers, rested and regrouped, would launch a devastating offensive. It had to be. But now there were these nagging, defeatist doubts. It was like the realization that however hard I prayed – and I prayed very hard – God might not keep my father safe.

During the next few days I did not see much of him. A number of transport troops, engineering battalions and anti-aircraft units were falling back on Lwów. My father had been put in command, and was told to sort them out. One evening, while out for a brief stroll with Mateczka, I saw some of these defeated soldiers marching towards the old city. They were wearing a variety of uniforms and different headgear. Some had helmets while others wore the stiff garrison caps that I had grown up with. Few of them carried weapons.

'Which way is the citadel, little one?' one of them asked me as he passed.

I pointed towards its large brick walls. You could hardly miss it.

'We're going to defend it,' said one of his companions.

I was astonished. Surely the enemy were not this close? I discussed the matter with my new friend, a Ukrainian boy of about my own age, named Zenek. His parents were schoolteachers and rented one of the apartments beneath my uncle's living quarters. Our playground was the surrounding garden with its immaculate lawns, winding paths and flower beds, and fruit trees laden with apples and pears. Inevitably, the game we played was war. Zenek contributed a small detachment of his own lead soldiers to our game. We excavated miniature entrenchments, using garden trowels and old spoons, and constructed cardboard aeroplanes. We particularly liked imitating the wail of sirens, only to be frequently interrupted by the real thing.

Sometimes our soldiers went missing in action, fatally buried by the handfuls of earth with which we simulated explosions. No doubt some of these casualties still lie there in their unmarked graves. By some unspoken mutual agreement the one thing we never discussed, let alone played, was the nine-month Polish-Ukrainian war that had occurred ten years or so before we were born and had established Lwów as part of Poland (though many Ukrainians continued to live there). The Polish and Ukrainian languages were close enough to make it easy for children like Zenek to become bilingual. And from the moment I first heard it, I could understand a lot of spoken Ukrainian.

On what, I distinctly remember, was the twelfth day of the war an afternoon air raid brought us into the cellar, where we remained much longer than was usual. Zenek and I longed to return to our garden campaign. Instead, afternoon turned into early evening and we were still there, listening to a rumble of explosions that sounded somehow different from what we had become accustomed to hearing. And when, from time to time, the noise subsided we listened in vain for the sirens to sound the all-clear.

It was hours before Mateczka considered it safe enough to take me back upstairs and get a breath of fresh air. Darkness was falling on the city. In the hallway of the house some of the tenants were gathered around a man who had ventured far enough out to acquire a copy of the city's evening newspaper. When I got close enough I had no difficulty reading the size of the headline above the biggest front-page story it had carried since the war began. 'ENEMY BEATEN BACK AT THE GATES'.

The Germans had succeeded in reaching the city where my father had imagined I would be safe while he got on with fighting. Most of the explosions we had been listening to were not aerial bombs but exchanges of fire between German and Polish artillery. Motorized infantry supported by a battery of big 150 mm guns had penetrated the city's suburbs before reinforcements, in the act of disembarking from trains, had the chance to be deployed. The day had been saved, the article said, when General Władysław Langner personally assembled a few platoons of police gendarmerie and army recruits, perhaps a little over a hundred men, whose artillery support consisted of two old French 75 mm guns. This ad hoc force held the enemy at bay until they could be reinforced and, for the time being at least, the Germans had withdrawn.

'Don't worry, your father and his railway warriors are safe,' boomed a familiar voice.

I looked up and saw that Uncle Józef, with his untidy beard, gold-trimmed armband and a walking stick, had just walked through the front door.

'I tried to intervene,' he said to nobody in particular, 'but they're morons. It's too late to stop the vandalism of my property.'

Clearly upset, he vanished into the building's elderly electric lift (which Mateczka always insisted we avoid in case a power cut stranded us between floors during an air raid).

She took my hand, and we walked cautiously outside to see what was happening. It was getting dark now but the narrow street was crowded with people – civilians and soldiers. Some of them were using picks, crowbars and shovels to rip up the pavement. They carried their looted trophies a few hundred yards to the street leading to the citadel where, we were informed, a massive barricade was being constructed.

As they worked, people were talking in a matter-of-fact way about the damage they were doing to my uncle's property.

'That garden will never be the same again.'

'I hear they're going to put a gun there, a big one.'

'No, they need free passage to the church. Soldiers are digging foxholes all around it.'

It was not difficult to spot what had particularly angered my uncle. Directed by an officer cadet, soldiers in steel helmets were busy dismantling the wooden fence that, for the last twelve days, had not only protected his garden from the real war but had also enabled Zenek and myself to create our private battlescape. Soldiers not actively engaged in dismembering the fence were carrying materials from a nearby building site and piling them up on both sides of the street, but not actually blocking it. There was a gap, the width of a vehicle, between the two piles.

'Why aren't you building a complete barricade?' I inquired of the young man in charge. (I had often heard my father and other experienced officers addressing officer cadets and knew how to talk to them.)

It was some time before he spoke. 'My friend,' he said slowly, 'I suggest you go back to your toys.'

For the first time I wondered whether my uncle's criticism of the military might not be as unfair as I had thought. Perhaps there were some morons masquerading in uniform?

It was well past sunset, but there was a red glow in the sky and the sound of periodic explosions could be heard. Did I hold Mateczka's hand a little more tightly? Possibly I wanted to comfort her.

A soldier mounted on a bicycle sped past us. He was shouting, 'More men needed for the barricades! Bring your own tools!'

★

That night I slept fitfully, but at least I slept. Apparently, Mateczka did not sleep at all. By first light the explosions had stopped and, seeing that I was awake, she suggested that we go outside and get some fresh air. It was a grey dawn and the only other person in the street was our usual local sentry, with his rifle slung. The garden fence had entirely disappeared. A short distance away, on the street parallel to ours – leading to the citadel, and visible because of a large vacant lot – loomed a massive barricade made up of two piles of jagged paving stones.

In the morning, I stood on my uncle's balcony and viewed the overnight defences of a city surprised to find itself besieged. It was an astonishing sight.

Everywhere I looked, streets were blocked by barricades. Some had been constructed around overturned trucks and other large vehicles. All were piled high with bricks, boards, heavy furniture and dug-up flagstones. A broad but fairly shallow trench had been dug across one street. I later discovered this was intended as an anti-tank ditch. Soldiers were visible on some nearby balconies and rooftops. I watched a heavy-machine-gun crew setting up their weapon in a position overlooking the garden where Zenek and I had once dug in our own troops.

Day after day the war seemed to get a little closer, until we reached the moment when the air-raid sirens fell silent. There was no point in sounding them. In one part or another, the city was under almost constant artillery fire and few civilians left cover for long.

One night, a shell exploded in the garden. There was a deafening noise, and the blast tore the blackout paper from the ground-level window not far from my bed. Perhaps for the first time in the war I was afraid.

'*Mateczka!* Do you think they're trying to aim at the citadel?'

But though she generally bore up well, in the circumstances, she was hopeless about military matters.

Except for lulls in the shelling, when we would dash upstairs to use the bathroom or eat a hasty meal, we lived in the cellar. It had acquired a certain familiarity. Most of its occupants behaved well, and there were few quarrels – although, in the way of things, some people were more prone to panic than others.

One night, during heavy shelling, a soldier joined us, ignoring a woman's arguments that he had no right to be there.

'It's not his place,' she said. 'This is a civilian house. If they come and find him here, we'll all be killed.'

'They' were the enemy. This was the first intimation I had that there were people who seriously believed we might be defeated and the city would fall.

It seemed that everything was against us, that fateful September, including the weather. It continued to be one of those warm and sunny Indian summers everyone yearned for in peacetime, whereas what was needed was enough rain to turn our unmade roads and farmlands into the kind of quagmire that would suck the panzers to a standstill. Instead, their dust clouds rolled remorselessly through our flatlands of swaying corn and started to encircle parts of the army that had promised to march on Berlin.

During breaks from the cellar I would sometimes look out of the sitting-room window and watch the steady movement of men and vehicles going to and fro between the citadel barracks and what I presumed to be front-line positions. Most of the vehicles were horse-drawn transport, but I occasionally saw automobiles carrying officers or small trucks pulling the artillery ammunition tenders that my father's generation liked to call gun caissons. Then a rather advanced-looking anti-aircraft battery arrived, its guns not pulled by horses but by squat little tank-like tractors.

A couple of days later, a column of trucks appeared, laden with rifles. And with them came my father, who had apparently played a major role in rescuing weapons and ammunition from an arsenal outside the city.

'Are we completely surrounded, Papa?'

'No, we still have open roads to the east and south-east.'

'Will the rescue come from there?'

'It may. Our forces are regrouping.'

The radio had even better news. Despite our setbacks there had been a discernible Polish victory. A counter-attack by General Tadeusz Kutrzeba at the important rail junction of Kutno, in central Poland, was correctly reported to have scattered two German divisions, taken some 3,000 prisoners and sent the Wehrmacht reeling. Polish cavalry, some in light tanks but most on horseback, raided the enemy's rear echelons and gave birth to the ludicrous legend that our lancers had tilted at panzers. Nonetheless, it took no more than a week for German air superiority and massive reinforcements to repair the damage and to force Kutrzeba to start withdrawing into the Warsaw perimeter.

Long before then my uncle was, of course, already throwing cold water over all the optimism the Kutno battle had engendered.

'Half the country is occupied. The industrial areas are gone, the capital under siege. We are besieged here in Lwów, and our air force hardly exists any more. And you ask me if I think we'll lose the war. We've already lost it.'

'So what's going to happen to us?'

'Oh, one day our city will surrender – in ruins, of course. Later, perhaps next spring, the French and the British will invade Germany and capture the Ruhr. The Germans will come to their senses, there will be peace talks, troop withdrawals by both sides, and we'll get our country back. With a better government, I hope.'

Then something happened that had never entered my uncle's head – and nor, to be fair, anybody else's. Soviet troops entered eastern Poland.

Most adults were aware that, eight days before the war started, the Russians had signed a non-aggression pact with the Germans. What they didn't realize was that the pact contained secret protocols negotiated by foreign ministers Molotov and Ribbentrop, which divided Poland into Soviet and Nazi spheres of interest. The implications of this latest development were unclear. Were the Red Army coming as friend or foe?

In desperation, my uncle called his younger brother. After he had put the telephone down he announced with obvious satisfaction, 'He doesn't know any more than we do.'

And yet, momentous though the Russian intervention was, a more pressing issue demanded immediate attention. Although electric power was still available, German shelling or bombing had destroyed an important filtration and pumping station and cut off most of the city's water supply. Fortunately, Lwów had a number of old wells, though some of them had not been used for years. Now people risked breaking cover and being caught by artillery or air attack. They lined up at these wells with buckets and almost anything else that would hold water. Civil defence officials assigned various streets and apartment blocks to different wells, and it all seemed to be reasonably well organized.

And to my great delight, I was given a role to play. On 17 September – the afternoon of the day we heard that the Soviets had crossed Poland's eastern border – I contributed to the replenishment of our water supplies. Carrying two small pitchers, I proudly accompanied Mateczka to our allotted well. It was near St Lazarus Church, and to get there we simply crossed my uncle's recently unfenced private garden, walked past a camouflaged anti-aircraft position, and entered the rear of the churchyard. The church itself was built on a slight mound that overlooked an important intersection. A number of soldiers were dug in around it in individual foxholes. Now the well had no doubt added to its tactical value. The soldiers joked with the women, who included my uncle's maid, and helped us draw the water. Mateczka made her usual impact, and one of them insisted on carrying her bucket all the way home.

Our taste of fresh air was short lived. That evening the city was subjected to a heavy artillery barrage, perhaps the most violent we had experienced.

First, two of the armoured trains my father so much despised had fought their way into the city and contributed their firepower to a counter-attack that drove the Germans out of the Zboisko district. But the enemy had responded by deploying their artillery in some hills overlooking the city, with excellent fields of fire. Several of the shells landed close enough for their explosions to shake the walls of my uncle's apartment building, and there was a certain amount of praying aloud.

Then, suddenly, the radio announced that there would be a brief ceasefire. Those who wished to leave the city could pass through the enemy's lines using designated crossing points. General Władysław Langner had agreed to it in order to withdraw and concentrate his

Polish defences on defending a smaller, less-populated perimeter in which we and the rest of the citadel area were included. At the same time both the Russians and the Germans were trying to persuade us that further resistance was useless.

On 18 September, the day after the Soviet intervention, the Luftwaffe littered the city with thousands of leaflets urging our garrison to surrender. Simultaneously, the commander of a Russian armoured brigade was busy telling a Polish envoy that the Red Army were there to fight the Germans and, in order to do so, required unhindered passage into Lwów. This, of course, was an enormous lie. Stalin's troops were there, though most of them were probably unaware of it, because of the secret clauses in the Molotov–Ribbentrop Pact.

We cellar dwellers were ignorant of these developments. All that had been announced on the radio was the news of the brief ceasefire for those who wanted to get out. There was a furious row between Zenek's parents over this. His mother did not want to leave but his father did. Finally, his father appeared with a briefcase, grabbed Zenek by the hand and strode off. His mother stayed behind, a crumpled, weeping figure.

In the morning the sky was cloudy and the explosions seemed more distant. Sometime before noon a large formation of planes flew over the city. They seemed different from the usual enemy planes – darker, noisier.

'Soviet,' somebody said.

Mateczka had been involved in long telephone conversations with my father. Now, after the last one, she rushed about packing our things. Then she took my hand and we walked down the stairs. 'Papa is sending a car for us,' she said.

It was a large black machine with a soldier at the wheel and an official-looking card with a stamp on the windscreen. The driver saluted, put our luggage into the boot, and we were off. My father had come to the conclusion that his headquarters were safer than an apartment block near the citadel, and we were going to stay with him there. Mateczka's relief was transparent, but for entirely different reasons – she did not get on well with my uncle and aunt.

This was my first venture into the city centre since the siege had begun. The streets were empty. Here and there, houses were in ruins, the debris spilling on to the pavement. In several places, barricades had been manufactured out of overturned tramcars. Twice I saw heavy gun batteries, their barrels elevated to a high angle to lob the shells over nearby buildings.

'Howitzers,' said the driver.

Some barricades were complicated, and he had to manoeuvre carefully to pass through their narrow openings which, he explained, would be filled at the last minute with some handy vehicle, should the enemy ever get that close. For the first time I understood why the haughty cadet officer had left a gap in his barricade. In the Jesuit Park I could just make out a huddle of military vehicles covered with leafy branches. Soldiers were digging narrow trenches in the lawns.

'Latrines,' said the driver.

My father was working out of the massive railway directorate building for eastern Poland. Now the military were in charge, and he had a staff of what appeared to be more than a score of officers. Accommodation had been prepared for us in what looked like a small library, its walls lined with bookshelves. There was a couch and a narrow bed in the room together with a basin full of water, a supply of towels and soap, and a chamber pot.

It was evening before my father could spend any time with us, when he escorted us to dinner at the officers' mess across the street. It was a simple meal of soup followed by a main course of some kind of meat served with mashed potatoes. There was no desert but tea was available. On my part it evoked a certain reluctant nostalgia for my uncle's dinner table which, thanks to the generous custom his wife had long given the local shopkeepers, had so far been immune to the war's shortages.

We had barely crossed the street and entered the directorate building when it was rocked by a juddering series of explosions followed by the musical sound of broken glass.

'What bad luck,' said my father. 'I thought you'd be much safer here than near the citadel.'

It must, to say the least, have been very frustrating. First of all he had sent me to Lwów in the belief that this easterly city was bound to have a much safer war than Maków – an assumption that turned out to be hopelessly wrong, though most people would have shared it. Then, when the city came under siege, he had moved me away from the citadel area in the logical belief that the railway directorate building was far less likely to be considered a worthwhile military target.

Nor was the shelter in the directorate as exclusive as my uncle's cellar. Two tiers of basements, equipped with some kind of dim emergency lighting, had been converted to accommodate what appeared to be hundreds of people. Next morning, when I walked to the breakfast room with Mateczka, we looked through a ground-floor window and glimpsed a large group of officers in a room so crowded there was not even sufficient seating. Some of them were leaning against walls while others literally sat at the feet of the man who was addressing them. As we got closer we saw that the speaker was my father. His audience did not look as if they were getting good news.

A couple of hours later I overheard a conversation between two officers who had apparently attended that meeting.

'Two days ago we could have broken through,' one was saying. 'We have enough cars and weapons. Nothing could have stopped a determined group of forty-five officers.'

'But Romania is far away,' said the other. 'And what about the Ukrainian guerrillas?'

'We could have coped. Now it's too late. We're trapped in this sack with the Germans and the Russians all around us.'

By lunchtime the mood seemed to have lightened. When my father took us into the officers' mess there were some distinctly optimistic rumours circulating. Romania, someone insisted, had declared war on Germany. West of Lwów a counter-offensive by three divisions had destroyed a large SS panzer formation. These victorious divisions were even now advancing towards the city and would shortly relieve it. There was no doubt about it. It was another Miracle of the Vistula!

That night we did not return to the directorate's basement but slept in our little library room with its water basin and chamber pot. The artillery fire seemed to have subsided. After a while, we realized there was no firing at all.

The next day was bright and sunny. Mateczka opened the window, and we looked out at some nearby gardens full of red and golden autumn tints. For a few minutes it felt like there had been no war, no destruction. It was almost as if the last twenty-two days had never occurred.

Then the door opened and my father walked in.

'At seven o'clock this morning,' he said. 'General Langner surrendered Lwów to the Bolsheviks.'

## 6.   Learning the Internationale

Soldiers were beginning to dismantle some of the barricades, but the streets were mostly empty. News of the capitulation had apparently not reached everybody. Through the sunlit city the same black car drove us back from the railway directorate to my uncle's apartment building.

Now that the siege was over, I could not understand why my father was unable to come with us. I asked Mateczka if he intended to fight his way to Romania?

'*Non, mon chéri*. Papa has to lead his officers to the headquarters.'

'Why?'

'To surrender to the Russians, *mon petit*.'

'What will happen to them?'

'Papa says there has been an agreement that they'll be released. The Russians aren't interested in Polish prisoners.'

'Has all the Polish Army surrendered?'

I was assured that this was not the case. There were several places where the fighting was by no means over. Top of the list was heroic Warsaw. Despite almost incessant artillery and air bombardment the capital's garrison continued to resist. Nonetheless, there were rumours that the Polish government was already in neutral Romania and that some cut-off army units, comprising thousands of men, had followed them there.

I wondered what my mother was doing. Was she in Warsaw, helping to build the barricades? Or had she fled to Romania, in an attempt to join her husband? (Mateczka had informed me that he was a defence attaché at the Polish embassy in Paris. I had no idea what an attaché was, but it didn't sound like a proper soldier. Certainly nothing like my father.)

It appeared that the surrender of Lwów had been our greatest disaster to date. After besieging the city for ten days, and failing to break through its defences, the Germans had withdrawn west of the San River to make a line that would cut the country in half. Everything east of it would go to the Russians, who had now arrived in great numbers and had halted at the city's outskirts. It looked like our worst fears were coming true: after twenty years of freedom, Poland was being partitioned again.

'But where were the French?' I asked Mateczka. 'Weren't they supposed to be helping us?'

'Soon, *mon chéri*,' she said. 'Soon they'll attack the Germans. The English too. Just you wait and see.'

When we got to my uncle's apartment building there were hardly any greetings. He and my aunt and their loyal maid, all covered in dust, were busy carrying broken bricks and other debris downstairs from the attic.

'Now a shell hits our roof,' he snapped. 'All because some idiotic general wants his honour preserved.'

'They won't do it again,' I told him, sensing that he had not heard the news. I don't think I had ever told an adult anything quite as momentous.

'What do you mean?'

'We've surrendered to the Russians.'

'That's brilliant! They turn our city into a ruin to fight the Germans, then they give it to the Russians. Real statesmanship!'

Nothing, it seemed, could ever be right for my uncle. The city was not in ruins – any more than a single small-calibre shell had irreparably damaged his house.

Before we had finished unpacking, news of the surrender was known to everybody. The first Soviet troops were to enter the city later in the afternoon. The radio kept broadcasting instructions to the population to remain calm and await further orders.

Mateczka never needed to be reminded to stay calm. 'Put your coat on, Andrzej,' she said. 'And we'll take a stroll outside.'

Reluctantly I put on my raincoat. It was a pleasant September day, and I was a robust child, but she was always concerned I might catch a chill. Overdressed as I was, we had hardly stepped out of the front door when the first thing we saw was an adult male taking his clothes off. Barely covered by the remnants of my uncle's gap-toothed garden fence, a policeman was in the process of shedding his dark blue uniform and putting on a crumpled civilian suit. Lying at his feet were his pistol and truncheon.

'He ought to hurry,' said a knowing voice.

I looked around and there was the apartment block's caretaker. He paused to take a drag of his cigarette before he told us, 'Officers and policemen. That's whom the Russians will go for first. Then it'll be all the rich shopkeepers and lawyers. It's going to be fun to watch.'

Officers? Lawyers? Fun to watch?

My uncle employed him in exchange for a small rent-free basement flat where he lived with his wife and son, a boy of about my own age. We had hardly ever spoken to each other. They were poor. It was probably a home with no books to read, no toy soldiers to play with. But I was shocked to find that here was someone who seemed to be relishing the prospect of life under our new masters.

I wanted to tell him that he didn't know what he was talking about. That the Russians were going to let my father and all the other officers go. But Mateczka whisked me away. A few hundred yards away, shaded by a row of chestnut trees, a cavalry squadron was waiting, their horses looking well groomed. Mateczka went up and patted one on the neck, murmuring a greeting.

Then a sergeant appeared and pressed something into my hand. 'I don't need it any more,' he said.

I looked down and saw it was a whistle.

By mid-afternoon the streets had emptied. I remember standing just outside my uncle's house wondering how it was that people seemed to know exactly how to behave. In the morning they had been milling about the streets, mingling with the soldiers and cursing all those who had dragged them into this mess. Now they had all gone home to await the arrival of Russian soldiers who had not set foot in Lwów since the Bolshevik defeat, eight years before I was born.

My first encounter with Stalin's Red Army was surprisingly benign. There were three of them, wearing khaki tunics with

matching round, peaked camps and black breeches with high boots.
They arrived in a looted horse cab, leading a second horse with a saddle on it tethered by its reins to the back. From our balconies and
doorways we watched them approach, ready to dart back inside at the
first sign of trouble, but they seemed not to have noticed us. The
most insouciant of this trio was reclining well back in the seat of
the cab, with his long legs outstretched, and smoking a cigarette.
He might have been the man who broke the bank at Monte Carlo.

They were heading in the direction of the citadel. The top of the
street was still barricaded, and shortly afterwards they returned the
way they had come. They were obviously a reconnaissance party –
brave men seeing if there was anybody left who was willing to fire at
them – before their comrades arrived en masse. These came on foot
and, despite the sunshine, they wore long grey overcoats, as if they
always brought snow. On their backs were small burlap sacks, and
fixed to their rifles were long spiky bayonets of a type I had never
seen before. They too went towards the citadel, stayed a while, and
then marched back again.

Then it began to get dark. Word was passed along the street that
the citadel contained a massive amount of supplies left by our troops.
There were no guards there. Why leave it all for the Russians?

Within minutes people started running towards the abandoned
barracks. They returned burdened by cans of tinned meat, packs of
coffee, flour, blankets and even bits of military equipment. Mateczka
and some of the other adults from my uncle's apartment building
watched with stone-faced disapproval. Was this how anarchy started?

Three smiling soldiers without belts, caps or any visible weaponry
joined us. Their uniforms were neither Polish nor Russian but of a
fairly well-cut grey-green material, with a spread-winged eagle
insignia on the right breast. Close up, I saw that in its talons the eagle
was clutching a small swastika. After my first Russians I was meeting
my first Germans.

They turned out to be newly released prisoners of war out for an
evening stroll, unguarded and unmolested. Mateczka spoke to them
in their own language, and they explained they were awaiting a Russian escort back to their own lines. After a couple of minutes'

conversation with her they bade us farewell and sauntered back towards the citadel.

'They said they had been well treated and regretted it all had to end this way,' she told me.

'Do they like the Russians?'

'I don't think so, *mon petit.*'

'So why are they on the same side?'

She didn't bother to answer. I doubt that she could. And, in any case, she had been distracted.

Approaching us through the falling darkness was a stooped figure dressed in the kind of long army overcoat worn by the Polish rank and file, but without the customary leather belt. My father's first kiss was for me, then Mateczka's hand. After which, with furtive glances in all directions, he ushered us back into the house.

'There aren't any Russians in here,' she assured him.

Colonel Borowiec was on the run.

Before General Langner had surrendered to the Russians he had negotiated generous terms. Most of the men who had defended Lwów were from locally raised units. All the non-commissioned ranks from sergeant-majors downwards, who made up the mass of the Polish prisoners, were allowed to hand in their arms and go home. Officers were to be permitted to keep all their belongings and leave for whatever country accepted them. Langner himself went to Romania and then, by boat, to France where just over 80,000 Polish soldiers would fight on as what remained of the Polish Army, and a government-in-exile was set up.

But the general was an exception. His signature was hardly dry on the surrender document before the secret police – the ideologues of the NKVD, the People's Commissariat of Internal Affairs – overrode the Red Army. Not only were officers who were already in Russian hands not to be released but the NKVD's militia began to hunt down those who, like my father, had evaded capture, together with senior policemen, university professors and anybody else whose class or politics identified them as an enemy of the people. It seemed that some of our caretaker's gloating predictions were fast coming true.

My father was able to escape because he was not only fluent in German but could also speak some Russian. During the first hours after the surrender a senior Soviet officer asked Colonel Borowiec to guide him and his aides through the mined Polish front line, so that he could make contact with the Germans. My father knew next to nothing about the minefields, but he readily agreed. He was determined to get out of Soviet hands. It had been a humiliating business because his captors also seem to have used him as a guarantor of their safe passage through any bands of Polish diehards who refused to surrender. He had been placed in the turret of an armoured car where his rank badges were in plain view of those civilians whose excessive expectations of their army had turned to notions of hideous betrayal, and who were eager to subject captive colonels to particular abuse.

At some point during the Russian envoy's conversation with the Germans, the colonel had slipped his escort and wandered away. As escapes go it seems to have been a low-key affair. There were no cries for him to halt, followed by shots that failed to find their mark. But it hadn't been entirely uneventful. When he passed a mob looting a brewery, a drunken sergeant had levelled an unsteady rifle at him, but the colonel had been able to disarm him. Eventually, he managed to acquire the happy disguise of an ordinary soldier's overcoat and made his way to his brother's flat.

I did not have the chance to talk to him that night. Mateczka said it was best to leave him alone. When she took me to say goodnight to him, before going to bed, he was sitting in my uncle's library with his head in his hands.

'Papa will have to leave the Russian zone,' Mateczka explained. 'Otherwise he will be arrested.'

'But if he goes to the German side, won't the Germans arrest him too?'

'The Germans respect officers. If they catch him, he'll go to a prisoner-of-war camp – an officers' camp. The Russians might send him to Siberia, or worse.'

Next morning he was waiting in the living room, dressed in one of my uncle's suits that was a bit too big for him.

'We'll go for a walk,' he announced.

At the time it did not occur to me that I had not been invited along entirely for the pleasure of my company. A man walking with a small boy was less likely to attract the attention of people looking for the fugitive officers of a proud army.

Dressed in leather jerkins and rather odd leather helmets – a bit like the kind pilots wore – the crews of some Russian armoured cars were trying to engage passers-by in conversation, but I noticed people seemed reluctant to linger. A more formal infantry column marched by with bayonets fixed. They were wearing large helmets with the red star in the front. Near the park was a horse-drawn artillery unit.

'Their animals are lean and neglected,' observed my father.

We walked over to where a crowd had gathered by a wall. They were reading a freshly pasted proclamation in Polish and Russian demanding the surrender of all weapons, including antique muzzle-loaders, sabres and bayonets. The punishment for failing to do so was death. It was signed by a Colonel Kotyakov.

'Remember that name,' said my father. 'He is your first Russian town commander.'

I never quite worked out why I should remember that name. Perhaps it was one of my father's little jokes, though the occasion hardly merited it. But remember the name I did, and here I am – no doubt many years after Colonel Kotyakov's own death – putting it down on paper as if I had learned it only yesterday.

There was something especially chilling about that poster. Suddenly I was living in a place where you could be executed for merely possessing the kind of decorative parade-ground cutlery that had always been part of our home. For the first time I realized what it meant to be occupied.

A coffee house was open, crowded with a mostly male clientele, many of them speaking Yiddish. I was served a glass of soda water and syrup, and when his coffee arrived my father questioned the waiter.

'What's the rate of exchange today?'

'One zloty, one rouble,' he was told.

'My God!'

The waiter shrugged and moved away.

My father looked shocked. 'Despite our economic difficulties,' he explained, 'we had one of the strongest currencies in Europe. It was backed by gold. The rouble is worthless outside Russia.'

'But where is our gold now?'

It was his turn to shrug.

On the way home he seemed preoccupied. We passed a stack of discarded military equipment guarded by a Russian soldier with Mongolian features. Whenever a crowd of onlookers got too close, he pointed his fixed bayonet at them and they retreated.

My father did not stay long in this occupied city. One rainy morning, dressed in a shabby overcoat donned for proletarian guise, he set out in a peasant cart with two demobilized soldiers returning to homes in western Poland. He appeared to have gone to war with a considerable amount of cash on him because Mateczka told me that he had given her and my uncle easily enough of his devalued zlotys to look after me. It was his intention to somehow make his way back to Maków and then send for me.

Whether Mateczka would come back and live with us was unclear. I was aware that there was some sort of rivalry between her and Ada and very much hoped that, in these uncertain times, her replacement might have opted to return to her own family. But there was every chance that my father might not get to Maków. He might join up with some of the Polish troops who were still fighting the Nazis. He might be taken prisoner and sent to Germany. He might even be killed, though I tried not to think about that.

For some days Lwów remained crowded with refugees and discharged soldiers shambling about the streets in crumpled uniforms. Soviet troops were everywhere. Tanks and trucks clogged the streets. And when these had moved on, they were often followed by long columns of infantry chanting their mournful marching songs, frequently responding to a brief solo supplied by a selected cantor. We found this rather novel.

On 6 October, the last conventional Polish resistance ended when the undefeated General Franciszek Kleeberg surrendered at Kock, in eastern Poland. About 200 German prisoners taken in Kleeberg's final counter-attack were freed. Mateczka wondered whether my father had been able to join this last stand by a man she thought was one of his Austro-Hungarian Army contemporaries. It was now almost three weeks since he had disappeared from our lives in the back of a hay cart.

By this time Lwów was returning to a semblance of normality. Shops were still well stocked with pre-war goods. Their best customers were Russian officers profiting from the favourable exchange rate. They bought everything in sight: toys, household utensils and, Mateczka informed me with a girlish giggle, any size of women's underwear they could get their hands on. I noticed they always carried holstered pistols but, with their hands full of purchases, they seemed friendly enough – although they must have known that this unabashed hunger for minor luxuries was not the best advertisement for their workers' paradise.

When we heard of the damage inflicted on Warsaw in a month of air attacks, shelling and street fighting, we knew that Lwów had been lucky. And yet, although the city was undoubtedly functioning, most of its Polish inhabitants were still dazed by the city's brief but violent war and Poland's partition.

According to my uncle, the non-Poles were much more ambivalent. The Ukrainians had adopted a wait and see attitude, and the Jews believed it much better to be occupied by the Communists than the Nazis. Whatever their other faults, the Russians were considered untainted by anti-Semitism. Many of the Red Army's political commissars were said to be Jews.

Around my uncle's table there was considerable discussion over the role Jews were now playing in his city. I learned that, apart from the very rich families, they had long been well known for their Communist sympathies. This was why they had flocked to join a police force renamed the People's Militia. Its old, dark blue uniforms had been modified by the victor's uncompromising red star on its caps, and members wore matching armbands. There was, as yet, no class warfare but 'bourgeois exploiters' like my uncle had no doubt it was coming and were determined to adopt a more appropriate exterior.

One day he turned up wearing a red armband with some kind of official insignia on it, explaining vaguely that he and several of his acquaintances had joined something called a Citizens' Committee. 'We must all work together to prevent chaos,' he informed us.

Mateczka and I thought him a dreadful traitor, quite likely to heap dishonour on to the Borowiec name. In the spring would come the great Anglo-French offensive and the restoration of Poland. Where would he be then?

Meanwhile, I went back to school. I had been enrolled in a local establishment almost as clean and modern as the one I had first attended in Kielce before moving to Maków. I was the only refugee in my class, and the other boys were indifferent to my presence, neither friendly nor unfriendly. The teachers seemed to adopt much the same attitude and left me alone. My only bugbear was the hour a day of compulsory Ukrainian the school had always been required to teach alongside Polish. All of the pre-war curriculum was taught, except for history. That had been suspended until the arrival of the new textbooks that taught a version of the previous 300 years of Polish–Russian relations entirely unknown to most Poles.

The anniversary of the 1917 Bolshevik Revolution was approaching, and the new authorities were preparing a huge parade with the participation of schoolchildren and factory workers. Householders were expected to fly a red flag. In order to comply most people simply tore their country's flag in two and, having disposed of the white half, flew the other. At my school the music master held auditions for a choir and my altar boy's voice was well received. But now it was being trained to sing the Internationale in a classroom where the Russian words of the Communist anthem were written in Latin script on a large blackboard. With the aid of the music master's violin we learned it in two sessions. A Soviet officer, with the usual pistol at his waist, turned up to hear us. He listened with a large smile on his face, nodding his head from time to time, apparently delighted at our progress.

But I never did get the chance to perform it in public, and perhaps that was just as well.

Several days before the anniversary, probably through ecclesiastical channels, word reached Mateczka that my father had arrived in

Maków. Apparently, the Germans had accepted him as a discharged reserve officer who, having spent most of his military career in the Austro-Hungarian Army, preferred to live under a German-speaking occupation. We were requested to attempt by all possible means to cross the partition line and join him.

So, early in November, we said goodbye to my uncle and aunt – no doubt with a certain amount of mutual relief – and boarded a crowded train at the central station. Our destination was Przemyśl, a town about a hundred miles away that straddled the San River. Its waters delineated a good part of the frontier between the two zones.

There, I was told, we would try to obtain a pass to cross.

# 7.   The Crossing

Dusk was falling but the outline of the person walking across the river on its snow-covered ice was quite clear. A few minutes before, somebody had partly opened a sash window to let some fresh air into the room where a corner wood burner was sometimes too effective.

My uninterrupted view of the ice walker's cautious progress was as good as watching a high-wire act. If the crossing could be achieved so easily, I wondered why we, and thousands like us, had been waiting here for weeks trying to acquire the right paperwork to get to the other side of the railway bridge.

Then I saw that somebody else was watching, and I immediately understood.

He was standing just below me, on the near bank. At that point his rifle was still slung over the right shoulder of a shapeless, ankle-length greatcoat. He had probably only just noticed. Perhaps he could hardly believe his eyes. The next thing I knew, the Russian had his weapon in his hands and was shouting something in the direction of the figure, who was now attempting to run – as much as you can run on ice – towards the opposite bank. I couldn't be certain whether it was a man or a woman. He, or she, walked on in defiant, tottering strides, their arms outstretched for balance. It was the action of somebody who had gone too far to stop.

The soldier put the rifle to his shoulder and slowly took aim.

When it came, the shot filled my ears.

I watched him work the bolt to eject the empty cartridge, then aim and fire again. The noise brought the other occupants of the apartment rushing to my side. By now the Russian's target was lying face down on the ice, though possibly still moving a bit. The light was fading fast and it was difficult to tell.

Mateczka firmly closed the window. Someone else drew the curtains. I was eleven years old and I had just seen my first person shot. I heard somebody say that a child should not be exposed to such things. No doubt the security radiated by these concerned adult voices was not entirely unwelcome. And yet, I don't recall being in need of comfort. After all, it was nobody I knew. In Lwów, I had been exposed to quite a lot of things. The air raids, the gunfire, the foxholes outside St Lazarus Church, the mob of disbanded soldiers on the day of the capitulation had all enlarged and considerably altered my understanding of military lore.

War wasn't sabres and bugles and colourful posters promising victory. War was the stench of my uncle's crowded cellar; enemy planes that hit their targets whenever they wished; officers without troops; troops without weapons; and the shame of surrender. And now, 200 metres away at most, war was a dark figure sprawled on the white expanse of a frozen river that separated the two armies occupying my country. If not already dead, or dying, whoever was out there would certainly freeze to death overnight.

Perhaps, like my father, their only crime was a desperate need to get home.

On arrival, the first useful Russian phrase I had learned was '*Davay nazad!*' It means 'move back'. In Przemyśl it was much used by the scruffy Soviet guards surrounding a massive building in which the Soviet-German Commission vetted everybody who, for one reason or another, preferred to take their chances under the Nazis. In theory anybody who could prove residence in the other zone was entitled to cross the river. In practice it was not as easy as that.

Throughout what adults assured me was the worst winter in living memory people would join the long line outside the building shortly before dawn. At first, they assembled in an orderly enough fashion. Then the German delegation would arrive, resplendent in polished jackboots and tailored overcoats of a noticeably superior cut to Soviet issue, and pandemonium would break out as everybody tried to petition their potential saviours.

Sullen soldiers stamped their feet, some showing the straw they packed into their short felt boots for extra insulation, and began their cries of '*Davay nazad!*', backing them up with menacing gestures from rifle butts and bayonets. A few minutes later there would be another surge, and the guards would start all over again. What we could not see were the Wehrmacht sentries on the other side of the river going through a similar performance with hundreds of Jews who wished to remove themselves from the expanding jurisdiction of the Nuremberg race laws.

Not surprisingly, the Germans were more inclined to speak to people who spoke their language, and though Mateczka's German was not as good as her French it was serviceable enough. It also helped if you were well dressed. Although we had travelled to Lwów at the height of a glorious summer, Mateczka had been prudent enough to pack an elegant fur coat, and this now came into its own. When we eventually pushed our way into the area where the Germans had parked their cars, she had no difficulty in handing a tall officer a letter explaining our predicament.

But this was only the start of it. Now we had to wait until both sides approved our petition.

Meanwhile, we had to stand in line every day just in case our names came up. If your name was called when you were not present, there was a good chance that you would have to start the whole process again. I soon added a new word to my Russian vocabulary: '*Nyet.*' I badly wanted to be reunited with my father, and to be denied such a simple request was baffling for a child. I must have driven Mateczka mad with my questions.

'Why is it so difficult?'

'I don't know, *mon chéri*. Perhaps a lot of people want to get away from the Russians, and the Russians don't want to let them go.'

'Are the Germans much better?'

Yes, she felt the Germans were a much more civilized, western people. One could reason with them, and they appeared polite. As for the Russians, well, almost anything could be expected from them.

The Germans might also be our enemies, but it was a sound decision to get away from the Bolsheviks.

At first, we stayed with a dressmaker, a woman who had owned her own shop before the war and now let out rooms. We shared the place with the wives of two Russian officers. One of them had a fourteen-year-old daughter, named Lala, with very blonde hair and a mischievous manner. We were all entitled to use the kitchen and the living room, which was the only heated place in the vast apartment.

One or two of the other rooms were still used by seamstresses who tried to copy frocks from a pile of dog-eared copies of old French fashion magazines. Their clients were mainly the wives of Soviet officers stationed in the area. Even I soon realized the wives were simple souls, lavishly lipsticked and childishly entranced by the drawings and photographs in the magazines that inspired their orders.

In the evenings, while the adults chatted among themselves, I played endless games of cards and battleships with Lala. As we played, we talked – or rather, Lala talked. She mostly told me about her boyfriends and what she got up to with them. I could never decide whether her tales were real or imaginary. All I knew was that these things excited and bothered me at the same time. Once she contrived to briefly press my hand to her nascent breasts, and I marvelled at how firm they were.

When we were not waiting outside the Commission we seemed to spend a lot of our time lining up for bread and other victuals. Food, or the lack of it, soon became the main subject of conversation in the apartment above the dressmaking shop, where the landlady's employees stitched and gossiped at the same time. There were various theories about how such a rich agricultural area could suddenly become so short of provisions.

'They're taking food by the trainload to Russia.'

'The Soviet officers here are buying everything for higher prices.' (This was said out of earshot of the two wives living with us.)

'The peasants are hoarding it for later.'

Whatever the reason, food remained scarce. Farmers from neighbouring villages brought in their produce in their horse-drawn carts, but the prices were staggering. The only cheap foodstuffs available were bread and the honey-butter sent from Russia.

The town had a number of pretty churches. And for the fur-hatted Orthodox and the more assimilated Reform Jews, who dressed the same as anybody else, there were two different synagogues. Both were rather grand buildings, designed by the same Jewish architect. Some smart residential areas still existed, and there was a park. But the overwhelming misery was only too apparent. There were scores of aimless refugees looking for someone to take care of them. Maimed and destitute soldiers from our defeated army were begging in the streets, long past disdaining the odd coin or cigarette tossed in their direction by a Russian. It was bitterly cold and, if you didn't have a full belly and a warm bed, the snow was anything but picturesque.

One day, Mateczka led me to a railway siding where a train of wooden cattle trucks with sliding doors was parked. Inside were the remnants of a Polish cavalry brigade, many of them still recovering from their wounds. There were no officers among them – any who had tried to stay with their men had most likely been arrested by the NKVD. The troopers had installed small wood-burning stoves in their wagons, and people from the town were giving them what food they could spare. Mateczka was reduced to tears, and I think she gave them some money.

Loudspeakers in the town centre blared the Internationale but on Sundays, and sometimes even midweek, the churches were packed. Some people even stood outside to listen to High Mass. God was merciful, the priest assured us during one sermon, and His mercy would once again shine on Poland. But first, the people had to expiate their sins, which were considerable. According to this priest Poland was populated by some of the worst sinners in the world. Our defeat was all to do with God's wrath. This was disturbing news, and I asked Mateczka if Germany's victory could be explained by the Nazis being much less sinful than we were?

She told me this was not the case. From all she had heard, Germany was a pretty sinful place too. I wondered if there were many women in Germany like the ones I had noticed standing on street corners in certain parts of town. Off-duty Russian soldiers took an interest in them, and I once drew this to Mateczka's attention. She told me not to look; I was much too young to ask questions about such things, and she refused all further discussion on the subject. Naturally, this only made me more curious, and so I asked Lala about it. She giggled and blushed and told me they were bad women who took money from men who wanted to see them naked. I wondered where they found anywhere warm enough to do this.

The Soviets were now in considerable strength in our half of the town and were looking for officers' billets. One day, the dressmaker informed us that a Russian officer and his family would be moving in and we would have to work out alternative sleeping arrangements. Mateczka and I transferred ourselves to the large room already occupied by the two officers' wives and the teenaged Lala, who between them occupied two beds. Now Mateczka and I slept in one bed, while the two women and Lala huddled together in the other. By early December, the temperature in the unheated room had plummeted and we woke in the mornings to find that water left in the china hand bowl was covered by a thin sheet of ice. No one wanted to get up.

The Soviet officer – a tall, dark Asian-featured senior lieutenant – was polite and friendly. Conversation was easy enough in the kind of pidgin lingo the speakers of close Slav tongues tend to adopt with each other. Some members of that crowded household already spoke enough Russian to do without it. I was soon able to communicate without too much difficulty.

This was the direct result of the arrival of the officer's two children – a daughter about the same age as Lala and her eleven-year-old brother, Refik, a Turkic name meaning 'close friend'. But whatever their Tartar origins might have been, their Soviet assimilation was complete and they always spoke Russian among themselves. They were bright children. Apart from chess sets they had few toys. What they did have was a genius for concocting games that merely required such items as an exercise book, old newspapers, pencils and scissors.

Refik shared my passion for things military. Whenever the crunch of marching troops was heard outside he would abandon our game of checkers, or whatever we were doing, and rush to a window. Addicted as I still was to the spectacle of marching ranks and long bayonets,

I would pointedly continue with our play and decline to show the slightest interest in the Soviet Army. This massive display of will-power was, I think, my first act of political defiance. And politics soon came between us.

Possibly because the commissars could not reconcile themselves to the idea that Poland's downtrodden masses might be better off than the average Russian, Moscow's interpretation of world events was undermined by the number of radio sets that still remained in private hands. Our landlady owned one. Every evening we were able to gather round and listen to the Polish language news bulletins and communiqués that were being broadcast from a studio used by our exiled government in Paris. And although there was no mention of the anticipated Anglo-French attack on Germany's western border, we all rejoiced whenever there was news of a major setback for one of our enemies elsewhere.

Little Finland, once part of Czarist Russia with border territories that Stalin was determined to recover, was giving the Russians a bloody nose. With its three and a half million citizens it was the smallest member of the League of Nations. The Red Army was clearly expecting the kind of pushover they had enjoyed when they stabbed Poland in the back, while most of its army was facing the Germans. They had a shock. In below-zero temperatures Finnish ski troops in white camouflage – the first time any army had used it in action – ran rings around the Russians. Enthralled, we listened to accounts of forest ambushes, of Finnish snipers picking off their brown-clad targets at will, of Soviet tanks destroyed by daring men who got close enough to jam tracks with crowbars and then finished them off with the petrol bombs the Finns called Molotov cocktails after Stalin's duplicitous foreign minister Vyacheslav Molotov.

One evening, we had just heard that the League of Nations had expelled the Soviet Union from its ranks when one of the Russian wives drifted into our room and, no doubt noting our smiling faces, asked what the radio was saying.

Somebody told her.

'Switch it off!' she screamed. 'Switch it off at once, or I'll report you to the authorities.'

The atmosphere was never the same after that, and I no longer played checkers – or anything else – with Refik.

At about the same time, the rumours started. The NKVD were raiding flats and houses at night and arresting reserve officers. We had one staying with us – a Jewish lawyer for whom there was no escape on the German side of the river. He started sleeping on the table in the living room, 'just until things calm down'.

One day, we went to a monastery crammed with refugees – or fugitives who wanted to become refugees – where the stench of unwashed bodies was nauseating. I didn't want to go in, but Mateczka insisted. She thought a priest might have a letter for us. And indeed, there was a letter. It was from my father. I have no idea how she knew it was there. I suppose one of the refugees had delivered it to a priest or monk. The clergy had somehow managed to set up a courier service that transcended these new frontiers.

My father's news was that he had been arrested, then released, and was now living back in our home at Maków Podhalański. He urged Mateczka to do all she could to bring me home, saying it was not as difficult as it looked.

'I have done it, and so have other people.'

She read it all aloud to me and was obviously upset by the reproach in that last sentence.

'How much more can I do?'

I could see the tears welling in her eyes, and I felt for her. Day after day, when she wasn't lining up for food, she was a shivering petitioner outside the Commission building. I thought my father was being very unfair. But perhaps he knew what he was doing, and some extra effort was made, because it was shortly afterwards that the miracle occurred. She came back with the magic papers signed by both occupying powers.

Apparently, in the end, it had all been quite simple. Up until then, though she had always described herself as a governess, she had never had the opportunity to explain my own background. This time she was asked for my details, and she had a brainwave that she acted upon – probably at some risk to both of us. She announced that my full name was Andreas von Neumann and that I was the child of wealthy *Volksdeutsche* parents who had sent me to Lwów, not only to keep me away from the fighting but also because of the growing hostility towards the German-speaking community in Kraków, where they lived. Unfortunately, my papers had been lost when one of our suitcases was destroyed in Lwów, during the fighting there.

Despite these happy developments it was not possible for us to leave immediately. The trains had been stopped because the rail bridge across the river had been damaged in the September fighting. The traffic it had carried since then had weakened it to the point where repairs were necessary before it could carry any more.

A few weeks before Christmas, we moved out of the crowded dressmaker's apartment where the atmosphere between the Russians and the other occupants had grown almost as frigid as the air we all breathed. Mateczka had discovered a young woman, deprived of her man by death or captivity, who rented rooms to refugees for a reasonable price in her clean and well-heated apartment overlooking the river.

It was from one of its windows that I saw the fugitive being shot on the ice.

At last, early in the New Year, we received word that the trains would soon start moving again. Mateczka had to go to another office with our passes, where she was informed that we would not be getting seats on the first train. But perhaps we would be allocated places on the second or the third.

Our turn came on another freezing mid-January day. We said our goodbyes and set out from the apartment on a horse-drawn sleigh with all our belongings, including Mateczka's hatboxes. She wore her fur coat with matching accessories and looked marvellous. I was dressed in a good-quality white sheepskin jacket, a second-hand bargain acquired locally.

At the railway station we had to fight our way into a vast room where blue-uniformed Soviet customs inspectors examined our luggage. They were not unpleasant or particularly difficult; our inspector even helped us close the suitcases and wished us bon voyage.

While we waited to board the train I broached a subject that was so painful to me I had pushed it to the back of my mind until then, but it could no longer be avoided.

What were her future plans?

She told me her immediate intention was to stay with some friends who lived on a large estate in the central part of the country. After that, she wasn't sure. Perhaps she would go to Italy, which was still neutral, and from there to her beloved France.

So she wouldn't be going back with me to my father's home in Maków?

No, she would not.

Once we got to the other side we would be taking an express train to Kraków, and there we would part ways. I would take a train south to the little town I had left over four months ago, to get away from the war. She would take another one, in the opposite direction.

I knew I was going to miss her, and miss her terribly. Since the outbreak of the war my mother – whom I had seen so little of since the age of six – had vanished from my life. She probably had no idea where I was. I certainly had no real idea where she was, other than in Warsaw somewhere, with my little half-brother. And Warsaw had been heavily bombed. Mateczka might have meant 'Little Mother', and this was a term of great affection, but we both knew that she meant a lot more than that to me.

Of course, I told her none of this. I was probably too close to tears. All I could get out was, 'Who's going to look after me at home?'

'You're a big boy now, Andrzej. Other boys of your age don't have governesses.'

'But they do have mothers!'

She did not reply.

Full of self-pity, I turned away.

Someone helped us get our luggage into an unheated cattle truck with glassless windows full of wretchedly cold people beating their arms against their thighs like penguins and blowing on their fingers. It was rumoured there was a reluctance to risk heavier and more expensive rolling stock because the bridge was still considered a little uncertain. The train waited for what seemed like an eternity. Then, with a high-pitched whistle, its locomotive rumbled slowly forward towards the river.

Within about the space of a minute I had my last glimpse of the Russian sentries, with their usual fixed bayonets, and then, as we crossed over to the west bank, I saw the first armed German soldiers that were not on some newsreel. Beneath their distinctive coal-scuttle helmets they were protecting the tops of their heads, ears, cheeks and jawlines against frostbite with woollen scarves knotted beneath their chins. It was a homely touch that somehow robbed them of their menace – although, like the Soviets, they had also fixed their bayonets.

The train stopped not far from a large barracks complex. There was a line of rusting Polish tanks partly covered with snow.

A German warrant officer with a fur collar on his overcoat walked briskly alongside the train.

'*Alle heraus!*' he shouted.

We were definitely on the other side.

## 8.   For Germans Only

Next day, on the Kraków express with Mateczka, there was a man standing in the corridor who every so often had to press himself against the side of the carriage to allow people to get by on their way to the toilet. I noticed he wore a crumpled white armband on one of the upper sleeves of his overcoat. There was some sort of insignia on it.

'Excuse me,' I said, 'but what does that armband mean?'

'Jew,' he said.

He almost spat the word out, as if he loathed Jews almost as much as the people who were making him wear it for being one. It was the first time either of us had seen the compulsory white armband with its blue Star of David, which all Polish Jews now had to wear. In Germany itself it was a yellow star with '*Jude*' written on it. Obviously the Nazis had imposed their laws just as fast as the Soviet commissars in Lwów had insisted that every schoolchild learned to sing the Internationale.

Our first night on the German side of Przemyśl had been spent with some people to whom Mateczka had somehow engineered an introduction before we left the town's Russian sector. The following morning, we had boarded the regular express train full of bedraggled civilians and various members of the Wehrmacht who had presumably been on duty over Christmas and were at last going home on leave. I noticed some of the Germans had bayonets with silver tassels attached to the scabbards. They were not unfriendly and helped us get our luggage on board before finding seats in the first-class cars marked '*Nur für Deutsche*' – for Germans only.

Our carriage was not heated, and we sat by a window in our buttoned coats watching Poland's snow-covered flatlands rush by. We rarely saw civilian passengers on the platforms of the stations we passed through. Sometimes there were German sentries trying to keep warm by walking briskly up and down, then stomping the snow off their jackboots when they turned.

It was dark by the time we reached Kraków, and we could not leave its main station because the curfew had already started. Poles needed a special pass to venture into the sub-zero streets outside in search of a warm bed for the night. Along with hundreds of others we huddled down among our luggage in a large waiting room that was crowded enough to be warmed by a fug of body heat and the tobacco smoke supplied by those who could afford it.

Throughout the night loudspeakers blared announcements in two languages. Uniformed Germans stepped over and, occasionally, on the sprawled figures with a brusque air of authority. Mateczka and I did not sleep a wink. She spent her time writing a long letter to my father. When she had finished she sealed it in a large envelope together with some documents.

'It explains everything,' she said.

I saw that her eyes were brimming with tears. This made it difficult for me to hold back my own, or even get my words out.

'Where are you going?' I eventually gasped.

'I will be taking a train north. But only after I've put you on yours.'

My father, she assured me, knew how to get in touch with her. It was all in the letter that was placed in my suitcase before I boarded the train for the two-hour trip to Maków. One of the other passengers, a near neighbour, recognized me and promised to keep an eye on me. Mateczka kissed me goodbye, and we both wept copiously.

Then I was aboard the train, and a railway official on the platform was announcing our departure by alternately shouting '*Abfahrt!*' and '*Odjazd!*' Suddenly the train jolted and began to move slowly away. Mateczka, in her matching fur hat and coat, was waving and then dabbing at her eyes with a handkerchief held in a gloved hand. I pressed my face to the window and waved until I could no longer see her, and probably beyond.

Never in all of my eleven years and three months had I felt so desolate.

1. *Top left*: My father, Colonel Stanisław Borowiec, *c.*1925, wearing the uniform of a newly independent Poland. 2. *Top right*: Myself as a six-year-old lieutenant making the old Polish salute in the cap provided by my governess, Mateczka. 3. *Bottom left*: My Uncle Józef and I collect our bread ration in the Russian-occupied city of Lwów, October 1939. 4. *Bottom right*: How I looked, not quite sixteen, at the start of the Warsaw Uprising.

5. *Top left*: Women seated before one of the Uprising's most popular posters, 'TO ARMS!'
6. *Top right*: The damage around the *Arbeitsamt* where I threw my first grenade.
7. *Bottom*: Some of the Zośka Battalion on the captured Panther tank they called 'Magda' and used to break into the small Gęsiówka concentration camp. I joined the battalion for the Czerniaków bridgehead fighting.

8. *Above left*: A new pistol and a new kitten. Pets soon became a luxury we couldn't afford.
9. *Above right*: Eleven-year-old Różyczka Goździewska helped us out in a field hospital.
10. *Below*: A playful sabre duel during a lull from more serious affairs.

11. *Above left*: Beware snipers. A crawl alongside one of the low and flimsy barricades typical of the Uprising's early days. 12. *Above right*: Barricades soon became much more substantial affairs and even included this knocked-out Hetzer tank destroyer. 13. *Below*: Stalking in the rubble-strewn no-man's-land between the barricades. Both these AK fighters wear captured German camouflage smocks. Mine was off a corpse.

14–15. *Top*: Two Ukrainians serving in an SS unit that massacred Polish civilians are led to their execution, to be buried in a common grave after their coveted boots are removed.
16. *Bottom left*: Their commanding officer may well have been Oberführer Oskar Dirlewanger, whose pensive features belied his rampant sadism. 17. *Bottom right*: Captured Wehrmacht were usually well treated. Two Poles lift a tall wounded German while his escort walks behind them with a pistol.

18–20. *Top*: Riflemen of the Kiliński Battalion engage an isolated German garrison who, for almost three weeks, staged a mini-Alamo in the tall PAST telephone exchange until they were literally smoked out after a fire engulfed the entire building. *Bottom*: They emerged with their hands up.

21. *Left*: Captured at PAST was this Waffen-SS Sturmscharführer, who failed to remove his distinctive collar tabs.
22. *Above*: Contrast his gunpoint interrogation to that of Wehrmacht Major Max Dirske, comfortably seated and smoking a cigarette. 23. *Below left*: Home Army soldiers handle a PIAT. PIAT stood for 'Projector Infantry Anti-Tank', a British hand-held weapon dropped in by the RAF. We couldn't get enough of them.
24. *Below right*: Our best tank-killing zones were in narrow streets with high barricades such as this one, which has been crowned with the embossed head of Hans Frank, Poland's hated Nazi governor.

25. *Above*: Engineers disarming then extracting the explosive from one of the huge bombs lobbed by the Germans' enormous siege mortars. 26. *Below*: Though the bombs were fused to explode immediately after they had penetrated reinforced concrete, multiple layers of thin civilian ceilings often failed to detonate them, thereby providing our grenade makers with an excellent filling.

I had been sobbing quietly to myself for some time when I became aware of the large and somewhat florid face of a uniformed German gazing down at me. He was saying something.

'He wants to know why you're crying?' translated the man who had promised to look after me.

Ashamed, I wiped away the tears with the back of my hand but made no attempt to reply. Then I noticed the German was holding something in his hand; it was a sweet wrapped in silver paper. For a split second I wondered whether I should accept a gift from the enemy. But I did not want to appear rude, so I took it and at the same time asked my interpreter how to say thank you.

'*Danke*,' he said.

'*Danke*,' I repeated, and I think I managed a smile.

The German beamed, patted me on the head and returned to his seat. On either side of him sat other soldiers of the Reich. The journey was the longest I had ever made without an adult; it seemed interminable.

It was four months since I had left Maków, driven to Kraków at the height of a glorious summer in the funny car without a steering wheel that could ride on rails. Now the town's sleepy streets had their winter coat on, and in them I spotted a couple of German uniforms. But, at first glance, the war did not appear to have touched the town – at least, not structurally. The neighbour who had boarded the train at Kraków with me insisted on carrying my suitcase to the door of my home, then disappeared before I had time to thank him properly. I suppose he did not want it to be thought that he was after a tip.

When I knocked on the door, our red setter, Mik, began his mad barking and then, to my immense delight, shut up as soon as I called out his name. Ada appeared, took one look at me and screamed. This was also nice and rather unexpected. Then, from behind her, emerged a bearded, crumpled and rather quizzical-looking figure in an old sweater.

It was several seconds before I realized I was looking at my father.

Winter remained unrelentingly harsh. In Maków, for adults and children alike, the dreariness was only relieved by our belief that spring would bring the Anglo-French offensive that was guaranteed to restore our freedom. We believed in it like we believed in the Resurrection, and it was obvious that Berlin and Moscow shared at least part of our faith because they had recently issued a joint statement advising France and Britain of the foolishness of continuing the war.

Meanwhile, the water pipes froze. We had to go to the wells that still functioned and collect our water in buckets, just as I had done with Mateczka during the brief siege of Lwów. There was no coal and little wood. In order to reduce our heating requirements we shut up our upper floor. I slept with my father in a room that had been temporarily converted into a kind of study cum dining room. Ada slept in an alcove off the kitchen, the warmest part of the house. No doubt my father joined her there from time to time.

Then, just when we thought things couldn't get any worse, the local committee in charge of rehousing refugees added to our misery by billeting a family of three on us. A middle-aged couple and their eighteen-year-old son moved into one of our downstairs rooms. They came from that 90,000 square kilometres of western Poland that before 1918 had been under Prussian administration. Now Hitler had returned it to East Prussia, and all Polish place names were changed to German ones. Thousands of Poles were expelled, often at short notice, with no more than they could carry on to the freezing freight cars.

Even so, my father soon resented our uninvited guests. Their son, who was probably the most able-bodied male in the house, had an irritating habit of absenting himself whenever there was snow to clear or water to fetch. I heard Papa complaining about him to Ada.

'A boy his age should be in Romania trying to find a ship that will take him to our army in France. He's idle, stupid. And God help Poland, because there's a lot more like him.'

My father had become a difficult, brooding person with little patience for a small boy's incessant questioning. Ada, sensing my bewilderment, told me about the difficult time Papa had getting back to Maków. How one day she had seen this slightly bent, unshaven figure dressed in an old suit and with a rucksack on his back, walking slowly towards his home.

'It was hardly the way he expected to be returning from this war,' she said.

Shortly after his return, the Germans arrived and arrested him. But less than two weeks later, he reappeared. He had been released on the grounds that he was a German-speaking former Austro-Hungarian officer and a reservist who had retired from the Polish Army some time before the war. All he had to do was report to the local military headquarters once a week and, as it turned out, this was staffed by a friendly Austrian unit who spoke his kind of German.

It seemed Mateczka had been right. Our conquerors knew how to treat an officer. However, there was a price. Colonel Borowiec was one of about twenty local notables – all retired officers and senior civil servants, including the mayor – who were listed as 'guarantors' that there would be no hostile acts against the occupying power. The implication was clear. They were hostages. The price of any act of armed resistance in Maków was their lives.

No one doubted that the threat was real. Some 10,000 civilians had already been massacred in various reprisal shootings for alleged 'acts of terrorism'. Then, just after Christmas, when Mateczka and I were in Przemyśl and longing to reach the German zone, came the first example of the gross retribution the Nazis were willing to exact for any attack on their troops. On the evening of 26 December 1939, two Wehrmacht sergeants were in a tavern in the Warsaw dormitory town of Wawer when a pair of Poles, who both had criminal records, gunned them down. The shooting may have occurred during a drunken row over a black-market deal that had gone sour.

According to their notions of 'collective responsibility' local German troops responded by rounding up the first 120 Polish males they could find. Some were dragged from their beds. Several were not even from Wawer but were Christmas visitors. After some kind of surreal drumhead court martial, five *Volksdeutsche* and a Russian were released and the remainder sentenced to death. One man darted into the night and escaped. The rest were led out into the frosty air and machine-gunned in batches by the light of vehicle headlamps. Seven wounded managed to play dead long enough to avoid a coup de grâce and were able to crawl away. The rest, one aged fifteen, were buried in mass graves.

Full details of the massacre emerged slowly. But the Nazis soon made sure that their basic arithmetic was understood: 2 dead Germans = at least 100 dead Poles. It was meant to be the kind of deterrent that terrifies a subject population into obedience. Then, after a while, Warsaw walls began to carry the words '*Pomścimy Wawer*'. ('We will avenge Wawer.')

I was aware that my father was considered important enough to be on some kind of list. Had he not been, I dare say I would have been offended. But even though I knew something of the events at Wawer, it never seems to have penetrated my eleven-year-old brain that, given Poland's proud tradition of resisting foreign usurpers, my father was in imminent danger of being taken out and shot. His very existence depended on there being none of the stirring acts of defiance I yearned for.

What I did know was that we were getting poorer by the day, and my father was turning what he could into cash: oriental rugs, his elegant fur coat, our wind-up gramophone and several paintings. Almost invariably the buyers were peasants from the outlying villages. In some ways they had never had it so good. While towns and cities were beginning to go hungry, the peasants charged a fortune for the food stocks they had prudently hoarded.

My old school had reopened, but it was decided that I would not be studying a curriculum imposed by our new masters. The Germans had devised an education plan that was far more radical than the one imposed by the Russians in their slice of Poland, and also much simpler. All secondary schools and universities would remain closed. Only a few vocational establishments teaching subjects such as carpentry, metalwork, electronics and plumbing were permitted to function.

'We are Slavs,' explained my father. 'Under the new order we're second-class citizens and a full education is wasted on us. We're allowed to read and write, and perhaps become craftsmen skilled enough to work in the factories of the Reich. But we are not to train as doctors, architects or engineers.'

Seeing my consternation, he added that this madness would, of course, all change in the spring when the enemy met their comeuppance at the hands of the Anglo-French and the large contingent of Poles who had managed to join them. Meanwhile, I would be continuing my studies according to a pre-war curriculum with an unemployed teacher who gave private tuition.

She turned out to be a pleasant young woman who gave me much of the attention that had been lacking since my separation from Mateczka. At home I read French with my father, who also insisted on teaching me German.

'But why bother, if they're going to lose the war?'

'They will lose the war, but their language will survive. It's an important language and you must learn it.'

I learned it fast, though I found the grammar tedious. My father's Austrian-accented German was excellent but he was a poor instructor, far too impatient. I dreaded the lessons themselves but enjoyed the homework. I did this on the massive mahogany table in our one-room living quarters, while my father either carved his wooden heads or paced up and down playing bits of Mozart on his violin. Our piano had been sold to the local tailor; he owned a house nearby and was making a fortune sewing uniforms for the German customs officials that were now living in the town.

Maków had now become a border town on the line between the occupied *Generalgouvernement* zone and the part annexed to the Reich, a few kilometres to the west. If we wanted to visit the nearest town that was big enough to support a cinema, we had to cross this new frontier, and that required a special pass.

There was news of Mateczka. She was staying with some friends who had a large estate somewhere on the central plain. I was told I must write her a letter in French at least once a month – another chore I didn't enjoy. Fond of her though I was, I could rarely think of anything interesting to say. In any case, there was a certain amount of self-imposed censorship; I suspected that my father wasn't reading my letters merely to check my French grammar. I was beginning to adjust to her absence, but some days it wasn't easy.

We were virtually cut off from the outside world. Within hours of the German arrival in Maków wall posters had gone up demanding on pain of death that all radios and weapons of any description be surrendered at designated collecting points. Ada, who was alone in the house, had handed over the radio as well as the service pistol my father had swapped for her smaller automatic. The old Russian rifle I used to play with had also gone from the attic.

Nonetheless, we knew that some brave souls had hidden their radios and were picking up the Polish language broadcasts from Paris. Passed by word of mouth, the stories often grew in the telling and, young or old, our spirits soared as once more we had it confirmed that a massive Allied army was about to descend on the Ruhr. Naturally, the enemy-controlled press, published in German and Polish, chose to ignore these developments. We almost felt sorry for the soldiers in their grey-green uniforms, getting happily drunk in our local bars and singing their song about a girl called Lore and the beauty of all girls of eighteen. Poor fools. How little they knew.

One of the taverns they frequented was the place where I had stayed with my father on our first night at Maków, only now it was under new management. The assimilated Jew who had run it then had apparently waited until he saw the first enemy tank pass his door and had blown his brains out. His replacement was a *Volksdeutsch*.

Identifying oneself as *Volksdeutsch* could be a mixed blessing. For along with extra food rations and well-paid employment, males of military age were also accorded the privilege of conscription into the Wehrmacht. Another factor was the hostility of the majority of people they lived amongst. For though there might be some sympathy for those with an obvious German name, there was none at all for people whose surnames were obviously Polish but who had gone out of their way to persuade the occupiers of their ancient German roots. The few people who did this in Maków were regarded as traitors and were the subject of considerable speculation.

'What's going to happen to them after the war, Papa?'

'They'll hang.'

'On lamp posts?'

'Don't ask stupid questions. Back to your work!'

My father was more cantankerous than ever. I don't think he could help it. He was preoccupied. In 1410, a Borowiec had fought in the great Slav victory over the Teutonic knights at the Battle of Grunwald. He knew where his duty lay, but he didn't know how to go about it.

I began to notice that people I had never seen before were calling on him. On one of these occasions I saw that, while he was closeted with a visitor in one of the freezing upstairs rooms, outside another man paced up and down along the garden fence, swinging his arms to keep himself warm and occasionally pausing to look around him.

One day, I plucked up the courage to ask him something that had been bothering me ever since his harsh words about our eighteen-year-old lodger. Why didn't he try the Romanian route to France himself?

'Don't you want to fight any more, Papa?'

I had dreaded the prospect that he might lose his temper – after all, I was almost accusing him of cowardice – but he looked me in the eye and calmly gave me two reasons. The first was that Romania had become closer to the Germans and some of the officers who, like himself, did not have the chance to be among the first wave of Polish troops to cross its border had found themselves interned there. The second one came as something of a shock.

'Some people are needed here too,' he said. 'That's all I'm going to say, and even that must never be repeated. Not to your old school friends because you want to impress them. Not to anybody. Understand?'

Almost feverish with excitement, I went away and mulled it over. Was my father involved in organizing an uprising against the enemy? And if that was the case, weren't we all in mortal danger? A recent rash of German wall posters had once again warned that any hostile act against 'the legitimate occupying power' was punishable by death. Now I realized what his mysterious visitors with their lookouts at the garden fence were up to. They were his fellow conspirators.

But how exactly were they planning to do it? Was it planned to coincide with the great Allied attack in the Spring?

Of course, it never occurred to me that my father had another very good reason not to go to France: his determination to keep me out of my mother's hands.

In March, the Finns agreed to give the Soviets 11 per cent of their territory, and a peace treaty was signed in Moscow. My father explained it was essentially a draw and the Finns could feel proud of themselves for hanging on to as much territory as they had. He considered it conclusive proof that Stalin's army was not as good as Hitler's army. But he thought the Finns wise to have negotiated when they did. Winter had been their biggest ally, and now it was almost over.

Spring saw Colonel Borowiec turning his much-admired flower beds into a vegetable garden. I was required to help: plants had to be dug up and fresh seeds planted with as much horse manure as we could find. We were going to become as self-sufficient as the peasants who had acquired enough spare cash to buy our gramophone and rugs off us. Several of our neighbours were doing exactly the same thing.

But it puzzled me. Why bother to make these long-term preparations if, any day now, everything was going to change for the better? Adults seemed to like making unnecessary work for themselves. It was boring too.

The weather was getting warmer and drier. In between gardening duties I was able to take long walks with my pre-war school friends. All of them had spent the brief campaign in Maków, where there had been no action, and they couldn't get enough of my war stories from Lwów. I regaled them with tales of air raids, artillery fire, even a shell that had exploded close enough to blow me out of the makeshift bed in my uncle's cellar. As for my account of the shooting of the figure trying to cross the frozen river at Przemyśl, their envy knew no bounds.

'You saw it? You were actually that close?'

They could only console themselves with the thought that very soon the French Army was about to go through Germany like a knife through butter and not stop advancing until they had liberated all of

Poland. This would also entail a swift victory over the Russians. My own experiences were no more than a dress rehearsal.

'We'll see it all soon,' they assured me. 'It's going to start any day now.'

But it did not start where we thought it would start.

And it wasn't the Anglo-French who started it.

## 9.   For Whom Our Bell Tolled

In April 1940, Hitler invaded neutral Norway. On the front page of the German newspaper that my father read were maps with arrows purporting to show various deployments, as well as pictures of Wehrmacht ski troops clad in the sort of white snow-camouflage overalls the Finns had worn.

According to the Polish radio station in Paris a Polish brigade under General Zygmunt Bohusz-Szyszko, an officer my father knew quite well, were fighting alongside French, British and Norwegian troops for control of the North Atlantic port of Narvik through which Sweden, another neutral country, exported its iron ore to Germany. The news bulletins from Paris stated that British ships and aircraft had trapped and destroyed a lot of enemy vessels while the German newspaper claimed similar success for the Kriegsmarine, whose tally was reported to include an aircraft carrier. Both were more or less right. Even so, we were a bit disappointed in the Royal Navy. We had expected the British to blow them all out of the water and win the day.

But it soon became irrelevant, because the next thing we heard was that the Allies were withdrawing from Norway and rushing their troops to France where, much to our amazement, the Germans had struck first.

Holland and Belgium – like Norway, both neutral countries – were quickly overrun. But these were small countries with small armies. France had one of the biggest armies in the world, and certainly the best. Her soldiers were as good as Poles, but there were lots more of them and they were better equipped. Soon the real war would begin.

And so it did. But not quite in the way we expected.

Day after day, the enemy's communiqués spoke of swift advances into a country whose martial prowess I had been brought up on.

Before long the German newspaper carried photographs of endless columns of morose-looking French prisoners guarded by grinning German soldiers, some of whom had impertinent spring flowers sprouting from the barrels of their rifles.

No one knew what to make of this. Was France caving in as fast as our own country? Impossible! I could hardly get a word of explanation from my father.

I overheard him talking to one of our neighbours, a retired lawyer. 'In a way it vindicates us,' he was saying. 'We're no longer the only country they've rolled over.'

'Yes,' said the lawyer. 'What a consolation.'

It was a brilliant day in June, a Friday, when we heard the church bell pealing in mid-afternoon. It was too late for a funeral and, in any case, the sound was different. These were loud, celebratory peals. A town policeman (weaponless, badgeless but nonetheless reconstituted in the same uniform) happened to be passing our newly planted vegetable plot.

'Why is the bell being rung?' inquired my father.

'The Germans are doing it, sir. Paris has fallen.'

My father turned as white as a sheet. Without another word he picked up one of his favourite carved-head walking sticks and left our garden, a stooped, greying figure with a shirt tail hanging out of his trousers. Fighting would continue for another week before the French agreed to sign an armistice, but for several days all the adults I knew acted as if the fall of Paris was the end of all our hopes.

A few days later we found ourselves looking at a front-page picture straight out of our worst nightmares: Hitler standing on one of the bridges across the Seine with the Eiffel Tower in the background. Inside were more tourist snaps of the Führer's day trip to Paris: Hitler at the Arc de Triomphe; Hitler at L'Opéra; Hitler at the Louvre; Hitler at Napoleon's tomb.

Our own summer, as if to make up for the cruel winter, was unusually warm. I swam with my friends on the beach at the bend in the river where I had watched Mateczka get into the first two-piece swimming costume I'd ever seen on a woman. We repeated to each other what all our parents were saying: that the Poles had held out longer than the French; that France had betrayed them; that it was no longer the victorious France of the Napoleonic conquests and the stubborn war in the trenches. France was now a cowardly nation. Marshal Pétain, the hero of Verdun, had agreed to collaborate with the enemy and in return had been allowed to set up a new French government in the spa town of Vichy. At least Poland had never formally surrendered by signing an armistice or sunk as low as forming a collaborationist government like the Vichy French and the people who were following Vidkun Quisling, in Norway.

On the contrary, there were whispers that a Polish language broadcast relayed by the BBC had reported that our government-in-exile had escaped from France and set themselves up in London. Many of the Poles who had been fighting alongside the French had also joined them there. The war wasn't over. Our liberation was going to come from England. My father clearly believed so, and his initial despair at the news of France's defeat seemed to have evaporated. He explained to me that the British owned half the world. Furthermore, they lived on an island and it was not so easy to conquer an island, especially when its occupants had a strong navy. They had not been invaded since 1066. Not even the Swiss could claim that.

According to our enemy none of this mattered. The Luftwaffe was doing to London what it had done to Warsaw exactly a year ago. The British capital was one blazing inferno. Newspapers showed pictures of tearful English children in strange hats carrying gas masks and waiting to be evacuated. Every day hundreds of planes bombed London. People no longer lived in their houses but were reduced to a troglodyte existence in underground railway stations where they apparently cursed the warmonger Churchill for rejecting the Führer's generous peace offer.

But somehow England was not caving in the way France had done. And unlike Warsaw, London did not have to contend with panzers and artillery as well as bombers. By late autumn the enemy had still not invaded. The BBC's Polish language broadcasts must have mentioned the contribution being made by Polish pilots flying British Hurricanes under RAF command because, before long, everybody seemed to be talking about them. They called themselves the Kościuszko Squadron after a formation that flew in the 1920 Polish-Soviet war.

I was listening avidly one evening to a conversation on aerial warfare between my father and a former air force officer, a *Volksdeutsch* called Gutkind.

'If they don't break them now, they will never break them,' Gutkind said. 'Imagine that power: industry, fabulously rich colonies and discipline. Do you know how many British it takes to run a huge country like India? Eighty thousand! That's all. Such people don't surrender easily.'

Nonetheless, our enemies were riding high on the crest of their victories. New slogans were being displayed on public buildings. '*Deutschland Siegt An Allen Fronten.*' By now I had enough German to translate this: 'GERMANY IS WINNING ON ALL FRONTS.'

When I asked my father where the front was now, he explained that in a total war it was everywhere: land, air and sea. Massive British armies were being organized in the Middle East and India. Their air force was already retaliating for the bombing of London. Apparently, there had been raids on Berlin, Hamburg and Munich. But I must not repeat this. Was that understood? The Germans did not want the Poles to hear of such things. If they discovered anybody was talking about these raids, they would guess there were forbidden radios in town and come looking for them.

Not everybody was buoyed by the idea that Poland was going to be saved by the small flame of freedom that still flickered on western Europe's largest offshore island. After the French surrender some people in Maków Podhalański made no attempt to disguise their loss of heart. More people than ever began to sign the list of people declaring themselves to be *Volksdeutsche*. Jews were increasingly terrorized. In Warsaw and Kraków the Nazis had begun to revive the kind of walled ghettos not seen in Poland for a century. Assimilated Ashkenazi were being flushed out of their verdant suburban homes and herded into the old slums which their Yiddish-speaking grandparents had worked so hard to get out of. But this time their chances of escape were slimmer. The newly built walls were topped by barbed wire and guarded by SS sentries who shot to kill.

Even in Maków Jews already had different ration cards. When I lined up for bread and milk, I used to see them. The *Volksdeutsche* had another kind of card that entitled them to German rations. Among the well fed was Gutkind, the friendly ex-airman who had rightly predicted that Hitler would never invade Britain as long as the RAF held off the Luftwaffe. He probably felt that, with a name like his, registering as *Volksdeutsch* was unavoidable, and at least he wouldn't go hungry.

Other people had less excuse for bad behaviour. Some of the local peasants were trying to ingratiate themselves with the enemy by selling them hams and chickens for prices they would never accept from a Pole. There were worse things too. It was said that unregistered Jews trying to hide out in the countryside had been betrayed and arrested. An SS unit in their black uniforms, with silver skulls as cap badges, had moved into our little town. They strutted about the place with an air of authority that was very different from the Austrian troops. Among them was a small detachment of Geheime Staatspolizei – the dreaded Gestapo – who mostly wore civilian clothes. They were billeted in a small hotel on a slope above the church with splendid views of the town.

As we entered the second winter of the war, we received a desperate message from my aunt. She was in Kraków. She and my uncle had somehow managed to smuggle themselves out of Soviet-controlled Lwów. But something had gone wrong, and now my uncle was in jail.

I was impressed. 'For patriotic activities?' I asked my father.

'No. Currency smuggling.'

It turned out he had been arrested by the Poles, not by the Germans, and within a few days he was released. He had been caught trying to exchange a small amount of dollars, but he still had plenty left. Just before the outbreak of war he had turned most of his zloty savings into gold coin and US dollars. When he and my aunt left the Soviet zone, some were sewn into the linings of their coats while the rest were hidden beneath the false bottoms of their suitcases.

These were not quite the kind of 'patriotic activities' I expected of my relatives but, increasingly aware of our own dismal finances, I was a little admiring. I even ventured to wonder out loud why we had not done the same when these magical currencies were apparently worth more zloty every day?

'Because I'm a soldier and not a clever lawyer,' came the answer, which was exactly what I wanted to hear; I'd much rather have a soldier for a father than a lawyer who was jailed for doing shady deals.

I received a similar reply when I mentioned that nowadays the parents of some of my old school friends seemed distinctly better off.

'They're all trading,' he explained. 'Buying food cheaply from the peasants and selling it at a profit in Kraków.'

I had no reason to ask more. Trade was obviously beneath us. An officer and a gentleman was not expected to have any aptitude for commerce.

All that was required was his willingness to die well for his country.

Ada suddenly announced one day that she had had enough and was leaving. She wept and assured us she would always think of us, but she insisted she just couldn't do it any more. She was a fluent German speaker, and she had to think of her future. Probably her relationship with my father was not what it had been and, like Mateczka before her, she realized that there was no future in it. Twice bitten, Colonel Borowiec was no longer the marrying kind. Whatever the reason, she went and we had to learn to fend for ourselves.

'It's wartime, you know,' said my father. 'I'll cook and you'll clean the house.'

I thought at first he was teasing me, that sooner or later he would introduce some obliging female who had come to our rescue. But as the days passed, I began to accept that this was it; we were on our own. While my father prepared our only hot meal of the day – soup or fried eggs or dumplings – I made beds and swept the three upstairs rooms we occupied.

We were now a little better off. Ada's small salary no longer had to be found, and our income had also begun to pick up slightly. The refugee family with the lazy son had moved out and a circuit judge presiding at the *Generalgouvernement* civil and criminal courts paid my father a small rent for the use of their old quarters.

We started raising rabbits, and the tool shed next to the house was soon filled with their cages. There was only one drawback. Colonel Borowiec may have been willing to dispose of his country's enemies but, being the essentially kindly man he was, he could no more bring himself to kill one of our hand-reared rabbits than I could. Whenever we had gone without meat long enough to bring ourselves to eat one, I had to convey the condemned animal in a basket to the tailor who had bought our piano. One of his apprentices at the shop would grab the rabbit by its hind legs and give it a karate chop on the back of the neck. I never stayed for the execution but handed the rabbit over and fled, returning only when bunny had become meat.

We also acquired some hens. I was required to fill in the chart we kept in the kitchen to record their individual egg count. Non-layers got a one-way trip to the tailor's apprentice. Flour and the occasional pork sausage were obtained by barter from peasants whose portraits Papa sometimes painted in gaudy colours. He might not have sunk to trade, but I was beginning to appreciate the ingenuity with which he was adapting to hard times.

Then, from a very unexpected quarter, came another small income. Somebody in Berlin had been persuaded that it was outrageous for former Austro-Hungarian officers, who had faithfully served alongside the Kaiser's forces in 1914–18, to be deprived of their pensions. So that part of my father's monthly stipend was restored. It was only a fraction of the full remittance he had received when it included the additional twenty years of Polish army contributions, but it all helped and he didn't hesitate to accept it.

'They're looting Poland,' he said. 'At least we're taking some of what they've stolen back.'

There was enough money to pay for more advanced private tuition. I had gone as far as I could go with the woman who had taught me during the final year of junior school. Although secondary education was officially banned for Poles in the *Generalgouvernement* zone, teachers everywhere eked out a living tutoring clandestine classes. In Maków it was a retired high school teacher. He looked the part – slightly unkempt, with his reading spectacles perched on the end of his nose. There were three of us in my group: myself, plus another boy and a girl, both from the annexed area. We followed the old curriculum, including Latin and Polish history. Our teacher was a kindly old gentleman who treated us like adults. This was important, and we tried to please him.

My father suggested that if I worked hard, learned languages and understood history, I should become a foreign correspondent rather than a soldier. I had read newspapers from an early age, but it had never occurred to me that writing for them might be almost as interesting as the lives of the people appearing in them.

The war my friends and I had so longed for had become, in the main, a tedious and boring business where hardship far outweighed adventure. War was now the effort of getting up with the cold dawn to feed the rabbits on dark autumn mornings, of making sure that the house was clean and making a mental note of what foodstuffs were running low.

Whereas the first winter of the war had been met with hope and expectation, the second was merely a matter of survival. Our country was partitioned, our enemies well organized and confident, and the war itself had become a distant concept. Somewhere, thousands of miles away, ships were torpedoed, bombs dropped, tanks churned desert dust. None of it seemed very relevant to the people of the newly impoverished mountain town of Maków Podhalański.

I suppose, in our separate ways, most of us were waiting for a miracle in an age without miracles.

# 10.   Our Enemies Fall Out

Throughout the winter and spring there had been persistent rumours that the unlikely alliance between Nazi Germany and Communist Russia was about to break down. As summer approached, the evidence increased. Eastward-bound troop trains clattered across the countryside with growing frequency. Motorized columns woke sleeping towns and villages at night, heading in the same direction. Word spread. All the signs were that the Germans were about to attack the Russians.

It started on a sunny Sunday towards the end of June 1941, rather like the day the previous June when our church bell had pealed to announce the fall of Paris. This time a loudspeaker truck toured Maków playing military marches in between periodic announcements that Christendom was at war with godless Communism. Together with his new Finnish and Romanian allies Hitler had attacked Stalin along a front that stretched for over 2,000 kilometres.

My father was much cheered by it all.

'So the Russians will defeat the Germans, Papa?'

He was vague about this. He explained that two enormous powers were locked in a historic fight. Germany had Italy on its side, but Russia was bound to ally itself with England. And since England was much stronger than Italy, this meant Russia would win.

I was puzzled. 'But when they came last time, you escaped from the Russian zone. You wanted to live with the Germans. Papa, if the Russians win, will we have to run away again?'

But it rapidly became apparent that this was not going to be a cause for concern. Just like the last summer, all the news was of German advances. The newspapers were again filled with photographs of helmeted soldiers moving behind tanks and of burning villages – the only difference being that this time the long columns of prisoners were not French, they were Russians.

When Lwów fell, it was discovered that the city's several jails were piled high with hundreds of putrefying corpses, a leaving present from the NKVD who had murdered Ukrainian nationalists, Poles, Jews and common criminals without discrimination. Some German reports also claimed that there were Poles on the German side too, massacring Jews who had been recruited into Soviet militias and assisting in the deportation of 'reactionary elements' to Siberia. In the shtetl town of Jedwabne the Germans claimed they had been unable to prevent over 300 Jews – men, women and children – being killed by irate locals.

My father thought there might be some truth in these reports (as it turned out, there was) and pointed out that one could hardly blame the Jews for preferring Soviet to Nazi occupation. 'After all, we couldn't protect them.'

As the Wehrmacht's relentless eastern progress continued, and further evidence of Soviet atrocities emerged, Goebbels' propaganda teams made sure the world was made aware of the service being rendered by Hitler's Christian soldiers. One headline simply read '*Gott Mit Uns*'. It was the old Prussian motto of divine preference that all Hitler's troops, except the SS, had inscribed on their belt buckles. The SS motto translated as 'My Honour is Loyalty'.

There was no denying it: Stalin's mighty Union of the Soviet Socialist Republics seemed to be collapsing faster than Poland, faster than France. The miserably equipped Yugoslavs and Greeks had put up a better fight in places. The BBC announced that Britain was sending Moscow a military mission to see what they could do to help. But if only half of what the Germans were telling us was true, it sounded as if they might be too late. Some citizens of the USSR were photographed welcoming the invaders. As the panzers rolled over the fertile Ukrainian prairie, its farmers rushed to greet this victorious army with bread and salt. Entire divisions, 15,000 strong, surrendered. According to our daily newspaper the Wehrmacht had taken hundreds of thousands of prisoners within weeks.

My father admitted that he didn't think they were exaggerating. German claims were corroborated by a number of Polish eyewitnesses who had been waiting at various rail halts in the high summer heat. They had seen freight wagons arrive, packed with Russian soldiers making heartrending pleas for water. Guards shot at any Poles who tried to bring it to them.

'They don't appear to feed them at all,' was the appalling observation I overheard one evening.

I was listening to a conversation my father was having with a rustic gentleman whom he rated a bit brighter than most. He quite often called in to pass on various titbits of information but, for sheer horror, this was by far the worst story he had ever brought us: some of the starving Red Army prisoners had resorted to cannibalism. Apparently, they had first been herded like livestock into a barbed-wire enclosure. Then they had been left there to rot – without food, water or sanitation – while somebody worked out when space would be available on trains to take them to camps further to the west. Meanwhile, the weakest died – either murdered or through illness – and some of the survivors had tasted their flesh. If the guards noticed, they did nothing about it.

I was utterly sickened by this story and a bit frightened. How could Europeans behave so badly? I thought cannibalism was something that happened on a South Sea Island or in Darkest Africa. Not in Poland.

But my father shocked me by saying that, in a way, stories like this were good news. 'They might not fight for Stalinism, but they'll fight for survival,' he explained. 'Once word of this kind of mistreatment spreads, the Russians will start fighting. Just you mark my words.'

Judging by conversations I had with my old school friends – whose views, like my own, mostly reflected their father's opinions – the citizens of Maków were divided about Germany's success. In a country where the antipathy we held for both our powerful neighbours was almost a way of life, some people were elated that the Russians were being given a drubbing. Had they not stabbed Poland in the back? But others were concerned that Germany might emerge as master of all Europe. This particularly applied to our Jewish population, now swelled by the arrival of their intelligentsia from the cities.

In their eyes, whatever their other political views, the Soviets were infinitely more acceptable than the National Socialists. They had expected their salvation to come from the East, and now they were getting alarmed.

The German steamroller, having in the space of a week captured Kursk and Kerch, had now got as far as Moscow, where Russian resistance at last appeared to have stiffened. Indeed, the Wehrmacht's latest communiqués were becoming reminiscent of the Polish bulletins of 1939 with their talk of 'consolidating' and 'regrouping'. There seemed little doubt that their advance had come to at least a temporary halt. True, it had stopped in the heart of Russia. But I was beginning to think that my father's optimism was not entirely misplaced. Nor was he the only one.

'Remember what the snow did to Napoleon,' people were saying. 'It's going to happen again.'

Winter came early, and we were pleased to see that it was as brutal as the two previous winters of this war. Yet there was no Napoleonic-style retreat from the gates of Moscow. Instead, Goebbels' daily propaganda sheet posted on the wall of our local post office showed determined-looking soldiers crawling about the snow in the white camouflage overalls German troops had first worn in Norway. Coal began to be strictly rationed. There was enough for the *Volksdeutsche*, very little for the Christian Poles, nothing for the Jews. All skis beyond a certain length were requisitioned. A special commission was set up to confiscate fur coats; even the peasants' rough sheepskins were not exempt. The slogan was '*Alles für die Ostfront*' – 'Everything for the Eastern Front'.

We waited for the outcome of the winter fighting, just as we had waited for the Allied offensive in the spring of 1940. We thought it might be the turning point of the war. In early December, the latest broadcasts from London mentioned the exploits in the Libyan Desert of the Polish Carpathian Brigade, which took its name from the range that included our nearby Tatra Mountains. Apparently, the brigade had played a major role in the relief of Tobruk after Rommel had besieged the port for 242 days.

But on the same day, this little victory was eclipsed by another event – though the time difference meant it took a while for the post office news-sheet to announce it. On 7 December 1941, the Japanese attacked the US fleet at Pearl Harbor, in Hawaii.

Four days later, Hitler, acting out of solidarity with his Asian ally, declared war against America.

In Maków the Gestapo diligently sought out the numerous enemies of the Reich. Our local postman was executed. It turned out he had been delivering more than just mail and my father's pension. A hidden radio had been discovered in his tool shed. He was one of the brave people who had been disseminating the BBC's Polish language broadcasts from London, which had done so much to keep our morale up. I wondered who had betrayed him. Colonel Borowiec was questioned several times but always released. Presumably, the fact that he had chosen to live in German- rather than Russian-occupied territory still stood him in good stead.

On one occasion they came to search the house. They spent most of their time in the colonel's study, removing in the process several elegant Biedermeier pieces – a couple of balloon-back mahogany chairs and a small desk – which they squeezed into the back of their vehicles.

My father was philosophical about it. 'All victorious armies loot,' he said. 'At least they left me behind.'

Then it was my turn.

I was summoned to report with my father to the town's old courthouse building. We were led into a large room pleasantly heated by a tiled, pot-bellied stove. Facing us from his chair behind a large desk was a uniformed German. He talked incessantly and loudly at my father, who tried to reply to something a couple of times. But the German dismissed these attempts with a wave of his hand. His words were coming out too fast for me to understand, but I understood enough to know that I was being accused of some crime.

Finally, the German finished and Papa was permitted to explain the charges.

'He says you are spreading rumours damaging the German war effort. He says you are telling people that there is hunger in Germany and that the Wehrmacht is retreating from Russia.'

'I have never –' I began.

'Say nothing!' snapped my father.

He continued speaking to our interrogator, while I began to sob. Eventually, we were dismissed with a warning from the German ringing in my ears.

If he ever heard that I had been spreading such stories again, I would immediately be parted from my father and sent to work in Germany. Did I understand?

Yessir, I understood.

Safely home, I loathed my thirteen-year-old self. How could I have squandered that opportunity to defy the enemy with my head held high? Why had I not behaved with the courage and dignity expected of Poland's long line of martyrs? I should have admitted it all – for, of course, I had said all these things to my friends and almost anybody else who cared to listen – but, instead, I had wept like a child and left the talking to my father.

He later administered one of his beatings, 'To teach you to keep your mouth shut.'

As far as he was concerned the situation was very clear. Someone who had something against him had reported his son to the Germans. One could not trust anybody. For the next few weeks I hardly left the house for anything other than my clandestine lessons with my teacher, who had a perpetual cold. We were only able to heat the house every other evening. When I did my homework I put on two sweaters. My father wore a faded velvet smoking jacket as he paced the floor, violin pressed to his chin, playing melancholy airs. Then he would stop and listen to me reading some of Goethe's poetry aloud while he corrected my pronunciation: '*Kennst du das Land, wo die Zitronen blühn . . .*'

'Lemons in bloom,' my father would say, with evident longing. 'Can you imagine Italy's almond trees in bloom, all white? Can you see the orange groves heavy with fruit? And the blue sky?'

I listened, hypnotized. Yes, I could imagine all that, despite the howling wind outside whipping clouds of snow across our frozen garden.

Sometimes my father would talk of the old war. His service with the Austro-Hungarian Army in the northern Italian Alps had come as a reward for being wounded in Russia. He did not have a high opinion of the Italian fighting man; when, at the beginning of the year, the British in Libya had captured them by the thousand, he had not been very surprised. But he did admire the hardiness of the Russian soldier.

Since our own questioning, there had been an increasing number of arrests in Maków. Many of its Jews had fled to remote mountain villages, where it was rumoured they paid enormous rents for the most primitive hovels. By now it was known that thousands of Jews transferred to concentration camps from the Warsaw and Kraków ghettos had never been heard from again. The same thing was beginning to happen to Jews in the ghetto they had established in Lwów, which the Germans now insisted on calling Lemberg, its old Habsburgian name. They were told they were being resettled, and that was the last anybody ever heard of them. It was possible that they weren't allowed to write. But why? Polish prisoners of war who had been in various Stalags and Oflags for almost two years now regularly wrote home. Their families even sent them food parcels.

Yet apparently not all the Germans were anti-Jewish – or, at least, not all the time. Suddenly Maków was rocked by a scandal involving a locally based Gestapo officer caught sharing a hotel room in Kraków with one of our young Jewish women. It was believed both had been executed. I had known the facts of life for about a year now, and my initial aversion to such unhygienic behaviour was beginning to turn to the obsessive curiosity of the young adolescent male. I knew that people might not always share a hotel bed because they needed a rest; but the idea that sex could be a capital offence had never occurred to me.

'But what crime did he commit?'

'The Nazis call it *Rassenschande*. It means something like "racial defilement", allowing your Aryan blood to be polluted.'

I was only too aware of these notions of racial purity and the assumptions they could lead to. Enemy soldiers often took one look at my blond hair and blue eyes and addressed me in German.

I was embarrassed, but before long my father would find it had its uses.

# 11. Train Trips and French Lessons

Having survived the Russian winter, the Wehrmacht launched a spring offensive. Once again, we were led to believe that the capture of Moscow was imminent and could do nothing but get on with our lives as best we could.

In Maków the Borowiecs were among several families replanting their vegetable gardens. By now I was old enough to make a useful contribution. My father needed this assistance, because he had invented a new source of income: writing petitions in German. These petitions mainly concerned obtaining permission from the district administrative office to plant certain crops, acquire livestock fodder or extend outbuildings. Petitions written in German tended to go to the top of the pile. As a result, our diet was much improved; payment was invariably in foodstuffs that cost a fortune in hard cash.

Then, towards the end of April 1942, my father announced that he wanted me to go to Kraków. Alone! I was astounded. It would be the first time I had gone anywhere on my own since Mateczka had put me on the local train from Kraków some two years before. He told me that he had received a letter from Ada complaining about her meagre rations there, and he wanted to send her a sample of the rewards his scribing had earned him. In return, she would send back some papers that were of interest to him. They were not to be mentioned or shown to anyone.

'What if the Germans search me?'

'Ada will make sure they're well hidden.'

'And if they find them anyway?'

He shrugged. 'I don't think you look like the kind of boy the Germans will bother to stop.'

I knew exactly what he meant. With my looks I could easily have been a thirteen-year-old member of the Deutsches Jungvolk, the junior Hitler Youth for boys under the age of fourteen. I suppose

I got my blondness from my mother, for my father was dark-haired – as was my Uncle Józef.

Carrying a small leather suitcase full of victuals, I set off next morning wearing the only suit that still fitted me. The train was crowded with shabby humanity, and I had to stand in the corridor. In my pocket were precise written instructions of the tramcar number I was to take from the train station, how many stops I should count before getting off, and the short walk I would follow after that. I stood at a window watching the spring greenery go by. Every time we stopped at a local station there were Germans on the platform looking for the '*Nur für Deutsche*' signs on their compartments.

At one station a blind man, wearing a pre-war Polish army jacket and field cap, was led on to the train and helped into the carriage by a boy of about my own age. Once inside, the blind old soldier almost immediately began singing. He had a good voice and it was a moving song about a gallant lancer, still in his bloody uniform, being borne to his grave by his loyal comrades of the Fourth. I very nearly burst into tears. When he had finished I handed him some of the money my father had given me for the journey.

'Watch out, little one,' said a voice behind me. 'There are plenty of specialists on the trains these days.' The speaker was a big, red-faced man, perhaps already slightly drunk (though it was not yet noon).

'You mean he wasn't in the Fourth Lancers?'

'Hell, no. I've been seeing him on this line since before the war. He got hold of those bits of uniform from somewhere to prey on patriotic schoolboys like yourself.'

I felt myself blushing.

'Don't worry,' he said. 'I would probably have done the same at your age.'

He chatted on, but by now I was cautious. I remembered my father's warning to keep myself to myself.

Then suddenly he shut up. I noticed a certain agitation among my fellow passengers in the crowded corridor. Some were crossing themselves. The train was passing a big marshalling yard on the outskirts of Kraków. Next to the track was a gallows, and dangling from it were three stiff shapes dressed in striped, pyjama-style uniforms.

Their stiffness was unnatural. It was hard to imagine they had ever been alive. Beneath them, in German and Polish, was a large sign: 'PUNISHED FOR SABOTAGE'.

The central station seemed huge – much bigger than I remembered it from January 1940, when Mateczka and I bade each other our tearful goodbyes – and there were several other trains in. The front of the locomotives were invariably decorated with big white V for Victory signs. Other notices on the wagons themselves proclaimed: '*Räder müssen rollen für den Sieg.*' I now had enough German to translate it: 'The wheels must roll towards victory.'

The crowd pushed its way slowly towards the exit. There were men with suitcases, peasant women with kerchiefed heads carrying large bundles, and people in city suits. And everywhere there were enemy soldiers moving briskly about, for this was one of the Wehrmacht's main logistical hubs for the *Ostfront*. In addition to their rifles, I noticed that some carried enormous rucksacks with an extra pair of boots strapped to them. Standing impassively at the exits, occasionally stopping soldiers and asking to see their leave passes or examining luggage, were the Feldgendarmerie with their distinctive crescent-shaped chest shields hanging from chains around their necks.

Without a second glance my suitcase and I were allowed through. As instructed, I found the tramcar stop and boarded the number 5, making sure I sat by the rear door. Part of the first car was always reserved for Germans, but I noticed that many of them ignored the sign and sat anywhere. I had not left the station during my first visit to Kraków with Mateczka. This was my first chance since Lwów to take a good look at a major city, and this time I was unescorted and over two years older – not quite six months short of my fourteenth birthday.

At one intersection I saw a column of men, with shouldered shovels, escorted by tall, black-uniformed guards. I did not need to ask who they were, and I doubt anybody else on that tram did; their haggard faces and white armbands with the blue insignia said it all. In a neutral, matter-of-fact manner some of the other passengers began talking about what was happening to the city's Jews.

'They took ten thousand from the ghetto last week,' somebody said.

'Treblinka or Oświęcim?' someone asked.

'There's no more Oświęcim,' the first man said. 'You have to call it Auschwitz now. It's part of their Germanification programme.'

I managed to get out at the right stop and followed my written directions to find Ada. Her fluent German had procured her a book-keeper's post in what had been a Jewish-owned furniture factory, and with it went the perk of a large room above the premises. Work finished early – curfew in Kraków was 6 p.m. – and in the afternoon she showed me around the crowded city centre. Here and there, a street band of three or four men, invariably dressed in remnants of uniform and sometimes on crutches, played the latest popular songs while one of them went up to anyone who had paused to listen and held out an upturned hat.

'Are they really war invalids, or specialists?' I inquired, anxious to prove to Ada that I was now a man of the world.

'Some are and some aren't,' she said.

This new Ada, away from Maków, was more communicative. And I soon realized that beneath her sometimes brusque exterior was a genuine warmth. To my mind she also had nerves of steel. She decided we would have dinner out and tried to get a table in a café full of people who all had the same idea and needed to eat before curfew. Ada didn't hesitate. Steering me by the elbow, she headed straight for the door marked '*Nur für Deutsche*'.

'Isn't this only for Germans?' I whispered.

'Leave it to me,' she said.

I soon found myself at a table with Ada ordering in German from the limited menu. Most of the clientele seemed to be uniformed members of the Wehrmacht, but from some adjacent tables I was picking up scraps of conversation in Polish. Were all these people blatantly disobeying enemy regulations?

'They were *Volksdeutsche*,' she explained after we had finished our meal and were walking back to her apartment. 'But a lot of them hardly speak the language. Nobody is going to ask for identification when they hear my accent.'

The next day, she took me to a cinema. The film was a German comedy with Polish subtitles. I didn't like it very much, though Ada laughed in places. I was much more interested in the newsreel that went with it. There was film of the Libyan desert war with blazing British tanks and captured infantry, wearing their odd-looking soup-plate helmets, being marched along a row of palm trees into captivity. There was a surfaced U-boat photographed 'off the American coast', according to the commentator, who boasted that its brave crew had been sinking Allied shipping within sight of Boston's city lights. And from the *Ostfront* came pictures of a smiling German officer receiving a glass of milk from a pretty girl with long blonde tresses as ecstatic Cossacks welcomed their liberators.

The narrator signed off with: 'Remember, Germany is winning on all fronts.'

(This newsreel would trouble me for several days, until the wife of one of my father's friends, a wise woman, told me, 'Think about it, Andrzej. If they're winning the war, why don't they let us keep our radios and listen to any station we want?')

Before I left, Ada put two tins of tea into my luggage. My father was a great tea drinker, but the cost was so high that he had been deprived of his brew for some time. I knew he would be delighted. They must have cost a fortune on the black market.

But there was something missing. 'Papa said you were going to give me some papers?'

'Not this time,' she said. 'Just tell your father I hope he enjoys his tea, and I'll be in touch with him soon.'

The return trip was uneventful. I saw no sign of the hanged men dangling on their gibbet. Either it had been taken down, or I was coming back on a different line.

Once I was through the front door, Mik's welcome was effusive even by red setter standards. And I could tell from the small hug he gave me that my father was extremely pleased to see me. I told him about the tea and expected an explosion of joy. What I got was a deep sigh of relief and a pat on the head.

'Ada told me she didn't have any papers for you.'

'She did? Let's have a look.'

I followed him into the kitchen, where he spread a newspaper on the table and emptied the tea on to it. There wasn't all that much tea. But there was quite a lot of paper – tightly folded sheets with type-writing on them.

'You didn't see this,' he said. 'And no matter how much you're tempted to show off, you mustn't tell your friends about it. If you do, it won't just be a telling off at the courthouse next time. You'll put all our lives in danger. Yours, Ada's and mine. Now go and get some sleep. You look exhausted.'

I went to bed, heart pounding. I knew now. My father was in the Organization.

Perhaps he had even had something to do with the train sabotage and the three men on the gallows?

And I had carried an important message. I was a man, almost a sol-dier! How I longed to tell my friends. But somehow I managed to resist it.

Apart from the war, I shared my contemporaries' preoccupations with two other things. One was sex, surely an unbelievable pleasure that must be just around the corner. For some unimaginable reason the nearest any of us seemed to have got to it were the chaste kisses on the cheek exchanged with the girls who somehow contrived to bump into us when we took our long Sunday afternoon walks in the mountains.

The other one was the acquisition of an *Arbeitskarte*. This was a work card that every male over the age of fifteen was obliged to carry. Those not employed in occupations that had been sanctioned by the *Generalgouvernement* were liable to be drafted for work in Ger-many. Some were employed on farms, others in factories. As an alternative to struggling in poorly paid jobs at home Poles were encouraged to volunteer for it. 'We're going to work in Germany!' declared a well-known poster of a trainload of happy-looking people, all waving their hats.

My father had given serious thought to my *Arbeitskarte* long before it was due. First, he decided the clandestine classes I rather enjoyed were getting too dangerous in a small town like Maków. Second, he

decided I was to be employed as a shop assistant. He had found work
for me at a small haberdashery that was based in Maków but served
the entire district. It was a family concern run by a couple who were
happy to do the colonel a favour, though it was understood that there
would be no question of wages. Nonetheless, I was excited by this
large step into the adult world. By the time my fifteenth birthday
came around I would have been in possession of an *Arbeitskarte* for
over a year and, with any luck, immune from the periodic round-ups
by an enemy in desperate need of manpower.

But before I started work I was sent back to visit Ada, in Kraków, and
deliver a suitcase full of butter and meat, including a rather pungent
garlic sausage. This time there was no mention of documents, and I
was to travel by a different route. At Kraków Central Station the
Feldgendarmerie, assisted by the Polish civil police, had started to
crack down on the smuggling of black-market foodstuffs into the
city. Arrests had been made and people deported to Germany.

But for the moment, probably because they were short of manpower, the police did not appear to have extended their operations to
the southern suburban stations. I was to get off at Bonarka and board
the blue and white tramcar number 6, which travelled a circular route
around the city. My father informed me that it should take about
forty-five minutes to reach the same stop where I had alighted the
first time for Ada's flat and workplace.

At Bonarka I boarded a tram with several other people from the
same train. For some time we travelled down streets with low
two-storey houses and front gardens. It was a warm day, the suitcase
was between my legs, and I thought I could smell the garlic sausage.
Then the buildings became taller, the gardens disappeared. I noticed
a tall barbed-wire fence dominated by towers that were occupied by
men with binoculars.

'So they still haven't rerouted the line,' I heard somebody say.

People were looking out of both sides of the tramcar. It was then
that I realized the line led straight through the heart of the ghetto.
On both sides the pavements were lined with barbed wire. There
were wooden overpasses to allow people to cross from one side of the

street to the other. My first impression was that it was like being in a zoo, only with people instead of animals in the cages. I was amazed to see that there were women behind the wire wearing colourful summer dresses in the sunshine. Some of them had their armbands lined with lace, while the men's armbands were often neatly starched. There were shops that seemed to be doing business, and I saw a Jewish policeman in his blue uniform with a Star of David on his cap. Jews were leaning out of the windows of their houses, staring at the slow-moving tramcar while we stared back at them.

'Can they leave the ghetto at all?' I asked Ada later. I was telling her about what I'd seen while she removed the garlic sausage and the other presents from the suitcase and put them away.

'Officially, no,' she said. 'But some of them do go to work in groups outside the ghetto. Some even get permission to go to another town. But it's becoming increasingly difficult.'

I told her about the women in the pretty dresses, about the shops and how surprised I'd been. It didn't look much worse than other parts of town.

'It's no holiday,' said Ada, shaking her head. 'You can't see everything from a moving tram. There are more than a hundred thousand people crammed into streets where twenty-five thousand used to live. They live three or four to a room. And every week hundreds of men are taken to the new concentration camp they've built at Oświęcim, the one they call Auschwitz. The Nazis are mad. They're like children trying to rearrange the universe.'

I returned home to find that my father had once again been addressing the problem of my French tuition. He was rightly concerned that, without regular practice, I would get rusty and had arranged for a young woman who had recently arrived from occupied Belgium to give me daily conversation. She lived with her mother in one large room they had rented on the ground floor of a somewhat dilapidated villa surrounded by a wild garden.

Nicole was dark-haired, buxom and wide-hipped. She usually wore long dresses. She was trying to lose weight, so the lessons usually consisted of a long walk during which we spoke about almost anything: the war; what was going to happen to the Jews; food prices; and the girls I knew.

'So you're having lessons with the Jewish woman,' a boy I knew said to me at about this time. It was more of a statement than a question.

I was amazed. It had never occurred to me. Neither she nor her mother wore an armband. But then quite a few people who had left the cities to live with the peasants were thought to be Jews who had failed to register with the authorities. Judging by some of the things Ada had told me, one could hardly blame them, but they lived at the mercy of anyone who felt like betraying them. And the terror against the Jews seemed to be increasing on a daily basis.

When I was due for one of my conversations I usually found Nicole waiting for me on a chair on the veranda. One afternoon she wasn't there. Somewhat puzzled, and perhaps slightly apprehensive, I knocked on the door.

'*Entrez*,' I heard from inside.

It was definitely her voice, so I opened the door. I saw her immediately.

Nicole was lying on one of the two beds, and she was stark naked. She had a white, ample body, enormous breasts with large, dark nipples and, most shocking of all, masses of black pubic hair through which I noticed she was moving the fingers of her right hand.

I felt like I was on fire. I stood there with an embarrassing erection stabbing against my ridiculous short trousers. I didn't know what to do. For a moment I considered running away.

'*Viens près de moi*,' she said.

I advanced towards the bed, trying in vain to conceal my erection. Nicole giggled. 'Sit down,' she said, pointing to her bed.

I did.

She opened her large thighs. 'Put your face there and lick,' she ordered.

I generally do what a lady asks me. Later, I did wonder at her confidence that I would do something that some of my friends had suspected some adults indulged in – though they were unanimous in declaring the very idea to be revolting. I suppose technically I was being abused by a female paedophile. It was marvellous.

As my excitement increased, I tried to extract my penis. It was too late; a quick, violent orgasm spilled over my short summer trousers.

'Continue,' she commanded, noticing my enthusiasm had begun to wane.

I did as I was told, until she started writhing and moaning and pushed my head away.

'One day,' she said slowly, looking at me with interest, 'you'll be a great lover.'

There were no more French lessons that day. She said she needed a rest.

I went home, covering the wet spot on my shorts with my hand. I wasn't sure whether what I had done counted as sexual intercourse but I was aware that I could probably consider myself more advanced in this area than any of my friends.

The trouble was, I knew I wouldn't be able to bring myself to tell any of them about it.

## 12.   Maków Loses its Jews

Towards the end of August 1942, in the weeks preceding my fourteenth birthday, the worldwide conflict seemed to hang in the balance. We were able to weigh against Berlin's propaganda what scraps of news we gleaned from those still brave enough to hide radio sets. At Stalingrad, on the Volga River, and at Alamein, in Egypt's Western Desert, German advances had for the moment been brought to a halt. In the Pacific, Australian and American ships had at last stopped the Japanese off New Guinea, in the Battle of the Coral Sea. But although Washington had been at war with Nazi Germany for almost nine months, the USA appeared to be in no hurry to get involved in the European conflict in any meaningful way.

Meanwhile, the war impinged on our own lives more than ever. We were among several families in Maków who were informed that our homes were being requisitioned because they were needed for bombed-out German citizens. Large-scale RAF night attacks on the Reich had begun in earnest in May with a 1,000-bomber attack on Cologne. A BBC Polish language broadcast had mentioned that over 100 Polish airmen flew in this raid. Were we being dispossessed as a reprisal?

I was surprised how calmly my father took the news. Our house and its well-tended garden, with its score of apple trees, were his pride and joy. Now we had been given two weeks' notice to get out. Even so, by the standards of wartime Poland this was generous. Families expelled from the annexed western areas had often been given a few hours to prepare their departure and could only take what they were able to carry.

Arrangements were made to rent two rooms from a Dr Mazaraki, a long-retired general practitioner who lived with his wife in a large nearby house. Our furniture was stored with other neighbours 'until the war was over'. We also had to find a new home for Mik, my faithful companion of many a mountain march. A friendly butcher took him in, but I was not allowed to take him for walks because it was thought this would confuse him and he would try to follow me home. My father tried to console me with the thought that our dog would probably survive the war better than we would. As things turned out, I only ever saw him one more time – and that was from a distance – and although I called him, I don't think he heard me.

A Jewish family who lived in a small house opposite ours watched our removal with sympathy.

'Hard times,' an old lady with red hair told me. 'Hard times for both of us.'

Then, a few days later, the times turned immeasurably harder for Maków's Jews.

We woke on Sunday, 23 August 1942 to find our alpine backcloth still bathed in its high summer sunshine and blue skies. But overnight Maków had been disfigured by a rash of printed wall posters. In German and Polish they ordered the entire Jewish population to assemble in the grounds of a sawmill near the railway station. Failure to report for *Umsiedlung* (resettlement) was punishable by death. A special train was being provided to take them to an undisclosed destination. Only essential personal belongings were to be taken. Anything not considered essential would be confiscated. All Jewish houses and apartments were to be left intact with their front doors open.

While our church bells tolled for High Mass, Jewish families began to move slowly towards the station. Despite the sunshine some were wearing heavy coats, for wherever they were going winter was at most only three months away. All were carrying bags or small suitcases. Several had handed vases, clocks and other treasures to astonished Gentile neighbours and asked them to keep these items safe until they came back. SS men at the sawmill made no effort to venture further into town and round families up at gunpoint. There was no need. The Jews made their own way there, grim-faced and largely silent.

Impassive peasants dressed in their dark Sunday suits watched them go by. Any doubts the old and the infirm might have had about their probable fate were soon dispelled. A man known as 'Old Weiss', who could no longer walk, was put in a wheelbarrow and trundled down to the sawmill by his family. His arrival was duly noted by the SS awaiting them. Bystanders watched one of these black-uniformed figures saunter over to Weiss and his relatives and, after solicitous inquiries about the old man's mobility, shoot him carefully in the head with a pistol.

In the afternoon I disobeyed my father, who was aware of the killing but had not yet told me about it, and sneaked out to see what was going on at the station. When I got there, Maków's town crier and his assistant had removed Weiss's body. Most of the Jews were already packed into a train made up of the wooden freight wagons often employed as cattle trucks. Along the top of each wagon ran a plank-sized horizontal gap to provide ventilation; in the summer heat parents were holding children to the gap so they could get some air.

Suddenly I made out the head of a boy I knew. His surname was Mülrad, and he had come to one of my name day parties. His father was the town's watchmaker and clock repairer. As a sergeant in the reserves, he had gone to one of the Wehrmacht's prisoner-of-war camps when his unit surrendered. And there, like so many other Jews captured in the uniforms of Germany's enemies, he stood a good chance of surviving the war. As far as the Wehrmacht were concerned, a soldier was a soldier – regardless of his religion – and Jews were treated no differently from anybody else. General Bernard Mond, the Jewish commander of Poland's 6th Infantry Division was probably the most senior example of this. But the mayor of Maków, no doubt thinking he was doing Sergeant Mülrad a favour, had successfully petitioned for his release on the grounds that he was an essential worker, necessary for the servicing of all public clocks and the punctual running of the town. Now Mülrad and his family had punctually reported to the SS.

The train left in mid-afternoon. Its destination was almost certainly Belzec, a small town about 200 kilometres east of Maków, where earlier in the year the Nazis had established the first purpose-built extermination camp, constructed close to its railway station. Within hours of arrival my friend Mülrad and all the other Maków Jews would have been dead, packed naked into locked 'shower rooms' and then slowly asphyxiated with carbon monoxide piped in from the exhausts of captured Soviet motor engines. Their winter coats were sent to Germany and distributed among the poor. There were no Auschwitz-style crematoriums, only mass graves.

We knew nothing of this. What we did know was that these men, women and children living alongside us had, with sullen acquiescence, assembled to start a foul journey towards an uncertain fate without a word of protest from themselves or anybody else. It was as if we all somehow accepted that the Germans had some unchallengeable right to do this. We were no more expected to object than we would have been able to interfere in the fate of sheep being herded into an abattoir. I would dearly have liked to shout some words of defiance to Mülrad before he left, but I didn't have the nerve. I felt ashamed.

When I got home, breathless and shattered, I poured all this out to my father.

'So you expect us to go out and fight for them?' he asked.

'We could have worked together –' I began.

'Don't you think there were efforts to organize joint resistance? Do you think you're the only one who ever had the idea? All kinds of approaches were tried. But the elders of their community, those in the long black coats and the *pejsy*, were against it. "Let us be patient and God will reward us," they were saying. Their people should tear them apart.'

As it turned out, not all the Jews from the Maków area had gone obediently to the doomed train. Some of them had fled into the forested parts of the mountains. Most of these fugitives were young men and women, but there were also some children. Their survival depended on the goodwill of peasant farmers. Sometimes they took payment, sometimes they did it out of charity. No doubt there were occasions when it was a mixture of both.

As usual, the Germans were quick to respond. New posters were pasted over the ones that had summoned the Jews to their *Umsiedlung* train. This time they announced that the penalty for anybody discovered giving food and shelter to a Jew was death. Within days emaciated figures were reporting voluntarily to the hotel where the SS and the Gestapo had established their headquarters. The Germans did not bother to put them on a train. A friend whose home overlooked the place told me that they were shot with a pistol after being made to dig their own graves.

I made sure I never went anywhere near the place we called the Gestapo Hotel though, like many people, I was certain that, from time to time, I had heard shots coming from that direction. Towards sunset one evening I did get a glimpse of some of the horror of it all. Just as the church bell began to toll the day's third Angelus, I was walking near the presbytery when I noticed two men and a young woman in its yard. They were sweeping dead leaves into neat piles with long-handled brooms.

Watching them, with arms folded across his chest, was one of our local town policemen, who was unarmed. I thought he looked embarrassed. Then the priest's housekeeper emerged with a steaming soup tureen and some bread. Within seconds all three of the sweeping party had dropped their brooms and were dunking their bread into the soup. I had no need to ask who they were.

'What will happen to them?' I asked the policeman.

By way of reply he turned and pointed in the direction of Hotel Gestapo.

'Can't you let them go? Nobody would know.'

'I didn't arrest them. They came to the priest and offered to sweep up the leaves in exchange for food. They said they were too cold and hungry to hide out any longer.'

'And the priest called you?' I was shocked.

'No, somebody else saw them here and informed the Germans,

and I was ordered to pick them up. Do you know what would happen to me if I didn't deliver them?'

I knew all right, but it didn't stop me hoping that, fortified by the soup and the knowledge that their escort was unarmed, they might make a run for it.

If they did, I never heard about it.

## 13.  My Father

Almost a month after my friend Mülrad and all the other Jews had
disappeared from Maków, I began my unpaid work at the haberdashery. My employers were a kindly couple, prepared to do my father a
favour by stating on my official application for an *Arbeitskarte* that
what they badly needed was a junior assistant. Entering into the spirit
of things, I sorted and shelf-stacked the knitting wool they sold with
fine attention to detail and did my best to look busy whenever anybody came in.

'Knowing commerce can always be useful, *n'est-ce pas, Papa?*'

It was the first time in months that I had used one of the French
phrases acquired from Mateczka, let alone the word 'Papa'. I knew he
liked to be called it but it sounded so childish, and I was anxious to
establish the fact that I was not a child. It was the day after my fourteenth birthday.

He did not seem to hear me. We were walking side by side, about
to enter our new home. Then he stumbled and leaned against the wall,
his face contorted. I grabbed an arm and tried to keep him from falling.

'*Papa! Papa!*' I shouted.

There was no reply. His lips moved but no words emerged.

Someone rushed up, and together we supported him across the
threshold and into our bedroom. Dr Mazaraki did what he could to
make his tenant comfortable and sent for help. He had never practised in the town and did not have a telephone. Maków then had a
population of about 2,500 and there were only 40 telephones in private hands – a figure that has always stuck in my mind.

It seemed like an eternity before a young doctor, a displaced person from one of the annexed western parts, turned up and examined
him. He decided that my father would be best looked after at a small
makeshift clinic staffed by a couple of nuns. It was located on the
ground floor of a house near the marketplace. The doctor left and

shortly afterwards returned with two men carrying a stretcher, who transported my father there on foot. At no point did anybody think it necessary to give me any indication of what might be wrong with him, or how long it might take him to recover.

It was some time before I learned that he had suffered something known as a stroke, and this was a serious affair.

The next day I tried to keep busy. Our house, from which we had been evicted, was still empty so I returned with a basket to pick the apples in our orchard. I delivered most of them to a neighbour who gave me a few zloty for them. Then I took a wheelbarrow to my father's office, placed in it the heavy typewriter he used to write the peasants' petitions and brought it back to our room at Dr Mazaraki's house for safekeeping. It felt like the right thing to do.

When I visited my father and told him about this, I discovered he could speak a little from the corner of his mouth – though I had to put my ear close to his lips to hear him.

'You didn't damage it?' he whispered.

'No, Papa.'

There were no more doubts: this was my Papa lying on a bed with nuns in starched coifs hovering over him like flights of angels.

That evening Ada, summoned by a telegram, arrived on the train from Kraków. I assumed my father had managed to give her address to the young doctor who was attending him, and had indicated he would like to see her. She patted me affectionately on the head, but I could see she was preoccupied. Later I saw her listening intently to something he was trying to tell her. Afterwards, she talked at length to the doctor and the nuns, and once I saw her put her hand to her mouth and shake her head at something they had to say.

A little later I overheard a nun murmur to one of the other sisters, 'What on earth is going to happen to that poor boy?'

That night I was allowed to stay in the clinic, and a bed was made up for me in my father's room. Quite late in the evening a priest came to my father's bedside accompanied by an acolyte in a white robe. I heard the priest grant my father an absolution in Latin while the acolyte knelt beside him, holding a lighted candle that bathed the room in a gentle glow. There didn't appear to be any electric lighting.

I don't think I got much sleep. I'm not sure what time it was when I watched two of the sisters approach the other bed. One of them bent over him, picked up his hand by the wrist and stood like this for a few seconds.

'He has finished,' she said, and gently put the hand down.

Then both of them knelt and in a soft murmur began to recite some Latin words, their voices growing stronger as they became more confident of their unison. I recognized it immediately.

It was the Prayer for the Dead.

In a daze, incapable of further weeping, I followed Ada and the same two stretcher-bearers that had brought my father to the clinic as they made their way back to Dr Mazaraki's house, my father's corpse covered in a white sheet.

En route a man inquired if I knew who had died?

'My father,' I said, hardly believing my own words.

And wide-eyed, the man whipped off his cloth cap and crossed himself.

The next seventy-two hours passed in a whirl. In the old doctor's basement my father's body lay in the temporary chapel of rest that Ada had furnished with flowers, candles and a wall crucifix.

The funeral itself took place on a sunlit day, though dry autumn leaves crunched beneath our feet. The mourners were summoned by the same bell that had celebrated the fall of Paris. There was a full congregation in the packed church, including two figures in the Wehrmacht's field grey – officers from the Austrian regiment. They would have brought an honour guard with them, had Ada not been firm that, whatever had gone before, Colonel Borowiec had died a Polish officer and would not have welcomed occupation troops at his funeral. Through a haze of tears I noticed the yellow piping around their silver shoulder straps, denoting a cavalry or reconnaissance unit. They delivered a wreath with a card announcing in Gothic script: 'FOR A COMRADE'.

Standing at the graveside, I watched clods of earth breaking on the coffin while the aristocratic priest who had heard my father's confession intoned, '*Memento homo, quia pulvis es, et in pulverem reverteris.*'

Afterwards, some people seemed undecided whether to shake my hand or pat me on the head. Some did both. My Uncle Józef was not present. He had returned to Lwów, which was now well behind German lines, and no one had thought to inform my father's only brother of his death.

The next day I departed on the train for Kraków with Ada, carrying all the possessions I could fit into a suitcase. These included my father's slim gold Lépine-style pocket watch and fob chain, and a framed photograph of him in uniform.

While she was making the funeral arrangements Ada had made it plain to me that, in the circumstances, she thought it best that I go to live with her in Kraków. She knew this is what my father would have wanted and – for the time being, at least – she was confident a job could be found for me in the furniture factory where she worked. I had accepted this as if it was the most natural thing in the world. Of course, it was nothing of the kind. The most natural thing would have been for Ada to ask my mother to come and collect me. But I suspect that my father, hoping to recover and fearing to lose custody of me during a lengthy convalescence, had extracted a promise from her that she would do no such thing.

I suppose I was old enough to try to get word to my mother myself. But it had been almost four years since I had last seen her and eighteen months since I had received any kind of communication from her. Later I could only conclude that my father, determined to punish her, had intercepted all the letters and cards she insisted she had written.

Perhaps I was in a state of shock. One day I was walking alongside a loving and attentive father, wondering if I wasn't getting too old to call him 'Papa', and the next day he was dead.

Before long I would know people who took longer to die from a bullet.

# 14.   Kraków

The factory where Ada worked was making furniture for the Wehr-macht's rear echelons. In the days immediately before Poland's occupation, its Jewish proprietor had managed to escape abroad with his family. As an abandoned Jewish enterprise it had been seized by the Reich and it was now under German ownership, though most of the ninety or so workers on its payroll remained Polish. They even included a few Jewish 'essential workers', who had been issued with passes that allowed them out of the ghetto. They were escorted back and forth by one of the Gentile Polish workers, whose badge of office was the stick he was required to carry in case his charges attempted to assault him and escape. There was absolutely no danger of this, because the Jews' families depended on them to smuggle food back into the ghetto as a way of supplementing their meagre rations.

Ada, with her fluent German, was highly regarded at the fac-tory and had no difficulty in persuading Georg Wimmer, its German manager, to give me a job as a messenger. Herr Wimmer was a veteran Nazi – he had been among the first 25,000 to join the *Nationalsozialistische Deutsche Arbeiterpartei* sometime in the early 1920s – and he wore a special enamel swastika lapel badge on his jacket to prove it. But he was hardly typical of the breed. A pleasant-looking man, I never heard him once raise his voice. He treated everybody, Gentile or Jew, with courtesy. I'm not saying he was another Oskar Schindler, who also had a Kraków factory and with whom he was probably acquainted. There were no lists of unsuitable Jewish workers employed at a loss to save their lives. But he did have Frau Halina – his buxom Polish mistress – who, like Ada, worked in the office. Although some Nazis race experts believed that not all Poles were subhumans, unworthy of Germanization, a blatant love affair with one was hardly toeing the party line.

The offices were next door to the factory, an extension of the same building. Above them were some small apartments for employees. Ada had a room and bathroom, and I slept on a narrow bed in the same room as her. From time to time she gave me a little pocket money. I assumed it came from what was left of my father's ready cash after his funeral expenses had been paid. In return for my board I worked as a messenger in the factory. But as there were not all that many messages to deliver, I was constantly being found other small tasks. Every Friday I would sit at a small desk in Wimmer's office writing the names of his ninety-two employees on a stack of envelopes that would become their pay packets. '*Schön schreiben* – nice writing,' he would urge as I dipped my pen in the inkwell provided, breaking the monotony with intermittent attempts at a calligraphic flourish.

I suppose he was a nice Nazi. God knows how aware he was of the industrial-scale mass murder being fine-tuned all around him.

I arrived in Kraków with Ada towards the end of September 1942, a few months after my first glimpse of its ghetto during the errand I had run to the city for my father. It was one of seven city ghettos the Nazis had established in Polish cities, including Warsaw and Lwów, by slightly expanding the traditional Jewish quarters and cramming thousands of people into them. Maków's Jews, like many from the smaller communities, missed the intermediate stage of the ghetto and went directly to an extermination camp.

About a month after I had joined Ada in Kraków, the SS started to move some of its Jews from the ghetto to the nearby Plaszów concentration camp, built on the site of two flattened nineteenth-century Jewish cemeteries in one of Kraków's southern suburbs. Plaszów was not an extermination camp as such. It did not have gas chambers or crematoriums. It supplied slave labour to local armament factories. Those judged unfit for work were either shot on the spot – there were shooting pits for group executions – or sent to Auschwitz, which was about thirty kilometres away.

Apart from being aware that Plaszów was a concentration camp, and its inmates almost certainly did not have an easy time of it, we knew none of these details. But it was about this time that one of the Jewish workers in the factory sidled up to me with a package.

'You collect stamps?' he asked. He handed me an album mostly displaying pre-war European issues. 'I don't think I'll be needing them where I'm going.'

Truthfully, they were not of all that much interest to me. I collected the stamps of the Second Polish Republic, year of birth 1918 – ten years before my own. I was particularly proud of a purple-coloured Austro-Hungarian stamp of that year on which the rebirth of a sovereign Polish state was announced in black capitals by the overprint 'POLSKA'. Nonetheless, gauche fourteen-year-old though I might have been, the stamps obviously meant a lot to him and I had the manners to accept his gift with profuse thanks. He was a tall, lean young man engaged in some kind of manual work in the factory and was probably unlikely to be selected for 'resettlement' in the immediate future. This was a task the Germans left to the ghetto's Jewish police whom the young man was already regularly bribing so that he could take food back into the ghetto.

Apart from Wimmer, a few other Germans worked for the firm. I think all of them were glad to be in Poland where their Reichsmarks went much further and they were away from the ever-increasing Allied bombing of their cites.

Among them was Frau Josie, a motherly woman who was small and dark and not very German looking. She was often rather warmer towards me than bossy Ada. On the other hand, Frau Josie was not responsible for me and didn't have to put up with my teenaged sulks and occasional tantrums.

One of the constant bones of contention between us was Ada's refusal to allow me to see the only friend I had in Kraków of my own age. This was a boy from Maków, the son of an officer in the Blue Police, who had come to Kraków after his father had been transferred there. In vain I pleaded that he was a Polish policeman, but Ada was adamant. The Blue Police, who were armed, were often obliged to work alongside the Germans and therefore couldn't be trusted. Perhaps her real concern was her own safety: twice I had acted as a courier between her and my father, and no doubt she also knew that in Maków I had attracted the attention of the Germans because

I could rarely resist telling anybody who would listen that the Nazis were going to lose the war.

And Kraków had become a very obviously occupied city. Quite apart from being the headquarters of the *Generalgouvernement* area, it was one of the transport hubs for the Russian Front. Polish street names were replaced with German ones. Almost all its motorized traffic belonged to the Wehrmacht. Most Poles used the trams or horse-drawn vehicles and were off the streets before the 6 p.m. curfew. Among the few exceptions were the Poles working in the cafés and bars patronized by soldiers travelling to or from Russia.

The city was full of German civilians too. Party apparatchiks had been seconded to the *Generalgouvernement* administration under its notorious Governor-General Hans Frank, who had once been Hitler's personal lawyer. After posters had appeared all over Prague announcing that seven Czechs had been shot for anti-German activities, he famously told the Nazi Party newspaper *Völkischer Beobachter*: 'If I did that for every seven Poles I had shot, there wouldn't be enough trees in Poland to make the paper.'

I began to kick against living in Kraków. Once Christmas was over and we had moved into the new year, my quarrels with Ada were becoming more frequent. At the end of one of them, consumed by an adolescent desire to shock, I demanded in my loudest voice to know how she could bear to live among these *Deutsche Schweine*? Most of the *Deutsche Schweine* in the building – who, in their various ways, had all been quite kind to me – could not have helped but hear it. Then I stormed out, announcing as I did so that I was returning to Maków.

This was easily accomplished. Rail fares were cheap, and I had my bit of pocket money. I had somewhere to stay too. Before leaving I had become friendly with two brothers from one of the refugee families that had been turfed out of their homes in western Poland. Their father had found full-time work on the extensive improvements the Wehrmacht were making to the Polish road network in order to facilitate traffic to the Russian Front. As a result, they were relatively well off and their mother had told me I could always stay with them if I wanted to visit old friends. But it was obvious that a short stay was expected, and I didn't tell them about my row with Ada.

Having left on impulse, I soon realized that I had no alternative. I had to return to Kraków. I had nowhere else to go, though God knows what my reception was going to be like. Shouting 'German pigs' at the top of your voice was not the wisest thing to do in Nazi-occupied Poland.

Before I left Maków, I decided that I should try to sell some of the possessions that had been left with various neighbours – just in case Ada showed me the door – but few people had any money to spare. In the end, I sold some of my father's collection of large pre-war photographic prints documenting troops on manoeuvre or parade to somebody who had always admired them.

Then, tail very much between my legs, I said my goodbyes and boarded the train for Kraków.

Ada was unexpectedly calm. There had been an exchange of telegrams with my mother. She was coming to collect me. I would be living with her in Warsaw.

'I think it's for the best,' Ada said.

# 15.  Living with Mother

The apartment block at 12 Opoczynska Street was a modern four-storey building, constructed in the mid-1930s in Warsaw's southern suburb of Mokotów. My mother and my four-year-old half-brother, Jerzy, occupied a one-bedroomed flat on the first floor. For the last two years they had been sharing it with my Aunt Olga, mother's unmarried younger sister, and my maternal grandmother. They had both been expelled from their home in Łódź, following the city's annexation by the Germans. My grandmother, Hermina Arct, was the widow of the man who had finished his career in charge of the Polish Army's medical corps. Her large house in Łódź was my birthplace, my mother having gone there for her first pregnancy.

A woman friend had accompanied her from Warsaw to Kraków to pick me up. Both had husbands they were very unlikely to see before the end of the war. Hers was in the Middle East with Polish forces under British command and her friend's had been captured in 1939. A few days after my return from Maków there was an amicable enough parting from Ada, whom I really quite admired, and the three of us took a tram to the central railway station. Our night train would not be leaving for another seven hours or so, but we had to be sure of getting there well before the 6 p.m. curfew started. It was nearly midnight before we began a journey that would take almost twice as long as it had done in peace time, because it involved a circuitous diversion to get around a tunnel that had been destroyed three years before by retreating Polish forces.

Ada had prepared sandwiches and a large flask of hot tea. As we travelled through the night, we had plenty of time to get reacquainted and tell our own stories of 1939. I recalled my evacuation to my uncle's house in Lwów, only to see the Russians move in, and the shooting I had witnessed on the frozen river before I left the Russian zone. My mother recounted the much more terrible siege of Warsaw that kept her and baby Jerzy in a cellar for the best part of a month while all around her 25,000 of its citizens died in relentless bombing and shelling that was obviously much worse than anything I had experienced in Lwów. After the ceasefire, it had been months before she received a Red Cross postcard from Paris where Major Władysław Michniewicz, her husband and my stepfather, was serving as a military attaché at the Polish embassy. After the astonishing French surrender there was more uncertainty before other carefully worded Red Cross missives indicated he was among those Poles who had managed to reach Britain.

From the moment we met, my mother behaved as if there was nothing unusual about not seeing each other for nearly four years. We merely had a bit of catching up to do. I gladly fell in with it. I suppose I shared with my mother a certain reluctance to display emotions. Even so, it must have been much easier for me than it was for her. After all, she looked much the way I remembered her. But however much she had tried to prepare herself for it, I must have come as something of a shock. I was ten when she last saw me. Since then there had not been so much as a photograph. Outwardly all that remained of that child in the adolescent she was now talking to was a fading facial resemblance.

We must have slept some of the time. But I was awake as the train slowed and under a cold, grey dawn we creaked through Warsaw's waking outer suburbs and into the central station. Most people had already left their seats and were reaching for luggage in the overhead racks, buttoning up overcoats, coughing over their first precious cigarette of the day.

As soon as we were out of the station, I spotted something I hadn't seen for years: a small rank of motor taxis. The exorbitant price of petrol meant that only Germans could afford them. They didn't appear to be doing much business and, along with almost everybody else from our train, we joined the line for the horse cabs. There was an alternative form of transport that appeared even stranger to my eyes than motor taxis. Almost as soon as our cab was under way, I noticed men peddling strange wooden contraptions fitted with bicycle tyres that could take at least two passengers. It turned out that they were locally built cycle-rickshaws, operating in the streets around the city centre, and what they lacked in comfort they more than made up for in economy.

We dropped off my mother's friend and shortly afterwards were in the Opoczynska Street flat where my grandmother and Aunt Olga, demonstrative in a way my mother and I were not, welcomed me to my new home with hugs and kisses. I would share the only bedroom with my mother and Jerzy. My grandmother slept in the dining room and Olga in what we called the 'salon'.

Olga was the only one who was employed. She worked as a secretary for a German who had been put in charge of a large Polish confectionary business. Once a month, a little three-wheeler van powered by a motorcycle engine would turn up outside our department building to deliver the best part of her wages: boxes of cakes and sweets, most of which were sold or bartered for other foodstuffs. Olga had got her job because she spoke good German, as did my mother and my grandmother, having all spent the last decade of the Austro-Hungarian Empire in Vienna.

The three women had adapted to their changed circumstances with a practised teamwork. The small flat rarely felt overcrowded and was really quite comfortable. There was a daily routine of restoring the sleeping quarters of my grandmother and Olga to their daytime function by throwing covers and cushions over beds and turning them back into sofas. Olga always feared she would be late for work, so after she had dressed and rushed out it was my task to go around the salon raising its window blinds. At night I would lower them and help return the room to its bedroom mode. For this small service she always insisted on paying me a few zloty.

We also had a maid – though not, of course, a live-in maid. Rozia lived not far from the ghetto and had to cross almost the entire city by tram and cycle-rickshaw to work for us. Apart from her cleaning duties, whenever possible she also answered our front door.

Shortly after my arrival, she opened the door and found two immaculate Wehrmacht officers on the threshold. 'Madame, there are some German gentlemen to see you,' she announced.

They were ushered into the salon, where they were no doubt

surprised to be greeted in my mother's lilting Viennese rendering of their mother tongue.

She never did divulge exactly what their visit was about. All she would say was that they were polite, and the matter was settled. But it seemed to have gone well enough, so I assumed it was something to do with the food parcels she had begun to receive from abroad.

These were assembled and started their journeys in the neutral cities of Istanbul and Lisbon. Their contents varied but usually included the kind of canned goods and waxed-paper packages that were unlikely to perish during a long journey: coffee, tea, sugar, sardines, corned beef, biscuits, chocolate and cheeses. They were sent by my mother's husband, who had discovered a company which – no doubt at considerable expense to himself – arranged to purchase these treats in Turkey or Portugal, then sent them overland by rail to Poland through countries that were either Nazi occupied or allied to Berlin. By far the shortest route was from Istanbul via Bulgaria's Thracian borderlands and on through Romania and Czechoslovakia to Poland. Thanks to Britain's naval blockade, even in Germany imported items such as Brazilian coffee were almost impossible to find. Most Germans drank ersatz brews made from chicory or even crushed acorns.

In Nazi-occupied Poland, where random reprisals by firing squads and the noose were constant reminders of the prevailing abnormality, it was hard to believe that something as reassuring as parcels from abroad got through intact, but they did. It could be that the delivery had something to do with reciprocal Red Cross agreements. As far as my mother could make out, the only losses occurred at the German customs office that mailed her the notification to go and collect the parcels. The *Volksdeutsch* in charge made it plain that considerable paperwork was involved and several more visits might be required unless he could be persuaded to give her priority. The usual price was some of the real coffee, though I believe at times there was a straight cash transaction. It was well worthwhile. Like Olga's sweets and cakes, most of the contents were sold.

As far as my mother was concerned, the downside to all this was that the parcels led to the loss of her telephone, because they indicated the existence of a contact outside German-controlled territory. Her line was now considered a security risk – even though all calls went through a switchboard operator who was forbidden to connect to anything but local numbers. Whether the visiting German officers were inquiring into the source of the parcels, or merely wanted to buy coffee, I never found out. Whatever they wanted, the matter was resolved. I think my mother felt that the less I knew about such things the better. No doubt Ada had mentioned that I could be outspoken, and I think my mother had resolved not to burden me with anything I didn't need to know.

Before long, I would be reciprocating in kind.

My mother certainly believed that the devil found work for idle hands. I had hardly been in Warsaw a week when she started to make arrangements for me to resume my interrupted education. To begin I would be getting private French lessons at the apartment. Any furtive hopes I may have entertained of the kind of extra-curricular activity the lascivious Nicole had provided soon evaporated. My tutor turned out to be an elderly lady dressed in black who was already well acquainted with the Borowiecs.

Some twenty years earlier, she had taught my father who, like a lot of his contemporaries, had decided that a good war record and fluent German were no longer all that was required. Poland's Francophile new army wanted officers suitable for staff courses at the *École Militaire* in Paris. After our first meeting she told me that I had obviously inherited my father's gift for languages and, provided I worked hard, I would be a credit to him.

This was encouraging, but much more exciting was my enrolment into several clandestine classes. My father had considered Maków much too small for me to risk arrest and deportation to Germany as a slave labourer by continuing to attend a secret school half the town could direct you to. Warsaw, with a population of slightly more than a million, was a very different proposition. Big and sprawling, even its 8 p.m. curfew came two hours later than the one in Kraków in order to give its commuters time to get back to the outer suburbs.

By denying a formal education to Poles above the age of fourteen,

the Germans made a big mistake. Whether as a teacher or a pupil, the
very act of attending one of these underground schools was a first
step to becoming part of the resistance. Classes were normally single
sex with no more than ten pupils at a time. For security reasons the
venues changed every couple of weeks with different people, often
the parents of one of the children involved, offering the use of their
homes.

We travelled to the classes on the old German tramcars the victors
had substituted for our smart new pre-war models, which had resembled railway carriages and were rumoured to be in Berlin. But the
antiques they had pressed upon us in exchange did give the averagely
agile fourteen-year-old boy one advantage: we were able to hitch
free trips by what we called 'riding the titty'.

The 'titty' was the breast-shaped connection mounted on a
wooden platform between the cars that were of a kind Warsaw had
not seen for years. Since the rear end of the last car wasn't connected
to anything, you could leap aboard. Leaving it as the tram slowed at
your destination was easy once you had mastered the technique of
stepping off the moving tram with your back to the tracks. It was
important to be leaning backwards as you did so. That way – if you
messed up – you fell on your back and were less likely to do yourself
much harm.

For short hops in the summer we sometimes clung to the ledges of
windows, but this was much more dangerous. There was a good
chance you would be hit by a tram travelling in the opposite direction, which often passed very close. Once, I found myself clinging to
the ledge of an open window in a '*Nur für Deutsche*' car that was just
about to depart when a hand firmly slapped my fingers and I dropped
to the ground, clutching my satchel of schoolbooks. It may not have
been unkindly meant.

From time to time the Gestapo would crack down on this blatant
defiance of the Nazis' master plan to turn Poland into a nation of
*Untermenschen*, fit only for keeping the Reich's industrial wheels turning. Towards the end of 1942, there was a coordinated effort to purge
the country's secret schoolrooms. (After the war it was revealed that
over 300 teachers who had been arrested during that round-up later

died in Auschwitz.) But during my first months in Warsaw the Germans seemed to have decided they had better things to do than chase schoolboys learning Latin and algebra.

Suddenly the war was not going at all well for them. On 2 February 1943, the last of Von Paulus's 6th Army surrendered at Stalingrad. Soon German military installations around Warsaw were within range of Russian night bombers. We could hear the drone of their engines, and the explosions that followed, but the results seemed disappointing and we rarely came across any damage.

In May the *Biuletyn Informacyjny*, the most popular of the underground news-sheets, reported from their monitoring of the BBC that the North African campaigns had ended in Tunisia with the surrender to the Anglo-Americans of 275,000 Axis troops, the majority of them German. More prisoners had been taken there than at Stalingrad. In those Warsaw cafés frequented by the Wehrmacht, Polish waiters overheard their customers referring to this latest defeat as 'Tunisgrad'.

# 16.   Between Katyn and Treblinka

For most Poles the previous month had already been tumultuous enough. On 13 April 1943, Radio Berlin announced that a mass grave had been discovered at the Katyn forest, near Smolensk, in which the bodies of 3,000 Polish officers were stacked like firewood, twelve layers deep. Photographs in the German press showed Allied prisoners of war, mostly British and American officers, who had been taken there to view the evidence. Almost all the dead had been shot in the back of the head. The Germans claimed that none of the documents discovered on the bodies, including personal letters, were dated after April 1940 – over a year before Hitler invaded Russia. The implication was clear. All the victims had been taken prisoner by the Soviet forces that entered eastern Poland in September 1939. Some seven months later, they had been murdered. From the moment we first heard of the Katyn massacre, I think most Poles knew in their broken hearts that this time Dr Goebbels wasn't lying. Stalin had never forgotten the humiliating defeat inflicted on the Bolshevik army that invaded Poland in 1920.

Moscow's immediate reaction to the disclosures at Katyn was to insist that all the Polish prisoners had been alive and well and engaged in 'construction work' before German troops overran their camps. I never met any Pole who believed this. But I did think how wise my father had been when he chose to leave me and Mateczka in Lwów and escape to the German zone on a horse-drawn cart wearing that shabby civilian suit. At least we were able to enjoy almost another three years together.

Before long, the Russians would break off relations with the Polish government-in-exile in London following their request that the International Committee of the Red Cross be allowed to investigate the matter. And it would turn out that Katyn was only part of the story. In the twenty months before the summer of 1941, when the German avalanche swept them aside, the NKVD had murdered about 22,000 Poles. The majority were killed after they had been transported to prisons and remote work camps far inside the Soviet Union. As many as 8,000, including the Katyn dead, were officers. The rest were middle-ranking policemen and above, as well as land-owners, industrialists and those with enough education to qualify as 'intelligentsia'. I would be in my sixties before Russia began to reluctantly admit Soviet responsibility. By then, the last quarter of the twentieth century had seen even greater crimes committed in the pursuance of Marxist–Leninist social engineering.

We had hardly digested the Katyn outrage when our maid, Rozia, turned up late for work one morning with news of something much more unlikely than the Bolshevik massacre. When she left her home she had been delayed by German roadblocks near the ghetto, from where gunshots and explosions could be heard.

'I think the Jews are shooting,' she said. 'And they are flying flags. I saw the blue and white Jewish flag flying next to the Polish one.'

It was true. The unbelievable had happened.

The Jews had had enough. They were fighting back. An uprising had started in the Warsaw Ghetto. At last, the sheep had turned on the wolves.

It should not have been as surprising as it was. By now our suspicions that the Nazis were not content to merely segregate the Jews were fast hardening into the realization that we were living alongside a killing machine whose efficiency exceeded even Soviet aspirations. In December 1942, the London-based Polish Ministry of Foreign Affairs had published a booklet, based on eyewitness accounts, entitled *The Mass Extermination of Jews in German-Occupied Poland*. 'It is not possible to estimate the exact number,' wrote Count Edward Raczyński, who doubled as both Foreign Minister and Polish Ambassador to Britain. 'But all reports agree that the total number killed runs into many hundreds of thousands.' Months later, these allegations were still being discussed in our underground news-sheets and, like Katyn, we believed them.

At about the time when I had been watching Maków's Jews

walking quietly to their deaths, the SS also began their *Grossaktion Warsaw*: the annihilation of Europe's biggest community of urban Jews. Between 23 July and 21 September 1942, thousands of Jews had been herded into the cattle trucks awaiting them at the *Umschlagplatz*, the ghetto's very own railway siding. They had been told that they were about to be 'relocated in the east'.

But their north-easterly journey along the Warsaw–Bialystok railway line ended a mere fifty miles away, at the village of Treblinka, where they were informed they had arrived at a transit camp. Sometimes the SS even distributed and collected postcards on which they could assure relatives and friends who would shortly be following them that all was well. But Treblinka was not a transit camp. It was a terminus.

The postcards were the idea of SS-Obersturmführer Dr Irmfried Eberl, an Austrian psychiatrist. Dr Eberl had graduated to mass murder through the Nazis' euthanasia programme, which had tidied away thousands of mentally disabled people. An ambitious man, at thirty-two he was the youngest commander of any of the extermination camps, and in order to impress the right people he asked for more trains to be sent.

Then, on the sixtieth day, when Dr Eberl had taken delivery of about 300,000 Jews, trains to Treblinka were suspended. The death machine they were feeding was choking. It had begun to vomit corpses. Each of the camp's ten gas chambers accommodated about 200 of the naked people who had just been told they were about to be given a shower. As at Belzec, they were choked with carbon monoxide and buried in mass graves. Soon the burial pits had brimmed their banks. Corpses were hardly covered. It was a hot summer. The stench of putrefying flesh was becoming unbearable. When fresh trainloads arrived, the Jews locked in the cattle trucks smelled it long before they arrived. Any hopes fostered by postcards from those who had gone before them vanished. Some contrived to die by their own hand, others by running at or away from the awaiting SS auxiliaries, many of whom were Ukrainian renegades recruited in prisoner-of-war camps.

When several of the gas chambers broke down, the guards began to attempt to shoot all new arrivals as a matter of course. But this was a slow process. Along the railway track leading up to Treblinka was a backlog of locked cattle trucks in which the very young and the very old had often already died of dehydration.

Warm summer breezes carried the stench of this charnel house for miles. Polish villagers scented it and shuddered. Eberl's superiors were furious. The eradication of the Jews was supposed to be a secret. He was sacked and returned to his euthanasia duties.

Back in Warsaw, the remaining 40,000 Jews were corralled into a ghetto that had shrunk to little over a square mile as street after street of empty apartment blocks were readmitted to the Christian side and adjustments made to the perimeter wall. SS-Polizeiführer Jürgen Stroop, a neo-pagan who believed Hitler was Wotan's personal gift to Germany, was appointed to finish the job. But some of the surviving rabbis were preaching that perhaps it was no longer God's will that good Jews should embrace their martyrdom. They pointed out that in past pogroms Jews could choose to save themselves by converting to Christianity or Islam. Those who chose death rather than deny their faith were truly martyrs. But the Nazis were not offering a choice: they wanted to wipe the Jews off the face of the planet.

Early in 1943, the problems at Treblinka were sorted out – news of which did not reach Christian Warsaw, let alone the outside world – and, under the direction of a few SS troops, the Jewish Police renewed the expulsions from the ghetto. About 5,000 people had already left from the *Umschlagplatz* when, in April, using a few pistols and Molotov cocktails smuggled in by the Polish resistance, some young men and women led a spontaneous revolt that brought the process to a standstill. The German response was simply to tighten their cordon around the ghetto and wait. Given this breathing space, the Jewish resistance built barricades and bunkers and shot some senior Jewish policemen and other alleged collaborators.

Stroop decided to bide his time until he could muster sufficient men from the hard-pressed post-Stalingrad Eastern Front to bring matters to a swift conclusion. On 19 April, Passover Eve, he entered the ghetto with just over 2,000 men, including 800 Waffen-SS infantry, Wehrmacht combat engineers equipped with flame-throwers, and Lithuanian and Ukrainian SS auxiliaries – men grateful to the Germans for liberating their countries from the Soviets and who shared a visceral anti-Semitism, partly based on a profound belief that educated Jews were pawns of Moscow (and educated, fighting Jews especially so). Waiting for them were about 600 poorly armed insurgents. Nonetheless, they not only made the Germans back off but even succeeded in setting one of their vehicles on fire.

From our underground news-sheets we soon learned that there were two main resistance groups involved. One was the Jewish Military Union (Polish initials Z W Z), who were far from being pawns of Moscow. Many of these right-wing Zionists had served as junior officers in the Polish Army and theirs was the blue and white ensign that Rozia had noticed with the hexagram Magen David design in the middle. Its horizontal blue stripes symbolized the tallit, the Jewish male's traditional prayer shawl. The other group called themselves the Jewish Combat Organization (ZOB) and their politics were probably more in keeping with what the Ukrainian and Lithuanian SS auxiliaries suspected, though their roots were in the trade union movement. They were socialists, not Stalinists, and at that time they preferred assimilation to Zionism.

In both factions their courage would be a weapon. They wanted to die fighting.

On the second night of the ghetto uprising there was a heavy Soviet air raid. As we listened to the explosions, I suggested to my mother that perhaps the Russians were trying to help the Jews escape.

'But where will they run to?' she said. 'They can't all go to the forests – men, women and children.'

She was right. Where were 40,000 people going to go? Thousands of Catholic Poles were already risking summary execution by succouring Jews hiding among the Gentiles outside the ghetto's walls. It was a precarious existence. As well as being hunted by the Gestapo, they risked being preyed on by Poles who specialized in blackmailing Jews. We called these lowlifes *szmalcowniks* – from *szmalac*, the slang for money, our equivalent of 'dough' or 'dosh'. Sometimes the resistance shot them and scattered leaflets on the scene to explain why.

While the ghetto revolt flickered on, the rest of Warsaw mainly went about its business and some found what pleasure they could – even if it was from the hand of the occupiers. My mother and Aunt Olga attended an afternoon showing of the latest Marika Rökk musical to reach the city. Rökk, who was half Hungarian, was the Reich's Ginger Rogers. Watching her singing and dancing her way through some romantic comedy defied resistance posters urging people to boycott German-controlled cinemas where Nazi newsreels complemented the more subliminal messages in feature films licensed by Dr Goebbels. Along with thousands of other war-weary Poles, especially if their German was good enough to understand the plot, my mother refused to regard her attendance as being any reflection on her patriotism. As far as she was concerned the whereabouts of her absent husband were ample proof of that.

The sale of my father's gold watch paid for the several weekly clandestine classes I attended, and my main activities revolved around my education and getting to know the other teenagers who lived nearby. Three of the teenagers in my apartment block and in the one next door, with which we shared a courtyard, were girls.

Two sisters, both blonde, lived below us on the ground floor. These were the daughters of a former sergeant in the air force who, like my father, had somehow avoided capture and now worked in a post office sorting station. He was an unusually fat man for wartime Poland, but his two daughters – one slightly older than me, and the other one younger – were attractive, lively girls. So was Lona, who lived next door and whose father, she was soon whispering to me, was 'a captain in hiding' whom she rarely saw.

After the surrender of the Warsaw garrison on 28 September 1939, a number of officers had not only evaded capture but managed to blend into the civilian population, biding their time. One of the most senior of them was Colonel Stefan Rowecki, who had commanded a motorized infantry brigade. By the time France had fallen, his stock had risen significantly among a nascent resistance that was now in regular touch with Britain. Władysław Sikorski, Poland's commander-in-chief in London, put him in overall charge and made him a general. His brief was to unite the disparate factions of the Polish resistance which, at its political extremities, ranged from Communist to Neo-Fascist.

This became the Home Army and was usually referred to by its initials, AK (for *Armia Krajowa*), though for a long time most of us called it the Conspiracy (*Konspiracja*). In Polish the word 'conspiracy' doesn't have the derogatory connotations it has in English because, so many times in our history, it has referred to secret and patriotic preparations for a revolt against foreign occupation. Long before he started his army career, Rowecki was well versed in conspiracy. Prior to the First World War he had grown up in that part of partitioned Poland that was under Czarist sway and had been a member of a dissident scout troop secretly coached by the Austro-Hungarians in skills Baden-Powell might have considered unsporting.

None of the teenagers who gathered in the courtyard of our flats in Opoczynska Street, the only place we could linger outdoors after the 8 p.m. curfew, had heard of Rowecki. Nor had the various adults we lived with. His identity was a secret. But we were beginning to learn of someone who called himself 'Grot'. It was the most enduring of Rowecki's several pseudonyms. It meant 'Spearhead' and was sometimes found at the foot of AK editorials in the underground's *Biuletyn Informacyjny*.

Eastern Poland was aflame. Guerrilla bands that regularly sabotaged the Wehrmacht's main road and rail supply routes to the Russian Front sometimes fought pitched battles with the enemy. But for over two years the AK had tended to avoided major actions in Warsaw itself, caching the weapons the RAF were beginning to drop for them and waiting until the Soviets got closer. But now Grot decided to stage some high-profile attacks in the capital. That spring and summer, my first in Warsaw, the war seemed all around us. Quite apart from the Russian bombing, hardly a night went by without the sound of shots in the dark. Even the well-disciplined Wehrmacht seemed to be getting trigger happy.

This new phase started on 23 March, almost a month before the ghetto uprising began, with Operation Arsenal. A closely guarded covered truck was taking some newly captured prisoners belonging to the Grey Ranks, one of the AK's young scouting formations, from the notorious Pawiak Prison to fresh terrors at Gestapo headquarters, in Szucha Avenue. As the vehicle turned into Długa Street and drew level with the Warsaw Arsenal building, one of the handsome seventeenth-century landmarks of the Old Town area, long used as municipal offices, a 28-strong ambush party were waiting for it with Sten sub-machine guns and grenades.

In the firefight that followed three of the ambush party and four Germans were killed. But all twenty-five prisoners – six of them young women – were freed, including a Grey Ranks officer whom they had rightly suspected was being badly tortured. Unfortunately, he needed the kind of hospital treatment that was unavailable to fugitive Poles and died four days later, though not before he had revealed the names of the two SS interrogators responsible.

The immediate German response was to execute 160 Pawiak inmates in reprisal: forty for every German who had died. Their full names, addresses and sometimes their ages – if they were young or old enough to shock – were listed on the printed *Bekanntmachung* posters that were put up, explaining that they had died for 'atrocities committed by Polish terrorists serving British interests'.

Before the end of May the underground's *Biuletyn Informacyjny* was able to announce that SS-Obersturmführer Herbert Schultz and SS-Rottenführer Ewald Lange had been executed for the fatal torture of the Grey Ranks troop leader. This time the tariff went up to 100 lives, most of the victims picked up at random in the street round-ups we called *łapanka*. Inevitably, some people said it wasn't worth it. The elder daughter of the post office worker living below us was one. Wouldn't it be better, she argued, to wait until liberation was at hand? And let's hope the British and Americans got here before the Russians.

Undeterred by these civilian casualties, Grot pressed on with his assassinations. He called this phase 'Operation Heads' after the silver skull death's-head cap badge his targets were so proud to wear.

One afternoon, towards the end of the ghetto uprising, I saw the SS at work in Warsaw for the first time. One of my clandestine classes took place in the apartment of a former high school headmaster that was probably even closer to the ghetto than the home of our maid.

From the room in which we worked we could see orange flames dart-ing above the ghetto's high wall and thick columns of black smoke rising into the air. The SS were using flame-throwers to try to burn out the last of the Jewish resistance, a few of whom would be taken alive. But on our side – the Aryan side, as we had learned to call it – Polish firemen in gleaming brass cuirassier-style helmets had arrived on their horse-drawn engine and were trying to stop the flames spreading to some nearby factories which, among other things, made German uniforms and spare parts for Wehrmacht vehicles. The logical way to do this was to hose down the flames on the other side of the wall. This was exactly what the firemen were doing, closely watched by a number of curious civilians.

Then an SS officer appeared waving a pistol. Perhaps he was the man in charge of the flame-throwers, and these ignorant Poles were undoing all his good work. He made it abundantly clear that the fire-men were not there to extinguish the fire on the Jewish side. For a while a silent crowd watched as the flames behind the wall took hold. Then some black-uniformed Lithuanian police auxiliaries turned up and moved them on. I thought a couple of women appeared to be weeping. There was an occasional shot or brief burst of automatic fire.

Somebody in the classroom said that if the Jews could do it, then so could we – and so much better.

## 17.  The Grey Ranks

'I pledge to you that I shall serve with the Grey Ranks, safeguard its secrets, obey orders and, if necessary, not hesitate to sacrifice my life.'

In the late summer of 1943, shortly before my fifteenth birthday, I joined the Conspiracy. Or, to be more specific, I became a junior member of the *Szare Szeregi* – the same Grey Ranks that had staged the rescue at the Arsenal.

I was invited to 'meet some interesting people' by Tadeusz Stopczyński, the son of schoolteachers and a couple of years older than myself, who had met me at one of my clandestine classes. He told me he thought I was 'the right material'. I could have walked on air.

I suppose the war was what we had instead of sports days and happy childhoods. Our concentration was rarely what it should have been, though I well remember a particular Latin lesson.

'*Utrum Bucephalus, equus Alexandri Magni, habuit rationem sufficientem?*' our teacher inquired of me.

I found it hard to focus and address his question. I couldn't care less whether Alexander the Great's horse was a rational creature. Eventually, I translated it correctly but our teacher seized the opportunity to admonish all of us.

'Put your hands on the table. I know exactly what goes on here. Your parents are paying for these courses, and money is hard to come by these days. Do your conspiratorial work later, if you please.'

And the lesson continued.

'*Ut homines mortem vel optare incipiant, vel certe timere desistant . . .*'

The text was well chosen. Were we afraid of death? Was our conspiracy a game at which we would fail once the danger became direct, real and murderous?

The Grey Ranks, like all the urban components of the Home Army, was organized on a classic cell system whereby people were encouraged to know as little as possible about one another and were required to adopt a nom de guerre. Tadeusz's was Mietek. Mine was Zych, after a character in an historical novel by the hugely popular and internationally successful Henryk Sienkiewicz, who is best known in the English language for *Quo Vadis*. I suppose Zych – an old soldier known for his pointed quips and jokes – appealed to my teen-aged ideal of the cynical warrior breed.

My joining came shortly after a sickening setback for the Home Army and a sharp reminder that, despite the code names and the obsessive secrecy, we were all vulnerable. At the end of June 1943, Grot was betrayed and captured. Gloating headlines in the Nazis' Polish language daily *Nowy Kurier Warszawski*, the Goebbels version of the old *Kurier Warszawski*, announced the arrest of our commander-in-chief. An old photograph of him in the uniform of a full colonel was captioned: 'The British-paid mastermind behind terrorist out-rages against the forces of the Reich'.

Mindful of the recent Polish success in rescuing prisoners, an air-craft was standing by to fly their prize prisoner immediately to Berlin and thence to the nearby Sachsenhausen concentration camp. But the wave of arrests that was expected to follow his interrogation and the examination of various documents left at the flat he had been visiting never happened. Most of us in the rank and file of the organization had to wait until after the war to learn the reason why. Grot had stashed the papers he had come to collect in the flat's safe, which was concealed in a hollowed-out sculpture of Christ's head, of a kind that decorated many Catholic homes. Either the Gestapo had not searched the flat carefully enough or, dizzy with triumph, they had not both-ered to search it at all.

Within days of Grot's arrest, the *Biuletyn Informacyjny* was inform-ing its readers that he had been replaced by a General Bór, who promised to continue the struggle 'until final victory'. The word *bór* means 'forest' in Polish and was an obvious pseudonym. Later, much later, we would learn his identity. Bór was Count Tadeusz Komorowski, a distinguished horseman trained in the Austro-Hungarian cavalry who led the Polish equestrian team that came second in the 1936 Berlin Olympics, where Adolf Hitler shook

Komorowski by the hand and presented him with Poland's silver medal.

Almost immediately after Grot's capture came an even greater loss, and one that was much more difficult to fill. General Władysław Sikorski was killed in an air crash. He died when the RAF B-24 Liberator bomber returning him to London from an inspection tour of Polish troops in the Middle East plunged into the sea while taking off from Gibraltar. Its Czech pilot was the only survivor. For most Poles the death of Sikorski, who was sixty-two, was the equivalent of the British losing Churchill. For almost four years the veteran politician and soldier, who was not only prime minister but also supreme commander of all fighting Poles – whether Home Army or overseas – had personified our spirit of 'No Surrender'. He stood for everything that made us different from the French and ensured that we would never have a collaborationist government, never suffer a split along Pétainist-Gaullist lines.

Once again, Dr Goebbels' *Nowy Kurier Warszawski* had a field day, calling Sikorski 'the last victim of Katyn'. It alleged that the RAF had shot him down, claiming that our London-based leader's belief that the massacre was the work of the Soviets was undermining Churchill's unholy alliance with Stalin. I doubt whether any Poles thought Churchill had Sikorski killed. Certainly, my mother and Aunt Olga didn't, though they did speculate that the Soviets might have done it. (More recently, it appears to have been accepted that, at a time when almost any flying was still an adventure, the general died because of a jammed elevator flap.)

Bruised as we were by losses of this magnitude in such rapid succession – Sikorski died only five days after Grot was captured – we were consoled by the general decline in the Wehrmacht's fortunes. So much had changed since I had seen my first Nazi newsreel in Kraków. The days when the news really did live up to the Nazis' oft-repeated slogan that Germany was victorious on all fronts were over. Now I had total confidence that the Germans would be defeated and the Anglo-Americans, who had just invaded Sicily, would surely curtail any territorial ambitions the Soviets might have in post-war Poland. If they didn't, we were beginning to realize we might have a problem doing it ourselves. It was obvious that, after their poor start, the Red Army had become a formidable fighting machine. As an encore for Stalingrad, Marshal Georgy Zhukov had given us Kursk – the world's biggest tank battle. The *Biuletyn Informacyjny* was full of it, the details mostly gleaned from BBC reports.

Distributing copies of the news-sheet I so assiduously read was the modest level of involvement in my country's struggle that the Grey Ranks reserved for youngsters my age. I was usually directed to go to a certain place and pick up my score or so of copies, and I rarely saw who had left them there. The *Biuletyn* was easy to conceal; it was a small format and never had more than eight wafer-thin pages. Sometimes I would drop copies at random into the locked postboxes in the hall of an apartment block. On other occasions I made deliveries to specific addresses.

I was also used as a messenger to tip off people who were about to be sent to work in Germany. It seemed the underground had agents in the *Arbeitsamt* (the local employment office) who were prepared to leak the identities of the next batch of deportees. This could usually be avoided if you had proof of employment or were engaged in something deemed to be useful to our occupiers. The *Arbeitskarte* that I was required to carry from the age of fifteen – something my father had been preparing for when he got me the job at the haberdasher's in Maków – had eventually been supplied by the father of one of my classmates. He ran a factory making furniture and prefabricated buildings for the Germans and was able to acquire the authorization to add names to his payroll. He said I was one of his apprentice carpenters.

The only real work I was doing with my hands was a little graffiti with a brush and a pot of white paint. The insignia for the Home Army was an anchor – in Polish, *kotwica*. It was formed by the merging of two letters: P and W. The P grew out of the central prong of the W, and the loop of the P could be taken as the anchor's eyelet for its rope. Originally the letters stood for '*Pomścimy Wawer*' – 'We will avenge Wawer' – and commemorated the 107 Poles murdered there during our first Christmas of occupation, hauled bleary-eyed from their beds to be told they were going to die for the killing of two

Germans in a tavern. It had been one of the first indications of what kind of people we were dealing with. And just in case we had any doubts, the 108th victim was the innkeeper himself, photographed hanging in the threshold of his own doorway. But the events at Wawer had since been eclipsed by so many other atrocities that the letters were increasingly understood to stand for '*Polska Walcząca*' ('Fighting Poland') or simply '*Wojsko Polskie*' ('Polish Army').

Not long before his capture Grot decreed that the *kotwica* should be considered the emblem of the spirit of Polish resistance, akin to the 'V' signs appearing all over the rest of Nazi-occupied Europe, and we painted our anchors with a will.

It was not entirely without risk. 'Careful, there's a German patrol about,' passers-by would murmur as they saw me approaching, paint and brush in hand. After a while I could almost feel the mood of a street, notice the underlying tensions when people began to move a little faster, melt away indoors. I knew when I should find some small hiding place for my equipment and walk on. I painted our sign any- where. Any blank wall where it could be easily seen would do. Sometimes I painted it on the pavement. The *kotwica* was an easy design – it could almost be done in two strokes – and I could paint a good one in less than a minute.

What I could not match was the coup pulled off the previous year by Grey Ranks scouts Jan Rudy Bytnar and Jan Gut. (Bytnar had been rescued in the Arsenal ambush, only to die of the injuries inflicted under torture.) One of the glories of newly independent pre-war Warsaw had been the sculptor Edward Wittig's statue, called the 'Pilots' Monument', unveiled in 1931. Wittig's airman, wearing helmet, scarf and overalls, stood on a tall plinth that dominated Union of Lublin Square. It was there to honour the pilots, several of them Americans, who had helped repulse the Russian invasion of 1920.

In 1940, inspired by the deeds of the Polish aircrew flying with the RAF, the citizens of Warsaw began to leave floral tributes at the base of the statue. The Nazis responded by getting some heavy lifting equipment and removing it. All that remained was the empty plinth. Then, despite its very public position, sometime in the autumn of

1942, Bytnar and Gut got close enough to paint anchors on two of the pedestal's four sides, and get away with it.

For every Pole that passed that spot, the anchors were an immediate reminder of the missing statue and all it stood for. Strangely, the Germans never bothered to remove them. Perhaps they considered these doodles no more than a measure of our helplessness.

By the autumn of 1943 – my first in Warsaw – violent death had become an inseparable part of our lives. Anyone who used its crowded tramcars was bound to see it sooner or later.

There was a young man who was shot near one of the city's leaf-strewn parks. He was running away when, from the back platform of the tramcar, I saw the German soldier aim and fire a burst from his sub-machine gun. The young man's legs, in those highly polished boots worn by officers before the war, bent in a strange fashion before he collapsed backwards.

Another day, en route to one of my secret classrooms, I noticed that people were pointing to the balcony of the massive pre-war courthouse building. I looked and saw that several hanged corpses were dangling from it, their feet just touching the large inscription beneath: 'Justice is the Foundation of the Republic.'

Other public executions involved the police rounding up as many people as possible to watch and be warned. The ratio of Poles killed per dead German varied but was rarely less than ten. The condemned were always referred to as 'bandits' and 'terrorists'. They came from a pool of prisoners who had often been arrested for no better reason other than to provide hostages. They were usually lined up in front of a wall, their mouths sealed with tape to prevent them from shouting patriotic slogans or screaming obscenities at their executioners before they were shot.

But the underground refused to be deterred. It continued to assassinate German agents and individual SS and Gestapo officers who had been condemned by our clandestine courts, regardless of the consequences. A few said it wasn't worth it, but most people kept their mouths shut. Not fighting back hadn't helped the Jews.

On 7 September it was the turn of SS-Oberscharführer Franz

Bürkl, the notorious deputy commander of Pawiak Prison where Rudy Bytnar had been tortured until he was near to death. Bürkl, who kept a German shepherd dog he called Kastor that had been trained to terrorize prisoners of both sexes, was a monster. In both Pawiak and in the ghetto Bürkl had been known to shoot people at whim. He died, along with Kastor and several of his colleagues, close to the Gestapo headquarters in Szucha Avenue, gunned down by an ambush party of five insurgents using parachuted Sten guns and our home-made Filipinka grenades. Their leader was Jerzy Zborowski, a studious-looking 21-year-old who wore large, round-framed spectacles and was an unlikely-looking assassin. Perhaps that was why he had been able to get so close.

Late that afternoon, returning home from a lesson and riding on the back platform of a ramshackle tramcar, I felt that something unusual was happening. I watched a man jump from the car, expertly leaning backwards. Then the tram started braking. I saw helmets, rifles and waiting trucks.

'*Alle heraus!*'

An officer with a pistol in his hand walked up and down as the passengers disembarked. Women with children were released immediately, followed by older passengers. All the others, including myself, were herded into one of the covered trucks that the citizens of Warsaw had nicknamed *buda* (meaning 'kennel'). Other trucks joined our convoy, each with its cargo of terrified men and three or four young women.

My heart was beating fast. I felt numb. But I remembered with some comfort that I had nothing incriminating on me.

'They didn't even search us or ask for our papers,' observed one of the men in my truck.

'In that case it's serious,' someone else said.

I asked why in a trembling voice.

'That means this is no ordinary round-up. They're probably taking us straight to Szucha.'

The Gestapo headquarters at 25 Szucha Avenue was in an area we called 'the police district', secured by barbed wire and machine-gun bunkers. To escape from there was virtually impossible. Soon the doors of the truck were swung open, and SS men with the silver skull and bones emblem on their peaked caps appeared. They had their Schmeisser sub-machine guns at the ready.

We were led through a series of corridors to a long basement room. In its centre was a double bench arranged so that those sitting on it were lined up back to back. The bench was too small for all of us.

'The women will sit first,' one of the Gestapo said in fluent Polish.

The remaining seats were taken by men. I was too late and the Gestapo man told me to stand, facing the wall. Next to me was a dark-haired, smallish man who was visibly trembling. His terror was so great that he seemed about to collapse.

Of course, the Germans noticed it too. A tall SS man with a horse-whip in his hand approached and examined the man's profile by gently raising his chin with the butt of the whip.

'*Jude!*' he shouted and slashed the man's face with the whip.

Jews who had somehow escaped the ghetto were hiding out all over the city.

Blood oozed from the man's wound. Then the SS man kicked him and he fell on me, staining my coat with blood.

'Sorry, sorry,' he murmured. Sorry for bleeding.

We stood next to each other for what seemed like an eternity. Some people were taken outside for what I assumed was interrogation. Some of those who were sitting were told to get up and give their places to those who had been standing staring at the wall. Finally, I was told to sit.

The suspected Jew was next to go. He cast a last glance at me and walked out, straight backed.

'*Was ist mit dem Junge?*'

I understood the German. I knew there was nobody younger than me in the room, so I turned my head slightly and saw a tall man who looked like a senior officer.

The Polish-speaking Gestapo man approached me.

'How old are you?'

'Fifteen.'

'Where do you work?'

I rattled off the name of the factory from which I had obtained my fake *Arbeitskarte*.

'What do you do there?'

'I'm learning to be a carpenter.'

'Show me your hands.'

I extended my hands, palms up. I knew I was lost: they were not a manual worker's hands.

The two Germans looked at each other. The tall man winked.

'Go home to your mother,' said the Polish-speaking Gestapo man.

I couldn't believe my ears. I suppose I could have been a very new apprentice carpenter, but I don't think the man who had winked believed a word of it.

'*Los*,' said the German, prodding me with his whip – the same kind of whip that had been used on the Jew, if that's what he was – and then shouting into the corridor, '*Er ist frei!*'

I was free!

Guards pointed the way out. I bounded up the narrow stairs, then through another guarded door. The crisp autumn air hit me. It was almost dark. Another guard at the adjacent bunker showed me the way to the exit. Beyond the barbed wire of the police district was the city. I still had half an hour to curfew and heard the clanking of the tramcar.

Then I knew I was going to make it. And they hadn't even searched me!

When I got home, I decided not to tell my mother what had happened. I was frightened I'd be kept in, and there was a lot I wanted to do.

# 18.   Training

By early 1944, I graduated to what we called 'Battle Schools'. I was the youngest in a *sekcja* – a cell of six. Our code was MG300. At our weekly meetings we studied the pre-war infantry manual *Combat*. We learned the theory of an infantryman's five basic tasks: to reconnoitre, advance, attack, defend and withdraw. We memorized the organization of a column with flankers and rearguard, and we studied the duties of a sentry and a patrol. From the careful examination of coloured drawings we learned all about the standard infantry rifle. Rather more satisfying was the actual feel of a captured MP40 Schmeisser sub-machine gun, which we learned to strip and reassemble in thirty seconds.

We also had an automatic pistol, Poland's famous Vis 9 mm, to train on – though we did not appear to have any ammunition for it. On one occasion, I was entrusted to take it home for safekeeping, for twenty-four hours, before it was passed to somebody else. This was a great honour. Nothing could have pleased me more. I was an armed Polish soldier walking home through the streets of occupied Warsaw with a pistol about my person – admittedly unloaded, but perhaps it soon wouldn't be.

Unfortunately, I could not resist showing it off to my younger half-brother, Jerzy, in the bedroom I shared with him and our mother. Jerzy, who was about six at the time, was sworn to secrecy, but he could no more resist informing on me than I could resist showing it off. I should have known better. Jerzy was unpredictable, a hyperactive, unstable child forever being reprimanded for jumping on and off furniture or suddenly shouting his head off. My mother blamed his behaviour on what people now call post-traumatic stress – in Jerzy's case brought on by the bombardment he had endured in 1939, as a two-year-old, during the siege of Warsaw. I always thought it was something more than that, but I never said anything – and, anyway, he was a nice kid. Sometimes it rankled a bit that no allowances were made for any erratic behaviour on my part resulting from my own experiences during the siege in Lwów and the nights spent with Mateczka in my uncle's cellar; or the sight of a sliding figure gunned down on a frozen river at dusk; or the groaning gallows glimpsed from a passing train while my travelling companions crossed themselves in horror. But my mother and I both knew we were very similar. We tended not to dwell on things we could do nothing about.

Bringing the gun home did make her angry – especially if the Germans began to suspect that her food parcels from abroad were of a military provenance and decided to keep an eye on us. The discovery of a weapon in our apartment would, at the very least, have got all of us sent to a concentration camp. Or seen my mother and aunt joining the pool of hostages in Pawiak Prison, available for execution the next time some SS thug got what he deserved.

But being the general's daughter she was, and on her second marriage to a regular officer, much of her fury was directed at the people who had handed me the gun in the first place. What sort of amateurs would allow me to carry an unloaded pistol on to the streets? A single German soldier or policeman could have stopped and searched me, and I wouldn't have stood the slightest chance of shooting my way out of trouble. And what kind of people recruited boys my age, anyway? She thought the only explanation was that I had fallen in with some Communist faction who liked nothing better than to shape young minds. The gun was not in our flat for very long, but neither was any effort made to curtail my activities. I suppose she realized it would be useless.

On the contrary, later in the year, when the weather became warmer, she prepared sandwiches for me to take on the training days that the Grey Ranks organized in the countryside. We usually went by train to Zielonka, a small town in a forested area several miles north-east of Warsaw, where the parents of one boy had a weekend villa. Flankers and rearguards would be appointed, and we would get into our column formation for what we hoped looked like an innocent ramble through the woods (often pretending not to notice similar parties, including contingents of girl scouts, encountered doing much the same thing). We sometimes collected large stones for use in grenade-throwing drills, always miming the removal of the ringed cotter pin that kept the real thing safe until you were ready to throw it. We were advised never to throw them uphill or up flights of stairs. The reasons for this are obvious, but it was explained to us that in a battle people sometimes got overexcited and did silly things. A young female medic from the Girl Scouts showed us how to make proper use of the pre-war field dressings the Polish Army used. Apparently, these bandages were something we had in abundance.

Probably the riskiest part of our field training was getting to and from Zielonka. In both directions it involved passing through Warsaw's central station, which was closely monitored by several different kinds of police, including the Gestapo. Polish Blue Police mainly tried to busy themselves with black marketeers, though they were sometimes attached to Germans in an interpreting role.

Weekend excursions on suburban trains to the city's surrounding countryside were popular. Like going to the cinema, it was a whiff of normality for a city that since the war's opening shots had known almost nothing but uncertainty and steady deprivation, interrupted by wicked bouts of terror. We travelled among this innocent throng, planning mayhem on their behalf. Some of us carried rucksacks, and I soon learned that adolescents with bags attracted attention.

Late one Sunday afternoon, I arrived at Warsaw Central from Zielonka in the company of Tadeusz Stopczyński, the young man who had been sufficiently impressed with me to propose my membership of the Grey Ranks. Slung loosely over his right shoulder was a small brown canvas rucksack containing, as I knew full well, various incriminating documents including a copy of the *Combat* infantry manual. As we walked together towards one of the exits, two men in long raincoats and wearing trilby hats approached Tadeusz, one tall and the other short.

'Where have you come from?' asked the taller one, speaking in Polish. He didn't bother to produce any identity and it was difficult to tell whether he was a German or a Pole. A lot of the Blue Police came from eastern Poland, and their accent was different from the capital's. Whatever nationality he was, he spoke with unmistakable authority.

'Zielonka,' said Tadeusz.

'And what's in the bag?'

'I'll show you what's in the bag,' said my military mentor.

I couldn't believe what he was saying. I was standing a short distance away, and I wasn't entirely sure whether the two men knew I was with him or not. The station was crowded. Shouldn't I just drift away? No point in both of us being arrested. But the fear of proving unworthy of my older friend's estimation of me, of being the kind of coward who abandoned him at the first sign of danger, kept me rooted to the spot.

By now Tadeusz had knelt down and was unbuckling the straps, saying, 'What I've got here is a glass jar, and a book, and –'

'All right, close it. You can go,' he was told before he could add to his list.

I waited until we were out of the station before I asked my companion what he would have done if the men had made him empty the bag.

'I suppose I would've had to think of something else fast,' he said.

I was very impressed. It was an amazing piece of bluff, and I told him so.

'You weren't so bad yourself,' he said. 'All it would have taken was for you to lose your nerve and make a run for it, and the game would have been up. But it obviously never occurred to you.'

Although I had been promoted to Battle Schools, I continued with my patriotic graffiti. Towards the end of May 1944, I was able to make a significant addition to my repertoire. As well as my *kotwica* insignia I was now painting a new slogan in block capitals: MONTE CASSINO.

The capture of the sixth-century monastery of Monte Cassino, 75 miles south-east of Rome, was Poland's most significant land victory of the war to date. It was even more exciting than our 1940 contribution to the Battle of Britain. After over a year of training

in Mandate Palestine and Egypt, General Władysław Anders' Polish
2nd Corps had at last joined the British 8th Army in Italy, in time to
participate in the Allies' fourth attempt to crack the Wehrmacht's
Gustav Line and capture Rome. It began on 11 May, when the Allied
divisions attacked along a twenty-mile front. The Poles' main objective was the crucial monastery position itself where, dug in among its
rubble, German paratroopers had doggedly fought off all previous
attempts to dislodge them. A week later, a foot patrol from the 12th
Podolian Lancers planted a Polish flag on the blood-soaked hilltop.
Getting it there had cost Anders almost 1,200 dead and over
3,000 wounded.

So two words, totalling twelve letters, had acquired a certain resonance for us. It was where we had beaten some of the best soldiers
Germany had to offer, and the Grey Ranks inscribed its reminders on
any suitable surface. This was partly done to boost Polish morale.
How much it tormented the Germans is uncertain. Perhaps it raised
the blood pressure of the Nazi fanatics in the SS and the Gestapo but
not, I suspect, the ordinary soldiers. Once, I was about to write it on
a fence running along one of our broader avenues when I became
aware that, interspersed between Polish civilian traffic, both motorized and equestrian, were some of the horse-drawn wagons the
fuel-starved Wehrmacht still used. They were packed with morose-
looking troops whom I immediately identified as Wehrmacht
infantry. And since they were heading in an easterly direction, I
assumed they were taking the ever shortening route to the Russian
Front.

I think I had got as far as MONT. I immediately put down my
bucket and brush and noted there was an escape route through a
nearby construction site that was actually being worked on – which
was unusual in wartime Poland. If they had been German police of
some kind, I would have scuttled off. But they didn't seem to be taking much interest in me, so I didn't run away. I suppose all they saw
was a blond Polish kid, wearing the short summer trousers that made
me look a lot younger than my fifteen years – and I looked young
enough to start with. I could have been working for the local municipality, so I slowly drifted away, tools in hand.

When I wasn't memorializing our famous victory I was distributing the *Biuletyn Informacyjny*, which was increasingly full of good tidings from abroad. Within a month the Monte Cassino triumph had been followed by the German withdrawal from Rome, and two days later that had been eclipsed by the D-Day landings in Normandy, where the British-based 1st Polish Armoured Division would shortly go into action with the Canadians. Meanwhile, General Anders' men had gone on to capture the central Italian port of Ancona, on its Adriatic coast, thus shortening the 8th Army's lines of communication and, a military commentator assured us, providing a springboard against the new defences the Germans were consolidating in northern Italy. Berlin called it the Gothic Line.

On its home news pages the *Biuletyn* was full of local war news. If only half our claims were true, the guerrilla campaign we were waging in eastern Poland must have been of considerable assistance to the Soviets. In our cities the AK went after the entire apparatus of occupation – not only the SS and the Gestapo but also the imported German functionaries whose job it was to ensure that the occupation profited the Reich. Recent assassinations included the Nazi mayor of Radom, the arms-producing town where the Vis pistol was now being produced for Göring's paratroopers.

In Warsaw itself we were probably killing about ten Germans a day. It had reached the point where they rarely walked anywhere unless they were part of an armed patrol or in regimental strength, like the soldiers I frequently saw near our flat. They were quartered in a former agricultural college no more than 200 metres from where we lived, and they used to march out to a nearby park for various drills and exercises singing '*Die Ganze Kompanie*'. It was one of the jollier German marching songs, entirely without menace, Teutonic Gilbert and Sullivan. The chorus went: '*Hussassa, tirallalla / Die ganze Kompanie, ach ja!*' If I had been given the chance, would I have happily dropped a grenade into this jolly choir? Yes, I suppose I would have. They were the enemy. Did I hate them? No, I don't think so. Nazis, real Nazis, were different.

Our biggest coup was the killing of SS-Brigadeführer Franz Kutschera, five months after he had been made overall head of

Warsaw's police. Kutschera, an Austrian notorious for terrorizing Soviet Belarus, was determined to prove worthy of his latest posting. He saw to it that the names and ages of hostages to be shot as a reprisal for German deaths were published daily. And when it happened, he made sure that passers-by were rounded up to watch them die.

Kutschera was difficult to get at. He lived less than 200 metres from his office but invariably took the precaution of being driven there. Shortly after 9 a.m. on Tuesday, 1 February 1944, his Opel Admiral limo with its whitewall tyres was just about to enter the gates at Aleje Ujazdowskie 23, when its passage was blocked by a two-door Adler Trumpf Junior, a humbler species of the German motor trade. Two more stolen cars – an Opel Kapitän and a Mercedes 170 – penned in Kutschera's car. Altogether it was a twelve-person team: three hit men, six more providing covering fire (for this was the well-guarded 'police district'), plus three young women acting as lookouts. One of their tasks was to indicate the approach of the target by casually adjusting a headscarf or tugging at the collar of a coat. Kutschera and his driver were both shot dead, riddled with two of the Sten guns the British had been parachuting into Poland over the last year.

In the prolonged gunfight with various SS sentries that followed the assassination, two of the team – including its leader, Bronisław Pietraszewicz – were mortally wounded and died in a hideout a couple of days later. Two others were killed when they hit a temporary roadblock on a bridge over the Vistula. They abandoned their car and, after a brief gunfight, were consumed by the river's winter waters.

Kutschera lay in state in the seventeenth-century Brühl Palace, formerly Poland's Foreign Ministry, while 100 hostages in Pawiak Prison were herded on to trucks, then taken out and shot in various public squares. Kutschera's body later went by special train to Berlin, from where it was decreed that the Warsaw municipality must also raise a collective fine of 100 million zloty.

Then, one balmy June morning, the war with all its laws, demands and punishment visited our own apartment block. As he was leaving home for his job at the post office, two young men shot dead the plump father of the leggy blonde sisters I liked to chat up in the courtyard. A note was found near his body announcing that the Directorate of the Underground Struggle had sentenced him to death for stealing food packages intended for Polish prisoners of war who had ended up in Germany after the 1939 campaign. A few days later, the *Biuletyn* printed a typical Home Army communiqué confirming that he had been tried in absentia by an underground court and its sentence had been carried out.

After their father died, his two pretty daughters disappeared from my life. There were no more evening chats in the courtyard – where a goodnight kiss that almost brushed the lips might be bestowed – and I never saw them again.

I was sorry about that – though not about their father, for I assumed that the organization to which I belonged was infallible in these matters. In any case, I didn't have time to dwell on it, because by now we were in the grip of extraordinary events and there were signs that the whole Nazi edifice was about to crumble from within and without.

In the 21 July issue of the Nazis' *Novy Kurier Warszawski* we read with some astonishment the official transcript of Hitler's radio broadcast about the previous day's attempt on his life. He had been attending a conference at Wolf's Lair, his military headquarters in our borderlands with East Prussia, when a bomb in a briefcase exploded two metres away from him. 'A very small clique of ambitious, unscrupulous, criminal and stupid officers formed a conspiracy to do away with me,' explained an indignant-sounding Führer, who went on to thank God for sparing him to continue with his life's work.

Some of us were astonished that the world's most notorious Austrian could be such a grateful Catholic, but it came as no surprise that elements of the German Army were tiring of him. It was obvious that they were losing the war. Their Atlantic Wall had proved no more impregnable than France's Maginot Line. After almost two months of hard fighting in Normandy, where the British and Canadians had borne the brunt of an armoured counter-attack led by the Waffen-SS, large cracks had begun to appear. The Americans had captured the port of Cherbourg, and the Allies were poised to break out of their bridgehead. On the Eastern Front the news was even more dramatic.

By mid-July an enormous Soviet offensive that had been going on for just over a month had at last succeeded in clearing the Germans out of all Russian territory. The Wehrmacht's Army Group Centre had almost collapsed. It was nearly another Stalingrad. As many as 31 of its 47 generals were said to be either prisoners or dead, a couple having died by their own hand. A *Biuletyn* article said that the BBC were reporting thousands of newly captured Germans being paraded in Red Square in a kind of Roman Triumph.

Meanwhile, the Red Army was advancing rapidly into eastern Poland. There was fighting near Lwów, which was on the brink of changing hands for the third time since 1939. And some Soviet units had already forded the San River, where I had witnessed the shooting of that desperate figure trying to cross its winter ice. In Lublin, Polish Communists travelling in the baggage train of the Soviet juggernaut were encouraged to set up a Committee of National Liberation. Even more ominous were rumours that some Home Army guerrillas who had been supporting the Soviet advance had been disarmed and their officers arrested. Yet Moscow Radio was broadcasting constant appeals for an uprising in Warsaw that would smite the enemy from the rear, and these were beginning to be reprinted in the underground press: 'The Polish Army calls on the thousands of brothers thirsting for a fight to smash the foe before he can recover from his defeat.'

This 'Polish Army', which was calling on its brothers to rise up, was not related to any of the forces loyal to the government-in-exile in London. It was what Moscow called the 'Polish People's Army', and we knew it as the 'Berling Army'. General Zygmunt Berling was born to Jewish parents who had converted to Christianity and, in 1920, had won a *Virtuti Militari* fighting the Red Cossacks at Lwów. But twenty years later, Berling, by then a lieutenant-colonel, was among those captured by the Soviets. Like General Władysław Anders, the commander of the 2nd Polish Corps in Italy, once in Russia he had somehow escaped the NKVD's brutal culling of Polish officers. Following Hitler's invasion of Russia and Stalin's release of Polish prisoners, Berling decided at the last moment not to follow Anders and his 40,000 men through the newly opened 'Persian Corridor' to British-controlled territory. Instead, he accepted Moscow's offer to form a Polish Corps within the Red Army. Anders was furious. Court-martialled in absentia, Berling was sentenced to death for 'deserting to a foreign power that desires the extinction of Poland as a sovereign state'.

By 25 July, the Russians had crossed the Bug River and were less than 100 kilometres from Warsaw. The Germans were obviously trying to fall back to a line along the west bank of the Vistula, but the central section of the line was hardly manned. South of the city, several Soviet point units had managed to cross the river. Further north, their leading tanks were on the outskirts of Praga, Warsaw's sprawling suburb on the east bank. In their wake were parts of Berling's Army, their numbers strengthened by press-ganging both partisans and untrained peasants into their ranks. There had been an article about it in the *Biuletyn*.

I wondered if they made them learn the Internationale, the way I had been forced to after the Russians captured Lwów the first time.

'The Polish Army, trained in the USSR, is now entering Polish territory,' Moscow Radio informed me and my *sekcja* in one of its broadcasts. 'Its ranks will be joined tomorrow by the sons of Warsaw. They will all, together with the Soviet Army, pursue the enemy westwards and expunge the Hitlerite vermin from Polish soil.'

We particular sons of Warsaw were sitting in a well-heeled apartment that a sympathetic concierge had made available to our cause. We assumed it had recently been occupied by a *Volksdeutsch* family because the radio was quite openly displayed, and we had never heard of a Pole getting a licence for one. Most of the *Volksdeutsche* weren't waiting to be expunged. With the Russians on the horizon, and the prospect of a Polish uprising in their midst, they were leaving in droves – and never mind the Allied bombers and the devastated state of many of the German cities that lay ahead. The Soviets too had stepped up their air raids, and for several days now we had also been hearing the comforting rumble of distant artillery as the Red Army and Wehrmacht exchanged fire outside Praga.

'No doubt Warsaw already hears the sounds of the battle which is soon to bring her liberation,' cooed the broadcaster from the Union of Polish Patriots, the Communist front organization that had set up shop in Lublin. 'Let those who have never bowed their heads to Hitlerite power join us for the decisive action.' Apparently, the 1939 Molotov–Ribbentrop Pact and the division of Poland between Communist Russia and the Nazis had never happened. Did they really think we had such short memories?

But the Germans were also reminding the Poles of old battles and pleading a common cause. Warsaw Governor Ludwig Fischer, who earlier in the year had narrowly escaped an attempted assassination for the many executions he had ordered, had announced the call-up of all males aged between sixteen and sixty-five. He explained that they were needed to help dig a deep anti-tank ditch and build other fortifications around the city's outskirts. 'Just as it did in 1920, Warsaw will defend itself and defeat the Bolshevik enemy,' promised Fischer, a plump and prosperous-looking lawyer still in his late thirties. Loudspeakers blared his appeal outside public buildings, and the text was printed on posters displayed throughout the city. It was as if all the horrors of the last five years were a mere spat between neighbours, and we were now being urged to get together to put out a fire that threatened both our houses.

At about this time there was a joke being told in Warsaw, in which the Archangel Gabriel drops in and asks the first man he meets whom he hates most: 'The Russians or the Germans?'

And the Pole replies, 'When?'

We were not exactly spoilt for choice. One side had given us Katyn, and the other Auschwitz. But however legitimate our grievances, however many Poles they had murdered, picking a fight with the Russians simply wasn't an option. We knew about the Lublin Committee, and about the Red Army disarming and even arresting some of our people, but that was in eastern Poland where the Russians or Ukrainians had always disputed our boundaries. In Warsaw it would be different. The Americans and the British would be watching. Whatever his dispute with our government in London, Stalin would have to accept us as his allies and treat us accordingly. And had not Radio Moscow already given us sons of Warsaw tacit recognition?

The Home Army decided it would issue its own demands for calm, urging total non-compliance with any German notions that we should be helping them dig their trenches. We produced our own posters to paste over Fischer's efforts. In Poland there is a tradition of poster pillars – usually tall steel cylinders with domed tops – positioned on strategic street corners for advertisements and official announcements. One afternoon, I noticed that a crowd had gathered around one of these, and saw that they were reading the latest German announcement on the approach of the Red Army. I retired to the shelter of a doorway to apply the glue to the corners of my sheet. When I had finished, I pushed my way through the crowd and covered what they were reading with the underground's reply. No one reacted except for a man leaning against the wall of an adjacent apartment building, who was watching me closely.

'*Dóbry Molodéts*,' he said as I hastened to leave the scene.

It was one of those Russian expressions Poles usually get to know, if only because it's the name of one of their popular folks songs. It means something like 'brave youth'. I paused for a moment and took a good look at him. He was tall and swarthy-looking, wearing a dark suit and a white open-necked shirt. I wondered if he might be an escaped Russian prisoner of war who, like some of the Jews, had been lucky enough to fall into good hands.

He murmured something, then walked away.

At first, I didn't quite realize what he had said. But then his words – spoken in Polish, but strongly accented – came back to me. I'd already heard them used a couple of times that week, as a kind of greeting.

'*Dzień się zbliża*.' It meant, 'The day is coming.'

## 19.   Summer in the City

Throughout July Warsaw enjoyed glorious weather and, along with the obvious nearness of the Soviet artillery, it seemed to be another harbinger of even better things to come. Pedestrians soaked up the sunshine and treated the occupying army as if it was already an irrelevance. Ten-man German patrols still walked the streets, but even their demeanour seemed to have changed. They lacked their usual deadpan style and sometimes tried to flirt with the mostly unresponsive girls in their flimsy summer dresses. One young woman who did permit herself to smile back was among those delivering cans of petrol for Molotov cocktails.

Wall slogans predicting our imminent victory multiplied, particularly the three parting words my Russian speaker had used. I don't think any of us doubted that the day was indeed coming, and coming fast. By now we all had the red and white armbands stamped 'WP' for *Wojsko Polskie* (Polish Army) that would identify us once the fighting started. From the moment we collected them at our various secret postboxes, we all knew that the countdown to W-Hour had begun. The 'W' stood for *walka* – combat – and was another of our watchwords.

'Zych!'

On the afternoon of Friday 28 July, dressed in shirt and shorts, I had just picked up my latest batch of the *Biuletyn* when I heard somebody shouting my code name. As I turned, Olgierd, the boy who headed our squad of three *sekcja*, each comprising six recruits, screeched to a halt alongside me on his bicycle.

'Alarm,' he gasped. 'Get your men to Dąbrowski Square 2/4, by seven thirty. The password is "Wilno". Have your emergency gear and armbands with you.' And without another word of explanation he vanished.

Get my men? But these were unpredictable boys. I was the youngest, not quite sixteen, but had been promoted to section commander because, in my unit, I distributed more copies of the *Biuletyn*, painted more anchors and passed on more potential recruits for assessment than anybody else. As usual, curfew was at 8 p.m. I had little more than three hours to locate my five comrades-in-arms and bring them to whatever awaited us among the eighteenth-century townhouses of Dąbrowski Square. Four of them lived within walking distance. One I could inform in a lightly coded telephone call from our corner shop. This was just as well, because he lived behind the barbed wire of an area that was supposed to be a secure German police quarter. A few carefully vetted civilians had been allowed to stay. In his case it was probably because his family name was Schmitt, though this didn't necessarily mean he was a *Volksdeutsch*. Many full-blooded western Slavs had the common German surname. I never asked what he was – I wasn't even supposed to know his real name.

All I asked was would he be interested in getting together for the weekend? If so, he should bring his rucksack and meet us at the usual place. He immediately understood and said it sounded like a good idea and he'd see me there. All but one of my *sekcja* turned up at this pre-arranged rendezvous for mobilization, and I knew the missing member wasn't coming. He was a recent volunteer who lived quite close to me. When I called, it was obvious that my news was the last thing he wanted to hear. It was, he pleaded, too early; there had not been enough time to prepare his parents. We didn't regret losing him. I suppose he made us feel braver.

One of the oldest among us was Romek, a tall dark-haired doctor's son who always wore the Polish schoolboy's version of the traditional peaked *czapka*. Despite his headgear there was a certain reserve and air of maturity about him that some of us lacked. I persuaded him that he was the ideal candidate for a sensitive mission. I needed the kind of young man older adults took seriously to call at my home, tell my mother I might be away for a couple of nights and persuade her to hand over my rucksack, which was already packed with my active-service kit of clean shirts, underwear, soap, towel, torch and at least a day's rations of tinned food. I was convinced that, if I went there myself, my mother would never let me out again.

Romek not only returned with the rucksack but also with an envelope containing 500 zloty. I had never seen so much money in my life.

'She told me to tell you not to spend it all at once,' he said.

Later, he rather enjoyed telling me something else my mother had said. 'A boy like you is almost a man. Andrzej is still a child.'

Dąbrowski Square 2/4 turned out to be a sturdy two-storey building housing a soup kitchen run by a voluntary organization for refugees who had fled the fighting in eastern Poland. It stood opposite what had been the premises of the Towarzystwo Kredytowe Ziemskie Bank, in which the Germans had installed an *Arbeitsamt* to procure workers for Germany's war industry. It was about a kilometre south of the Old City and, like a lot of old Warsaw buildings, it had a massive entrance gate. Inside it stood a man holding a Russian light machine gun, the equivalent of an American Browning Automatic Rifle or a British Bren – an excitingly candid display of arms. He told us to go up to the first floor, where we had to wait in a large room. People came and went; in an adjoining room we saw a man in a pre-war Polish officer's uniform, with a captain's insignia, examining a large wall map of Warsaw; a woman introduced another woman to him, and they both stood to attention. It was all very exciting, except that nobody knew what to do with us.

Then suddenly there was a minor commotion. Several boys staggered into the room carrying between them two heavy sacks of ammunition. They were from our platoon. 'We're upstairs,' they said, and we all helped to carry their wonderful burden up the remaining steps.

The first thing we saw was ample evidence that there had been similar deliveries. A large table was laid out with pistols and two sub-machine guns plus a box full of what looked like brand-new British Mills grenades, with their distinctive pineapple-patterned casing to give the thrower a better grip.

Hovering over this small arsenal was a short, nervous-looking man wearing a black beret and the plus-four style of knickerbocker trousers tucked into socks that, in Poland, were known as 'Pumps'. He introduced himself as Lieutenant Bohun, our company commander, and told us to find a place to sit. There were two platoons in his company, and ideally there were at least four companies to a battalion. In theory Bohun's best platoon was 116, whose members were all mature working men. This platoon was unusual in that it included a few veterans of the 1939 fighting. Unlike the countryside guerrillas, most of the Warsaw units of the Home Army consisted of people who had never fired a shot in anger.

The number of my platoon was 101. It was almost entirely made up of teenagers whose duties were intended to be confined to various auxiliary roles, such as messengers. We were thirty-four strong, and were supposed to be almost twice that number, but it soon became apparent that mine was not the only *sekcja* with a missing member. Nonetheless, the adjacent corridor was full of boys, and some young women as well.

Waiting in a corner of the room was a worried-looking, middle-aged couple who had had the bad luck to be visiting the building when we began to assemble and now, for security reasons, were forbidden to leave. It was past curfew and they had no choice but to stay the night. They clung together, longing to get home.

Things eventually settled down, and various sections took turns to snatch some sleep in a room that had several camp beds. When it was our turn, sirens heralded the nightly Soviet air raid, followed by the thump of German flak guns and then the angry crump of bombs exploding nearby. We occasionally heard the searching drone of the planes themselves, and we told each other they were targeting the central railway station. Ammunition trains from Germany came through there – at least, that's what we thought.

No one explained what our future plans were. We knew something had to happen. But we didn't know what, where or when.

Saturday 29 July was a working morning in Warsaw. The apartments where we had spent the night were still full of young people – though, as yet, the only weapons issued had been given to the sentries, who were changed every few hours. Our squad commander, Olgierd, and my mentor, Mietek (Tadeusz Stopczyński), had been among the chosen few permitted to patrol the extensive inner courtyards with sub-machine guns at the ready.

It was not until about noon, after scenes of feverish activity among our leaders, that we received our first clear order. Disperse! Pick up your rucksacks, vacate the building immediately, scatter to various designated locations throughout the city and await further orders. This did not inspire confidence. What was going on?

Later, we learned what had happened. At some point during the night one of our sentries had killed a lone German officer as he tried to enter the building. His body had been placed in the basement and plans were afoot to try to bury it somewhere. But it was unlikely that his death could be concealed for long. Meanwhile, several hundred conspirators gathered in the block could not risk discovery before the designated W-Hour – whenever that was.

In the mass exodus that followed the dispersal order, the area surrounding the block buzzed like an overturned beehive. Groups of young men and women headed their separate ways, each carrying rucksacks or clutching some kind of hastily wrapped package. Incredibly, German patrols somehow failed to register this panic, and we all got safely away. Mine was one of two *sekcjas* that spent the next three days in a large apartment near the Warsaw Polytechnic, not far from the big twin-spired Church of Our Holiest Saviour in which, the following day, some of us attended Sunday Mass.

One prayer had already been answered. My sudden mobilization had discovered me in shorts, and I found this acutely embarrassing. However hard I tried, I tended to look younger than my almost sixteen years, and bare knees didn't help. My comrades-in-arms were of the same opinion. All agreed that a potential fighter looked silly in short trousers. It was obvious that my turnout was in danger of undermining my authority, such as it was, as their leader. But when we got to the other apartment, all was resolved. I was able to borrow some items of clothing from one of the boys in another section. They were a pair of plus fours with a pair of long socks to go with them – exactly the same Pumps-style knickerbocker trousers that our company commander Lieutenant Bohun was wearing, and therefore beyond reproach.

At last, I felt properly accoutred for battle. Or almost. My ruck-sack still lacked a few essentials. Once again, I asked a colleague to collect them from my mother's flat while he was visiting his own family who lived nearby. He came back with a message. My mother had offered her 'word of honour' that I could visit her without fear of incarceration, which I did that afternoon.

They were all there: Aunt Olga, Grandmother and Jerzy, who wanted to know if I had shot anybody yet. There was a certain amount of hugging and kissing but my mother, true to form, was not overtly emotional. As far as she was concerned there was nothing to get all that emotional about. All our local news was good. It was a pity the Anglo-Americans weren't as close to us as the Russians, but one couldn't have everything – and at least nowadays we were on the same side. Only ten days earlier, German officers had come close to killing Hitler. The *Volksdeutsche* were leaving in droves. Perhaps a demoralized Wehrmacht would follow them home. Meanwhile, the weather was gorgeous. I was taking a few days off with my Boy Scout troop, still almost a child and hardly likely to be exposed to much danger. If there was to be an uprising, the consensus was that the Red Army would cross the Vistula and it would all be over in a couple of days. I can honestly say that, when the time came to say our good-byes, I might as well have been leaving for one of the peacetime summer camps that I had never had the chance to attend.

Just before I left, my mother asked me if I could let her know when something was due to start because she and Olga wanted to stock up on groceries. I promised I would do my best. I could have stayed a bit longer but, apart from giving myself plenty of time to get back to my *sekcja* before curfew, I was frightened of missing some-thing.

On Sunday evening we played ping-pong and talked about what we were going to do 'after victory'. Among the possibilities was a return to full-time education, a prospect some of us viewed with mixed feelings.

Next day, we lunched at a soup kitchen while above us Soviet bombers etched white contrails across a clear blue sky. Sometimes they were pursued by the black puffs of exploding anti-aircraft shells, though the German gunners never seemed to hit anything – at least, not while we were watching. From across the river the artillery noise was getting louder.

The weather remained balmy and that night we decided to sleep under some trees in a park. Shortly after dawn, we saw a German soldier and a girl emerging from what I imagined to be the huts where the municipality kept its mowers and rollers. It was Tuesday, 1 August 1944.

We went back to the flat and received a message that we should collect rations of tinned food from a specified shop. En route we saw a German soldier sprawled, apparently lifeless, in the middle of the road next to his fallen motorcycle. We hurried on, uncertain whether it was the result of a road accident or a sniper's bullet. Were we about to be caught in a round-up, dragged off to Pawiak Prison, unable to defend ourselves because we still hadn't been issued with arms? Or was the time for round-ups over? The pavements were crowded with hurrying people, many the same age as ourselves, wearing rucksacks and determined expressions. There was a febrile atmosphere. You could feel the tension. A couple of times we saw open trucks with heavy machine guns mounted on the back, slowly touring the streets. But incredibly they ignored us, and we got back to the flat unchallenged.

I went out to St Saviour's where, in its incense-laden gloom, I found a priest prepared to hear my confession – mostly, I imagine, the normal solitary sins of the male adolescent. I also located a barber because my hair had grown longer and blonder – bleached, perhaps, by the sun – and I resented this Aryan stigma.

Sure enough, while I was in the chair, a swaying figure entered and demanded, 'Why are you cutting a German's hair?'

I could smell the drink on his breath. There were a lot of illegal stills in Warsaw, producing a rough approximation of vodka that we called '*bimber*'. Sometimes the Home Army destroyed them.

'He's not a German,' said the barber over his shoulder. 'He's probably a better Pole than you are. Now get the hell out of my shop and come back when you're sober.'

At about 2 p.m. we received the order we had been waiting for. We were to return to the Dąbrowski Square address we had so hurriedly evacuated four days earlier. The password was unchanged. We were no more than ten minutes' walk away from it when we saw our first Germans. They were sitting in an open-top Daimler-Benz command car, parked outside a café in Zbawiciela Square. Approaching them was a Polish waiter in a white apron, carrying a tray with the four ice creams they had ordered.

When we arrived at our destination, little seemed to have changed. The same man with the same light machine gun was still behind the main gate in the lobby. Upstairs the same weapons waited on the same table, but there was one addition. Somebody had added a stack of our locally made Sidolówka grenades. Officially designated the R-42, they were manufactured in our underground factories. Each grenade held 250 grams of Ammonite, stuffed into one of the distinctive cans in which the German company Henkel had long exported the metal-cleaning fluid they sold under the brand name Sidol: hence Sidolówka. I had never seen one before – just as, until my first visit, I had never seen a British Mills grenade – but I knew a bit about them. Once again, none of the weapons were distributed, and we waited uncertainly for orders. Some of us kept our rucksacks on our backs, ready for action.

It was just as well we were unaware of the agonizing that had taken place during the last four days. We certainly didn't realize we had been on standby whilst Bór and the Home Army's general staff thrashed out whether or not an uprising was worth it. It then had to be put officially to the man the London government-in-exile had appointed as its Warsaw representative. Code-named Sóbol, Jan Stanisław Jankowski, founder of the National Workers' Party, was sixty-two. Like Bór and his officers, he had been in hiding for the past four years and eleven months.

Those against an uprising pointed out that the paltry amount of weapons available had been even further depleted because the Germans suspected something was brewing and had made strenuous efforts to nip it in the bud. As a result, two major weapons caches had been discovered and, among other things, thousands of grenades and several hundred of our home-made flame-throwers had been lost.

Those in favour argued that the 'spirit of revenge' that filled the Home Army would compensate for these setbacks, and the losses would be replenished by arms captured from the enemy and fresh supplies dropped by the RAF. They also argued, once again, that the blatant Soviet attempt to crush Home Army units in newly liberated eastern Poland required them to liberate Warsaw and confront the arriving Soviets with the army's own authority.

Eventually, the general staff was divided straight down the middle: five for and five against. Bór could have overruled them anyway, but whatever he decided would align him with the majority. He came out in favour, telling Sóbol that an uprising in Warsaw would cut the enemy's lines of communication and turn their recent reverses on the Central Front into 'a total catastrophe'.

Sóbol asked a few questions about the Home Army's readiness, then he told its supreme commander, 'Very well, in that case begin.'

Bór set our W-Hour for 5 p.m. This was usually the time people started going home from work, and he thought he could take advantage of the organized chaos any city's rush hour brings to deploy his troops. But the first clashes started some three hours earlier – either because people bumped into German patrols while they were openly carrying arms, or because they simply could not wait. So, to some extent, the advantage of overwhelming surprise was lost as the sound of small-arms fire began to crackle across this city of almost a million people, rather like the first murmurings of a great forest fire. The streets emptied; passers-by rushed into the massive doorways of the houses; conductors fled their tramcars, which were later manhandled off the tracks for use as barricades.

For a while we listened anxiously to exchanges of fire from somewhere nearby and tried to identify the weapons. 'That's one of our Stens,' somebody said, after a burst of automatic fire had been heard, but how he could tell the British sub-machine gun from anything else was hard to say, because none of us had ever been lucky enough to fire one. Lieutenant Bohun, who had been observing proceedings on the roof through binoculars, came in and told us that what we were hearing was an attack on a German command post in the Europejski Hotel.

It was about 4 p.m. when the first shots rang out in Dąbrowski Square. They seemed to come from just in front of the building. Squad leader Olgierd and his deputy – the only two who were armed – dashed to the windows and began firing with a sub-machine gun and a pistol. These were their first shots at living targets. The rest of us ran in the opposite direction – charging into the corridor that led to the kitchen – then just as quickly, and rather shamefacedly, came back. Apparently, some SS had suddenly turned up in trucks and had hardly got their feet on the ground before they were fired at from one of the windows below us. Two were killed outright and their bodies lay in the courtyard for some time.

Soon gunfire seemed to be coming from all directions. Bohun came back and asked me if I knew anybody who could use a Schmeisser?

'I can,' I said.

I might never have actually fired one but all that time learning how to pull one apart and put it back together again had certainly left me with an intimate knowledge of the weapon's innards. If blockages were the problem, I was their man.

'Follow me,' he said and led me downstairs.

Outside, on the roof of a nearby building, a group of men with armbands on their civilian jackets were looking at something through binoculars. I followed Bohun up a wobbly ladder to a second-floor window. I didn't like this much. I've never had much of a head for heights, but this wasn't the time to give in to it. On top of the ladder, I climbed through the open window and the first thing I saw was a young priest in a black cassock standing next to a bed on which a wounded man lay covered in blood.

The priest approached me. 'Take this,' he said, and handed me a small card.

It was about the size of the pictures of famous sportsmen and the like that tobacco companies once put in cigarette packets to give collectors another reason for brand loyalty. Only, in this case, it was

a portrait of St Andrzej Bobola, the seventeenth-century Polish martyr whose remains had found their final resting place in Warsaw the
year before the war started.

'Perhaps he'll bring you luck,' said the priest.

I thanked him and tucked it into my shirt pocket – though I
couldn't help thinking that the aristocratic Jesuit, tortured to death
by marauding Cossacks, had not been all that lucky himself.

Bohun directed me to a room with several men in it. Then there
was a long burst of firing from one of our other positions, and he ran
off to see whether this was a justified expenditure of ammunition.
This was the last I saw of Bohun for a while – and I heard nothing
more of the Schmeisser. But one of the men in the room did have
what looked like a British Sten and was firing short bursts at some
targets below him in what appeared to be a professional manner.
Crouched beside him were two loaders refilling empty magazines.

A man lying on the parquet flooring skidded a Mills grenade in my
direction, and I picked it up. For the first time I felt the heft of the
real thing and tried to persuade myself that some of the practice
stones I had thrown had been heavier. With a firm grip on its metal
pineapple casing, I examined the cotter safety pin that had to be
removed before throwing. Under my palm I felt the spring-loaded
curved lever that had to be kept pressed hard against the case and
would keep it inert until it left my hand. Then, and only then, would
the lever fly off and start the bomb's five-second fuse – providing, of
course, somebody had remembered to unscrew the base plug and
insert a detonator.

I was told that the SS had gone into the *Arbeitsamt* building but,
unless they were trying to trick us, they now seemed to be trying to
get back to their trucks. A small group of them had already tried to
dash across the courtyard, and at least one was thought to have been
hit – which, with any luck, meant we had another rifle in our
armoury. Now we were hoping they would risk running our gaunt-
let again before the late summer dusk set in. It was still the best part
of three hours away. Meanwhile, both sides tried to provoke the
other to give away its position with single shots. I noticed there were

shards of glass on the wooden flooring and large holes in the windows, though by no means all the glass was out.

Behind me I could hear two of the older members of 116, the sister platoon in our company, grumbling about Bohun's tactics.

'He's trying to capture the *Arbeitsamt* with pistols and grenades when what's needed are mortars and heavy machine guns,' one of them said.

Suddenly the Sten gunner yelled, 'Here they come!' But after a couple of bursts, he stopped firing. Cursing, he tried to clear the jammed weapon.

Somebody shouted, 'Throw the grenade!'

I looked around and then realized his command was directed at me. In one action I rose to my feet, pulled the pin and hurled the Mills through the nearest window. On its way it hit some of the unbroken glass, and for a moment I thought I'd just wiped us all out, but all that fell back on to the highly polished floor on our side was a scattering of fresh splinters.

The explosion seemed to take much longer than the five-second fuse setting. When it came, I found it surprisingly loud. It filled my ears. Perhaps it was the echo effect of the courtyard. I peered below and saw several helmeted Germans running across, stooped under their heavy packs but obviously intact.

Had they charged out as soon as the grenade went off? That would have been the clever thing to do. We should really have thrown another one. Nonetheless, at last I was a soldier. I'd just tried to kill some of our enemies.

The Sten began firing again.

I remember thinking: I'll never be able to live back with my mother after this.

## 20.  A Mixed Beginning

Not long after I had thrown my grenade I heard a shrill voice from downstairs shouting, 'We've captured our objective.'

And so we had; the Germans had cleared out. We got down to the lobby just as some women were emerging from the cellar. One of them gave me a bowl of cherry preserve. It was very welcome. I hadn't eaten since breakfast, though only now did I notice how hungry I was. An elegant, silver-haired man confided to my benefactor that he had just returned from the Victoria Hotel, the headquarters of Colonel Monter who commanded the entire Warsaw area and was answerable only to Bór.

'The news is simply excellent,' he assured her.

Monter was the nom de guerre of Colonel Antoni Chruściel, who had once taught tactics at staff college. In truth, the news was mixed – and Monter knew it. On the first day we had done well in the city centre – where I had played my small part – in the cobbled streets of the Old Town and the western working-class suburb of Wola. This was mainly because there were fewer Germans in these places than anywhere else. By 8 p.m. the eighteen-storey art deco Prudential Tower near Napoleon Square, the city's tallest and most modern building, was in our hands. We had also managed to confine to the rococo extravagance of the Brühl Palace both Governor Ludwig Fischer and Generalleutnant Reiner Stahel, the city's new military commander, who had also based himself there.

Stahel, an Austrian, had arrived in the last major city between the Red Army and Berlin only forty-eight hours before. His orders were to prepare it for a siege. Now he found himself in intermittent radio contact with his command, but quite unable to visit any of it because he was surrounded by Polish insurgents. All he could do was hope that he would be rescued by the reinforcements he had requested before the ragtag militia he was examining through his binoculars grew strong enough to break in.

Then the Zośka Battalion did something that literally changed the appearance of much of the Home Army overnight. A fight for a warehouse ended with the death of a young SS officer who had barricaded himself and a lot of ammunition behind some big sacks of flour and sugar. Behind him they discovered boots, helmets and thousands of the latest leopard-spotted camouflage smocks usually issued to the Waffen-SS. Another haul was found in freight wagons being readied to leave a nearby railway siding. We considered these smocks – which we called '*panterka*', meaning 'panther outfits' – to be the last word in military chic, and eventually most of us had one. We were not all lucky enough to have a pristine issue; I would take mine off a corpse.

All this was good for morale, but few major objectives had been captured and held. After some initial success we had been driven out of the east bank of the Praga district, the nearest point to the Soviet advance. The leafy northern borough of Żoliborz, much favoured by the pre-war officer class for its modern villas, trim gardens and small parks, had also been abandoned. A 1,000-strong AK battalion commanded by Lieutenant-Colonel Mieczysław Niedzielski, who used the pseudonym Żywiciel, had been supposed to hold and secure the area. But his plans quickly unravelled after some of his men started the battle about three hours before the scheduled W-Hour, when they shot at a Luftwaffe foot patrol. Whether this was by accident or design depended on who you were talking to. All over the city there had been cases where young hands full of loaded weapons for the first time could not resist taking a potshot or lobbing some infernal device at the closest German target.

In Żoliborz this led to several truckloads of SS-Polizei, closely followed by three tanks, coming to the Luftwaffe's aid and, long before they were ready, this soon sucked in most of the rest of the battalion of whom just under half were armed. Eventually, with casualties going up and ammunition and morale coming down, Żywiciel decided that all he could do, to put it politely, was disengage and regroup. This entailed making an overnight march under driving rain into the Kampinos Forest, where there was a strong partisan unit which could at least replenish their British ammunition with parachuted supplies. They could also fill the gaps in their ranks with eager volunteers anxious to follow Żywiciel back to Żoliborz.

A more serious failure was that the two main bridges across the Vistula remained in enemy hands, as did the airports. (Some of Bór's staff dared to dream that the RAF might soon fly in the British-trained and equipped Polish parachute brigade who were, as yet, uncommitted to the Normandy fighting.) The fragmented start to the Uprising meant that, in all but the early skirmishes, the advantage of surprise was lost and the Germans were able to stick to their contingency plans for dealing with a city-wide insurrection by withdrawing into well-fortified buildings, some of them almost bunkers, and awaiting the arrival of reinforcements.

At that point few Home Army units were strong enough to capture these places in daylight frontal assaults, because even the few weapons we did have had not yet been properly distributed. A cache of 678 British Sten guns in an outlying district was so jealously guarded by its quartermaster that it outlived Nazi Germany by two years. In my own company Lieutenant Bohun could not arm every man, and on the first day I was lucky to get to throw a grenade.

But compared to some we were well off. At W-Hour, one 600-strong battalion assembling in a tree-shaded area off Kolonia Staszica found itself going to war with 300 grenades, thirty pistols, three sub-machine guns and three rifles. Repeated attempts to capture places including the well-guarded Gestapo headquarters complex in Szucha Avenue, where I had spent a terrifying half-hour the year before, were doomed to failure. Various buildings changed hands but the Germans almost always won them back, and the cost was horrendous. The same applied to the bridges, the city's two airports – which were defended by Luftwaffe anti-aircraft gunners, using their four-barrelled 20 mm flak guns in a ground role – and also the large SS barracks the Germans called '*Staufer Kaserne*', which had once housed the Polish General Staff. In all these places the Germans usually had excellent fields of fire when aiming at the Poles who were trying to get close enough to throw their Sidolówka grenades. On a couple of occasions, they were machine-gunned by tanks passing through the city en route to meet the Soviet armour across the river. About fifty young Poles who were cut off and surrendered were shot out of hand.

Almost to a man the people doing the planning had, in 1939, witnessed some of the best Polish divisions melt like candles against the panzers. Surprise night attacks might just have worked. But allowing these poorly armed novices to stage such ludicrous set-piece assaults surely smacked of criminal folly? One of the companies that had tried to take on the Luftwaffe's flak gunners had started the day with 120 men and ended it with fewer than twenty. Others suffered almost as badly. A lot of courage had been squandered trying to get past fast-firing machine guns set in concrete. I suppose taking on our enemies with little more than our bare hands is something of a Polish tradition. In 1794, at the Battle of Racławice, scythe-wielding peasants from the Kraków region captured an entire battery of twelve Russian guns. Like the Irish, we were all so steeped in this kind of history that what we had embarked upon seemed a natural progression.

Towards dusk I found myself on the roof, one of a group surrounding an unlikely-looking roly-poly figure with a holstered pistol strapped around a buttoned three-piece suit. This was Colonel Radwan, code name for Edward Pfeiffer, who some thirty-four years earlier had started his revolutionary career when he was about my age by distributing books forbidden by the Czar's censors. Radwan was the man in command of our sector but he had only just managed to join us, having been cut off when the fighting started in its haphazard, unplanned way. So much of this sort of thing had happened. Bór himself had almost been killed or captured when the headquarters he had set up in Kamler's furniture factory, in Dzielna Street, was discovered by some fifty German soldiers who were protecting a nearby tobacco factory. (In 1952, I met Bór-Komorowski in New York. He told me that the platoon assigned to protect him, mostly Kamler employees, shared a total of fifteen rifles and thirty grenades between thirty-three of them.)

Now here was Radwan, at last able to examine the sector he was responsible for from the roof of our building in Dąbrowski Square. I watched as he examined Warsaw through his binoculars. It was a city lit up by the glow of fires near the central railway station and the flashes of explosions around the compass of the horizon. He pointed and told one of his aides that in order to secure his sector he needed to capture the Central Post Office and the PAST telephone exchange – a tall, belle époque building which, in 1910, had been one of the first reinforced-concrete buildings in Europe.

In the morning we awoke from rough slumber to discover that it was raining slightly, and the citizens of Warsaw had hijacked our Uprising. Their enthusiasm for it was unquestionable. However badly we had started, there was obviously no going back. The civilians had realized that we controlled the largest part of the city, and during the night they had come on to the streets to ask our sentries where they should build the barricades to defend it. On a much larger scale it reminded me of what I had seen with Mateczka during the siege of Lwów at the beginning of my war, almost five years earlier. We were becoming a fortress. Deep trenches were dug; pavements were torn up; abandoned tramcars were manhandled into place, then over-turned to provide the framework that could be filled with enough earth and rubble to stop a Tiger tank.

Platoon 101 was ordered to help them. And as we worked we had music. Technicians from our propaganda department had been repairing the street loudspeaker system that the Nazis had attached to lamp posts, trees and balconies to tell us their lies, issue their ultimatums and announce their barbaric reprisals. It had been slightly damaged in the fighting but now suddenly burst into song, and we stood stock still, throats constricting, eyes moistening. For the first time in almost five years we were listening to a public broadcast of our national anthem *'Jeszcze Polska Nie Zginęła'* – 'Poland Is Not Yet Lost'.

Later in the day there was another treat. Bór used the system to address his soldiers.

'After nearly five years of continuous and difficult underground struggle,' he told us, 'you now stand openly, weapons in hand, ready to restore freedom to our country and punish the German criminals for the terror atrocities committed on Polish soil.'

Platoon 101, not for the moment having any weapons at hand, got on with building barricades. There was almost a holiday mood. Polish flags were unfurled, girls kissed front-line troops in their newly acquired leopard-spotted camouflage, housewives brought glasses of cold tea, bakers offered bread. And all the time the news got better.

We had captured the Powiśle Power Station on the west bank of the Vistula, and thus ensured that we had the electricity we needed to run our hospitals and arms factories. This was despite a recent strengthening of its defences when SS-Polizei reinforcements had brought the strength of its garrison up to about a hundred. But twenty-three of the Polish workers at the plant belonged to us and had smuggled in weapons and explosives. They announced W-Hour by exploding a large bomb beneath the guards' living quarters while, at the same time, their sentry posts came under heavy fire from outside. The surviving SS-Polizei barricaded themselves in. A fierce fight ensued, in which about twenty men were killed on each side. It ended at noon the next day when seventy-eight Germans, some of them technicians, came out with their hands up.

From the outset the Home Army had decided that, instead of paying the Germans back in kind, we would uphold the Geneva Convention, to which Poland was a signatory, and take prisoners. Apart from ethical and propaganda considerations there were good tactical reasons for this. The most obvious one was that soldiers who knew their lives would be spared were more likely to surrender a hopeless position and make our victories less costly. Another reason was that it might encourage the enemy to take prisoners too, if only so that exchanges could be arranged. Even so, as far as most of the Home Army were concerned, this applied only to the ordinary soldiers of the Wehrmacht. Whether or not an SS man was busy in the Totenkopfverbände, breaking records in human suffering, or engaged in more military pursuits was immaterial: they were all shot. A private and deadly cycle of daring assassination followed by cold-blooded reprisal had been going on between the SS and the Polish underground for so long now, they knew what to expect. And yet, at the Powiśle Power Station the SS-Polizei – who, in many ways, were the backbone of Nazi counter-insurgency operations against eastern European partisans – had chosen to surrender rather than fight to the death, and their surrender had been accepted. Were we being magnanimous in victory?

Undoubtedly we felt that we were on a roll. True, there was the occasional shower, but the sun was still shining. And though Monter had decided, for the time being, to stop costly attacks on bridges and airfields beyond our perimeter barricades, we continued to overpower isolated German detachments and consolidate our positions.

The capture of the State Securities Building and the Arsenal (near the place where Brigadeführer Franz Kutschera had been assassinated) meant that most of the Old Town was now ours. In the city centre, urged on by Colonel Radwan, Kiliński Battalion had begun their assault on the strongly defended telephone exchange building owned by PAST (*Polska Akcyjna Spółka Telefoniczna*). At one point, they had succeeded in establishing themselves on one of the lower floors when a hole suddenly appeared in a ceiling and they were ejected by a shower of grenades. Hostilities switched to sniping duels with the enemy, who were able to take advantage of their higher levels, while the battalion tried to work out how they were going to get back inside the building and put an end to it.

To date the insurgents' greatest success had been their attack on the main post office, where they killed about twenty of its defenders before the remaining sixty surrendered. Booty included two armoured cars and a Hetzer tank destroyer (basically a tracked but turret-less tank with high velocity anti-tank artillery and a machine gun mounted in its front hull). All three vehicles had been damaged by Molotov cocktails but the Hetzer, made by Skoda in occupied Czechoslovakia, was still mobile enough for it to become part of one of our barricades.

The Germans had already discovered that, even if our attacks on their fixed positions were not always very sensible, our ability to defend what we had was not to be underestimated. Our latest issue of the *Biuletyn Informacyjny*, never openly distributed in the city before, carried heartening reports of instances where enemy attempts to use tanks against well-made barricades had resulted in humiliating failure. The first occurred when two battle-scarred Panthers – recently discharged from intensive care in 19 Panzer Division's Warsaw repair shop – had been dispatched to rescue the marooned Generalleutnant Stahel from the Brühl Palace. Stahel had just been allowed to add Swords to his Knight's Cross for his distinguished handling of the rearguard in Vilnius, where he had denied the Red Army the Lithuanian capital for several crucial weeks. Cool in a crisis, the previous year he had served with distinction against the Anglo-Americans in Sicily. He was considered the ideal man to hold Warsaw, and Berlin badly wanted him in a position where he could start to do his job.

On Karolkowa Street the tanks attacked a barricade manned by members of the Zośka Battalion, procurer of the wonderful *panterka* camouflage dress and rapidly acquiring a reputation as being among the best we had. Success breeds success. Unlike some of the other barricades, they were well equipped with hand-held anti-tank weapons, as well as bottles of petrol. They had both *Panzerfäuste* (a light one-shot rocket fired from a throwaway tube) and the more cumbersome British PIATs. These compensated for their size and weight with a lack of back blast that allowed them to be fired in the enclosed spaces encountered in house-to-house fighting, and they were used against a wide range of targets.

Most of the Polish positions were in buildings behind and on either side of the barricade, and the enemy tanks approached without infantry cover. After a rapid succession of direct hits, a Molotov cocktail burst into flames that penetrated a vision slit and blinded the driver. The wounded crews abandoned the Panthers and were taken prisoner. To their delight the Zośka barricade discovered that the enemy tanks were more or less still in working order. One was quickly mended (partly by cannibalizing the other), christened Magda and would soon be making a name for herself.

The Panther was a medium-size tank, probably more vulnerable to close-quarters fighting – though, in this case, the real fault might have been the quality of the crews, who turned out to be mainly technicians from the workshop. Even so, forty-eight hours later, the

Germans had no more success when they sent a Tiger tank, the heaviest the Wehrmacht possessed, and an old Panzer IV to try to breach another barricade. Both tanks were disabled and abandoned by their crews. The Tiger was salvaged, though it never worked very well.

Buoyed by these successes, the mood in the city centre remained euphoric. If the war wasn't quite yet over, then the occupation of Warsaw certainly was. Everywhere there were Polish flags and wall posters appealing: 'To Arms in the Ranks of the AK!'

And all the time the news got better.

Żywiciel and his refurbished battalion had returned to Żoliborz, and the southern borough of Mokotów had been similarly reinforced by an intake of well-armed volunteers from the countryside. To help accommodate them the Home Army's no-nonsense bureaucracy emerged from the underground complete with secretaries, typewriters and detailed and well-prepared directives. Hospitals and food distribution points were set up. Home Army canteens were organized where we were entitled to one hot meal on production of our identity cards showing our code names and platoon numbers, which were carefully entered in a ledger. Mere possession of an armband was not enough – anybody could get hold of an armband.

There was always the sound of some shooting and explosions, as skirmishing continued between the insurgents and the shrinking number of German outposts in our midst. But these early August evenings were warm, and people kept the windows of their apartments open. Occasionally one might hear a tinkling piano or the voice of a BBC announcer coming in loud and clear over radios that had spent five years in hiding. I began to wonder if I would ever be required to do any more fighting. Was one thrown grenade really going to be my only contribution to Poland's freedom? My only consolation was that it was already one grenade more than most fifteen-year-olds had thrown.

Then, at exactly 2 p.m. on 4 August, we received our first indication that the Germans were still capable of surprises. For the first time since September 1939, the Luftwaffe bombed Warsaw. As air raids go it was not a heavy one, carried out by a few Junker 87 Stuka dive-bombers. The gull-winged aircraft – emblematic of invincible Nazi

Germany's string of blitzkrieg victories – was now rather out of date, though still frightening enough with the shriek of its near vertical dive. Most of their targets were in Wola, where Zośka Battalion had captured the Panthers, and in the city centre. They hit the area around Monter's headquarters, at the Victoria Hotel, and also targeted the Polish positions surrounding the little Alamo the Wehrmacht were staging at the PAST telephone exchange.

Our sector commander there was concerned that the Stukas might have been trying to provide the kind of close air support that would enable its stubborn German garrison to stage a breakout. He wanted help to strengthen his street barricades, and Platoon 101 was sent to put themselves at his disposal and round up all the civilian help we could muster.

On the way we started picking up some Polish language pamphlets the Luftwaffe had distributed with their bombs. One purported to be from Bór himself and, above what looked to be a reasonable copy of his usual signature, ordered us to stand down, return to our 'alert quarters' and await further orders. Another urged the population to demand our capitulation before their city was destroyed in an unnecessary battle.

When we got close to the telephone exchange, we saw that the bombs had damaged a corner building in Kredytowa Street. We walked down the street in search of civilian volunteers to help with the barricade building. When we reached Number 9, we heard a commotion in its cellar and discovered several men dressed in tuxedos and women in long dresses who had been having a celebratory lunch of some kind. A slightly inebriated gentleman explained they would be happy to help as soon as they had changed their clothes.

That night, we were woken by the din of several large-engined, low-flying aircraft. We could hear that the Germans were trying very hard to shoot them down. Next morning we learned that these had been four-engined RAF bombers (they were flying from bases in southern Italy) which, for the first time, were parachuting arms directly into Warsaw instead of the surrounding countryside. Their dropping zone was a protestant cemetery in Wola and, for the most part, they were surprisingly accurate.

At first we had assumed that these night visitors marked the return of the Soviet bombers, which had not been seen over the city for several days, though the lack of any bomb explosions had been a bit puzzling. Even more bewildering was the absence of a more familiar sound, which had now entirely faded away, though people couldn't make up their minds exactly when it had stopped: all we knew was that we could no longer hear the pounding of the Russian artillery from east of the river. And despite their earlier pleas to rise up against the common foe, Radio Moscow's announcers had yet to mention that an uprising had started in Warsaw.

## 21.    Stalin's Revenge

On 13 August, about a week after the Soviet guns on the other side of the river fell silent, any hopes we held that this was just a temporary blip, were dispelled by a communiqué released by the official Soviet news agency TASS, quoted in the *Biuletyn Informacyjny*, which refuted concerns raised by London's Polish government-in-exile that the Red Army had abandoned us to our fate. It read:

> TASS has been authorized to say that such foreign press reports are either a misunderstanding or an insult against the Soviet High Command. TASS has been informed that the Polish émigré circles responsible for the Uprising did not try to coordinate their action with the Soviet High Command. Polish émigré circles in London must bear the responsibility for these latest events in Warsaw.

The 'events in Warsaw' that TASS was so obliquely referring to was the slaughter by the SS of thousands of civilians in the western suburbs of Wola and Ochota. East of the Vistula the famous panzer theorist General Heinz Guderian had had some limited success with a counter-attack staged by four under-strength armoured divisions. Meanwhile, Heinrich Himmler had been given a free hand to use his SS troops to extinguish this bothersome insurrection being carried out in Guderian's rear. And he knew exactly who was needed to organize it. All of them could have comfortably auditioned for the Sack of Rome. All of them had already wallowed in mass murder.

In overall command was Obergruppenführer Erich von dem Bach. In 1919, in the chaos that followed Germany's surrender and the disintegration of the Austro-Hungarian Empire, he had first fought Poles during a local uprising against Prussian rule in Silesia. Yet this SS equivalent of a lieutenant-general was himself a mixed product of the Prussian-Polish Pomeranian borderlands. His surname had originally been Zelewski and, though his father retired as an insurance clerk, there was a time when he was happy to claim descent from Polish nobility. A veteran of trench warfare, with two Iron Crosses and gas-damaged lungs, by 1931 he was calling himself von dem Bach-Zelewski and had become a Nazi – though, to his intense embarrassment, all three of his sisters had married Jews. By 1939, he had dropped the Zelewski altogether and was a rising star in the SS.

After the Polish surrender, Himmler gave him the job of making Silesia as German as the Ruhr, and I would later meet some of the 20,000 Poles he ejected from their home in Maków. But at least he didn't kill them. It was not until the German invasion of Russia, in the summer of 1941, that von dem Bach, a bespectacled figure with a deceptively affable demeanour, became truly embroiled in the wholesale murder that so endeared him to the Nazi hierarchy. His crowning achievement was the extermination of the ancient Jewish community in Minsk, but this came at a price. Ostensibly evacuated to Berlin for a stomach complaint, he appears to have suffered a nervous breakdown; one doctor reported that he was suffering 'hallucinations associated with the shooting of Jews'.

By July 1943, he felt well enough to accept command of all the anti-partisan activities on the Eastern Front. He conducted a series of operations in which civilians could count themselves very lucky indeed if they were merely displaced from their homes. When, a year later, Himmler gave him a free hand to deal with the Warsaw insurgents it was merely a continuation of this role. It had already been decided that the Wehrmacht's General Stahel would not take up his appointment as the city's military commander. Once he was extracted from the Brühl Palace he would be transferred to Bucharest, where he was needed to help the Romanian Army prepare their capital's defences against another Soviet spearhead.

At von dem Bach's disposal were the forces of Kampfgruppe Reinefarth, commanded by SS-Gruppenführer Heinrich (Heinz) Reinefarth. He was another Prussian from the borderlands, born in 1903 at what his parents called Gnesen and their Polish neighbours knew as Gniezno. A lawyer by profession, he had studied at the ancient Jena University where, along with his degree, he had acquired a stunning duelling scar on his left cheek. Kampfgruppe Reinefarth included police and training units and even some X-ray technicians from an SS hospital in Posen. But its main components were two blood-soaked and mostly non-German formations that between them had killed thousands of Russian civilians in what were supposed to be counter-insurgency operations.

One was the SS-Sonderregiment Dirlewanger, partly a penal unit and named after its commander, Oskar Dirlewanger. The larger of the two, though so poorly disciplined it was far the less effective, was the Waffen-SS Sturmbrigade RONA – the letters being the Cyrillic acronym for Russian National Liberation Army. It was commanded by Bronislaw Kaminski, a former Soviet political prisoner who had been born in Belarus of a German-speaking mother and, most likely, an absent Polish father (because he made a great show of loathing all things Polish).

With German backing, and a 10,000-strong locally recruited militia, Kaminski had run with warlord brutality something called the Lokot Autonomy. This semi-autonomous region had a population of about 600,000 and was slightly bigger than Belgium. All the surrounding collective farms were privatized and their produce sold to the Wehrmacht. Himmler regarded it as a blueprint for the way the Germans would run rural Russia once the war was won.

It lasted until August 1943 and the Soviet victory at Kursk. Beset by large-scale defections to the partisans, Kaminski and his dwindling band had then joined the retreating Wehrmacht on their long march westwards. Awaiting his arrival was von dem Bach, who knew Kaminski of old and regarded him as no more than a political brawler – mainly interested in women and loot, and given to vodka-fuelled soliloquies about how one day he would be Czar of a new Fascist Russia. A powerfully built man, he is alleged to have once strangled a recaptured deserter with his bare hands while in a drunken rage.

Drink, a sadistic sex drive and the opportunity to indulge it at whim also played a large part in the life of Oskar Paul Dirlewanger, the commander of the other anti-partisan unit in Kampfgruppe Reinefarth. But while von dem Bach was contemptuous of Kaminski, he had a certain admiration for Dirlewanger – as did Himmler, who described his confidence in him as 'limitless'.

Dirlewanger was five years older than the century and had seen enough close-quarters combat to last several lifetimes. Between 1914 and 1918 he had been wounded seven times. He was then wounded once more in the post-war fighting between Freikorps and Communists, when a bullet grazed his head, and three more times in Spain, fighting for Franco. Behind his back his men called him 'Gandhi', because he was tall and thin beyond mere wiriness – and nicknaming him after the apostle of non-violence probably seemed like a good joke. Although he denied himself none of his perverted pleasures, there was an ascetic look about him, with thin lips, and eyes sunk deep into his long macrocephalic skull. Although he was clever – he had a doctorate in planned economics – he was also fearless, drunken, amphetamine-dependent, unspeakably cruel and utterly depraved. He was surely the only serving SS officer to have ever been an inmate of a concentration camp: in 1934, he had been sentenced to two years' imprisonment for sex with a fourteen-year-old girl who was discovered in a government car he had drunkenly crashed. By his standards, this was a minor peccadillo.

Dirlewanger's eponymous regiment had originally been recruited from convicted poachers, in the belief that men who could track and shoot deer and wild boar were exactly what was needed to hunt down eastern Europe's forest partisans. Hitler, who was an admirer of Karl May's westerns, was said to be fascinated by the idea. But the supply of convicted poachers soon dried up. They were replaced by the dregs of military and civil prisons, granted licence to rape and pillage in exchange for an ability to kill the weak and defenceless with no more hesitation than they would show towards an armed enemy.

In the early summer of 1944, thousands of German troops were captured in Russia, but Dirlewanger and Kaminski's men – sometimes fighting, sometimes running – got out. By the time they were ready to go into action in Warsaw, as the vanguard of Kampfgruppe Reinefarth, their combined strength was just over 2,500 men of whom 881 were under Dirlewanger. Five per cent of these were the regular

SS cadre, who held officer's rank, and about 45 per cent were German, or at least *Volksdeutsche*. The rest were former citizens of the Union of Soviet Socialist Republics in all its startling variety: Russians, Ukrainians, Cossacks and the whole range of Turkic-speaking central Asians from Azerbaijanis to Uzbeks.

They had been recruited from some of the Reich's worst prisoner-of-war camps and their motivation varied. Perhaps a few were genuinely opposed to Communism – or, at least, the Stalinist interpretation of it. They may even have been inspired by a visit from the turncoat Lieutenant-General Andrey Vlasov who, before his capture and defection in July 1942, had been decorated for his role in the defence of Moscow. But the majority probably saw it as the surest way to avoid dying of starvation or disease, since their captors continued to use Moscow's failure to sign the 1929 Geneva Convention as an excuse to devise fresh hellholes for them.

And no doubt the recruiting sergeants who visited their camps and spoke of earthier things than the iniquities of Marxist–Leninism made service in the regiment sound fun: as much drink as you wanted, and any woman you could hold down – as long as she wasn't German. Possibly some of the nationalists among them – Ukrainian or Turkic speakers – had once been convinced they had joined the winning side and hoped the new rocket weapons falling on London would yet prove them right. Otherwise their prospects were bleak. If they deserted, either side would be entitled to shoot them.

These, then, were the men who were about to be unleashed on what remained of one of central Europe's most sophisticated cities.

## 22.  Massacre

New wall posters had appeared in the city centre urging those of us who were lucky enough to have a weapon to make every shot count. They showed a skull inside a German helmet with the slogan: 'Every bullet – One German.'

In our thinly defended outlying western suburbs of Wola and Ochota, SS-Gruppenführer Reinefarth was having the same problem. 'What shall I do with all these civilians? We have less ammunition than prisoners.' (General Nikolaus von Vormann, supreme commander of the remnants of the 9th Army, would recall these words, spoken into a field telephone, in written testimony presented at the Nuremberg war crimes trial almost exactly two years later.)

But Reinefarth's question was a rhetorical one. He had already decided what to do with the civilians. Indeed, he was already doing it. By the end of the first day of the counter-attack, Reinefarth had presided over the deaths of at least 10,000 men, women and children. By the early evening of 5 August, he was to be seen standing next to his communications vehicle, which was parked under a railway viaduct in Wolska Street, Wola's main road. Beside him was the sallow-complexioned Oskar Dirlewanger who was easily identified because, despite the sunny weather, he was wearing his trademark ankle-length black leather overcoat.

Apartment blocks on either side of them were being emptied and set on fire, though not necessarily in that order. SS troopers were busily igniting piles of broken furniture and bedding with flame-throwers and incendiary grenades. Frightened-looking people were milling about outside their homes, most clutching suitcases and bags stuffed with any valuables they could grab at the last moment. Some of the younger children must have been holding their favourite dolls and stuffed toys, because these were later discovered lying around the burst baggage. All able-bodied males were marched off to dismantle barricades. Those incapable of doing so were usually shot on the spot. The others were not killed until their labours had been completed, and some managed to save their lives by getting accepted for the *Verbrennungskommando*. These were the work details who first collected the bodies and then cremated them on pyres built from the debris of smashed homes, soaked with petrol and anything else that would help them burn. Bodies were everywhere: on the streets, in the houses, and piled up in the basements where people had sheltered from the air raids that preceded the arrival of Dirlewanger's killers, who liked to deliver grenades down cellar steps.

While the surviving men were organized into working parties, the women and children were being herded past Reinefarth and Dirlewanger to the places where the overworked firing squads topping up on vodka were waiting for them. One of them was the main factory yard of the Ursus tractor company. Outside the factory gates their victims were divided into batches of twenty and then, when their turn came, shoved with rifle butts through the yard's big doors. Families got split up. Children became hysterical at the sight of freshly killed parents and siblings and were swiftly silenced. Most of the people pulling the trigger were the Red Army renegades we usually referred to as 'Ukrainians' or 'Vlasov's men'.

The SS obviously intended to organize the killing the way a well-run abattoir tries to avoid letting the livestock scent the blood before it is too late. But it soon became an utter charnel house. A few people did survive to bear witness – mostly because their executioners, some of them singing, were too drunk to shoot straight. Wanda Lurie, the wife of a Home Army man who was away with his platoon, was in the last stages of pregnancy and accompanied by their three children: Wiesław, a boy of eleven, his younger sister Ludmila, who was six, and three-year-old brother Lech.

I came last and kept in the background, continuing to let the others pass, in the hope that they would not kill a pregnant woman, but I was driven in with the last lot. In the yard I saw heaps of corpses three feet high, in several places. The whole right and left side of the first and biggest yard was strewn with bodies. We were led through the second. There were about twenty people in our group, mostly children of ten to twelve. There were children without parents, and also a paralysed old woman whose son-in-law had been carrying her all the time on his back. At her side was her daughter with two children of four and seven. They were all killed. The old woman was literally killed on her son-in-law's back, and he along with her.

We were called out in groups of four and led to the end of the second yard, to a pile of bodies. When the four reached this point, the Germans shot them through the back of the head with revolvers. The victims fell on the heap, and others came. Seeing what was to be their fate, some attempted to escape; they cried, begged and prayed for mercy. I was in the last group of four. I begged Vlasov's men around me to save me and the children, and they asked if I had anything with which to buy my life. I had a large amount of gold with me and I gave it to them. They took it all and wanted to lead me away, but the German supervising the execution would not allow them to do so, and when I begged him to let me go he pushed me off, shouting, 'Quicker!' I fell when he pushed me. He also hit and pushed my elder boy, shouting, 'Hurry up, you Polish bandit!' Thus I came to my place of execution, in the last group of four, with my three children.

I held my two younger children by one hand, and my elder boy by the other. The children were crying and praying. My elder boy, see-ing the mass of bodies, cried out, 'They're going to kill us!' and called for his father. The first shot hit him, the second me; the next two killed the two younger children. I fell on my right side but the shot wasn't fatal. The bullet penetrated the back of my head from the right, then exited through my cheek. I spat out several teeth. I felt the left side of my body growing numb, but I was still conscious and saw everything that was going on around me.

For almost thirty-six hours Wanda Lurie lay with her children's bodies under an untidy and growing heap of the dead and dying. From time to time the killers returned to snuff out any signs of life and inspect their work for any missed loot. Once, Wanda felt some-body gently lifting her hand and realized her visitor was undoing the strap of her wristwatch. She kept still and let her arm go limp. Only when she felt the baby inside her begin to stir did she force herself to make the effort to escape and, fighting off nausea and dizziness, began to crawl away on her hands and knees hoping that help would arrive before the Germans.

For much of the Uprising it was perfectly possible to live a comparatively peaceful existence in one part of Warsaw whilst in another, and just far enough away to be invisible, occurred the kind of horrors that are normally only experienced in your worst nightmares.

For those of us approaching the end of our first week in the liberated city centre, life was becoming quite orderly. We still had water, electricity and food. There were soup kitchens and regular distributions of flour, ersatz coffee and other foodstuffs normally controlled by the Germans. There were also outdoor cafés where insurgents could sip their make-believe caffeine while reading the latest *Biuletyn Informacyjny* or even be entertained by singers wearing the same red and white armbands as ourselves. One might have thought it was all over, and we were merely awaiting the arrival of the Russians who had somehow been unavoidably delayed but were due at any moment.

Several times a day, sometimes piped over the captured public address system, we would hear the opening bars of the '*Warszawianka*' ('The Song Of Warsaw') that celebrates one of our failed attempts to throw off Russian rule. The chorus goes: 'Forward, Warsaw, to the bloody fight.' It was the signature tune for a new radio station called 'Błyskawica', which means 'lightning' and was also the name of a successful sub-machine gun produced in our clandestine factories. Radio Błyskawica did its best to moderate expectations of imminent Soviet rescue and get us used to the idea that we would probably have to hold out for a week or two yet. Its announcements reminded us: 'The nearest Russian troops are still almost twenty kilometres away from Warsaw.'

It also dismissed reports put out by Radio Moscow that all the real fighting was being done by the Communist People's Army. They and their inevitable Trotskyist schism, the Polish People's Army, did make a small contribution. So too, for that matter, did the National Armed Forces (known by their Polish acronym 'NSZ'), who were sufficiently right wing and anti-Semitic to qualify as Fascist. But in total all three armies could not have fielded more than 2,000 combatants.

The remaining insurgents were all members of the Home Army, which at this point was trying to repair the inconsistencies wrought by its chaotic mobilization and was attempting to sort itself out. Before they started any fine-tuning our leaders might have been better employed deciding exactly what territory they wanted to hold and deploying their troops accordingly. But there seems to have been a general belief that the Germans were too hard pressed by the Russians to make a counter-attack. Instead, an attempt was being made to tidy up and ascertain exactly what our ration strength was. Efforts were being made to adjust platoons to a uniform strength, by either reducing or increasing their numbers, and there was an attempt to keep people under eighteen away from the front line – though this rarely lasted for long.

The commander of Platoon 101, a tall, willowy young man in his early twenties whom we called 'Lubicz', saw to it that I was among ten of the younger ones transferred to barricade building and civil defence. Lubicz and I did not get on. In 1939, he had been a cadet sergeant – the lowest commissioned rank in the Polish Army – and during this time he had acquired an enthusiasm for the more arcane housekeeping rituals of peacetime barrack-room soldiering. Our relationship had never quite recovered from an early exchange of views concerning the right way to fold a blanket.

Romek, still wearing his student cap, was also transferred with me, as was Wacław Tarlowski, a boy of about my own age and size who had chosen the code name 'Wacek' and possessed my own bookish instincts, so I was not lacking for company. And in charge of our small unit, with the rank of acting sergeant, was none other than Mietek, the young man who had recruited me into the Conspiracy in the first place and whose nerve I had so admired when – in what now seemed like another world – he had invited the police check at the main railway station to examine his bag full of incriminating literature. Mietek had received some shrapnel wounds at one of the city centre's barricades and we had lost track of him for a couple of weeks while he was in and out of hospital. He was a couple of years older than the rest of us, possibly as old as eighteen.

One of our tasks was clearing rubble and occasionally trying to dig people, alive or dead, out from underneath it. Another was clearing rooftops of the kind of combustible materials (wooden laundry tubs and the like) that might ignite in an air raid. I disliked heights, and it was not my favourite job – especially on roofs without a proper parapet, where the naked edge seemed to be inviting a careless step into space.

I don't suppose it had occurred to any of us that we would find ourselves under air attack, let alone from the Junker 87 Stuka dive-bombers that had so often starred in the Nazi newsreels. In this fifth year of the war the Luftwaffe considered them a bit old hat, and they had long been reluctant to expose them to British Spitfires. But we didn't have any Spitfires, and it had been several days since we had last seen their Soviet equivalent over Warsaw. Nor did we have any anti-aircraft guns to speak of – people would persist in trying to shoot them down with various automatic weapons, despite the screams of protest from our officers at this blasphemous waste of ammunition. By far the most terrifying thing about them was the banshee wail of the siren attached to the Stuka as it went into its near vertical attack dive. They were intended to induce panic, and they were very good at it.

I can vouch for this. Sometimes I helped deliver mail between the centre's southern and northern parts which, to avoid snipers, required using the trench dug across Jerozolimska Avenue, one of the city's main thoroughfares. New postage stamps had been printed, though the old occupation-issue stamps were accepted – as long as Hitler's face was crossed out. Making my rounds, I was once caught crossing a large courtyard when one of these raids started. The insistent scream of the Stuka's siren, getting louder by the second, seemed to confirm that the pilot had me – and only me – in his sights. I bolted for the nearest open doorway, only to be halted by an angry-looking major who accused me of behaviour likely to cause alarm and despondency. And sure enough, despite my fears, the bombs did land some distance away. Nonetheless, I made sure it didn't happen again; I decided I'd rather die than be thought a coward.

In the city centre our first indication of the attack on Wola and Ochota were Stuka raids that were not only targeted on the suburbs themselves but also ranged east of them, towards the Old Town with its fortress-like views of the Vistula. Many of the refugees were heading there, knowing that the narrow lanes between its fifteenth-century buildings were easily barricaded and believing the Home Army would surely make it a stronghold.

Reinefarth had deployed his troops on a broad front, which was probably not the way the Wehrmacht would have gone about it with its love of the *Schwerpunkt* maxim: concentrating forces on one point of maximum pressure. Dirlewanger was in the middle with Kaminski on the right flank, in the more southern suburb of Ochota. On the left he had placed Attack Group Schmidt, a formation named after Oberst Willi Schmidt, the commander of the Wehrmacht security unit Sicherungs-Regiment 608, which was its nucleus. It was predominantly German, about 1,400 strong, with only one sizeable foreign attachment – an SS battalion recruited from Azerbaijani Muslims. But though Schmidt and his security troops were not SS, neither were they Rommel's chivalrous Afrika Korps. They tended to be middle-aged, married men who were older than the average infantry soldier, and their history was almost entirely composed of counter-insurgency operations behind the Eastern Front, with all the persecution of defenceless civilians that such activities usually entailed. Just like the SS, they regarded themselves as the bulwark between western Europe and the Judeo-Bolshevik subhuman horde to which the notoriously fickle Poles had now aligned themselves.

Opposing Schmidt's troops from their positions in the Jewish and Protestant cemeteries, where the RAF had made its first arms drop on Free Warsaw, was the Radosław Group. Just behind them was the Kamler furniture factory, where Bór himself had his headquarters. These were some of his best troops – better armed and better trained than most. Their commander was the eponymous Radosław, who was actually Lieutenant-Colonel Jan Mazurkiewicz. Like my father, and most of the officers of that generation, he had been in almost continuous action between 1914 and our victorious conclusion of the Polish-Bolshevik war in 1920. Only in one respect did Mazurkiewicz differ: he was from a working-class background, his father was a carpenter, and he was commissioned from the ranks for the courage and competence he had demonstrated.

Between the wars he had taught tactics to junior officers until shortly before hostilities started in 1939, when he was promoted to the rank of major and attached to the Polish General Staff as an intelligence officer. In this capacity he joined a team invited to think the unthinkable. They were to imagine that Nazi Germany had somehow succeeded in defeating and occupying Poland and draw up contingency plans for an armed resistance movement. It was, simply enough, to be called the Secret Military Organization (*Tajna Organizacja Wojskowa*) and when it came to pass, Mazurkiewicz was among those ordered to remain behind and set it up.

Schmidt's war-weary killers had probably never come up against anything quite like the Radosław Group. They were reasonably well armed with plenty of sub-machine guns and grenades, though their field training was rudimentary. Like the rest of us they were obliged to learn the basics of infantry fighting on the job, where learning from your mistakes depended entirely on how lucky you were. But they were well led, and their high morale more than made up for what most of them lacked in experience. Everybody knew the Germans were almost finished. All we had to do was show them the way home. We were particularly determined to protect Bór's headquarters and the cemeteries, where we were expecting more RAF arms drops – and, in our wildest dreams, perhaps even the leading elements of the 1st Polish Independent Parachute Brigade (which the British still hadn't used in Normandy and were obviously saving for something important).

The Germans were confident that the insurgents facing them would be so shaken up by the Stuka dive-bombing, they would be easily overrun. Instead, lining up at the edge of the Protestant cemetery, Radosław's forces had waited until they were close enough to use their sub-machine guns and then enfiladed the enemy's left flank with concentrated bursts of fire. They began to move forward, throwing their grenades and trying to divide the Germans into small groups before they had a chance to organize themselves into good

defensive positions. Schmidt's men were taken aback by the unexpected quality of the resistance. They retired, leaving behind three
dead and several of their wounded who, not being SS, were taken
prisoner.

Unfortunately for Wola, this was Reinefarth's only setback. In the
streets to the south of Schmidt's aborted sortie the only thing slowing down the troops under Dirlewanger and Kaminski's command
was their appetite for looting and rape. Dirlewanger's progress
towards the Saxon Garden and Brühl Palace, where General Stahel
was besieged, was particularly fast. Radio Błyskawica's reports soon
revealed why.

> Tanks came through streets with women tied on to them to prevent
> action from Polish troops. In Królewska Street many private homes
> have been bombed out. Some people have succeeded in escaping
> through the cellars to houses in AK hands. In Jerozolimska Avenue,
> to prevent AK troops from shooting at them, they drove before them
> 500 women and children. Many of them were killed and wounded.

Dirlewanger was implementing the same human shield tactics that
his brigade had used to good effect in Russia, and in a sector of the
city where he faced much weaker opposition than from the Radosław
Group. Among his Wehrmacht reinforcements was a detachment of
about thirty Assault Engineers (*Sturmpioniere*). The SS unit attached
three to each platoon to assist in things such as breaking down heavy
doors with crowbars or detonating clusters of grenades. One of them
was Mathias Schenk, an eighteen-year-old Catholic from the
German-speaking border village of Büllingen, which had been
annexed by the Reich in 1940. Somehow a tank, or some kind of
self-propelled gun, was blown up and Schenk noted the cap of one of
its crew members flying high into the air. Then the astonished con-
script watched as the SS began to force civilians to sit on a second
tank. Among those being forced to board was a woman clutching a
little girl. People already on the tank tried to help them up.

'Someone persuaded her to give him the child while she climbed
on board,' Schenk later recalled. 'But as he was handing her back, the
tank suddenly jerked forward and the girl was dropped and crushed

to death beneath one of the tracks. Her mother started to scream. One of the SS looked at her and frowned. Then he shot her in the head.'

As more survivors reached our lines, accounts of atrocities like these began to appear in the *Biuletyn Informacyjny* and its growing number of rivals. A woman who had already narrowly escaped rape when her assailant was distracted by gunshots attributed her own survival as a 'living barricade' to divine intervention.

> With our backs turned to the insurgents we knelt or crouched and the Germans placed themselves on the ground behind us, or knelt on one knee, firing over our heads. Including two children there were twenty-three of us, and we were mostly young women. It lasted for two hours. Shots whistled over our heads. The noise of the Germans' rifles so close to our heads nearly deafened us. We were all trying to prepare ourselves to die and saying the Rosary aloud. But as if by some miracle, the incoming bullets only hit our enemy. When the first Germans started to fall we were paralysed with fear. We thought they would take their revenge on us. Stupefied and astonished, they looked towards the insurgent posts, and then at our quiet, resigned attitude with the weeping children clinging to their mothers' necks. In the end, they let us go.

Oskar Dirlewanger got his men the best part of three kilometres down Wolska Street, Wola's main thoroughfare, before they encountered their first meaningful barricade. It happened to be manned by a platoon of Trotskyites from the Polish People's Army and might have proved a serious obstacle, had they not left themselves vulnerable to an attack from the rear by failing to block a crucial side street.

Dirlewanger made sure that they paid a heavy price for this and then started to encourage his men to slaughter all the civilians they could find. Assault Engineer Schenk watched the Poles running away.

> Civilians were getting out of cellars with their arms up. They were screaming at us in German that they weren't partisans – *Nicht Partisan!* I didn't see what was happening behind me because we were exchanging

fire with the Poles. But I did hear the SS commander in the leather coat screaming at his men to kill everyone: men, women and children.

Those of us in the city centre formed an eager audience for the first openly distributed and, by now, increasingly varied media for five years. And yet, the first accounts of these events were misleading. There was no doubt that bad things were happening. But initially there was no real understanding of just how awful they were.

'In many cases the Germans have torched entire streets of houses and shot all the men living in them,' reported Radio Błyskawica. 'As battles rage all around them, women and children have been turned out into the street to find their own way to safety.'

The reality, as the pregnant Wanda Lurie found out, was much worse than that. At this stage women and children were by no means simply being ejected from their homes and left to take their chances in contested areas. If they weren't immediately required to play the part of human shields and assist the enemy to proceed to the next barricade, they were being rounded up and led to slaughter. Recent Nazi propaganda had made much of the new pilotless V-1 flying bomb, developed as a reprisal weapon and fired blindly at Greater London as revenge for German civilians killed by Allied carpet-bombing. In Warsaw some of the SS executioners appeared to believe that they were engaged in a more personal interpretation of the same thing.

'We were in no doubt about our fate,' said Aleksandra Kreczkiewicz (whose evidence, like Wanda Lurie's, would be heard at the Nuremberg war crimes trials). When a woman walking alongside a German soldier asked what was going to happen to them, he replied: 'Our women and children are perishing by your hand. Now it's your turn.'

Kreczkiewicz escaped with a flesh wound. She had been among about 500 people living in apartment blocks in Górewska Street who were herded from their homes into a nearby field which, as a wartime expedience, had been put to growing potatoes.

The shooting started without warning, and I fell. When I recovered consciousness I heard them finishing off the wounded, one shot at a time. I played dead. Then I saw that only one of our executioners remained on guard. The others were setting fire to some huts on the field and there was quite a lot of smoke.

I was hidden by a potato basket, and when this German was looking in another direction I pushed the basket in front of me and crawled along for a few yards behind it. Suddenly the wind blew a cloud of smoke in my direction so that the sentinel could not see me. I ran into the cellar of a burning house where I found several people, slightly wounded, who had succeeded in getting out from under various heaps of corpses. The men decided that we were going to have to tunnel our way out of this cellar to somewhere safer, a difficult task amidst fire and smoke. We had one coal shovel and the rest of us did what we could with our bare hands. After several hours of superhuman effort the passage was finished. It brought us to the courtyard of a neighbouring house, not yet on fire. It was now about half twelve at night. I could hardly keep on my feet.

By now news of the Wola massacre was growing. More people reached our lines in the Old Town or the city centre, bursting to tell their stories. After its initial restraint Radio Błyskawica was quick to get on air and broadcast details of the atrocities committed against the wounded and the sick. Dirlewanger and Kaminski's troops had murdered and raped their way through the patients and staff in four hospitals. Three were in Wola, and the fourth was the Maria Skłodowska-Curie Institute of Oncology in Ochota, where Kaminski's men ran amok, drank the rubbing alcohol and gang raped nurses and cancer patients.

In total some 1,200 patients and staff were killed by Dirlewanger's thugs in the Karola i Marii, the St Lazarus and the main Wola hospital. Worst hit was the St Lazarus, where many of the victims had been sheltering from artillery fire in the basement. They died after a fire was started with grenades and petrol.

The Belgian Schenk witnessed the start of the rape of the nurses from the main Wola Hospital, where he saw the *Sturmpioniere* called 'Dirlewangers' tearing the women's clothes off them before the Wehrmacht ordered them outside on guard duty.

We heard women screaming. Then, in the evening, there came the kind of roar you sometimes hear from a boxing ring. Me and my friends had to climb a wall to see what was happening. Soldiers from all units – Wehrmacht, SS, Kaminski's Cossacks – most of them drunk, were there and making a lot of noise: whistles, exhortations. Dirlewanger in his long leather coat was standing with some of his men, laughing. The nurses were rushed through the square stark naked with their hands on their heads. Blood ran down their legs. A doctor was dragged behind them with a noose around his neck. He wore a rag, red maybe from blood, and a crown of thorns on his head like Christ at Easter. All were led to a roughly made gallows where a few bodies were already hanging. When they were about to hang one of the nurses, Dirlewanger personally kicked away the bricks she was standing on. After that I couldn't watch any more.

In the space of thirty-six hours, Reinefarth, Dirlewanger and Kaminski between them oversaw the murder of thousands of unarmed civilians. Years after the war the consensus among historians was that even more Poles died at Wola and Ochota in the week of 5–12 August 1944 than the 33,371 Ukrainian Jews who perished at a much better known massacre near Kiev, in a ravine called Babi Yar.

These were battlefield casualties, but the Nazis made no attempt to claim that they fell into that accidental category nowadays referred to as 'collateral damage'. Civilians were being deliberately targeted in order to break Polish morale and turn the inhabitants of Warsaw against the insurrection. If at the same time they happened to kill a few insurgents, then so much the better. At this point the German casualties were very low indeed. On the first day, six were killed and about forty wounded.

After the Wola massacre, Reinefarth's troops stormed down Chlodna Street and broke the siege of the Saxon Garden, adjoining the Brühl Palace. Reinefarth, who had won a Knight's Cross in France in 1940, squeezed himself inside a self-propelled assault gun and was one of the first at the palace gates. Afterwards, he claimed to have personally liberated the unfortunate Stahel, trapped at the outset in his headquarters without a chance to show what he might have achieved as Warsaw's newly appointed commander. (Nor did his luck get any better. He arrived at his next posting in Bucharest just in time to see the Romanians change sides and hand him over to the Soviets. Ten years later, aged sixty-three and still a prisoner, his excitement at being told he was about to be repatriated to his native Austria brought on a fatal heart attack.)

Bór was now threatened on his left flank and abandoned the Kamler factory. He followed the refugees into the Old City, where he established his new headquarters. Communications were a problem from the start: when he wanted to order Colonel Monter to relieve the pressure on Wola by launching an attack from the east, the only way to tell him was to send one of his staff officers to the colonel's city-centre headquarters. Not that it did any good. Monter told the commander-in-chief's envoy that he did not have the weapons and ammunition to waste on 'irresponsible undertakings'.

An operation that had nothing whatsoever to do with the plight of the Wola civilians was undertaken. Not far from Pawiak Prison, in the midst of the ashes and scorched rubble that had once been the Warsaw ghetto, stood a collection of intact single-storey barracks buildings with eight watchtowers and a high connecting wall between them, all made of nineteenth-century brick. This was Gęsiówka, in pre-war days a Polish military prison and now perhaps the smallest of Germany's concentration camps, containing some 400 prisoners. They were being kept alive to scour the rubble of the ghetto for salvageable items – the Nazis were obsessed with notions of Jewish gold – and also to locate and remove from beneath the debris any bodies whose putrescence was suspected of contributing to a lingering outbreak of typhus. A crematorium had been installed to dispose of these corpses. None of the Jews who fed it, and they came from all over Nazi-occupied Europe, had any doubt that once their labours were done they would also be fuel for its flames.

But rescue was on hand. Despite the desperate need for reinforcements in Wola, Radosław was permitted to use part of his Zośka Battalion and the captured Panther tank they called Magda to break into Gęsiówka. A certain amount of sniping since the start of the Uprising had alerted the SS guards to the fact that they were more or less surrounded by insurgents, and they were awaiting help. When they saw Magda approaching their main gate, immune from snipers with its turret hatch closed, they naturally assumed that the cavalry had arrived.

Only when their visitor disdainfully brushed aside the barricades they had built in front of Gęsiówka's imposing portcullis-style entrance did the penny drop, but by then it was too late. Impervious to machine-gun fire from the watchtowers, Magda flattened the gate and then, commanded by one Wacław Micuta who had served in tanks in the 1939 campaign, proceeded to pound the towers with its 75 mm cannon and machine gun. As it did so, Zośka's foot soldiers rushed in and began shooting at every black uniform in sight. Some of the SS attempted to make a stand in their administrative building. But by the time an amazingly intact grandfather clock in the corner of the dining room was chiming 11 a.m., the fighting was over. It had taken exactly half an hour. Polish casualties were two killed and one wounded.

There were no SS prisoners – or if there were, they didn't last very long. Some of Gęsiówka's guards were cut down as they fled towards Pawiak Prison where, shortly afterwards, the survivors probably joined in the massacre of its remaining 700 political prisoners. Another 500 prisoners had been summarily executed in Mokotów Prison where, on the first day of the Uprising, a single platoon broke in and managed to free about 300 people before they were driven out and had to leave the rest to their fate.

In Gęsiówka the Zośka contingent discovered they had liberated 348 Jews of whom 259 were foreigners, including citizens of Belgium, Czechoslovakia, France, Germany, Greece, Holland, Hungary and Romania. The remaining 89 were Polish Jews and even included a few of the surviving fighters of the ghetto uprising. Almost all of them, regardless of nationality or sex, volunteered to fight with the Home Army. Few would survive.

Operation Gęsiówka may have been tactically irrelevant, and the number rescued a drop in the ocean compared to the slaughter going on in Wola, but it was a tremendous morale booster. Nobody had ever sprung an entire concentration camp before. Reading about it filled us all with a tremendous sense of pride, and I remember feeling deeply envious of the Zośka Battalion. The *Biuletyn Informacyjny* published photographs of the newly released prisoners, still wearing their death camp stripes, and of Magda covered with freshly cut leafy camouflage. The jubilant crew and others were sitting on its turret, and a young woman with a broad smile on her face was straddling its big gun.

There was not much to smile about in the western suburbs, where it had seemed that nothing could stop the killing. Only in Ochota were we able to extract a measure of revenge. When Kaminski's RONA troops first arrived in the neighbourhood some joyful local residents, hearing Russian spoken and seeing their old Soviet uniforms, assumed the Red Army had crossed the Vistula and had rushed out to greet them. They soon learned their mistake. These were some of the 1,600 unmarried men specially selected by Colonel Ivan Frolov, Kaminski's Georgian chief-of-staff, for the Warsaw operation. This happy band of bachelors murdered and raped as if it was as natural as breathing, and between times they drank as much alcohol as they could find.

But, unlike Dirlewanger's brigade, one thing they didn't do was fight very well. They were not only undisciplined – too mesmerized by the loot to be had, both carnal and material, in a western city that possessed such novelties as indoor plumbing – but the majority had scant, if any, knowledge of urban warfare. They had received very little in the way of any kind of unit training, and they had probably never met an enemy so anxious to kill them as the Poles.

Two Home Army redoubts held out in Ochota. Both were connected by tunnels to the sewers and through them to the city centre which enabled them to be resupplied. One was close to the Radium Institute, and they were well aware of some of the atrocities Kaminski's troops had committed there. Some had watched through binoculars as they poured petrol over screaming captives and burned them alive in its grounds. About a hundred or so of these Russians, commanded by a Major Yuri Frolov (a cousin of the chief-of-staff) then began looting some buildings that were perhaps a little closer than they realized to the nearest Home Army position. Its commander could hardly believe his luck and immediately attacked. Among the weapons used was one of the flame-throwers we manufactured in our underground factories. Surprised, and probably drunk, the Russians were soon put to flight. No prisoners were taken, and Major Frolov was among the dead.

In the first week of the fighting RONA lost 500 of its 1,600 men and, time and again, took its revenge against those unable to fight back. We were later amazed to learn how passively some people had gone to their deaths, clambering up on piles of warm bodies to kneel and await their turn for a shot in the back of the head, just like the Jews.

'We were so obedient,' admitted Krystyna Błońska, who was seventeen and survived a shot that grazed her scalp and bled profusely. To the last second she had been praying and holding hands with her parents, who were standing on either side of her. 'They shot a man with a child in his arms. I was saying, "Mother, don't look." I was thinking a bullet straight in the head means nothing. I was only afraid that they would throw grenades and tear us into pieces. I didn't hear the shot.'

By the time she came round, it was dusk and the shooting had stopped. Covered in blood, Krystyna lay next to her parents. When she touched them she realized they were dead. It was about this time that there came the first surreal indications that the Germans might wish to put an end to the killing. Officers began to turn up at various execution sites and announce to their handiwork that anybody who could still hear them had nothing to fear and should show themselves.

These Lazarus invitations must have taken some believing, but those survivors who could stand up slowly got to their feet. At one of the Wolska Street killing grounds Wacława Galka had lost her teenaged daughter and six-year-old son, who had survived for some time but got a second bullet when he started crying because his leg hurt.

'I got up and, immediately after me, my husband,' said Mrs Galka. 'Then he saw our dead children. "You killed my children, kill me as well," he screamed.'

So they did. A couple of other men were also killed.

But the Germans could not make up their minds what to do with Wacława Galka and three other surviving women. On three occasions the women thought the executioners were about to finish what they had started. But they were eventually sent to a new transit camp that the Nazis had opened at Pruszków, the railway repair depot on the Warsaw–Vienna line some ten kilometres south of the capital's city limits. At that point only a trickle of evacuees were going there. Eventually, it would hold well over half a million.

Among them was the pregnant Wanda Lurie who, after teaming up with another wounded woman, had escaped the execution site at the Ursus factory yard only to be recaptured by some of the same Russian renegades responsible for murdering her children. But this time they evidently had different orders. The women were delivered to a shelter of sorts in Wola's St Stanislaus Church, though there was no medical assistance available for her terrible head wound during the two days she spent there. Nor was there any assistance in Pruszków. But on 11 August, a week after she had been shot, she was transferred to a small clinic in the woodland town of Podkowa Leśna and received medical attention for the first time.

Nine days later, it was there that she gave birth to a healthy baby boy she called Mścisław. The name means 'he who vows revenge'.

## 23. 'The Worst Street Fighting Since Stalingrad'

On the day that Wanda Lurie gave birth to her only surviving child, who grew up to become a chemist, I happened to be watching a dishevelled column of 115 newly surrendered German prisoners. They had just emerged from the PAST telephone exchange. After a twenty-day siege, the eleven-storey building had finally fallen to the Kiliński Battalion whose weapons included some of our locally made flame-throwers.

The siege had ended when somebody informed us about a little-used subterranean entrance into the basement and wondered if the enemy might be equally unaware of its existence. This proved to be the case.

The Kiliński Battalion had got in at night and immediately inflicted heavy casualties when they opened fire at point-blank range on the astonished ground-floor guards. The survivors fled to the upper levels and trickled grenades down the stairways. The intruders responded by starting an enormous blaze beneath them, using a fire-engine pump to flood the place with petrol and then igniting it with their flame-throwers. Once it had taken hold, they quit the building, covered the exits and awaited developments. At 1 p.m. the Germans began to come out of the smoke-blackened ruin with their hands up.

During this last fighting the German garrison of the PAST building lost thirty men, bringing their total fatalities there to fifty-six. Over the same period fifty-eight members of the Kiliński Battalion had been killed or wounded, of whom eight died during the final assault on the telephone exchange.

I joined the crowd who were watching the German prisoners being marched off to captivity in some school buildings. There were no catcalls, no fist waving. People just looked curious. So this is what defeated German soldiers looked like? The various leather straps to which their equipment was attached had been removed. Disarmed, helmetless, unbuttoned and unbelted they almost looked like civilians. They no longer had their hands up, and they walked normally. I noticed some of them felt relaxed enough to smile at the younger women in their audience, who sometimes smiled back.

Shortly before their capitulation, intercepted radio messages revealed that they were becoming quite desperate and were running out of food, water and ammunition. There had been earlier attempts to use armoured vehicles to resupply them. When these couldn't get through our barricades, attempts were made to drop ammunition on to the roof of the telephone exchange from a Fieseler Storch spotter plane. But the Luftwaffe's nimble little high-wing monoplane was too slow to risk many attempts. In any case, they could never have dropped enough to make a difference.

Towards the end of the siege, the morale of this small garrison had plummeted, and afterwards there were reports of at least one suicide. The German soldiers would probably have given up sooner, if they could have been certain that we would accept their surrender. But how could any German soldier be sure of this after the relentless diet of atrocities they had served us since 1939? As it was, we remained determined to demonstrate that we were better than they were. To prove it photographs of the surrender of the PAST garrison appeared in the *Biuletyn Informacyjny*, which somehow always got into the hands of the Germans. There they were for all to see, clearly acknowledged and recorded as prisoners of war. General Bór had not heeded the advice of the old lady whose open letter to him – urging that, as a deterrent against air raids, enemy prisoners be detained on flat rooftops – also appeared in the *Biuletyn*. Nor did they look like people who feared they might be about to be taken to some factory yard and shot in the back of the head.

The incredible volte-face that had seen the executioners in Wola and Ochota revisiting the condemned and reprieving some of those lucky enough not to have received a fatal bullet was entirely due to the intervention of Obergruppenführer Erich von dem Bach. His motives, to say the least, were mixed. In Russia he had presided over the liquidation of thousands of *Untermenschen*, both Gentiles and

Jews. Admittedly, in the process he had suffered what sounded like a nervous breakdown – though he soon recovered, and went back to work with a vengeance.

Possibly he felt that Poland was different from Russia – after all, it had produced a fervent Catholic Church, a Roman alphabet, his beloved Chopin and even part of his own surname (which he never used in Poland) – or possibly, as far as von dem Bach was concerned, we western Slavs could not quite be classed as *Untermenschen*. After the war he made much of what he called his 'historic deed for humanity', and it certainly helped to save his neck. Thanks to the Americans and the British his only appearance at the Nuremberg trials was as a witness. The Russians were longing to hang him, but the Allies saw to it that extradition requests from the USSR and Poland were turned down. However, he was eventually convicted of murdering a German citizen during the Nazis' pre-war rise to power, and died in prison.

Von dem Bach tried to give his American and Bristish interrogators the impression that he was at heart no more than a professional soldier who liked a tidy battlefield. 'A military force which loots and massacres ceases to fight,' was one of the pearls of wisdom he offered them. Shortly after he assumed command in Warsaw he is reported to have leapt out of his open-top staff car to halt the shooting of civilians who would already have been dead if their busy executioners were not having difficulty relighting a funeral pyre clogged with their previous butchery. It was after this that he gave the order that all mass killing of civilians must stop. *Banditen* like myself remained a different matter. We would soon be hearing of the three captured teenaged scouts from our own Grey Ranks who were forced to stack corpses in a burial pit until they were told to stop because there was only enough space left for themselves.

But while at this point he seemed content to execute captured Polish insurgents with the same regularity that he applied to the Russians, he had concluded that murdering their women and children was counterproductive. Some survivors were transported in a westerly direction to the Germans' new refugee camp at Pruszków. But others – often Jews who had been posing as Gentiles – evaded capture and reached our liberated areas, which were becoming smaller and easier to defend. Far from terrifying us into submission the tales these escapees carried only hardened our resolve to hold out until even Stalin could no longer ignore us.

Himmler would soon be telling Waffen-SS officer cadets that the street fighting in Warsaw was the worst since Stalingrad. From the beginning von dem Bach had realized that there were not going to be any short cuts. Afterwards, he was proud of the way he had turned down an offer from the Luftwaffe to withdraw his troops and let them bomb us into submission. At this stage of the war it was not really such a hard choice. The Luftwaffe was not what it was, and even the Allies – with their much stronger air power – had discovered that aerial bombardment could never win a land battle on its own. Monte Cassino had been a case in point: bombing alone had failed to budge the stubborn German paratroopers. It had required Anders' Polish infantry to do that.

Von dem Bach was far from happy with the state of some of his own infantry. He was especially dubious, as well he might have been, about the effectiveness of Bronislaw Kaminski's Russians. 'Every unit firing in different directions, and nobody knowing really where to shoot,' he reported. Numerous complaints about their extra-curricular activities, the most repulsive being the rape and murder at the cancer hospital, came from Wehrmacht support units, parti-cularly the artillerymen manning the Sturmgeschütz (StuG) self-propelled guns – basically a 75 mm cannon mounted on a tank chassis and entirely enclosed with armoured plate.

Aware that the quality of some of his troops left much to be desired, von dem Bach was pleased to acquire an experienced former Wehrmacht divisional commander. In May 1940, Generalmajor Günther Rohr had distinguished himself by taking a key French position in the Ardennes. But since then, his career prospects had been blighted by acute attacks of rheumatoid arthritis. Nonetheless, between long periods of sick leave, he had taken what jobs were on offer and had built up a reputation for making the best of unpromis-ing material. Rohr had been stationed most recently in Lwów, where I had my own childhood memories of being besieged. Fortunately for him, he was sent to what the Nazis preferred to call '*Festung Lem-berg*' too late to be blamed for losing it but in time to get out before the Soviets completed their encirclement.

A month later, he found himself in southern Warsaw in command of something rather grandly called Attack Group Rohr. Various Wehrmacht units, including a small amount of infantry, were about to reinforce it. But apart from the StuG gunners and the rear-echelon troops responsible for transport, logistics and communications the bulk of his command was composed almost entirely of Kaminski's men. This time, Rohr was unable to weave his usual magic; the rene-gade Russians were as incompetent as ever.

An attempt to use them to guard and administer a new civilian transit camp and processing centre for Pruszków, which had been established on the site of the walled Zieleniak vegetable market, was treated as yet another invitation for robbery, rape and murder. No effort was made to provide even basic sanitation or drinking water. This enraged von dem Bach and Rohr, because the camp was sup-posed to be a magnet that would attract civilians away from Polish Home Army territory. When Rohr visited Zieleniak, some dis-traught young Polish women approached the general and begged his protection only to have their molesters try to pull them away. Kamin-ski's men were eventually dispersed by a burst of overhead fire from Rohr's Wehrmacht escort. As far as Rohr was concerned, this was the last straw. He persuaded von dem Bach that there was no place for Kaminski and his brigade in Attack Group Rohr, and some alterna-tive employment should be found for him.

But Kaminski had fallen too far out of favour to be given a second chance. Looting was a capital offence and the Belorussian warlord had become too much of an embarrassment for Himmler to continue to turn a blind eye to it. Towards the end of the month, it was announced that SS-Brigadeführer Bronislaw Kaminski had been killed in an ambush by Polish terrorists en route to a command con-ference at Łódź. Despite their numerous media outlets at home and abroad his alleged assassins failed to trumpet this singular success. But when Colonel Frolov and his senior officers were taken to inspect their fallen leader's bullet-riddled car, they appeared to believe the

official version. In truth, they had very little choice. Not long afterwards, von dem Bach sent them to the sparsely populated Kampinos
Forest, on the northern outskirts of the city, where he was trying to
build up a cordon that would prevent arms and men reaching central
Warsaw.

But this was certainly not von dem Bach's priority. For the Germans the most important objective was to prise us away from the
positions we held along the west bank of the Vistula, which would
provide the Red Army with an unopposed crossing. The most
important of these, running north to south, were the crucial riparian
districts of Żoliborz, the Old Town, Powiśle and Czerniaków – at
least three kilometres of riverbank. A little to the west of them was
the city centre, where I would spend the first five weeks of the Uprising. We also controlled part of Mokotów, to the south, though not
the part where my mother lived.

Von dem Bach decided to start with the Old Town, with its sweeping views of the Vistula and its bridges. Attack Group Reinefarth,
with Dirlewanger's brigade in the lead, were already at its gates. But
they were finding it a very different proposition from Wola, and were
beginning to take heavy casualties. They were badly outnumbered.
About 7,000 Polish combatants, of whom the majority were from
the highly motivated Radowan Group, were defending some
100,000 civilians (half of them refugees from the western suburbs).
Reinefarth had less than half this number, and his troops were
expected to fight their way through well-constructed barricades.
These were usually built about a third of the way down a street so
that during their approach the Germans were funnelled into a killing
zone where they could be shot at from three sides. If territory was
lost, we usually won it back and sometimes even captured a few of
the enemy's wonderful MG-42 quick-firing light machine guns
and other treasures. Typical of Bór's terse reports to the Polish
government-in-exile in London at this time was one which ended: 'In
the evening we redressed the situation by a series of counter-attacks.
Heavy losses in personnel and destruction.'

Reinefarth's armoured support was beefed up in order to overcome the barricades. In addition to the StuG self-propelled guns,

they were equipped with Hetzers, loaned to them by Nikolaus von
Vormann's 9th Army, who were struggling to keep the Russians east
of the river. These were the Wehrmacht's latest tank destroyers
which, like the StuG, were another turret-less tank with a high-
velocity cannon. Fortunately for us, the Hetzers mainly carried
armour-piercing shells which usually went straight through barricades without exploding – so unless they scored a direct hit on a man,
they were relatively harmless. In any case, both these clumsy tracked
vehicles were made more vulnerable than ever at close quarters when,
on the night of 12 August, the RAF made two arms drops on the Old
Town. Inside some of the weapon containers were PIATs, the British infantry's equivalent of the bazooka. PIAT stood for 'Projector
Infantry Anti-Tank', and with each one of them we got six hollow-
charge armour-piercing rounds. There were never enough of them,
but together with our Molotov cocktails and home-made Filipinka
grenades they could make life very uncomfortable for the crews of
the Hetzers and StuGs.

As it happened, this direct delivery of the anti-tank weapons to
the Old Town garrison coincided with their first serious setback. In
the early evening, there was another attempt to breach the important
Podwale Street barricade. This time three StuGs had shelled the
insurgents without much effect and the infantry behind them had
failed to press home their attack. Then the Germans brought up what
looked like a small open-top tank, rather like a tractor, with a large
square engine housing. Its only visible crew was its driver. When he
started to come under machine-gun fire, the driver jerked to a halt
well short of the barricade and ran off.

The unit responsible fell upon their trophy with glee. After some
experimentation, they discovered the vehicle had two gears: forward
and reverse. A gap was briefly opened in their barricade and, accompanied by a growing crowd – for this tractor hardly went above
walking pace – they proceeded towards Bór's headquarters.

Bór had been out and was returning on foot with his aides when
he became aware of the commotion ahead and hurried to see what
was going on. A minute or so later, at almost exactly 7 p.m., the
1,000 pounds of high explosive contained in what looked like the

engine housing went off. About 120 Home Army soldiers were killed and the civilian fatalities were estimated to be half as much again. It was hard to tell. Many of them were torn to shreds. Bór and his aides were unscathed, though the blast had blown them off their feet and some were concussed.

The machine that had caused this mayhem was a Borgward demolition vehicle. The Germans also had something we would see a lot more of: the Goliath, which looked like an attempt to make a scale model of a First World War tank. It was much too small to be manned and was guided by remote control at the end of 600 metres of cable. After the operator had steered it as close as he could to his target, he pressed a button and a charge less than a quarter of the Borgward's blew the vehicle to pieces along with most things in the immediate vicinity. Put in the right place it could do a lot of damage.

The Borgward, as Bór had found out, could be even more effective. But it was much harder to operate, because it was intended to be recoverable. Once the driver had got as close to his objective as he dared, he was supposed to run back to where its radio-control operator was edging it a little closer, releasing its charge and then waiting until he had reversed the Borgward a safe distance away before detonating it. He then returned to the vehicle and drove it away.

At Podwale Street it was unlikely that the Germans intended to turn the Borgward into such a devastating Trojan Horse. The summit of their ambition was almost certainly to blow a big enough hole in the barricade to send a tank through it. Most likely the radio controls failed. After that, the explosive either went off because it was unstable or because an irate operator, having witnessed his Borgward's capture, persisted in sending the detonation signal.

Apart from this fluke, which very nearly killed Bór, Reinefarth was having little success. Time and again, even when reinforced with light anti-aircraft guns and flame-throwers, his attacks were being contained. And in the process the PIAT launchers were taking a steady toll of his armour. His response was to lay on as much indiscriminate bombardment as could be managed in these stretched times for the Reich. The Old Town's ancient timbers were extremely combustible, and incendiaries dropped from Stukas started fires in the market square. But behind their old stone walls civilian morale usually remained high, and they were not calling on Bór to surrender. On the contrary, they told each other that it would not be long now before the Russians crossed the Vistula.

All they had to do was hang on for another couple of days.

By the second half of August the city centre was also beginning to come under what artillerymen like to call 'harassing fire'. After the attention the Old Town was getting, we almost welcomed it. There were two types. The Nebelwerfer was a multiple rocket launcher. Once in flight, the missiles, which were either high explosive or incendiary, made a distinctive groaning sound. American and British troops sometimes called them 'moaning minnies'. We nicknamed them 'moo cows'. These rockets were quite small, but they were very good at starting fires on upper storeys.

At the other end of the scale were the two-ton bombs being lobbed at us by Karl-Gerät siege mortars. These had been designed with France's Maginot Line bunkers in mind but were first used in 1941 against the Soviet fortresses of Sevastopol and Brest-Litovsk. They were self-propelled on a huge tracked chassis, almost twelve metres in length; they needed several modified tanks to carry their ammunition, and an accompanying crane to lift and load it. The mortar itself required a crew of twenty. In the entire Wehrmacht there were only six of these guns and each had a name. There was Adam and Eva and the other four, like a Wagnerian opera, all celebrated the old Norse gods: Ziu, Thor, Odin and Loki.

The first one to arrive in Warsaw was Ziu. It was set up in one of the parks on the western side of the city, and was ready to fire by 19 August. Eventually, there would be three guns in place but most of the time the Germans made do with two. They were ponderous things to prepare and load and needed a lot of maintenance. They usually fired no more than three rounds a day, which was quite enough. A single bomb could collapse an entire building and leave us searching the rubble for hours at a time, listening for survivors trapped beneath the ruins.

What most of us didn't realize was that it could have been much worse. The Germans were using ammunition intended to penetrate thick reinforced-concrete bunkers before exploding inside the target. In a city of brick-built apartment blocks the bombs often crashed without exploding, falling through one floor after another before ending up in a basement. Home Army sappers would then arrange for us to return the best part of it to the enemy by extracting the explosive and donating it to one of our arms factories. One was enough for over 3,000 grenades.

Obviously we could not always expect to be that lucky, and the number of civilian fatalities in the city centre was going up. Sometimes I helped remove bodies from buildings, and not always with as much dignity as I would have liked. I remember the sickening thwack of a head dropping from step to step as I pulled an elderly man downstairs by his legs. We buried our dead in courtyards, gardens and, as we became short of space, beneath the pavements. Before the Uprising the only dead person I'd ever seen close up was my father, and I was surprised how quickly I got used to this sort of thing. It was, of course, essential work. We had to find the bodies before the rats did.

As the artillery strikes and air raids increased, a warren of subterranean walkways began to develop. It started with residents in neighbouring buildings punching through cellars so that they would not have to walk the increasingly dangerous streets above. But what began as holes in basement walls became signposted routes with whitewashed street names and arrows indicating directions.

There was, however, a downside to this. Some people, especially parents with small children, were beginning to live a stubborn troglodyte existence, refusing to leave their basements and the passageways that connected them. People began calling it 'cellar disease'. Attempts to persuade them up to ground level to do something useful – such as scavenging interesting bits of scrap metal for our grenade shrapnel – usually came to nothing. These were people who had had a long war, starting with the 1939 siege of the capital, continuing through the uncertainties of the occupation and reaching a nadir in the Wola massacre, and now they'd had enough. They simply yearned for some semblance of a normal life. When the Uprising started, they had not been alone in thinking that it promised a swift victory and a return to peace. But this was clearly not the case. And unlike the Old Town, with its back to the river and the Russians not far beyond, deliverance seemed a lot less tangible.

Occasionally, we would hear, 'You started the fighting. You stop it.'

We shrugged it off. We felt sorry for them, but we knew we were going to win. Whenever we weren't working we drilled and sang patriotic songs. Where there were fires to be quelled, we often found ourselves part of the bucket chain. But towards the end of August the buckets contained sand more often than water; the main water pumping station had remained in German hands and important conduits were no longer working, sometimes because they were choked with corpses. Warsaw had faced the same problem in the 1939 siege. The wells they had dug then were reopened, sometimes with German prisoners of war doing the digging. In addition, the Home Army issued an edict instructing all janitors to try to divine old wells in the backyards of apartment houses built on land where there had been human habitation for centuries. Even so, there was never really enough water to go round. The number of baths and showers one would have normally taken during hot summer weather were certainly a thing of the past. But neither was there any recorded instance of anyone dying of thirst.

The Home Army slipped into the role of civil governance when it had to and, for our own security, we also policed the city against infiltrators. Everybody, civilians and military, required passes for travelling from one area to another, and a dusk to dawn curfew was enforced. Internal barricades were manned around the clock.

Anyone who moved after the evening curfew was challenged with the traditional cry of, 'Halt, who goes there?'

The password and answer changed daily and usually started with the same letters: *demokrata – doktor*; *Wilno – Wolność*.

From time to time we were sent to bolster squads manning external barricades. This was a much more exciting proposition. Although there was usually a small amount of no-man's-land between us, the enemy did sometimes venture near enough for us to trade insults.

This frequently happened with those Ukrainians serving with the SS, because our languages were so similar.

'Come any closer and you can suck my rifle,' one of us would shout.

'Let me in, I think I left my shoes under your mother's bed,' would come the reply.

We would crouch there, gripping our weapons, hoping they would push their luck. But they rarely did. We were aware that in the Ukraine itself a nationalist militia, sometimes fighting alongside the Nazis and sometimes against them, had exploited wartime chaos in western Galicia to murder thousands of unarmed Polish-speaking peasants and drive the survivors off their land.

And yet, I had fond memories of the miniature battles with our toy soldiers that I had played with my Ukrainian friend, Zenek, in my uncle's garden in Lwów – where my opposing general had called the city 'Lviv', and a real war was being fought above our eleven-year-old heads. So I found it hard to hate Ukrainians. I think I found it hard to hate anybody really, even the Germans. I certainly hadn't hated the prisoners I watched being marched away from the PAST telephone exchange. But I did want to get involved in something that was a bit more exciting than what was generally on offer in the city centre.

Towards the end of August, I got my chance.

## 24. Into the Sewers

Volunteers were needed for a special mission and I was one of five boys selected for it. We all had certain things in common: we were not too tall, rather skinny and determined to get involved in something more exciting than our civil defence duties. Our task was to carry a single delivery of important dispatches to the besieged Old Town. We were to get there through the sewers.

The construction of Warsaw's sewer network started in the middle of the nineteenth century. By 1939, it consisted of two types of sewers: storm sewers, which carried the overflow after heavy rains or spring thaws, and small oval-shaped sewers reaching almost every corner of the city. The storm sewers were relatively lofty affairs, eight feet high in places, so that even a tall man had no need to bend. To assist maintenance workers some were equipped with wooden pathways, and because we had not had much rain that summer they were fairly dry. The Old Town was connected to the city centre by one of the main storm sewers, but the staff at Bór's headquarters, which was still operating from there, were reluctant to sanction its regular use. Unbeknown to us a withdrawal from the Old Town was under active consideration, and they didn't want to draw attention to what might become their main escape route. So we had to use one of the egg-shaped sewers, which were often as low as three feet high and never more than five. These were the ones that carried the shit.

It was a glorious summer morning and our guide was a stocky girl of about nineteen. She wore old rubber boots and a dappled German camouflage jacket that reached down to the middle of her thighs. Her hair was pinned up beneath a filthy beret. Our deliveries, wrapped in waterproof cloth, were waiting for us. She showed us how we must carry them: this would not be rucksack-style on our backs but strapped firmly over our chests and stomachs. Each of us was then issued a short, sturdy stick.

Before we set out there was a final briefing. Our particular sewer, she explained, was about a metre high and sixty centimetres wide (just under two feet). Sometimes it passed under German positions.

'Occasionally they watch through manholes and drop grenades inside,' she said. 'So a peep out of any of you could get us all killed.'

We had to wait for the end of a mercifully brief delivery of German mortar fire on Świętokrzyska Street and Napoleon Square. Exchanges of fire were becoming more common on the city centre's northern front as we tried to relieve the pressure on the Old Town. Once this had subsided, we sprinted across to a small open manhole and one by one descended its iron ladder until we could no longer feel or see the bright August sunshine. For a moment the contrast, with its stench, total silence and sense of utter isolation, was overwhelming. The girl produced a torch and counted us, then used its beam to point out a small black hole. It was the entrance to the sewer.

She led us towards it then handed her torch to one of the boys, telling him to point it at her. Now we saw what the short sticks were for. She entered the tunnel and, holding her stick in front of her, leaned on it until it stopped at the lower part of the egg-shaped sewer, thus supporting her. She extricated it, moved forward with her back touching the top of the sewer, and continued. Her movements resembled those of a rabbit.

We followed her in the same manner and eventually each of us developed a certain rhythm. We advanced slowly in the slime and after a while the smell did not seem to be so overwhelming. We crossed several intersections where the sewage moved swiftly and light penetrated through open manholes. At one of these places we noticed, lying face down, a dark-clad corpse. We paid no attention and continued to move along the sewer, heading north. Our hands, our shoes and the backs of our jackets were soon covered with faecal slime. Periodically, we rested.

It seemed to go on for ever. But it turned out to be no more than three hours, and probably less, before I heard our guide announce, 'Old Town!'

And there it was, a light at the end of the tunnel, growing bigger as we bunny-hopped towards it. We climbed to the surface by another

iron ladder. When we got to the top, the light blinded us at first and
it was a few seconds before we were able to take in the narrow street
lined with gutted buildings, piles of bricks and crushed masonry.
Pieces of broken furniture were scattered around graves marked by
crude wooden crosses. The air was heavy with dust, and somewhere
nearby salvoes of artillery were exploding with industrial regularity.

Near the manhole a bored-looking man in a Wehrmacht greatcoat,
with a Home Army armband, sat on a dining chair. A sub-machine
gun lay across his lap. 'What's new in Centre?' he asked.

'There's been more and more artillery fire,' one of us told him.

'More and more, eh?' he said with a grin. 'Poor Centre.'

Nowhere had been as badly shelled as the Old Town, and its
defenders didn't like you to forget it. The quietest district of all,
almost throughout the Uprising, was the northern suburb of
Żoliborz.

'In Żoliborz,' we used to say, 'they play volleyball.'

This was a bit unfair because they had their bad moments too, notably when they were asked to assist in relieving the pressure on the
Old Town by joining a pincer attack from the north and the south.
The main contribution of the Żoliborz contingent was to be a night
attack on the enemy-controlled central railway station, for which
they lacked both arms and training and, as a result, suffered heavy
casualties. We could be solid in defence but we rarely succeeded in
pulling off any set-piece, large-scale attacks. Frankly, I doubt whether
our senior officers were up to it. Brave and honourable men though
many of them were, all they had known was defeat and five years on
the run with the prospect of being tortured and executed if betrayed.
It was hardly the best preparation for open battle.

We spent the best part of a day in the Old Town at the headquarters of the unit, where we delivered our dispatches. While new
packages were prepared for us to take on the return journey, we
rested in a long barracks-like building listening to mortar-bomb
shrapnel rattling on its corrugated-iron roof. Men were sitting on the
floor playing cards and eating chocolate, of which there seemed to be
an inexhaustible supply. From time to time we heard the unmistakable high-pitched whine that Stuka dive-bombers make once they

have gone into their vertical dive. Hardly anyone paid any attention to them.

Our return to the city centre was set for the late afternoon. We walked through the same debris-littered streets, past half-ruined houses with empty window sockets, past graves with makeshift plaques bearing the pseudonyms adopted by the fallen when they joined our Conspiracy. I thought I noticed another Zych, but didn't take a closer look. It seemed unlucky. Certainly I was aware of a couple of living ones – I couldn't expect to acquire exclusive nom-de-guerre rights to one of Poland's most popular authors – but at least I was the only Zych in Platoon 101.

There was a group of people, both men and women, already waiting at the manhole. Home Army military policemen checked everybody's passes, presumably on the lookout for deserters. One of them was carrying what appeared to be a brand-new British Sten gun. We often wondered what law of military science decreed that fighting units should always be short of weapons and MPs always armed to the teeth.

In addition to our guide from the morning we were joined by two more young women in German camouflage smocks, one of them a stunning brunette. She entered the manhole first and we all followed her down. We walked slowly in what seemed like a long procession, stooping in the small sewer, most people managing without the helpful sticks. This sewer seemed to be going in an easterly direction towards the Vistula, rather than due south in the direction of the city centre. Even more alarmingly, it was somehow filling up with smoke from burning buildings. It was beginning to make our eyes sting.

The cortège was halted and the pretty brunette pushed us back, whispering, 'I made a mistake.'

We turned round. The sewer seemed endless but we recognized the place where, on our outward journey, we had seen the body lying face down and started heading in the right direction.

It was night when we emerged in the city centre. In the distance we could hear someone firing a machine gun in long bursts. We knew it must be German fire because we were under strict orders to conserve ammunition. We were particularly warned not to waste it on low-flying aircraft – though I imagine the man at the Central Post Office who succeeded in shooting down a Stuka was forgiven. It was our only recorded success against the Luftwaffe.

Even with this sporadic machine-gun fire, the city centre seemed like an oasis of peace compared to the Old Town.

'Look,' marvelled the brunette, pointing to a building. 'Look at their windows! They still have glass.'

She must soon have felt at home. As the bombardment of our district increased, intact glass did not remain a common sight much longer. The very next day Ziu, the giant mortar, managed to land one of its two-tonners on top of the Prudential Insurance Building – the concrete and glass tower from where, in 1936, Europe's first television broadcasts had been transmitted. Perhaps the Karl-Gerät specialists had changed the fusing because this one exploded on impact, though the skyscraper's innovative steel frame stopped it collapsing (a posthumous tribute to the genius of construction engineer Stefan Bryła who, nine months earlier, had been murdered by the Gestapo for teaching a clandestine polytechnic class).

But even with its skyline dominated by the sight of its vandalized tallest building, the city centre was not as damaged as the cramped Old Town, where the defenders had fought too well for their own good. By 29 August, most of von dem Bach's losses – 3,961 killed or wounded – had occurred at the edges of the ancient bastion's narrow lanes of half-timbered houses. He responded to these casualty figures by acquiring enough additional artillery support from Nikolaus von Vormann's 9th Army to turn this minuscule target, barely three-quarters of a square mile, into a little Verdun. Heavy mortars and howitzers plus a battery of six 150 mm field guns, as well as his existing tanks and assault guns, combined with the Luftwaffe's small but frequent contributions to wear down both buildings and morale.

Against all odds Colonel Wachnowski's poorly armed garrison held out for almost four weeks in the hope that the Russians would cross the Vistula and the British would send enough arms to keep the enemy at bay until they arrived. Instead, the Russians stayed away while, with growing frequency, the BBC's Polish language service played 'Choral', a heart-rending nineteenth-century piece about (what else?) failed rebellion and Poland's longing to be free. It was the signal not to expect a parachute drop the following night, and we heard it too often.

By the last days of August, the situation in the Old Town was becoming intolerable and morale was beginning to crack. Some of the civilians crammed into the cellars beneath its cobbled streets had now reached the point when all they wanted was for it to stop.

'This rising is a service to the Soviets,' was the message on one of several propaganda leaflets that regularly fluttered down to earth from the planes that had just bombed us. On the same paper were calls for a temporary truce. Civilians were invited to leave the Old Town and take advantage of German offers of good treatment at the refugee camp at Pruszków, which von dem Bach had now opened for inspection by the Swiss Red Cross. Refugees from Wola and Ochota no doubt found this hard to believe, but some were fast getting to the point where they might be persuaded that those atrocities were an aberration.

Even some of the fighters were asking themselves how much more they could take. The only full bellies belonged to the rats feeding off unburied corpses, and wounded comrades who should have recovered died because of thirst and infections. As I was making my own trip through the oval-shaped sewer to the Old Town, the decision to give it up had probably already been made. Bór and his headquarters staff, with its female secretaries clutching files and portable typewriters, had already left. They had reached the city centre by walking along the roomy storm sewer, which we had been forbidden to use.

This left Wachnowski, Commander of Group North, which included both the Old Town and Żoliborz, to work out how he was going to gradually disengage and extricate some 4,500 of his troops down almost two kilometres of sewers. There was also the problem of the wounded. Wachnowski (the pseudonym of Karol Ziemski, who had been wounded himself while commanding an infantry regiment in the 1939 campaign) was determined to take as many with him as he could. At this stage nobody had much doubt about what was likely to happen to those who were left behind. But Colonel

Monter – who, as supremo of all Home Army troops in Warsaw, was Wachnowski's immediate superior – had issued explicit instructions that the colonel's priority must be armed men fit for further combat. The unarmed and the wounded would have to take their chances with the civilians.

Wachnowski had other ideas. Since it would, in any case, be impossible to take scores of stretcher cases down into the sewers, he decided he would make a corridor between the Old Town and the city centre. Some 500 of his best troops were sent down the main storm sewer and made their way to the city centre. Their orders were to start the corridor with a surprise attack from that direction while he tried to link up with them from the Old Town. After some initial success it failed, with heavy losses among his exhausted and dispirited ranks, who mostly had little faith in the feasibility of the operation.

Wachnowski had already started sending some of the walking wounded and auxiliary units, such as medics and messengers, down the main sewer. He set 8 p.m. on 1 September as the starting time for evacuating his troops in platoon-sized groups of fifty. Some of them refused to leave their wounded comrades, which considerably slowed things up. A few of the stretchers were carried by German prisoners who were among a group of around 100 to be evacuated. About the same number were left behind to regain their freedom and, it was hoped, regale their compatriots with tales of good treatment at our hands.

Although a rearguard was essential, it was probably inevitable that, once word of the evacuation spread, not everybody would be prepared to wait their turn. One of these was a certain Major 'Pelka' (his code name). He ordered the surviving seven officers and thirty-eight men of his battalion to abandon their position, then led them to one of the sewer openings. On arrival he was almost immediately arrested by the Home Army's military police, who had been briefed to look out for this sort of thing. After a drumhead court martial, he was sentenced to death for desertion in the face of the enemy. But Wachnowski felt the verdict had been reached too quickly and, taking into account the unhappy major's honourable record, he reprieved him. He probably felt enough Poles were dying without killing each other, though there were a couple of executions for what was termed 'systematic looting'. We read the announcements in the *Biuletyn Informacyjny*.

By mid-morning on 2 September, Wachnowski had got about 4,500 people to the city centre. Some 1,500 were armed combatants. Most of the remainder were also Home Army but, as was often the case, were unarmed because they were sharing a weapon with somebody else. The rest were civilians, some of them refugees from Wola. Despite the best efforts of the military police, who had beaten them back and fired shots in the air to secure an unhindered passage for the Home Army, a lucky few had managed to join the evacuation.

Instead of going to the city centre, about 800 of Wachnowski's men escaped by using a sewer link that led in the opposite direction, to the northern suburb of Żoliborz. Among them were members of the Communist People's Army who had clashed with the Home Army's military police when they abandoned two barricades they were supposed to hold.

Some 2,500 of our wounded were left behind with about 35,000 civilians, of whom 5,000 were also injured and mostly bedridden. For all its last-minute chaos Wachnowski's withdrawal seems to have been smartly done. Several hours after the last of his troops had departed, the Germans were still unaware that the Old Town was no longer defended. Yet more salvoes were fired into its stricken stonework, where the stoutest walls had been built with no more than cannonballs in mind. German infantry, watching out for snipers, cautiously followed this barrage over the rubble. Only when civilians approached, waving white sheets and assuring them that not only were they '*nicht Partisan*' but that all the partisans had gone, was a message sent to the gunners to cease firing.

Von dem Bach kept his word as far as the civilians were concerned. They were sent with their bundles to the transit camp at Pruszków where some, usually young adults, were selected for forced labour in German factories. An unlucky few went to concentration camps because vigilant Gestapo interrogators had determined they were either fugitive Jews or members of the Home Army, sometimes both. But the majority, particularly children and the elderly, were sent to

the Polish countryside. The living conditions were cramped –
sometimes a couple of single mothers and their children lived
together in one room – but after surviving the Old Town fighting
most of them thought they were in paradise.

Eight-year-old Krystyna Johnson (née Dobraczyńska), whose
absent father would soon be in action at Arnhem with the Polish
Parachute Brigade, had fond memories of living with plenty of play-
mates in a large country house on a big estate with its own lake. Yet
her first night at Pruszków was one of terrifying uncertainty, spent
wearing her mother's rings on a string around her neck to trade for
food and shelter in case they were separated. Then next day, Krystyna
found herself part of a surprisingly haphazard selection procedure.
Shortly before her death from cancer in 2003 she wrote an account of
it which her British husband contributed to the BBC's 'People's War'
website.

> We were all lined up. The officer doing the sorting was a nice young
> German who was pleased to hear me say *'meine Mutter'* and put us
> together to be sent to the countryside. I tried it on, saying 'grand-
> mother' and 'grandfather' for the Jewish couple, and that worked,
> then 'aunt' for the next lady, without success. She was put in the line
> to be sent to a work camp.

But two Jewish lives had been saved. The couple in question had
rented a room in Krystyna's family's small flat in the Old Town – a
risk her mother took because, apart from anything else, she needed
the money. Krystyna had been left in no doubt that, if the Germans
ever discovered who the old couple were, they would all be killed.

This was exactly what happened to the wounded people whom
Wachnowski had been unable to evacuate. They were murdered in
the beds they occupied in overcrowded field hospitals, mostly by
Dirlewanger's men who had been lashed into one frontal assault after
another and taken heavy casualties. The killing happened despite the
pleas of Germans who were lying wounded alongside them and
shouted out that they had been well treated by the Poles.

Assault Engineer Mathias Schenk, who later deserted and was

sheltered to the end of the war by a Polish family, was with the troops
when they stormed what turned out to be a hospital.

> I was setting explosives under big doors. From inside we heard '*Nicht
> schiessen! Nicht schiessen!*' The doors opened and a nurse appeared with
> a tiny white flag. We went inside with fixed bayonets. It was a huge
> hall with beds and mattresses on the floor. Wounded were every-
> where. Besides Poles there were also wounded Germans. They begged
> the SS men not to kill the Poles. A Polish officer, a doctor and fifteen
> Polish Red Cross nurses surrendered the hospital to us. The Dirle-
> wangers were following us. I hid one of the nurses behind the doors
> and managed to lock them. I heard after the war that she had sur-
> vived. The SS men killed all the wounded. They were breaking their
> heads with rifle butts. The wounded Germans were screaming and
> crying in despair. After that the Dirlewangers ran after the nurses,
> ripping the clothes off them.

## 25.  Joining the Elite Zośka Battalion

Not everybody escaped the Old Town through the sewers. One of them was Captain Jerzy, nom de guerre of Ryszard Białous, whose Zośka Battalion liberated the Gęsiówka concentration camp with its captured tank.

Jerzy and sixty of his men had been part of the rearguard when they found themselves cut off and unable to reach any of the man-holes. He decided that their only chance was to escape through the nearby Saxon Garden. These forty acres of trees, rolling lawns and fountains, overlooked by the Brühl and Saxon Palaces, formed one of the oldest public parklands in the world. It was also one of the few places where the enemy's front-line encirclement of the Old Town was dug in on open ground.

It was well after dark, and Jerzy was hoping that the German hel-mets and camouflage smocks worn by most of his men would enable them to get well into the parkland before they were identified and the shooting started. After that, they would have to charge through and hope for the best. It would be every man for himself. With any luck, he thought a few of them might make it and, anyway, nobody seemed to have a better idea.

They had moved in a loose formation, trying to look like men returning to the fold who knew they were no longer in much danger. Those who could muttered the kind of German phrases that seemed appropriate and generally tried to act like some weary Wehrmacht company returning from action. They had ambled through the park unchallenged and got almost as far as the first Polish barricade on the other side when a German sentry behind them opened fire.

The Poles manning the barricade shot back.

Jerzy's men began shouting: 'Don't shoot. We're Poles. *Starówka* (Old Town).'

Gradually, the firing died down.

Against all odds and for the loss of only one man – and that almost certainly from friendly fire – Jerzy had got away with it.

I first laid eyes on Jerzy a few days after he got out of the Old Town. He had been badly hit in both legs during the siege of Warsaw, in 1939, and had been hospitalized for four months. Whenever he could, he liked to take the weight off his feet. He was lying on a couch, resting these old wounds, when I was paraded before him along with the nine other teenaged members of Acting Sergeant Mietek's squad. The remnants of the Zośka Battalion, which by now was probably not much more than 100 strong, was about to be redeployed to the riverside suburb of Czerniaków and was looking to build up its strength with suitable replacements. Mietek thought he had the perfect answer, and we all agreed that joining the famous battalion was an excellent idea.

But would they have us?

Our sergeant made his pitch, explaining to his recumbent audience that, apart from our other duties, we had all seen a little fighting and were anxious to do a whole lot more. As he spoke, Jerzy – just turned thirty and every inch the soldier – lay there looking us up and down. Standing by the couch, a couple of his officers were doing the same. We were dismally aware that our appearance was not very martial. Only Mietek had a camouflage smock. Several of us, including myself, were by now wearing some of the grey-green Wehrmacht trousers the Home Army had acquired – though, as yet, I had been unable to get the boots to go with them so was still wearing civilian shoes. Romek wore his usual student cap. The rest of us were mostly without headgear.

'Well, shall we take them?' said Jerzy, turning to his officers. 'What do you think? At least they're used to gunfire.'

We stood there holding our breath.

'They'll do,' said one of them.

'I think so,' said Jerzy.

So we were in and on our way to Czerniaków.

It was common sense for Bór to reinforce whatever parts of the Vistula's west bank we still held. Our only hope was that the Soviets would come to our rescue when their desire to possess these potential bridgeheads eventually outweighed their indifference, to put it mildly, to the fate of the nationalist Polish forces clinging on to them. Mietek and the rest of us were going to Czerniaków as a direct result of Bór's decision to send the river suburb what was left of the Radosław Group, of which Jerzy's veterans were a crucial part. With replacements like ourselves the entire group numbered about 500. It had originally been 3,000.

We assembled during the evening of 5 September in the garden of a once fashionable restaurant at Aleje Ujazdowskie 37, which is near the site of today's US Embassy. Its lawn was crowded with tables and chairs. Almost everybody was wearing a German camouflage smock, and I promised myself one at the first opportunity. Weapons were stacked, and from the restaurant's kitchen came a strong smell of cooking. I poked my head through the door and heard the men working around the stoves talking to each other in a very foreign-sounding language.

A blonde girl carrying a sub-machine gun noticed my curiosity. 'Dog goulash again,' she said. 'The cooks are some of the Hungarian Jews we rescued from the Gęsiówka camp.'

I hoped she was joking. It smelled delicious.

We were fed and then led to a pavilion where, in various shapes and sizes, a regiment of military footwear was on parade. I tried on a pair of German jackboots, decided they were a good enough fit and left my old shoes in their place. At dusk we began to form up in the garden. There was a certain amount of firing going on. Lazy lines of tracer floated overhead. A flare lit up the darkening sky. Reinefarth was trying to follow up his success in the Old Town with probing attacks on the city centre's northern front. Fighting was going on around the strongholds we had created in what had been the Colosseum and Studio Movie Houses and the nearby Cristal Café.

We waited as one by one the names of skeletal battalions now reduced to weak companies were called out: Broda, Czata, Parasol, Zośka. All these units had fought from the western suburbs of Wola and Ochota, then across the ruins of the ghetto and into the destruction of the Old Town before escaping through the sewers. Mietek reported his men to a Lieutenant Szczerba and a woman who was introduced to us as Pani Zofia. ('Pani' is the honorific title for addressing women, the equivalent of 'Madame'.) Both she and the lieutenant were wearing German camouflage and carrying Schmeisser sub-machine guns. None of us had yet been issued with arms, though Mietek might have carried a pistol. Romek had somehow acquired one of the enemy's handy little egg grenades (*Eierhandgranate*) which, unlike their better known stick grenades – so called because of their attached throwing handle – fitted neatly into a tunic pocket. Also with us was a silent, tall and lean officer in a beautifully tailored pre-war Polish captain's uniform, the empty left sleeve tucked into a pocket.

At the rear of our particular column were the Hungarian cooks with their pots and pans. Romek was trying to converse with them in Yiddish. It was only recently that we had discovered Romek was Jewish. One night, we happened for some reason to be discussing the Jewish failure to rise up sooner against their tormentors. I suppose we said the usual sort of things. How their rabbis had taught them to accept God's will and go passively to their deaths, etcetera.

Then Romek, who had been unusually quiet, said suddenly, 'I quite agree with you. That's why I'm here. I'm a Jew.'

It came as a bit of a shock. Since we always addressed each other by our pseudonyms, we did our best to avoid revealing our real names let alone our family backgrounds. I suppose we all assumed Romek was a Catholic, most likely born and brought up in Warsaw. It turned out that he had spent most of his life in Lwów. His mother and father, who were both practising doctors, had moved there from the capital when he was a small child. His parents, he said, were an assimilated couple. They were not very kosher. They hardly ever went to synagogue. They had brought him up to believe he was a Pole who happened to be a Jew, not the other way around. None of which had saved them from arrest and deportation to an unknown destination after the Nazis captured Lwów as they swept through Soviet-occupied eastern Poland on their way to invading Russia itself.

He was fourteen at the time and would certainly have gone with them, had it not been for a miraculous and largely unexplained stroke of luck. One of the Gestapo agents who was taking his parents away had drawn him aside and asked him if there wasn't somebody he knew outside Lwów who might take him in? He told him that his father happened to have some Catholic doctor friends in Warsaw and, from time to time, he had visited their apartment with them. To his amazement this Polish-speaking German, possibly a locally enlisted *Volksdeutsch*, pressed some money into his hand, told him to use it to buy a ticket on the next train bound for Warsaw and to ask his parents' friends to take him in. Without a moment's hesitation this was exactly what they did, though every Pole knew what the penalty was for hiding a Jew. It turned out that they were already part of the Conspiracy and had a daughter of about the same age who was in the Grey Ranks. This was how he came to join up and how, on the evening of 5 September 1944, he happened to be trying out his very rudimentary Yiddish on some amiable if baffled Hungarian Jews.

We crossed the tree-lined Aleje Ujazdowskie, running as firing around us intensified. There were the usual barricades, a half-burned church, an empty square that appeared eerie in the moonlight. Soon we were in a complex of apartment buildings, then in a park sloping down towards the river. Every so often Pani Zofia stopped us and did a head count. We were not going to Czerniaków through the sewers. Physically this route would be an easier passage, though it had its dangers. The tricky part took us into one of our cellar mazes and through holes that had been knocked through adjoining walls to avoid the hazardous streets above, overlooked by the enemy.

Once we were in the cellars, Pani Zofia stopped us again and whispered into the ear of the first man, telling him to pass it on: 'Total silence from now on. Germans on the upper floor.'

In case some bobbing chink of light gave us away, the prolific use of torches was discouraged. We held on to the back of each other's belts, a legion of the blind, in order not to get lost in the darkness.

And then, with hardly any warning, we found ourselves, like a scene from *The Wizard of Oz*, in a different world. It was a planet of silent streets lined with small apartment houses. There were gardens and the humid night was permeated by the scent of greenery. We were led into an empty apartment on an upper floor, where we found ourselves enough floor space to remove our new footwear, put our heads on our rucksacks and fall instantly asleep.

Next morning, we discovered we could wash. Here, instead of having to line up with a bucket at some uncertain well, water still came at the turn of a tap. Some of the empty homes we were occupying had full tanks of water. And there was more. Not all the civilians had run away from a place that, as the Red Army neared, fully expected to be in the front line, with or without an uprising. Incredulously, we stared through two windows with their glass panes still intact and watched the family next door have breakfast. Below us there were women walking along a sunlit street carrying shopping bags. From somewhere far away we heard a long and pointless-sounding burst of heavy machine-gun fire.

None of the people we were watching paid it the slightest attention. Clearly Czerniaków would prefer not to know there was a war on.

## 26.   The Czerniaków Bridgehead

Those early days in Czerniaków were a strange interlude. From the start it was apparent that this leafy suburb with its well-spaced houses, gardens, orchards, vegetable allotments and public parks was going to be much harder to defend than the apartment blocks of the city centre and the Old Town. For the first time we found ourselves digging shallow communication trenches so we could stay under cover while moving from one position to another. For a while my friend Wacek and I were excused these labours. Instead, we were sent on foraging expeditions to the various allotments from which we returned to our squad with enough potatoes, onions and tomatoes to make our absence less unpopular than it might otherwise have been. It was our first fresh fruit and vegetables for weeks.

More members of the Zośka Battalion arrived, among them a short, brown-haired girl who was wearing a camouflage smock but with a skirt and white knee-length socks rather than shorts or trousers. She was assigned to our squad as a medic. Lidia Markiewicz-Ziental, who liked to be known as 'Lidka', was younger than any of us and had seen much more. A doctor's daughter, she was still a good four months short of her fifteenth birthday. Her parents didn't know it yet but they had already lost their eldest son and daughter, listed as missing, who had both followed their father into medicine. They had been killed in the massacre at Wola's Karola i Marii Hospital. From the beginning Lidka had pestered Captain Jerzy to allow her to join the battalion. Eventually, on the third day of the Uprising, he relented – though the commander of the company she was assigned to, a Lieutenant Mirosław Cieplak, had accepted her under protest, telling Jerzy he should send her home to play with her dolls.

Cieplak, who used the pseudonym 'Giewont' (after the mountain of that name, not all that far from my father's house in Maków), had by all accounts quickly learned to value her. She had been with them throughout the fighting in the Old Town. By the time she reached us, all three of Zośka's company commanders had been killed. Giewont was the last to go, crushed beneath a pile of rubble with thirty or so others when his headquarters in the Old Town received a direct hit from some large-calibre projectile. Lidka should have been with him but, just before it happened, she had been obliged to rush to a prior emergency.

In common with all those surfacing like submariners through a city-centre manhole Lidka had appreciated the cleanliness of its streets, the intactness of its glass, the general lack of death and defecation. Nonetheless, as von dem Bach tightened his grip, its fringes were undeniably becoming frayed. Czerniaków was the new paradise. Lidka and the rest of us in Mietek's squad thought it was in a league of its own, a veritable holiday camp, and certainly the place for the weary survivors of the Old Town to catch up on their sleep.

What none of us knew, and doubtless this included Radosław himself as he settled into his new headquarters close to the river at Wilanowska Street 5, was how desperate our position was. Bór was close to surrender. On 3 September, two days before we even set out for Czerniaków, our supreme commander had told London that most of his forces were running out of ammunition, food, sleep and hope. Unless they were immediately rescued, they would have to capitulate. 'Our soldiers' endurance is reaching the bounds of human possibility,' he informed Stanisław Mikołajczyk, prime minister of the government-in-exile.

Only nine days earlier, on 25 August, the Home Army had congratulated Paris on the success of their uprising, which had lasted not quite six days before the insurgents were relieved by a couple of divisions detached from General Patton's 3rd US Army – one American and the other LeClerc's Free French 2nd Armoured. For us it was a bittersweet occasion. While the Free World was celebrating the liberation of Paris, and Hemingway was reporting the capture of the Ritz Bar, we were coming towards the end of our fourth week of a much bloodier struggle. The situation was getting worse by the day and nobody seemed to care less. Yet we had expected to be at the barricades no longer than the Parisians before we found ourselves throwing flowers at the conquering heroes of the Red Army, welcoming them as members and allies of the Polish armed forces who had risen up at their behest. It seemed incomprehensible that the Anglo-Americans could not somehow shame them into entering the city and driving the Germans out.

Our leaders did not always confine their anger to the Russians. A sceptical General Kazimierz Sosnkowski (who had succeeded Sikorski as Poland's commander-in-chief in London) informed the Home Army leadership that, 'The lack of help to Warsaw is being explained to us by experts citing technical reasons.' In a message to mark Poland's fifth anniversary of the German invasion, delivered on 1 September, he pointed out that, 'The loss of twenty-seven aircraft over Warsaw during the last month means nothing to the Allies, who have many thousands of planes of all types. We should remember that Polish airmen suffered 40 per cent losses in the Battle of Britain.'

Bór was already corresponding, in the fluent German most former Austro-Hungarian officers had acquired, with the Wehrmacht general Günther Rohr. Originally Rohr had been negotiating through Countess Maria Tarnowska, head of the Polish Red Cross, about arranging local ceasefires and crossing points, which could be used by those civilians desperate enough to take the Germans at their word when they guaranteed safe passage to the Pruszków transit camp and beyond. But Rohr hoped to build on this. It would be a tremendous feather in his cap if, despite all the SS brutality that had preceded it, he could persuade the head of this insurrection that further resistance was futile and for the sake of the civilians caught up in the fighting he should lay down his arms.

Bór insisted that there could be no surrender unless he received public assurances that his command would be regarded as regular soldiers entitled under the Geneva Convention to be treated as prisoners of war, just as uniformed Poles captured in 1939 had been. This was a big ask. Ever since the Franco-Prussian War of 1870, when the term *francs-tireurs* (free shooters) was first coined, the German army had always refused to accept any kind of irregulars as lawful belligerents, however openly they were armed. If captured, they faced the death penalty. During their occupation of parts of France in the First

World War they had again rigorously applied this rule. They had also shot hostages in reprisal for casualties allegedly inflicted by the *francs-tireurs* – though not on the same scale as the Nazis did, some thirty years later, in all their occupied territories.

In the summer of 1943, the London Poles were trying to persuade Churchill's government to secure the release of Stefan Grot-Rowecki, Bór's captured predecessor, by swapping him for one of three German generals captured by the British in North Africa. As a first step they had already confirmed his post-capture promotion to full general. Churchill was initially in favour but Foreign Secretary Anthony Eden turned him against the plan. Eden pointed out that while Grot-Rowecki was, indeed, a senior Polish officer he was technically a *franc-tireur* and, according to international law, had forfeited his right to be treated as a prisoner of war. The British Army were also against an exchange: German generals were hard to come by.

Grot-Rowecki spent over a year in Sachsenhausen concentration camp, north of Berlin. He continually turned down invitations from Himmler to participate in the creation of an autonomous Polish state that would join Germany in the fight against Bolshevism. A few days after the Uprising started in Warsaw, some fourteen months after his capture, Berlin announced that Grot-Rowecki had died but did not reveal the circumstances. One theory is that Himmler had him murdered for refusing to make a public broadcast calling for the Uprising to stop.

Eden seems to have been quite shocked by the death of the man he might have saved, and there was no more talk of Polish *francs-tireurs*. Instead, he threw himself behind Polish demands that the Home Army be recognized as part of the Polish Armed Forces under British command whose personnel were covered by the Geneva Convention. A statement Eden made to the House of Commons on the subject was translated and broadcast on the BBC's Polish service. We all read the full text in the *Biuletyn Informacyjny*.

In it Eden stressed that the Polish forces in Warsaw wore distinctive badges, or Polish uniforms, and carried out their operations according to the rules of war, which had included accepting the surrender of German soldiers and tending their wounded. Then he pointed out that Germany was also required to uphold these laws, and the massacre of prisoners would not be tolerated: 'His Majesty's Government warns all those who participate in such outrages, or are responsible for them, that they will be held responsible for such crimes.'

It would be good to report that, in the face of His Majesty's displeasure, our enemies immediately mended their ways. But perhaps they didn't listen to the BBC. On 6 September, exactly a week after Eden's warning, Generalleutnant Otto Heidkämper signed a German communiqué issued by Army Group Centre on the capture of Powiśle, the west bank area between the two road bridges just north of Czerniaków. Almost in passing it noted: '152 bandits were liquidated by two machine gunners from the Dirlewanger Brigade.' The main verb does not suggest they were killed in action, but the numbers do more or less match our own reports of a massacre in and around a field hospital that was ultimately set on fire. The survivors lay for almost twenty-four hours amidst charred corpses, driven so mad by thirst – the weather was unseasonably warm – that one died an agonizing death from drinking iodine. Even some of those who crept out to tell the tale the following morning had moistened their lips with peroxide solution.

Bór's threat to surrender had at first met a mixed reception in London. Some members of the Council of National Unity reluctantly agreed it was the only thing to do to end the suffering. Others begged him to try to hang on, because they were still hoping that the Anglo-Americans would somehow persuade the Red Army to intervene. This became the majority faction.

Late on Saturday, 9 September, they felt they were able to justify their stance when they messaged Bór: 'Today Marshal Stalin promised help for Warsaw.'

Nor was he kept waiting. On that Sunday, the forty-first day of the Uprising, for the first time in almost five weeks we heard once again the sound of Red Army artillery from the east bank. It heralded a large-scale attack on the German positions in Praga, where parachute flares lit up the night sky. The main infantry component of this force was the Red Army's 1st Polish Army Corps under General Zygmunt Berling (the man who had deserted Anders and decided to stay with Stalin rather than join the British in the Middle East). Soviet fighter aircraft also reappeared, surprising the two-man Stuka crews who, apart from our one lucky hit from the gunner in the Central Post Office, had flown with impunity over Warsaw for so long now. There were reports that five of them had been shot down.

From Czerniaków we got glimpses of all of this: the white contrails etched into the clear blue September sky; a dark spiral of oil smoke heading remorselessly to earth. Once, I thought I could make out a white parachute. That night we heard the sound of four-engined aircraft and learned next morning that the RAF's American-made B-24 Liberators, flying from one of their Italian bases, had parachuted weapons into the city centre. It was the first Allied delivery for thirteen days and was desperately needed because we were running out of everything, including 9 mm ammunition for our Stens.

There was, however, a new source of arms. The Soviets had also started sending us weapons, but not at the end of parachutes. Along with sacks of dry bread, porridge oats, canned meat and other Red Army rations they were dropped at hedge-hopping heights by single-engined Polikarpov Po-2 biplanes. Their pilots and almost anybody else who had anything to do with them, including ourselves, called these planes '*kukuruzniks*' – Russian for 'maize dusters'. Originally designed for spraying wheat fields, they had a very reduced stalling speed and their ability to fly slow and low had made them ideal for locating the forest clearings used as dropping zones by Russian partisans.

The biplanes delivered little but often. We sometimes saw them three or four times a day. In this way we received small quantities of rifles, grenades, mortars, a long-barrelled anti-tank rifle that was good for penetrating buildings, and the sub-machine guns Soviet soldiers called '*pe-pe-sha*' that had proved so effective during the street fighting at Stalingrad. Unfortunately, the weapons were often damaged on landing, when their flimsy wooden cases tended to burst open and scatter the contents. Some people seemed to think that the Soviets were making sure they delivered us damaged goods, but I don't think this was the case. They were flying too low when dropping them to use parachutes. The RAF parachuted its gifts at 500 feet and 140 mph, and their metal containers were rarely recovered damaged. But sometimes they were not recovered at all – or, at least, not by the Home Army. A minor navigational error or some capricious nocturnal breeze, or both, quite often caused them to land well within German lines. And as von dem Bach began to draw on more reinforcements from the 9th Army and our perimeter began to shrink, it became harder for both the British and the Russians to be sure they had got it right.

Nonetheless, the arrival of the *kukuruzniks*, the reappearance of more lethal Soviet hardware, the return of the RAF and the reports of the exploits of Poland's 1st Armoured Division in Normandy had all helped raise our spirits. We also had word of a small local victory. Some veteran partisans who had recently arrived in the Kampinos Forest from eastern Poland had partly avenged the victims of the Ochota atrocities when they fell upon a battalion of the late Kaminski's SS-RONA at their usual drunken revelry. Although badly outnumbered, the partisans had killed at least a hundred of the Russian renegades, at little cost to themselves, and scattered the rest.

A writer in the *Kurier Stołeczny*, one of our new newspapers, encapsulated the mood that we could and must hold out a little longer.

> Who will break down first: Berlin or Warsaw? Who will help us first: Moscow or London? How long will our nerves last and the walls of our remaining buildings stand? Sunday brought a respite. Daytime the Soviet air force, at night the British planes. From the graves scattered on Warsaw's streets come the voices of our friends: don't waste our sacrifice.

As Czerniaków awaited the impending storm, von dem Bach allowed the attacks on the northern part of the city centre to continue. RAF Flight Lieutenant John Ward, who had been shot down in 1940 and contacted the Polish resistance after escaping from a prisoner-of-war camp in western Poland, was sending English language reports over Radio Błyskawica.

On every conceivable little piece of open ground are graves of civilians and soldiers. Worst of all, however, is the smell of rotting bodies which pervades the whole centre of the city. Thousands of people are buried under ruins; it is at the moment impossible to evacuate them and give them a normal burial. Soldiers fighting to defend their battered barricades are an awful sight. Mostly they are dirty, hungry and ragged. There are very few who have not received some sort of wound. And on and on, through a city of ruins, suffering and dead. The morale of the soldiers is also going down in most cases.

When a Home Army company commander in the city centre pleaded for a rest for his exhausted men, he was told: 'Only those on stretchers are allowed to withdraw.'

In the end, it was von dem Bach who stopped it by pulling out most of the units involved in the city-centre fighting, in preparation for the assault on our positions. It was always his intention to leave the city centre until last. Nothing was more important than prising us out of the bridgehead that offered the Red Army the best chance of getting across the first of only two big river obstacles between them and Berlin.

For his attack on Czerniaków von dem Bach had managed to put at Rohr and Reinefarth's disposal seven combat infantry battalions, totalling about 4,000 men. One of these battalions belonged to the Dirlewanger Brigade. The infantry, who had plenty of small mortars, were supported by a total of about sixteen tanks and tracked 75 mm assault guns. In addition there was a unit of *Sturmpioniere* who were controlling some of the remote-controlled Goliath mines. His artillery support consisted of a regiment of sixteen self-propelled 155 mm guns, Nebelwerfer multiple rocket launchers and the huge Karl-Gerät siege mortars. He could also call on the Luftwaffe's Stukas – though, with the Soviet air force back in the air, they wanted to keep their time over the target to a minimum.

Facing them were about 1,600 of us, under Radosław, who had now been formally put in charge of the sector. The 500 or so combatants he had brought with him, of which I was very proud to be one, were supposed to be the hard core. Some, including their commander, were still visibly bandaged from the wounds they had received in the Old Town. Our heaviest weapons were a few Soviet 50 mm light infantry mortars dropped by the *Kukuruzniks* but we had very little ammunition for them. Rohr and Reinefarth had as much as they wanted.

Six days after we arrived, our bucolic settling-in period came to its expected violent end with a combined artillery and air bombardment. It fell all along the line we held with our backs to the river: north, west and south. Under the bombardment our enemy cautiously advanced, probing for our weak spots as we emerged from the wreckage and did our best to show them that they could take nothing for granted.

My first action in Czerniaków was at night. A Lieutenant Szczerba had gathered about thirty of us in a front-line position for some ill-defined purpose, possibly to provide a diversion for a weightier effort elsewhere. I had been issued with a Schmeisser and was longing to use it. Much to my disappointment whatever we were supposed to be doing was called off (at this stage, this sort of thing was happening all the time). Perhaps we were being a bit noisy because suddenly we came under automatic fire. We could hear some of the shots passing low over our heads. Then, no more than 100 metres away, I spotted the orange flashes that revealed the source of the fire, and shot back. I squeezed off a couple of short bursts, probably no more than six rounds, just the way I had been instructed to do in my training class-rooms, where all we had was an empty weapon to play with. I doubt whether I hit anybody, but the firing stopped. On our side I was the only one who had worked his weapon.

'Was that you Zych?' inquired Szczerba.

'I saw their muzzle flashes,' I said, expecting to be reprimanded for wasting ammunition. This, after all, was the Zośka Battalion. Even in the dark they probably waited until they saw the whites of their enemies' eyes. But nothing was said.

Later, I realized this had been a compliment. They liked people who fired back.

The Germans began stepping up the tempo of their artillery and air strikes. As soon as they finished in one place, they started in another. The awful bovine mooing that warned you Nebelwerfer rockets were heading your way became more frequent. We were accustomed to throwing ourselves on the ground. The Mariawitów Church was burning. So were several buildings in Okrąg Street, where our front-line positions were located. Couriers trying to get there from Radosław's command post in Wilanowska Street, which was just behind Okrąg, were constantly having to find new routes through the rubble. Reproachful civilians, the same people we had so incredulously watched only a few days before enjoying their breakfasts and out shopping, now huddled in stinking cellars wondering when they would be reduced to squatting on the communal bucket in the corner.

'When are the Russians coming?' they asked.

'Soon,' we said.

One of our makeshift hospitals was hit. The nurses managed to get about 120 wounded to the nearby gas works, a solid building, only to discover that it had changed hands. Worse still, it was garrisoned by men from a Dirlewanger unit who promptly began beating and raping the nurses. But for once help was at hand. Shturmovik fighter bombers looking for targets, probably opportunistically, began to machine-gun and bomb some nearby tanks, and the Dirlewanger detachment fled. Amazingly most of the nurses were still alive and, with the aid of some local civilians, were able to carry the wounded to a place well behind our lines.

Russian air activity was definitely on the increase, and we began to see less of the Luftwaffe. Apart from the ubiquitous fighter bombers, the best indication of Moscow's newfound resolve to keep us in business was the frequency of their *kukuruznik* deliveries. Sometimes they would make them at night, briefly glimpsed as they appeared over our rooftops before we heard the thud of their presents landing nearby. Once, a drop at dusk left a large brown canvas sack tantalizingly just beyond our position in Okrąg Street, where the Germans were about 100 metres away. We crouched there staring at it.

What could it be? Ammunition? Grenades? (Grenades wouldn't go off if they weren't fused, no matter how hard you dropped them.) Perhaps a couple of the sturdy *Pe-Pe-Sha* sub-machine guns wrapped in blankets? We were like children staring at the parcels beneath a Christmas tree.

The sack was no more than ten metres from us. In the end, I decided it was dark enough for me to go out and get it. I crawled for some of the way, then ran in a kind of half-stoop. When I got my hands on the sack, I realized it was damn heavy. I had to drag it. Surely the Germans would hear something now? See signs of movement? But no. Nothing. I'd got away with it.

'Bravo, Zych!' Somebody patted me on the back.

It was difficult to open, well stitched together, and we were too close to the enemy to risk a light unless we dragged it down to the cellar. The contents felt knobbly. Like coal. Eventually, we got it open and put our hands inside. It was bread: small pieces of hard black bread. Enough to feed a hundred very hungry men. For this three people had risked their lives: the crew of the *kukuruznik* and me. It was certainly as hard as coal. Somebody suggested that if we spotted any of the enemy not wearing their helmets we could always throw it at them.

Next day, Mietek wanted a private chat with me and a couple of other members of his squad, both of them older than myself. It turned out that he had some good news for us. We had all been pro-moted to lance corporal. He had just had it confirmed by Jerzy himself. It was, of course, intended as a morale-boosting exercise. And it worked well for Lance Corporal Borowiec, who was still ten days short of his sixteenth birthday.

Not far away from me, in his cellar headquarters in Wilanowska Street, about a two-minute stroll from the Vistula's west bank, Radosław had also received some good news. The Red Army was about to attempt to cross the river – or, at least, its Polish component was. Berling had ordered elements of his corps to cross the Vistula along its entire length facing Warsaw. While some divisions were to make diversionary attacks in the northern part of Warsaw, the task of relieving our battered sector was given to the 3rd Division's 9th Infantry Regiment.

A small advance party, including wireless operators to keep in touch with Berling, had arrived on 14 September. Radosław was now anxious to coordinate artillery support and supplies: less bread, more bullets. At the same time, our commander kept his options open.

What if all this was no more than a symbolic gesture on Stalin's part to show the Anglo-Americans he had tried but failed?

Radosław sent a patrol to check out an escape route down the sewer connection to Mokotów. When they returned with the news that it worked, he immediately sent his walking wounded along it so that it would reduce the jam if we had to get out in a hurry.

# 27. Goliath!

After a sleepless night in the fire-damaged building in Okrąg Street, a dawn mist shrouded the no-man's-land we were watching. There was hardly any shooting in our immediate vicinity – though there was something going on around the river behind us, from where we could hear the explosions of mortar bombs and the noise of heavy machine guns. Much closer to us, loud and repetitive, was the sound of somebody revving up a tank engine. It seemed to be coming from just behind the ruins that were the backcloth to the German front line. We tried not to worry about it.

The battle din from around the river subsided, and shortly afterwards we heard the shuffling of feet on the staircase and voices speaking in the soft, almost Russian accents of eastern Poland. The first wave of Berling's troops had set off well before daybreak. They came in a flotilla of flat-bottomed river craft that had been assembled at Praga's little east-bank port of Saska Kępa, where pre-war success stories in the arts and commerce had left a legacy of handsome villas with lawns sloping down to the river.

At first, the boats had managed to remain undetected by the Germans but this didn't last. The last elements of the assigned battalion had come ashore, lit up by parachute flares and taking casualties from the machine guns and mortars we had heard. Nonetheless, at 4.30 a.m. Major Franciszek Mierzwinski was able to report to his superior that he had got 300 men across the Vistula with fourteen heavy machine guns, sixteen anti-tank rifles, eight mortars, five anti-tank guns and enough rations for four days.

Some of the wounded from the landing were carried down to our cellar, where a field-aid station had been set up. Meanwhile, one of our officers led a heavy-machine-gun crew to a first-floor firing point. They took up position behind a sandbagged window that I was manning with some of the squad. Their weapon was the Red

Army's famous belt-fed Maxim mounted on a small pair of wheels. Eager to avenge the casualties they had incurred, and to show what they could do, they immediately placed a handy table against the window sill and set the Maxim up on it. One of their number went outside and returned with some house bricks that he placed behind the wheels, to stop the gun sliding about.

A soldier who looked to be no more than a year or so older than myself asked me to indicate the enemy's position. At this stage, this wasn't all that easy to identify. The tank we could hear being revved up sounded close by, but we had no idea exactly where it was. We knew for certain that there had been some Germans in a house on a slight rise about 400 metres away, perhaps closer. It was a difficult rifle shot but easily within range of their Maxim. I pointed the house out to him. He crouched behind the gun and started to fire long and, in that confined space, enormously noisy bursts. Whatever his other merits as a machine-gunner, conserving ammunition was not one of them.

But it seemed to have the desired effect. Frantic figures were seen fleeing the vicinity, and we assumed that others were no longer so mobile. The gunner grinned at his handiwork and fired at the runners. Our sandbags began to take some incoming fire. The gunner gave whatever was out there another long burst. I noticed he had these frothy red bubbles on his lips. For a moment I wondered what he was eating. Then he collapsed on to his back and was dragged away. Either a sniper had worked out which window he was in, or it was just a lucky shot. I noticed nobody was in a hurry to take over his weapon.

His friends were tearing his clothes off and trying to apply a field dressing of some kind, though I doubt there was much point. In the end, they carried him as gently as they could down the stairs to the cellar. When they had gone we saw an army paybook of some kind and a letter in an envelope. Both were splattered with blood. They must have fallen out of his pockets when his comrades were trying to get at the wound. The paybook showed he was seventeen, born in 1927. The letter was written in the Cyrillic alphabet used by the eastern Polish minorities living among the Ukrainians, who had long known fluctuating fortunes and shifting frontiers.

Berling's men looked and acted differently from our idea of a Polish soldier. True, the cut of the long khaki coats they wore was the familiar pre-war pattern, and some men had four-cornered Polish field caps. But most wore big Soviet helmets with white Polish eagles stencilled on them. A closer look revealed that the eagle had been stripped of its crown. Even more disconcerting, they addressed us as 'brothers' or 'citizens' and referred to their 'political education officer', whom we assumed to be their Commissar.

Their commanding officer was a Major Latyshonok – a Russian on attachment from the Red Army, as were a couple of his junior officers. Despite the similarities in our languages his men could not always understand what he was saying. All of this made it hard for us to feel comfortable with them. And while their weapons sometimes included quite advanced-looking semi-automatic rifles and carbines, other pieces of their equipment and clothing were a bit primitive. Instead of socks they wore rectangular flannel foot wraps. Instead of rucksacks they carried their things in the kind of hessian bag you might use for newly dug potatoes. In the main, they were freshly conscripted peasant boys from the eastern plains and marshes who had never been in a city before. Now they found themselves thrust into a dangerous ruin.

Later that day, Soviet artillery from across the Vistula started bombarding German positions. It lasted less than an hour but it was said to have disrupted a counter-attack on this precarious landing we were protecting. Some of Berling's wounded soldiers who had been hit making the crossing were being sent back the way they had come. We helped get them out of the cellar and down to the boats. I noticed that one of them still had his rifle, the bolt-action Mosin-Nagant that was the Red Army's standard issue.

'You taking this with you?' I asked, my hand already around it.

'Take it,' he said with evident relief. 'I won't be needing it any more.'

He hadn't fired a shot, and he gave me all the ammunition he had brought over for it. Some of the other wounded men, seeing what he was doing, followed suit.

Napoleon could not have been happier. I had never possessed my own personal weapon. All the shots I had fired in anger had been with sub-machine guns, and they always had to be handed over to somebody else when I came off duty. I had received some theoretical training in the use of the kind of bolt-action rifle used by most European armies. But underground organizations tend to be short on target practice, and I had never had the chance to fire one.

My opportunities to rectify this would shortly be limitless.

I suppose men must have fought over river crossings since the first tribes disputed each other's territory. The Vistula is 1,047 kilometres (651 miles) in length. It rises at Barania Góra at the western end of the Carpathian Mountains, near the Czech border, and empties itself into the Baltic at Gdańsk. By the beginning of August, the Red Army had already established two bridgeheads across it. But these were about 130 kilometres south-east of Warsaw, at the small towns of Dęblin and Puławy. The prize was a crossing in the capital itself, which was almost on the same latitude as Berlin and not more than a day's drive (574 kilometres) away. Now, for the first time, the Red Army had a toehold west of the Warsaw stretch of the Vistula, and it seemed obvious that the city's suffering must be coming to an end. All we had to do was hold on, wait for Russian reinforcements, and victory would be ours.

The fight for the Czerniaków bridgehead would become one of the bloodiest battles of the Uprising. Most of the Zośka veterans considered it at least as bad as the Old Town. Lidka, our fourteen-year-old medic, thought the battalion had its 'blackest days' there. The Germans mostly preferred to fight in the daytime, but we could never assume that this was always going to be the case. They knew this, and had enough men for a night shift. We were kept awake by regular bursts of machine-gun fire, interspersed by the odd mortar bomb, and swaying parachute flares that stripped us of the cover of darkness.

Deprived of sleep, we fought in a daze and acted almost like robots. During the day we automatically rushed to whatever position was indicated to us, took cover and fired. Sometimes we saw the enemy and sometimes we just fired in his direction. We had enough ammunition

after the arrival of the Berling Poles to squander some of it on targets
such as truckloads of Germans 500 metres away, without achieving
any visible result. On other occasions we were either immediately
above or below the enemy, engaged in house-to-house fighting, and
things got really close.

'*Banditen, Hände hoch!*' they would cry, then try to shoot with their
Schmeissers through the floorboards of the upper rooms we usually
occupied.

But none of us would have dreamed of putting our hands up.
Quite apart from our unwillingness to surrender in the first place, we
knew very well that once taken prisoner *Banditen* could rarely expect
the military courtesies of *Soldaten*.

Once, a few of us were in a cellar under the command of one of
the Jewish Ghetto fighters Zośka had rescued from the Gęsiówka
camp. He was a tough-looking man named Neumann – or that's
what he called himself (just as, in another world, Mateczka had once
decided that I would be a von Neumann to get us into the German
zone). The idea was to ambush any Germans who managed to enter
the ground floor via the cellar. When Neumann gave me the nod, I
rested my rifle against a wall and gave them a grenade to share. At
least, that was the idea. It was a loud enough bang, but I didn't hear
any screams of pain. The people upstairs said the Germans had
dropped a white smoke bomb and retreated under the cover of it
with their wounded. I remember I was very careful to make sure my
grenade landed on the top of the cellar steps. One thing we were
always taught about grenades was not to throw them uphill or
upstairs – not unless we really had to.

At night we really did keep our eyes open by propping up the eyelids with matchsticks. Whenever they could, the girls – the couriers
and the nurses – brought us the food they had prepared. If we were
lucky, it was pickled herring or sugared orange peel discovered in
nearby grocery stores. Less welcome was an indigestible horsemeat
served with pasta. Hungry though I was at times, I can recall at least
one occasion when I just couldn't face it.

Men fell around us, and we had become virtually oblivious to it.
Once, I found a soft place to sleep in a crowded cellar and woke

a couple of hours later to be told I had been sleeping on a body. Corpses were everywhere and, at last, I acquired a camouflage smock from one. I don't know whether it was from a German or a Polish body, but I knew it was fairly fresh because when I turned it over to undo various buttons – there were no zips – it didn't smell. I also got hold of a German helmet I found lying around. It had a small hole in one side and people would look at it incredulously, marvelling that the present wearer was still alive. I tried to persuade Romek to get hold of one, but he still insisted on wearing his soft student's cap.

Our junior officers were expected to lead from the front, and they did. Their casualties were high. Often, we had hardly got to know them before they were gone. Companies and platoons that were under strength were constantly being amalgamated. I never understood how we held on to some buildings. I could only assume that those in charge of us knew why the defence of one place was more important than another and felt able to justify such casualties. We were starved of news. The few copies of the *Biuletyn Informacyjny* the couriers brought in from the city centre did not get much further than Radosław's headquarters. It would be days before we learned that our brave Polish paratroopers would definitely not be coming our way: they were reinforcing the British parachute drop at Arnhem.

Our world was reduced to the ruined buildings we were told to defend, a bite to eat and snatching enough sleep – though it was never quite enough, and the waking was almost invariably brutal.

'On your feet. Your turn!'

Only, this time, it was, 'You there!'

I was lying in a packed cellar where a good deal of the floor space was occupied by sleepers, like myself, and the wounded. Among the latter was a silent boy of about my own age who had refused to go to one of the makeshift hospitals. He was lying on some sacking, staring at the ceiling. Sometimes people brought him sugared orange peel and chocolate. I think they were waiting for him to die.

Reluctantly, I forced my eyes open and, in the light of the carbide lamps, found I was looking at the shoulders of somebody squatting close beside me. The shoulders carried epaulettes and on them were the two stars of a lieutenant.

'C'mon, wake up,' he said. 'You're being assigned to an observation post. Follow me.'

'But I've just come off duty!'

'You won't have to do much. Just glance at the terrain from time to time. If you see any movement, let me know. Just shout "Lieutenant Kos".'

The officer led me to another cellar room with a narrow window near the ceiling. To get to the window I had to step on a sandbag. The window sill was large, and I settled down on it in a comfortable position. I couldn't see much from the window, except for some old ruins and a large vacant lot. There was a much better view from the upper floors. But were there still people up there? Perhaps they were taking too much fire.

It was early evening and the shadows were lengthening. Soon it would be dark. I had been up since dawn and had difficulty staying awake. Several times, I briefly nodded off, only to wake with a start, confirm with relief that nothing had changed, then fall back to sleep. The last time this happened, I snapped out of my doze to discover that the view from my basement window had undergone a distinct and worrying change. In the middle of the vacant lot something was undeniably moving. It was about the size and height of a large coffee table with no visible sign of wheels or propulsion, yet palpably mobile. And there was something else. I rubbed my eyes and looked again. About 400 yards away, the unmistakable outline of a tank turret had become clearly visible behind a broken wall.

In normal circumstances that would have been bad enough. But even more alarming was the fact that this sinister object was zigzagging relentlessly towards Okrąg Street in a beetle-like series of furtive spurts and pauses. As it got closer, its miniature caterpillar tracks became plainly visible. It looked just like the photographs I had seen in the magazines my father kept in the loft at Maków of British soldiers on the Somme standing around their country's formidable contribution to the evolution of twentieth-century land warfare: a working model of a 1916 tank.

I had never seen a Goliath before, but I had heard all about them. Packed with sixty kilograms of high explosive, they were attached to a mother tank by 600 metres of cable in three strands. The operator guided it with a joystick. Two of the strands were for stopping, start-ing and steering and the third for detonating the explosive. Once the operator had manoeuvred it as close as he could to his target – usually a building – he simply pressed a button, and that was it. No more Goliath. And usually not much left of the target. One way to stop the tank was to somehow get behind it and cut its control wire. Some people had done this. Some people had even lived to talk about it. Otherwise, the best thing we had to defend ourselves against them at Czerniaków was the long-barrelled Soviet anti-tank rifles the *kuku-ruzniks* had dropped and the Berling soldiers had also brought with them. Designed in the 1930s, they were no longer much good against full-size 1944 tanks, but they were ideal for exploding these lightly armoured miniatures at a safe distance.

My Goliath was now moving fast and heading straight for us. I tumbled down from my window sill, just about remembered to grab my rifle, and rushed into the crowded cellar corridor shouting, 'Gol-iath! Goliath! Lieutenant Kos! Goliath! Lieutenant Kos!'

But Lieutenant Kos was nowhere to be seen, and my cries brought mixed reactions. Most people moved away from me. Some began talking among themselves, almost as if I wasn't there at all.

'Where is it?'

'Who saw it?'

'This young idiot says he saw it.'

In the light of the cellar's carbide lamps I saw bottles of vodka and men with Home Army armbands embracing the Berling soldiers in their long khaki overcoats. Some people looked drunk. They were celebrating the arrival of another small contingent from the east bank. Their presence was seen as added proof that the Red Army was not – or, at least, no longer – delaying its advance in order to give the Nazis time to butcher a pesky bunch of Polish nationalists. Not with the whole world watching. And that was, indeed, something to cele-brate.

Now I was spoiling the party with my bad news. Tired as I was, I was sure I hadn't been imagining it. And I expected it to go off at any moment.

'What Goliath? Who saw it?'

This time the speaker was wearing a doctor's white coat. His hands were covered with blood. He looked tired and nervous.

'I did.'

'I suggest you shut up. No one reported anything from upstairs. You are causing concern among my wounded. You are creating panic. Get lost.'

By now they were shouting at me from all directions. Drunk or sober, the atmosphere was clearly hostile.

Could I have been so shamefully wrong?

As ordered, I kept my mouth shut. But I kept moving along, as far away as possible from the wall towards which, if I had seen what I thought I had seen, something very nasty was heading.

When it came, the blast was enormous. It ripped through the cellar. I felt the heat of it on my face. The carbide lamps hanging from nails on the wall flickered and died. Great dust clouds billowed from the ceiling, and I started coughing. Around me men and women were also coughing. Some shouted and moaned. But I felt a strange sense of relief: I hadn't been imagining things, after all, and those who had ridiculed me were fools.

Then, over the din, I started to hear bursts of machine-gun fire and explosions from above. I had to get out, and pushed my way towards the staircase leading to the ground floor. Two others from my platoon, also coughing, were doing the same thing. They were white with dust, and I realized this is what I must look like.

'Everybody out! They're attacking!'

This was a tried and tested tactic that the enemy had been employing since the fighting in the Old Town: exploit the Goliath explosion to get in among us and finish us off. I rushed to the ground floor, fled across the debris-covered courtyard and saw my good friend Wacek, whom I had first met in a Latin class. He was letting off short bursts with his sub-machine gun, firing slightly stooped and in a professional manner, never more than four or five rounds at a time.

'Upstairs, for God's sake, fast!'

Stumbling over several corpses on the staircase, I reached the second floor – or what was left of it. The Goliath had collapsed the middle section of the building and half of it had tumbled down. Smoke was still trailing over the street below. From the other side of the street, enemy soldiers were running towards our building firing their weapons from the hip.

There were grenade explosions and more machine-gun bursts.

'*Banditen, Hände hoch!*' came the usual cry from below.

'Fuck your mother!' I heard behind me. In German as well, which was impressive. (Sometimes we shouted: 'Hitler is a dog fucker.' We thought this was pretty good too.)

I turned my head and saw a man from our group, a butcher in peacetime, firing a big Russian heavy machine gun – a present from the *kukuruzniks* – while one of the boys from our squad held the ammunition belt and fed it into the breech.

'For God's sake, fire!' someone shouted at me.

I lay down on a pile of rubble, took careful aim at one of the approaching figures and squeezed off a shot. To my amazement the figure fell over. It was rare to be that successful with a first shot.

'I got one!' I shouted.

'Shut up and keep shooting,' said somebody, probably the butcher. 'You're not at a fucking funfair.'

I struggled to work the bolt of the dusty rifle, eventually succeeded in ejecting the empty casing, and fired again. Once I had finished the five-bullet clip, I reloaded and used the next one up. By this time I had run out of targets. I believe several of my shots were as effective as the first one.

Apparently, all the upper floors were in our hands. From below us came the sound of competing bursts of automatic fire – Stens and Schmeissers – and confused situation reports. First, someone shouted up that some of the Germans were still holding out in a corner of the building. Then, we heard that they had been thrown out of part of the cellar. Finally, the shooting subsided and an officer came up to tell us that all the remaining Germans had withdrawn. We were ordered downstairs to help clear the rubble, because there were wounded combatants stuck in the cellar.

Mietek and Lidka were already there. She had a rough bandage around one of her hands and later admitted to a cut across her abdomen that had to be treated, but she was desperate to try to reach the people in the cellar. We all were. We could hear some groaning, and there were occasional shouts for help or pleas for water. I thought of the silent boy, sucking at his orange peel and staring at the ceiling. Frantically we pulled at the rubble with our bare hands, but every time we excavated a hole more rubble closed it. It was useless.

Mietek and I were called outside. The German tank that had been parked near our barricade had started up, but it was merely moving away to an accompanying shower of petrol bombs and grenades that did it no visible harm. We appeared to have run out of ammunition for the British PIAT hand-held tank destroyers. But where were the five anti-tank guns and sixteen anti-tank rifles Major Mierzwinski had brought over? Why hadn't some of them been rushed to our sector? We decided that Berling's soldiers were not very impressive. We were better motivated, better led and had much more initiative.

As dusk fell a German flare went up and illuminated the vacant lot in which I had first spotted the Goliath. Violent bursts of automatic fire followed, then silence.

I was a week short of my sixteenth birthday. Never for one moment did it occur to me that I was in any danger of missing it.

After all the horrors of the Goliath attack, we were treated to a heart-warming sight the next day. On 18 September, shortly before 2 p.m., dozens of silver planes began to appear in the clear blue skies above us. The Americans were lending a hand. We could not count them with any accuracy, but we later learned that we had been looking at 107 B-17 Flying Fortress long-range bombers accompanied by a fighter escort of Mustangs and Lightnings.

Since early June, the Soviets had permitted the Americans to station ground crews at three air bases that had recently been recaptured in the Ukraine. The idea was to enable them to refuel and rearm bombers based in Britain or Italy so that, on their way home, they could attack previously inaccessible targets in Hungary and Romania. It had not gone well. Inadequate Russian airfield defences enabled the Luftwaffe to destroy 47 B-17s on the ground. Then relations were further soured when Stalin refused to allow any aircraft that was dropping supplies to us to refuel at his bases. The cargo on the RAF flights from Italy was much reduced by having to carry a round trip's weight in fuel.

Stalin had now relented. As part of this apparent volte face – which had produced the *kukuruzniks* as well as Berling's soldiers on the Czerniaków bridgehead – he was allowing the Americans to drop us weapons and to refuel. It was an incredible spectacle. Suddenly the sky was full of coloured parachutes. We weren't exactly sure what they were but one overwrought officer was in no doubt.

'Open fire to support the paratroopers!' he ordered.

We promptly delivered a magnificent fusillade against the nearest known German positions, probably a terrible waste of precious ammunition. We soon realized that the parachutes were not supplying men but containers. We could also see that, since they had been dropped from a great height and had been caught by an unfavourable prevailing wind, most of them were being delivered to the enemy. Only about a quarter of them – to be precise, 288 out of 1,284 – fell into our hands.

Nonetheless, we felt much better. We told each other there would be a lot more where that came from – and, no doubt, next time they would get it right. As it happened, this was the last we would see of the Americans, and there would be only one more British night drop.

On the day the Flying Fortresses came over, Bór declared in an Order of the Day: 'We will survive until the entry into our capital of the victorious Red Army. You must overcome your fatigue with fighting.'

But we were tired, desperately tired. And, to put it mildly, the Red Army was still taking its time.

## 28.   Wounded and Captured

It was clearly a Russian voice, a rather hoarse and exasperated Russian voice. I moved quietly towards the door of one of the basement rooms at Wilanowska Street 5, where I realized I had just discovered where Radosław had housed the two Red Army artillery spotters.

'Elektron, Elektron, give me supporting fire to the coordinates indicated previously,' the man was saying. '*Elektron, Elektron*, why don't you answer? Please come in *Elektron.*'

The cigarette smoke was industrial. Suddenly, one of them sensed I was there, turned in his seat and angrily waved me away. But it was too late. I had heard enough to confirm the gossip. The Red Army was losing interest in us again.

After the Goliath explosion at Okrąg Street, the remaining members of our squad had been posted to the security platoon at Radosław's headquarters. This was Mietek, Romek, Wacek and myself – four out of the original ten of us who had auditioned before Captain Jerzy for the honour of belonging to his Zośka Battalion. The others were either dead or wounded. Lidka was facing fresh horrors in another cellar hospital where we would visit her from time to time. She was trying to deal with a new type of burn wound caused by the phosphorous bombs the Stukas had started dropping, and they were short of everything: painkillers, ointments, medicines, bandages, food and water. She wrote in her own short account of these times:

> I was in despair, despite Zych's efforts to console me. I have no idea how I survived those days. Our chaplain, Father Pawel, was with us, praying and trying to comfort us. All around us were the corpses of our colleagues and of Berling's soldiers . . . and one by one boys from my squad were falling.

The next to go was Romek. Not, as we all expected it might

happen, because he refused to wear a helmet but because of a stupid accident.

The bridgehead measured about 1,000 metres wide by 500 metres deep. We had hardly anything in the way of field telephones or radios. One of the duties of the security platoon was to provide runners between forward positions and Radosław's headquarters. Romek had been sent to an advanced Berling unit, a sort of listening post, who were dug in around what might in happier times have been some kind of hut or lean-to for machinery. The sergeant in charge got chatting to him about the Home Army, there was a reciprocal curiosity, and the sergeant asked if he could see Romek's army identity card.

Romek kept it in the same large breast pocket where he normally stored the German egg grenade he generally carried with him. Probably because he was in a front-line position, he seems to have already unscrewed the dome cap on top of the grenade for easy access to the coiled pull-cord that primes it. Somehow, while feeling for his card in the same pocket, the cord got caught on something. As he lifted the grenade out of the way, it became taut enough to click and activate the four-second fuse.

Romek immediately realized what he had done and rushed out of the hut, screaming, 'Grenade! Grenade!'

Unfortunately, before he could dispose of it, he ran out of time. It was a terrible waste of all the good luck that had saved him from a concentration camp.

I heard how it had happened from the Berling sergeant himself because, in the late afternoon, I was the one sent to replace Romek. I showed him my own Home Army identity card, to satisfy his curiosity, but not before I had revealed that I kept it with the little cigarette-card portrait of St Andrzej Bobola that the priest had given me on the first day of the Uprising. I was beginning to rate St Bobola's powers of protection and never travelled without him.

'Good Catholic?' he said when he spotted it.

'Good Communist?' I replied. I wasn't going to take any shit from a Berling sergeant.

'Good as I have to be.' He grinned and looked at my identity card.

'Zych?' he said. 'Is that your real name?'

'No, it's Borowiec.'

'Is it now?' he said, raising his eyebrows. 'I knew a Colonel Borowiec before the war, when I was stationed down at Chelm.'

'You were in the 7th Infantry Regiment, then?'

'I was.'

'My father commanded it.'

'He had a young wife.'

'My mother.'

'We all thought he was a very lucky man.'

'Yes.'

'And how is your father now?'

'He died.'

'I'm sorry to hear that.'

Shortly after this chat, we started to come under fire. The sudden nerve-shattering crack of small mortar bombs was followed by machine-gun bursts. Berling's conscripts scuttled about looking very sorry for themselves. I decided this was no place to be if it developed into a serious attack. I didn't trust them. They might scatter, turning it into every man for himself, or even take it into their heads to surrender. Red Army prisoners might be worked hard and badly fed, but they were not generally shot out of hand like *Banditen*.

'I think I'd better get back to headquarters and tell them about this,' I said, picking up my Mosin-Nagant.

'I suppose you better had,' agreed the sergeant. Perhaps he thought he had enough on his plate without looking after Colonel Borowiec's son. 'Tell them to send us some tanks.'

I ran back amidst a lot of small-arms fire. A couple of times, what sounded like single shots from a sniper cracked above my head. As I approached Wilanowska Street, I saw that Mietek and some of the others were already manning the barricade before the main entrance.

'C'mon!' yelled Mietek. 'They're thirty metres away. I'll give you cover.'

That lent me wings.

I don't know what happened to the sergeant and his men at the makeshift listening post, but the enemy were quickly surrounding us. Towards dusk, I spotted a crawling line of German helmets coming through a hole in a garden wall. They were heading towards our ground-floor entrance. For a moment I thought they might be Poles who were coming in from a patrol and were unwilling to stand upright in an area where an enemy sharpshooter might be watching – after all, enough of us were wearing our enemy's distinctive headgear, including myself. Then I decided this particular line was suspicious. In a Polish line there would always be the odd soft cap à la Romek, or perhaps one of the old French helmets in which most of our army went to war in 1939. I dropped a grenade on them and thought I heard a faint scream.

Beyond my immediate target I could make out some other figures running across a patch of open ground, perhaps 150 metres away. I rushed upstairs to the second floor, where I thought I'd find a better view. It was getting dark inside the building by now and along the corridor on the next level it was difficult to see where you were putting your feet. I trod on somebody, who let out an agonized screech of pain. I knew exactly what I had done: I'd trodden on a wounded man. I apologized profusely but he didn't say anything. I ran on and took up a position at the window. From here, even in the fading light, I could easily make out a row of figures trying to scramble back under cover. I fired two clips of five and saw at least two of them stumble and fall.

I was told to go back downstairs because we were expecting another attack, and more people were needed at ground level. On my way down, I paused to apologize again to the wounded man. For the first time I saw there were two of them, lying alongside each other in this corridor. One of them looked to be in a bad way and didn't say anything, but the other one was staring at me in a rather quizzical manner, as if he couldn't really understand what I was saying. He was quite young, probably only a few years older than myself. Then the penny dropped, and I spoke to him in German. He and his companion were wounded prisoners who had been captured earlier in the day. He told me it was all Hitler's fault and we should be fighting the Russians together. While we were speaking, a short man wearing a French helmet came up and gave both Germans some water. I wished them luck and went downstairs to prepare for whatever was coming next.

I noticed somebody had left a Sten lying around. Abandoned Stens were an increasingly common sight because we were running out of ammunition for them. I checked it out and, sure enough, its magazine was empty. But I decided to keep it, anyway. A sub-machine gun would be handier for house-to-house fighting, and somewhere or other I might find some 9 mm ammunition for it (the Wehrmacht's Schmeissers used the same calibre).

As usual, I wasn't getting enough sleep. I certainly wasn't enjoying the ten hours a night to which most adolescents feel entitled. Once the adrenaline rush of a firefight wore off, all I usually wanted to do was curl up in a ball somewhere. When I wasn't tired, I was hungry – rations, like ammunition, were something else we were short of.

The day before, I had heard Radosław bellowing down a telephone, 'How am I going to feed my two hundred men?'

I propped myself up at the top of the cellar steps, above the rooms where Radosław had established his headquarters and where the Russian artillery liaison had their radio. After a while, with my rifle slung over my right shoulder and the newfound Sten across my lap, I began to doze off. Suddenly I was conscious of people hovering over me. It was Lieutenant-Colonel Radosław himself, accompanied by one of the Russian officers.

'Look at this man,' he was saying. 'He's armed to the teeth. And instead of fighting, he's sleeping.'

I slunk away. I think he was joking, but tired teenagers are rarely famous for their sense of humour.

Later that night, Radosław announced we were pulling out of Czerniaków. We were going to withdraw down a sewer to Mokotów, the suburb to the west of us where my mother's flat was located – though it was now well beyond what had become German lines. This did not come as a surprise. During the last forty-eight hours, one could not help but become aware of the growing despondency around Radosław's headquarters. It was quite obvious that things were going from bad to worse. Artillery support and air cover were

becoming increasingly hard to acquire. Sometimes, as I had overheard, gun batteries and ground controllers simply refused to reply,
though radio operators could listen to plenty of other traffic and
were convinced their sets were in working order.

A few more boatloads of Berling's troops had arrived at the shrinking bridgehead that morning, but these troops were hardly enough
to make a difference. And although the Soviets had covered a long
stretch of the river with a thick smokescreen, no significant reinforcements were seen weaving their way through it. The only
beneficiaries were some of our wounded and a few civilians who
managed to go the other way and reach the sanctuary of Praga, on
the east bank. The truth of the matter appears to have been that Stalin was only interested in placating his Allies and making useless
gestures, such as allowing the Americans to make an air drop in the
Uprising's seventh week. Berling's landing at Czerniaków was possibly considered a gesture too far. He would shortly be dismissed
from his command and sent to the War Academy in Moscow to
relearn his trade – a humiliating but mild punishment, considering
Stalin's homicidal pre-war purges of his less fortunate generals. Even
Marshal Konstantin Rokossovsky had had nine of his teeth knocked
out and his big toes hammered flat by NKVD interrogators. But at
the time, Stalin needed Berling for his vision of a compliant post-war
Poland.

Among those left behind in Czerniaków was Captain Jerzy who,
together with some of his closest associates from the Zośka Battalion,
remained with Major Latyshonok and his troops. They seem to have
developed a camaraderie, for Latyshonok – who would later be taken
prisoner – admitted to the Zośka commander that his task was simply
to demonstrate 'fraternal help' for the Poles. Moving only at night
and accompanied by a woman courier (who refused to leave his side),
two Home Army insurgents and a Berling sergeant, Jerzy managed
to fight his way back to the city centre's YMCA building, which was
still in insurgent hands.

My own departure from the river bridgehead was somewhat less
heroic, following an initial false start. I was at the head of a group

that arrived at the sewer manhole only to be turned back by Radosław himself, who was standing in the muck with his rolled-up trousers revealing a bandaged leg.

He shouted up, 'Next convoy at 01.00 hours!'

We retreated to a house near the river that was packed with people, many of them wounded, while outside the incoming artillery fire was becoming more intense.

After an hour, someone shouted, 'Out to the sewer!'

But as soon as we had formed a line, shells started exploding along the riverbank. The line rapidly turned into something much more disorderly with a crowd of pushing, cursing people making their way to the manhole. I don't know how I managed it. But somehow, still clutching my rifle and sack full of ammunition and grenades, I managed to lower myself down the steep steel ladder that took me away from the shells.

It was a storm sewer, so I could walk in it comfortably without bending. Parts of the sewer were even lit by electric lights, presumably powered by a generator. At the places where the main sewer connected with the smaller ones there were the usual efficient young women, rather like air stewardesses, warning us that the water level at the next section was higher because the Germans were trying to drown us by damming various channels with sandbags. It turned out that the water was never too high and rarely reached my thighs. I had more trouble with 'Blondyn' – the pseudonym of the man ahead of me – who accused me of treading on his heels and threatened to hit me with the sack of machine-gun ammunition he was carrying. I think it might have been Blondyn's first time in a sewer. Only on the last stretch was there any real difficulty, when we had to go through a small oval-shaped passage where a woman got stuck and had to be pushed until she could free herself. I missed the stick I had been given to help me during my first sewer trip to the Old Town, and my rifle and ammunition sack didn't help matters.

After about four hours, we surfaced into a bright and cheerful early morning full of sunlight and birdsong. Eastwards, towards the rising sun, was a line of trees and small houses. Beyond them a machine gun chattered and there were some mortar bomb explo-

27. *Top*: On 28 August 1944 German gunners eventually managed to explode a two-tonne bomb from a siege mortar on top of the 18-storey Prudential Tower. 28. *Bottom*: We could respond only with much smaller quantities of high explosive. Here, a stick grenade is about to be lobbed over a buttress during an Old Town skirmish. I acquired one at Mokotów but was wounded before I had the chance to throw it. I hope somebody else had the pleasure.

29. *Top left*: Exposing as little of his body as possible, one of our snipers uses his detached scope to search for targets from a large casement window. 30. *Top right*: A remote-controlled Goliath demolition vehicle being prepared for action. One of them wrecked the house we were defending at Czerniaków. 31. *Bottom*: After an engagement we always tried to collect the bodies of both sides for burial.

32. *Above*: By mid-September the territory we controlled was shrinking on a daily basis. A German machine-gun section, equipped with two of their tripod-mounted MG-42s, take over a captured barricade partly composed of street traders' carts.

33. *Left*: Often the only escape was through the sewers, which were relatively safe though usually disagreeable, and not for the claustrophobic. Here an exhausted man is helped out of a narrow manhole into the fresh air. I know the feeling only too well.

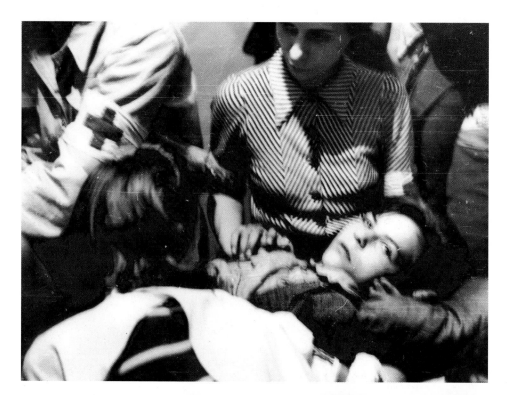

34. *Above*: His head cradled
in a woman's arms, a young
boy is about to have his
wounds dressed. Boys a lot
younger than myself were
sometimes used as
messengers, and few places
were entirely free from
hostile fire. In my prison
camp there was a badly
injured thirteen-year-old we
called 'The General'.

35. *Right*: Capitulation.
Women help a surrendering
fighter step out of the ruins
on his way to an uncertain
fate.

36. *Top*: Hungry, homeless, exhausted: for this elderly couple lying in the rubble and thousands like them, Stalin's treacherous refusal to support the insurrection turned it into a disaster. Thousands died. 37–8. *Bottom*: Makeshift graveyards rapidly filled and coffins soon ran out. Crouched in a communal grave, a woman can only wrap a sheet around a loved one's body.

39. *Top*: On 2 October 1944 it all ended with a handshake between SS–Obergruppenführer Erich von dem Bach and Bór, who now revealed himself as General Count Tadeusz Bór-Komorowski. In the official photograph Bach stands head and shoulders above our short commander, who had stalled until the last minute in the hope that the Soviets might yet cross the Vistula. 40. *Bottom*: Bór extracted a promise that we would all be treated as prisoners of war and the Germans kept their word, though some of these surrendering female auxiliaries must have had their doubts. As it turned out, they were much safer in Germany than they were in Poland, where our Russian 'liberators' raped thousands of women.

41. *Above*: Home Army prisoners boarding the freight cars that would take them to stalags in Germany. Most of the wounded, including myself, went in ambulance trains. I fully expected to be shot out of hand, but from the moment I was captured I was treated decently.

42. *Below*: However, inspired by the punishment Rome visited on Carthage, Hitler did his best to see that those buildings not wrecked in the fighting were destroyed anyway, and Warsaw was levelled.

43. *Above left*: The beautiful Lidka, her face quite unscarred from the wounds she received in Mokotów when she was trying to bandage me, aged about seventeen in a studio portrait she sent me in England.

44. *Above right*: The picture I sent back shows me in British battledress with the Home Army's *kotwica* emblem, given to all those who had fought in the Warsaw Uprising, sewn on my left pocket. The single bar on my epaulettes shows I'm a lance corporal, the promotion I received during the fighting at Czerniaków.

45. *Left*: And here I am a year or so later, sailing into the sunset aboard the RMS *Mauretania* bound for America, the Columbia School of Journalism and the beginnings of my new life as an English language journalist.

sions. I sat down on a log and emptied the muck from my boots. Watching over us was a smiling insurgent dressed in grey Luftwaffe overalls and armed with a pistol. Girls with clean hair distributed mugs full of warm liquid. It could have been tea or coffee. It didn't matter. It was warm.

And I just wanted to look at the sky.

Mokotów turned out to be quiet, as von dem Bach concentrated his resources on securing victory in the river suburb of Czerniaków. It was not until 23 September that the German 9th Army reported that the fighting in Czerniaków had ended, and added 'the insurgents fought until the last bullet'. Perhaps this was meant to explain why so few prisoners were taken – though it would transpire that some Home Army personnel, perhaps because they were able to pass themselves off as Berling's soldiers, had been taken prisoner. Otherwise, as far as Dirlewanger was concerned, it was business as usual. Polish civilians who were rounded up to collect the dead reported that thirty of our men, easily identified because they were still wearing their Home Army armbands, were discovered hanging in a riverside boat shed.

Meanwhile, on the day we arrived in Mokotów, Bór did something that was part of his plan to ensure we were treated as prisoners of war in the event of capitulation. To establish our status as an integral part of the Polish armed forces, no different from the men who had fought at Monte Cassino or our 1st Armoured Division (now serving under Montgomery in Belgium), it was announced that we had become the Warsaw Army Corps. The corps was to be made up of 'divisions' based on their pre-war locations: 8th Infantry in Żoliborz, 10th in Mokotów and so on. Senior officers were identified by their names rather than their pseudonyms. Thus Colonel Monter, the corps commander, was revealed to be Antoni Chruściel who had been given the acting rank of brigadier general.

None of this was of much interest to me, though it probably should have been. At 8.15 a.m. on 24 September, the morning of my sixteenth birthday, the battle for Mokotów started with the usual combination of artillery fire and Stuka dive-bombers. Shells exploded in front of and behind our billets, in a two-storey housing complex. Terrified inhabitants rushed to the cellars. Our platoon commander ordered most of us to follow them – except me. As I was a lance corporal, I was appointed 'observer' and told to remain on the upper floor. I wasn't sure what I was supposed to observe. All I could see were explosions, smoke and the local Mokotów unit in the distinctive grey-blue overalls they had looted from Luftwaffe stores. They were running down a tree-shaded avenue in small groups, heading directly towards the shell bursts. I wondered how much action they had seen.

The artillery preparation and the air raids went on for about two hours before von dem Bach, who had been reinforced by elements of the Hermann Göring SS Panzer Division, attacked from the west and south with his infantry and armour, which included Goliaths. Two nights before, in what would turn out to be our last air drop, the RAF had delivered some of the PIAT anti-tank rockets, so the enemy didn't have it all their own way. A massive school building on Woronicza Street, which the Germans had been using as a barracks and had painted in camouflage colours, was captured but then almost immediately recovered in a counter-attack. But most of the terrain we were trying to defend was Czerniaków all over again. There was too much space, too many gardens and parks. What we needed were the narrow lanes and built-up areas of the Old Town.

By the second day of the Mokotów fighting it was decided that our only option was to retreat to the city centre, the solidly defended heart of Warsaw. I found myself at the low wall of a small factory, protecting the evacuation of command personnel and some lightly wounded combatants who were making their way to the start of the inevitable sewer escape route. A few hours after we had been deployed, an SS-Polizei unit that specialized in urban warfare attacked us. We had rarely confronted them before, but we recognized them by their uniforms and helmets and were impressed by the speed with which they occupied the buildings opposite our positions.

We soon came under the kind of accurate machine-gun fire that made us keep our heads down and allowed the braver of our adversaries to get close enough to hurl stick grenades. One of them exploded close by, and I noticed blood dripping from my right hand; it also appeared to be trickling along my right leg into the German boot I was wearing. Stunned as I was by the idea that they had finally got me, neither of these wounds hurt very much. I refused to leave my position for treatment, waiting instead for Lidka. She was attending Mietek, who had also been hit in the hand, and was more seriously injured.

I seem to remember feeling rather pleased with myself. I was literally lubricating the rifle with my own blood, which was all over the bolt and breech, but I managed to squeeze off a couple more shots – though I don't recall firing at any specific target. This didn't last for long. Without warning there was a series of tremendous cracks, louder and much closer than the grenades: mortar bombs. Almost immediately I felt this stinging blow in my right leg, just below the knee. It hurt like nothing has ever hurt me, before or since. I would later discover that it had hit a nerve ending. At the time the only way I could think of reducing the pain was to roll about on the ground. I'm fairly sure I groaned, but somehow I managed to restrain myself from screaming.

Although I never quite lost consciousness, the rest of the morning remains a haze. Lidka appeared and, having pulled the boot off my wounded leg, we got into an argument about whether she could cut away or remove my trousers, through which she could see a large red stain growing. I don't know whether this was to do with my great fondness for my army trousers – such an improvement on the shorts and plus fours in which I had started my campaign – or some innate modesty. Certainly, at this stage, my underwear was unlikely to meet the exacting standard most mothers require of their sons in case of accidents.

Whatever discussion we had on the subject ended when Lidka suddenly jerked backwards, struck in the face by fragments from yet another of the dreadful mortar bombs that appeared to be exploding in airbursts. She had been hit in the right cheek and the side of her nose, but she insisted on dressing her own wounds. Amidst continuing exchanges of fire, another female medic replaced Lidka and stopped my bleeding with paper bandages. We had long since run out of the cloth sort. She assured me that the shrapnel in my right leg was neither fatal nor sufficiently lethal to require amputation.

It still hurt like hell.

Apart from my wounds, I soon became sick. Mietek had brought in a can of some sort of stew. We managed to open it with a bayonet and shared it with Lidka, all using the same spoon. But later I had a high fever and diarrhoea. I had to remove some of the paper dressing on my wounded hand to use as toilet paper when I limped out on one of my frequent trips to the garden. There was no water for the lavatory. My hand, covered in dried blood, looked filthy.

Mietek, Lidka and I had all opted to remain with our unit rather than go to one of the makeshift cellar hospitals. At one point Lidka, who also had a high fever, lay next to me on some sort of cot. I watched her periodically lift the bandage on her face to inspect the hole in her cheek with the aid of a pocket mirror. A friendly doctor promised her plastic surgery 'after the war', but it turned out there was no need for it.

Unfortunately, the quarters assigned to us were on the ground floor of an empty apartment. Someone had punched a large hole in the wall to communicate with the adjacent apartment. Instead of a quiet room, intended to help us recuperate, the three of us found ourselves in a transit area. At night, in the dark, I found something soft on the floor of the neighbouring apartment – a mattress, or some kind of duvet – and settled on it to sleep. Lidka and Mietek slept nearby in each other's arms. They said it was to keep warm.

During a lull in the shooting a Lieutenant Tomek, who always wore a black SS uniform, came in and gathered us around him. He said the walking wounded would be included in the planned evacuation through the sewers to the centre of the city. We would be called as soon as an accessible manhole was secured.

In my present condition I found the prospect of another sewer trip deeply worrying. Exposing wounds covered by flimsy paper bandages to that filth was about the easiest way I could imagine of developing gangrene. But if my unit left, I would have to fend for myself among strangers in a sector where we had spent only a week.

And were the Germans still shooting prisoners? I went back to bed, or what passed for one, and awaited the summons in a state of considerable foreboding and indecision.

'Come on now . . . slowly.'

My thoughts were interrupted by the voices of two girls. Both had fresh, pretty young faces. How could anyone look so clean? They were helping me to get up.

'My name is Bozena, and I will stay with you. Don't worry,' said one of them.

They took hold of my arms and I limped obediently between them. My wounds – hand, right leg and thigh – did not hurt much. No one had changed the bandages, but they were hardly more than a day old.

Outside, in the courtyard, I saw Colonel Radosław leaning on a cane. The colonel's leg was heavily bandaged. Other men in captured German camouflage waited in doorways for the Nazi planes to finish their business. When they had gone, the artillery salvoes resumed. We waited for what seemed like hours, the two girls at my side.

We filed out well after dark, a mixed group with some carrying weapons and cases of ammunition – though several of the wounded were unarmed, including myself. Soon we were in a tree-shaded street – Szustra Street, I was told. A barricade loomed to the right and armed men directed me to a trench. I saw a large manhole and one of the men from our unit lowering himself into it.

I was next, about to lower myself down into that stinking labyrinth, facing the prospect of hours without light, perhaps even rubbing my wounds into its filth.

'C'mon!' someone shouted. 'Are you going or not?'

Soon they were all yelling at me, some from the barricade and others from the end of the long line waiting their turn.

An officer approached and looked at me. 'Going into the sewer with your wounds? You must be out of your mind.'

'I'll stay,' I said, suddenly decisive, and I moved aside.

The girls who had helped me get this far prepared themselves for the descent by knotting up their skirts, to make them shorter. I watched them all go down, one by one, companions of previous skirmishes and previous retreats. Some were telling me to take care as they headed for the manhole. Others told me I must be out of my mind.

'The Germans will kill you,' said a phlegmatic lieutenant.

'I don't care,' I said, and I think I meant it.

I had refused to get into the lifeboat. It was as simple as that. The lieutenant didn't try to change my mind.

I was soon alone in the September drizzle. For the first time since I had gone into action, I cried. I was sixteen years and three days old, and I just wanted to be left to die in peace.

After a short while, I decided this was ridiculous. There I was – in my German helmet with a hole in one side, camouflage jacket and Wehrmacht jackboots – a soldier crying! That wouldn't do at all. What would my father say?

There were machine-gun bursts nearby followed by grenade explosions. Someone shouted that the Germans were attacking, chasing women in front of the tanks. Armed men raced by without paying me much attention. Somebody had long since taken my rifle, and there was nothing I could do. Dragging my injured leg across the wreckage of a garden, I headed towards the nearest building.

Then I spotted it. A miracle.

Above one of the entrances to the building was a large Red Cross flag. I limped as fast as possible towards it and went inside. The corridor, the stairs and the basement were packed with young men. All appeared to be wounded, and some were on crutches.

'Who are you?' demanded a middle-aged woman with a strong, determined face.

Wearily, I told her I had been wounded, gave the name of my unit and said I had decided to stay rather than go through the sewers again.

'What do you mean "again"? Have you made the trip before?'

'Yes,' I said, and I gave her a brief description.

'Child,' the woman said when I had finished, 'you're just what I need. Come and tell these fools why you won't go back to the sewers in your condition. They won't listen to me.'

I had a job to do, and somehow my strength returned. The wounded men here were mostly local. They had not left Mokotów since the fighting began, so had never been down a sewer. I went from one basement corridor to another, repeating my description of the sewers, the darkness, the hazards involved, the filth. Various voices followed me as I limped along.

'The kid is right. It's madness to go.'

'You stay. I'd rather try my luck than wait for the Germans.'

'The Germans control the manholes.'

'Do you know what they do when they capture a building? They throw grenades into every cellar. I'd rather take my chances in the sewers than wait here for the Germans to kill me.'

All of them wore bandages of one kind or another. I wondered (silently) how they were going to cope, especially in those narrow egg-shaped connecting sewers.

Someone shouted for the walking wounded to start moving and, despite all I had said, most of the men advanced towards the exit.

'I've done everything I can,' said the woman.

She took me down to a candle-lit cellar where a small ground-level window space, perhaps a coal chute, had been filled with sandbags and several wounded men were lying on mattresses. She found me an empty mattress and left me there.

I took off my German helmet and lay down. I didn't want to move through more trenches, more courtyards, more barricades. I wanted peace. I dozed until I heard voices.

'For God's sake, look at this one,' said a male voice, presumably a doctor's. 'He's wearing German uniform. They'll shoot the lot of us, if they find him.'

Two nurses started taking off my camouflage jacket with the Polish armband, my belt and my holed and bloody German trousers looted from captured stores. They also took my Home Army identity card and several photographs that had been shot and developed in the first days of the Uprising, when it had almost seemed like a holiday and the vestiges of normal life lingered on. I was allowed to keep my little portrait of St Bobola. I decided his powers were not on the wane – after all, I might have been killed or lost a leg.

I dozed again, until they woke me to make room for a freshly wounded man. We shared the mattress for the rest of the night. One of the wounded men was having nightmares and was shouting orders to attack. Another man conducted a monologue describing his various adventures. His low, somewhat hoarse voice rocked me to sleep. At dawn there was another artillery barrage and the building seemed to shake. Then came sporadic bursts of small-arms fire followed by a few single shots and an eerie silence.

The same woman who had asked me to dissuade the wounded from going into the sewers entered our cellar. 'This sector has surrendered,' she announced. 'The Germans have guaranteed that all those who took part in the action will be treated as prisoners of war.'

'I know what German promises are like,' said the tireless man with the hoarse voice.

'I forbid you to spread panic!' the woman shouted. 'If you don't shut up, I'll have you removed from this hospital.'

There was the sound of hobnailed boots in the corridor. German voices spoke and a woman's voice answered in what sounded like halting German. Timid light from outside was seeping through the barricaded cellar window. Two helmeted Germans peered into the cellar. Their uniforms looked brand new and were hung with grenades.

'*Hier alle Soldaten?*' one of them asked.

'Yes,' answered a nurse, 'all here are soldiers.'

I couldn't believe my ears. Had she gone crazy? Was she too terrified to lie?

But the Germans moved on. Furthermore, they had called us *Soldaten*. Not *Banditen*. *Soldaten*. They were taking us prisoner. That's what you did with *Soldaten*.

A few hours later, a Polish doctor told us that all the Home Army prisoners were being taken to a neighbouring apartment block. They put me on a stretcher, and the doctor and a nurse took some time to carry it upstairs to the exit. The day was cloudy and very autumnal, the courtyard covered by dead leaves. The first thing I saw was a stack of our abandoned weapons guarded by a middle-aged German soldier. He helped the doctor and the nurse to manoeuvre the stretcher carefully outside, puffing a little and saying, '*Langsam, langsam.*' ('Slowly, slowly.')

We were taken to the ground floor of a place that was full of mattresses and even some beds. I was left there for a while, wearing just a sweater, my underpants and a black pair of women's stockings I had found somewhere and wore to keep me warm at night. Then one of the nurses appeared with a pair of dark trousers from a stockpile of clothes that had been collected from abandoned apartments.

'Let's try these on you.'

I sat up, and together we pulled them on me.

'Perfect fit,' she said, folding the bottoms up a bit. 'There's a jacket too, it's a suit.'

When she held it up to show me, I saw the satin lapels.

'They're evening clothes,' she explained. 'Very smart.'

'Thank you,' I said, as politely as I could.

She folded the jacket and laid it down beside me. In the circumstances, I would have preferred any kind of uniform than the one worn by the leisured classes, but I didn't want to appear to be ungrateful.

There was a commotion in the corridor and a German general appeared, dressed in a long, well-tailored greatcoat with red lapels. I later found out this was Günther Rohr himself, the man who had negotiated the surrender with Bór.

He spoke briefly, praising our combat performance and regretting that 'such brave opponents did not fight Communism on Germany's side'.

Just as he finished, artillery salvoes exploded nearby.

'Your Russian friends,' he said as he left.

## 29.   Stalag XI-A

*Altengrabow, Germany*

'Father's name?'

'Mother's name?'

'When did you join the army?'

Did they mean the date I joined the Conspiracy?

I couldn't exactly remember. 'First August, 1944.' The day the Uprising started and I threw my first grenade. That would do.

The men asking the questions were other prisoners, and the documents were being prepared for both the camp administration and the International Committee of the Red Cross in Switzerland. Once we were properly registered in both places we would receive Red Cross parcels full of fabulous things: chocolate, corned beef and cigarettes (the camp's main currency). Meanwhile, the prisoners from several nations who happened to be in the camp's hospital when the Warsaw wounded arrived had all donated something from their last package as an act of solidarity.

Captive British medical orderlies had met me off the ambulance that transported me from the train. They had led me into a clean ward where my wounds were examined by a tall, handsome man with three pips on his epaulettes. This was Captain John Burton, a doctor in the Royal Army Medical Corps, who had been taken prisoner in Italy a few months earlier while searching for British wounded in a forward position on the Anzio beachhead. Burton tended to be well disposed towards Poles, having struck up a close friendship with Stalag XI-A's most distinguished Polish prisoner, Konstanty Ildefons Gałczyński, a widely published absurdist poet and former cultural attaché at the Polish embassy in Berlin, who had been a prisoner since 1939. Gałczyński's German was fluent, and Burton had managed to get him appointed to the hospital staff to work as both an interpreter and a paramedic – a role for which he was probably less qualified.

'How old are you?' Burton asked in German.

When I told him, he muttered something in English.

Burton himself was twenty-eight. Years later, when he published an account of his time in the camp, I discovered his first exposure to medical surgery had been as a medical student volunteer on the Republican side in the Spanish Civil War.

The British orderlies helped me undress and wash myself; the evening suit and the rest of my clothes went to be deloused. We communicated in German and French. Dr Burton, it turned out, preferred to speak French.

*Lazarett A*, as the huts that comprised the Stalag's hospital accommodation were known, was truly a European community. The Germans were very much in charge but often preferred to stay in the background. The hospital itself was run entirely by the prisoners. There were French, British, Yugoslavs, Greek, Dutch, Belgians plus a pleasant Russian dentist and what were soon referred to as the 'Old Poles' in order to distinguish them from us, the 'New Poles'.

Situated some ninety kilometres south-west of Berlin in a long-established military training area near the small town of Altengrabow, the nucleus of Stalag XI-A had once been a brick-built barracks for Prussian cavalry. The old stables were easy to identify by the concrete troughs lining their two main walls. Its first prisoners were some of the 400,000 Poles captured in 1939 who, by the following summer, were vastly outnumbered by a contingent from the million or so captive French whom the Third Reich had acquired. They arrived at about the same time as small numbers of Norwegians, Dutch, Belgians and British. Then, in the wake of Hitler's Balkan Blitzkrieg, came the Yugoslavs and Greeks. They were followed, within months, by the first of thousands of Russian prisoners who had somehow survived the torment of their crammed and waterless rail journeys across Poland.

By the time I was limping off the ambulance at Altengrabow, Stalag XI-A held some 50,000 prisoners. In addition to my own Warsaw contingent, the autumn of 1944 also saw the arrival of mutinous Slovakian soldiers, who were supposed to be serving a pro-Nazi regime but preferred to fight Germans rather than the Russians. There were also some Italians who, until the previous year when Italy surrendered and left the Axis Pact, had fought alongside their German Allies on the Eastern Front. Before being transported to Germany they had been held in a camp in Poland, and held the Poles in high esteem because some of the locals – who found it hard to regard their Latin fellow Catholics as enemies – had helped them eke out their meagre rations by bringing them food. In addition to these, most of the 2,000 British and Americans in the camp had, like Dr Burton, been captured relatively recently during minor local reverses in North Africa, Italy and Normandy. The latest included D-Day paratroopers who had been delivered into the hands of their enemies.

As far as the Germans were concerned, the Stalags were a valuable source of cheap labour. These camps were entirely for what the Americans called 'enlisted men' and the British 'other ranks'. Signatories to the Geneva Convention agreed that they would not oblige their officer prisoners to work. They were usually held separately, the commonest exceptions being medical officers, such as Captain Burton, and chaplains. In Germany, officers went to Oflags (*Offizierslager*) where it was rumoured they plotted daring escapes in between rehearsing elaborate amateur dramatics and learning foreign languages.

Work parties, or *Arbeitskommando*, were sent to mines, farms and factories and usually lived under guard at their place of work. But they were still administered from whatever Stalag they came from, which delivered their Red Cross parcels and mail. If they became sick, or were hurt in industrial accidents, they were sent to the nearest Stalag hospital with the facilities to treat them.

Until our arrival, the only recently wounded prisoners treated at *Lazarett A* were Allied bomber crews who had been shot down. They were kept in isolation, lest they gladden hearts with news of the war that somehow contradicted Dr Goebbels' latest version of events. Several of the Warsaw wounded were operated on by British doctors, but my injuries didn't appear to need any special treatment. I was walking better – though I still limped, and I had difficulty controlling my right foot.

'It'll improve in time,' Burton assured me, and he was right.

Like most people in the camp my main problem was getting enough to eat. The donations we received from other people's Red Cross parcels when we first arrived had long since been eaten, and although we had registered we had yet to receive the first parcels of our own. In Warsaw, especially during the last couple of weeks of the Uprising, we had mostly been too busy – and, no doubt, from time to time too scared – to notice how many meals we had missed. A lot of the time we craved sleep more than food. I suppose nowadays we would say we lived off adrenaline, but in 1944 we weren't all biochemists. Once we got to the camp, we were never exactly starving but we were almost always hungry.

They gave us ersatz tea to drink for breakfast, a thin soup for lunch and a dark liquid, which some charitably called coffee, in the evening. To eat with these three liquids we received a daily ration of one Wehrmacht-issue loaf and some margarine to be shared between six men. I soon learned to eat my portion at breakfast time and in the evening, and to let the soup suffice for lunch.

We were told things would get much better when the Red Cross parcels arrived with their tins of corned beef and sardines – not to mention the cigarettes, which could be exchanged for a host of other good things. Only the Russians didn't receive Red Cross parcels. Apparently, in 1929, the Kremlin had considered it unnecessary to sign the Geneva Convention since, unlike capitalist conscripts, the soldiers of the Revolution never surrendered. Once liberated, those who had surrendered were often sent to Siberia to learn the error of their ways. Even aircrew captured after being shot down over enemy territory could expect to find themselves facing hostile interrogation from Commissars demanding to know why they hadn't fought to the death.

By the time the Warsaw contingent arrived at Altengrabow, the Germans were estimated to have captured 5.7 million Soviet prisoners since the summer of 1941. Over half – 3.3 million – had died of starvation, epidemics and forced marches or had been massacred because, in one way or another, they were considered inconvenient. In the autumn of 1944, about half the inmates of Stalag XI-A were Russians who were held in their own compound. There should have been more, but we learned that many had perished in a typhus epidemic during the winter of 1941–1942. Apart from the Russian dentist, the only ones I saw in the hospital were the working party that emptied our latrines. They were always asking us for cigarettes and scraps of food. And while few of us doubted the justness of our dispute with the Soviet Union, it was hard not to feel pity for these abandoned soldiers.

Compared to these Russians, my own treatment as a prisoner was irreproachable. After two months of bitter fighting the concessions the Germans granted the Warsaw insurgents were unprecedented. None of the partisans operating in any of the other countries occupied by the Nazis had ever before been recognized as combatants entitled to the protection of the Geneva Convention. Nine days before the liberation of Paris, SS firing squads in the city's Bois de Boulogne were still executing members of the French Resistance.

The surrender document agreed between our leadership and the German military was unique. It was an amazing volte face in their treatment of the occupied nation that had suffered more deaths than any other per head of population. Those of us captured at Mokotów on 27 September were among the first large group of Home Army combatants to be treated as prisoners of war. Although we had got rid of it, the Germans knew full well that most of us had fought them wearing Wehrmacht uniform, including their helmets, but this clear breach of the rules of war was never mentioned. Instead, outfitted in our unlikely civilian clothes, stretcher cases like myself had been taken in a convoy of horse-drawn wagons to a railway siding south of the Warsaw racetrack. Here, under a persistent autumn drizzle, we awaited further transport. We had no idea where we were going but another sign of our enemy's good intentions was the appearance of a field kitchen, also horse-drawn, from which we were fed the standard thick Wehrmacht soup with hunks of bread. Delicious.

At this point, fighting was still continuing in the city centre and in the northern suburb of Żoliborz (the last place where the Home Army still held a stretch of the Vistula's east bank). Having missed their opportunity at Czerniaków, the Red Army might yet have turned this into a bridgehead had they cared to try, but they didn't. And von dem Bach concentrated his forces on Żoliborz to deny them the opportunity.

On 30 September, a German communiqué reported that 'after stubborn street fighting' Polish resistance in Żoliborz had ended. The communiqué made it plain that, whatever had gone on before, the Nazis were now willing to take prisoners. Listed among the captured were: '60 officers, 1,300 armed insurgents, 130 women fighters and 400 wounded'. There was no mention of *Banditen*.

Meetings to agree the surrender of all areas held by the insurgents had formally begun in Warsaw the day before, when Bór sent two officers under a flag of truce to von dem Bach's headquarters with a proposal to begin 'exploratory negotiations'. But the SS general knew that Bór would procrastinate while he still believed there was the faintest chance of the Russians crossing the Vistula, and so he imposed his own timetable. The capitulation document was signed four days later, on 2 October 1944, and consisted of twenty-three articles. Its most important paragraphs not only conferred prisoner-of-war status on all combatants but also guaranteed an amnesty for any anti-German activities prior to the Uprising. It was accepted that we all belonged to the same army as the Poles who had been taken prisoner at the end of the 1939 campaign.

Most surprisingly of all, SS-Obergruppenführer Erich von dem Bach-Zelewski had also agreed that our guards would be the German Wehrmacht. There was to be no question of us falling into the hands of the Ukrainian, Cossack and other non-German renegades who had been recruited as SS auxiliaries. Von dem Bach praised our bravery and related how he had personally persuaded Hitler to treat us as soldiers rather than terrorists. Presumably he had convinced his

Führer that it would otherwise take weeks to winkle the last of us out of the ruins of Warsaw, and this might somehow tempt the Russians into making a crossing.

The final act came on Thursday, 5 October 1944. It took place in the city centre, and an eyewitness account from one of its correspondents appeared in the Nazi Party's newspaper, *Völkischer Beobachter*, copies of which were available at Stalag XI-A.

At 10 a.m. six men, three in the pre-war uniforms of Polish officers and the others in civilian overcoats and hats, approached the German lines at the fire-damaged Warsaw Polytechnic Building, which had been much fought over. First one, then all six of them, began to sing '*Jeszcze Polska Nie Zginęła*' ('Poland Is Not Yet Lost') and, as the soldiers and civilians who lined the street joined in, this defiant singing of a defeated army's national anthem swelled. At the last Home Army barricade they were saluted by an imposing figure in full-dress Polish uniform wearing medals he had won in 1920, during the miraculous victory over the Soviet Union at the Vistula. This was General Antoni Chruściel, who had fought the Uprising under the nom de guerre Colonel Monter.

The six Poles then advanced towards a group of waiting German officers. The three in civilian clothes had all lost whatever scraps of uniform they had managed to preserve since 1939 in the last nine weeks of frantic moves from one collapsed building after another. One of them was the most senior man there: General Count Tadeusz Bór-Komorowski as he now styled himself by joining his best-known pseudonym to his aristocratic surname.

An immaculate Wehrmacht major stepped forward and shot up his right arm in the Nazi salute once confined to units of the SS. After the attempt by dissident officers to assassinate Hitler in the July bomb plot, it had become mandatory throughout the armed forces.

'Herr General,' announced the major, 'I have the honour of taking you into captivity.'

The general in question raised his hat and the others, according to their dress, either saluted or followed his example. Bór-Komorowski and some twenty of his senior officers, all of them selected by the Germans, were then driven to the railway station in a fleet of open cars and put in a closely guarded first-class carriage. It was the first stage of their journey to a Bavarian Oflag, where they joined hundreds of Polish officers who had spent almost five years in captivity.

The last pre-war census estimated that 35 million people lived in Poland. By the autumn of 1944, almost six million had been killed. Approximately half that number were Jews – about 90 per cent of their community. The rest were mostly Catholics. The widespread atrocities that occurred in the early part of the Uprising were typical of the prevailing brutality. Including the 15,000 combatants the Home Army counted who were killed in action, casualties are usually put at 150,000 – though some have insisted that a combination of massacres and indiscriminate bombardment makes 200,000 closer to the truth. And remember, this was in sixty-three days.

Estimates of German casualties have varied enormously over the years. But given that the heaviest ground weapons they faced were mortars and anti-tank weapons, and that Soviet air activity was negligible, a post-war German estimate that their losses were in the region of 11,000 dead and wounded – of whom some 2,000 were killed – seems reasonable.

About 16,000 of us – of whom 5,000 were wounded – ended up in the kind of prison camp in which I found myself. There were also in the region of 1,000 female prisoners who, according to Paragraph 11 of the surrender agreement, were to be accommodated 'in camps corresponding to Oflags'.

Lidka, who had taken the sewer trip I refused to go on, had experienced a nightmare fourteen-hour journey to the city centre in passages filled with panic-stricken civilians, some of whom were trying to bring along their suitcases and fur coats. She was among several of the Home Army's female couriers and nurses who avoided captivity by simply changing their clothes and joining the civilians who were being expelled en masse to the Pruszków transit camp. This was in preparation for Hitler's plan to demolish the entire city. Its surviving buildings were to be levelled and Warsaw was to be reduced to nothing more than a Wehrmacht transport hub to the Eastern Front, to be rebuilt as a model German city once this tiresome resurgence of the Red tide had been properly contained.

Meanwhile, Burning and Destruction Detachments (*Verbrennungs-
und Vernichtungskommando*) were set to work on the beginnings of
Himmler's grand design. In a more precise and risk-free way he was
doing to Warsaw what the Anglo-American air forces were doing to
Berlin and Hamburg. Areas like the Old Town, where many of the
eighteenth-century buildings had already been wrecked, were to be
turned into a sinister desert of rubble. Post-war damage assessment
found that 42 per cent of Warsaw's buildings had been destroyed, and
most of the remainder needed major repairs.

In the space of a week, between 1 and 7 October, the Germans
noted that a further 155,519 men, women and children had obeyed
their orders to leave the last parts of the municipality held by the
insurgents. Some Home Army fighters mingled with this exodus and
evaded capture. One was Radosław and his wife, Anna, who had
been alongside him in both the Old Town and Czerniaków. Warsaw
may have surrendered and been emptied of its people, but the Home
Army intended to continue its resistance in those western parts of
Poland that the Nazis still occupied. Just before the surrender, Bór
had appointed General Leopold Okulicki, his former chief-of-staff,
to succeed him as head of the Home Army. Okulicki was *Cichociemni*,
one of 'The Unseen and Silent Ones' – the nickname for those who
had been taught how to set occupied countries alight by Britain's
Special Operations Executive, then dropped back into Poland by the
RAF to find out how much of their training worked.

German intelligence was surprised not to find Okulicki with Bór –
his name was on the list of officers who were to accompany him into
captivity – and were looking out for him. He was picked up and put
on a night train for Kraków for further interrogation. On the outskirts of the city the commando-trained Okulicki managed to escape
with a daring leap into the dark, located a local Home Army cell and
was soon in radio contact with London. Few were capable of making
this sort of luck for themselves, if things went wrong.

Of the half a million or so people from Warsaw who entered the
Pruszków transit camp about 90,000 were sent to Germany as forced
labour. Many of them were young women. Several thousand more
ended up in concentration camps, usually because they were sus-

pected of being Jews who had managed to avoid being corralled in the various ghettoes. The majority were allowed to relocate in the areas of Poland that the Germans still controlled. I later discovered that my mother had found shelter in a convent at Pruszków for herself, Jerzy, Aunt Olga and my grandmother.

The treatment of Home Army prisoners being transported to various Stalags varied greatly and often depended on the whim of quite junior officers. Some were pummelled with rifle butts as they were packed, without food or water, into cattle trucks with standing room only and not even a bucket for bodily functions.

My own treatment, together with the other wounded combatants from Mokotów, was very different. First we were taken by rail to Skierniewice, a town some forty kilometres west of Warsaw, once famous for a railway station that was supposed to be one of the gems of the old Warsaw–Vienna line. The German 9th Army's headquarters had been there for the last three months, ever since the Red Army had pushed them back to the Vistula. We arrived at a transit camp, where we were taken on stretchers into a large barracks and laid with other wounded men in rows on the floor. It was there that we learned for the first time that both the northern suburb of Żoliborz and the city centre had surrendered, and the Uprising was over. I don't think any of us expected it to end like this, and I remember none of us wanted to talk about it. I think we were quite numbed by the news: all that effort, all that sacrifice.

Prisoner-of-war doctors, mostly Russian and French, examined our wounds in a somewhat cursory fashion before we were loaded into freight wagons equipped with wooden cots and lavatories. Our Wehrmacht guards did not prevent Polish civilians reaching the train and handing us baskets filled with food. There was one guard to each wagon; as well as carrying rifles they each had a couple of stick grenades thrust into their belts.

At the royal and ancient Polish city of Poznań, which had been annexed by the Third Reich, our wagons were shunted into a siding when another ambulance train, replete with red crosses, drew up alongside us. We could see bandaged German soldiers inside, and they could see us, because the walking wounded, like myself, had been allowed to gather at the open door to get a breath of fresh air. For a while we examined each other with evident curiosity, perhaps more on their part than on ours because, in the main, we were wearing an odd assortment of civilian clothes.

Then one of the Germans asked where we were from.

'*Aus Warschau,*' we said.

'*Wir sind auch aus Warschau!*'

So now it was established. They were also from Warsaw, and we were each living proof of the other's combat skills.

There was some fraternization.

'Czerniaków?' they asked.

'*Und die Altstadt,*' some of us replied.

The Germans threw a couple of packs of cigarettes and what appeared to be a small bottle of schnapps over to us. Then their train started to pull out. Some of us wished each other goodbye and good luck, and then they were gone.

Not long afterwards we were also on the move. We rattled across a rail bridge over the Oder, and were soon in Germany. It occurred to me that I was on my first trip abroad. At our first stop the doors to our wagon were opened and we saw a small group of passengers waiting for a train: elderly men and women wearing felt hats, a smattering of uniforms. It all looked so orderly and peaceful.

The train creaked slowly out of this country station and most of us drifted off to sleep. The next time we stopped, it was dark. Someone asked the guard where we were.

'Berlin,' he said.

We had been stationary for some time when air-raid sirens began to wail, followed almost immediately by the thumping sound of heavy anti-aircraft fire and the nearby thud of bombs. One exploded close enough to shake our wagon. We smelled smoke from burning buildings, which was drifting towards the train, and heard the hiss of the coal locomotive as it built up steam, anxious to get away.

'*Deutschland kaputt,*' said our guard, words we would hear more often in the coming months.

The Americans usually bombed by day, the British by night. Had our luck finally run out? Perhaps the RAF, whose attacks on

German cities we had always so applauded, would see that we were *kaputt* long before *Deutschland*? We lay there in the dark, noting brief bomb flashes or the flicker of searchlights through various small cracks and gaps in the sides of our freight car.

Then the sirens sounded the all-clear and our train moved slowly off into an uncertain dawn.

## 30. The Melancholia Patient

Once a week a monocled German doctor, who dictated his notes to an assistant equipped with a clipboard, inspected the wards and interviewed patients.

'Attention!' one of the British orderlies would cry.

Upon hearing this command the bedridden were supposed to lie motionless on their backs, arms outside their blankets. Those who could were required to stand by their beds and adopt some approximation of a parade-ground posture. The Wehrmacht doctor usually made a beeline for the latter category. He seemed interested in only one thing: weeding malingerers out of the hospital and into the camp, where they would join the labour pool available for assignment to an *Arbeitskommando*.

At the end of my second week in the hospital, the German doctor asked Captain Burton about my wounds. The British surgeon answered at length, but the two men were speaking in English and I didn't understand a word – though when they had finished, I thought Burton looked unhappy with the outcome. I soon realized why, for I had no difficulty in comprehending the one German word our visitor dictated to his assistant: '*Lager*'.

I was going to the camp and I would be leaving the following day. I still limped, and my wound dressings had to be changed regularly, but there would be no more attentive British orderlies looking after me. Some of the other patients took it upon themselves to warn me that I would not find the camp as pleasant as the hospital. I did not find this difficult to believe, but I consoled myself with the thought that I'd undoubtedly been in worse places of late.

Next morning, I stood on a windswept sports field with all the other unfortunates who had been found fit enough to leave our cosy niche. A tall Frenchman in a rakish kepi read out the roll call. When he reached the end of it, my name had not been called. He looked at his list again, but the more he looked the more my name wasn't there. He shrugged, and I walked back to the ward.

Not long afterwards, Burton appeared.

'Remember, you're not well,' he told me. 'You have suffered a shock. You are now suffering from melancholia.'

Melancholia was what the medical profession used to call clinical depression. Like most mental illnesses there are no conclusive physical symptoms for it – though, in the 1940s, there was still an abiding belief that one indicator was dilated pupils.

I immediately understood what was happening. Burton was going to do his best to keep me in the hospital.

A few days later, the German doctor made another inspection. I stood at the head of my bed, heart pounding. He headed straight for me.

'*Was ist mit dem Junge?*'

The words stung like a whip. I suppose the best translation would be: 'What's up with the kid?'

Once upon a time somebody had asked that question about me in another place, and the memory of it sent a chill down my spine. But where was it? I could think of nothing else and my mind remained a blank.

The German lifted my left eyelid and gazed into it. Then he did the same with the right eyelid. The monocle glistened. His breath smelled of coffee and tobacco. He gave Burton a thoughtful look.

'*Ja, ja, die Melancholie,*' he said at last. Then he told his assistant to note that I would be remaining in hospital.

As he walked out, I remembered where I had last heard the words '*Was ist mit dem Junge?*' It was at the Gestapo headquarters, in Warsaw's Szucha Avenue, when the terrified man accused of being a Jew had been struck in the face and had apologized for bleeding over me. On that occasion they let me out. This time they were letting me in. Once again, I was the baby-faced *Junge*.

But how many Germans had I killed? Two or three? Perhaps more. Perhaps none. Perhaps, like me, the ones I had hit were all recovering from their wounds in hospital.

I had no idea. Nor did I care very much.

★

We were all issued with printed Red Cross forms in order to inform our families that we were alive, if not always well.

> Dear father/mother/brother/sister (cross out inapplicable). I am well/ in hospital. Write to me by tearing off the other half of this form.

The other half was similarly brief. The forms were intended to facilitate the first contact with your family since capture. But who was I to write to? Warsaw was an empty shell manned by a German garrison exchanging sporadic shots with the Russians on the other side of the river. There was no point in writing to my mother's flat. She and Jerzy would have left the city along with everybody else, assuming they had survived – and I saw no reason to believe otherwise, because there had been no fighting in their part of Mokotów. Even so, accounts in the one-page Polish language propaganda sheet the Germans distributed made no secret of the scale of the retribution that had befallen Warsaw, mentioning the 150,000 dead but making no attempt to explain how so many had died. Instead, they blamed the whole business on 'agents of Moscow and London'.

So who was I to inform of my own survival? It was important that someone should know because I was also allowed to supplement my Red Cross parcels, when they started to arrive, with individual food packages that any well-wishers might care to send me. Suddenly, I thought of Ada. Was she still book-keeping for her affable old Nazi Georg Wimmer? Would life be carrying on as normal in Kraków and the rest of occupied Poland despite Warsaw's destruction? Well, there was only one way to find out.

Ada's answer came within two weeks, and I was able to write back at length. Shortly afterwards a large parcel arrived that contained smoked ham, sausages and warm underwear. I shared the victuals with two of the British orderlies who had been particularly helpful. They were amazed how good the Polish ham was. Other Home Army wounded were receiving similar packages from the western part of the country, which was still occupied by the Nazis. The non-Poles just couldn't understand it. How could a defeated, downtrodden country, occupied within the first six weeks of this long war, still be capable of producing such fare? Even the French were not doing as well as this. And since the U-boats were still trying to starve Britain to death, packages from that tightly rationed island were notoriously pathetic. There was rarely ever any food in them. Instead, Burton's orderlies got hand-knitted mufflers, socks and the ski hats they called 'balaclavas' after a nineteenth-century battlefield involving a gallant, if foolish, cavalry charge against Russian cannon. Yet here was this motley crowd of wounded from a lost battle in a lost country being showered with smoked pork and other delicacies. It just didn't fit.

Those who couldn't spare any treats for me – and some people back home were as hungry as we were – wrote letters, which were the next best thing. I had written to everyone whose address I remembered in Maków and received several carefully couched replies expressing a guarded admiration. All prisoner-of-war mail was stamped *Kriegsgefangenenpost*. It was one of those composite German words that sound oddly menacing to foreign ears, but one Polish prisoner – whether Old Pole or New Pole it was impossible to tell – was moved to write an anonymous tribute in verse and pin it up on one of the hospital's noticeboards.

> *Kriegsgefangenenpost*
> It sounds like a secret lore.
> Your name, your street, your home.
> The whistle of a distant train,
> The constant wracking of my brain.
> The love that cannot take the strain.
> *Kriegsgefangenenpost . . .*

Then the Red Cross parcels started to arrive. The distribution system varied. If you were lucky, it was one package a week divided up between two prisoners but sometimes four of us would be sharing one. As long as people had strong preferences for different things – chocolate rather than a can of corned beef, for instance – dividing them up was quite easy. Otherwise we would draw lots for various items. Everybody wanted their share of the parcel's ten packs of American cigarettes – 200 in all. A loaf of bread was worth twenty cigarettes; a tin of sardines ten; a complete British battledress of trousers

and jacket cost eighty; British-issue boots were forty. American uniforms were also available, but there were not enough to go round, so
some of us got the brass-buttoned jackets and others got the trousers.
A pair of US Army trousers (to match the jacket I had already been
given) cost me forty cigarettes. Later, I also acquired a British battledress top after selling the dinner suit I had arrived in to one of the
British orderlies. He had worked as a waiter in London's West End
and was confidently preparing to resume his civilian occupation in
the not-so-distant future.

It took me a while to realize exactly how much purchasing power a
non-smoker possessed. By then I had already given away my first cigarette ration to one of the British orderlies who had taken particular
care of me. His name was Arthur Smith and, at first, the pronunciation
of his name took considerable tongue-twisting for someone unaccustomed to English sounds. But before long I found I could put together
some simple sentences. I noticed the British prisoners liked us to learn
English, even though their own linguistic abilities rarely went beyond
a few words of pidgin German – a language I already spoke reasonably
well, and French even better. Now I had added to these accomplish-
ments the ability to inquire, in English, about the price in cigarettes of
a bar of Red Cross chocolate. And understand the answer.

It was a beginning.

I also began to do a few odd jobs around the hospital. The big
piece of shrapnel behind my right knee, the one that had really hurt,
was still there. I was told it would work its way out. (Almost seventy
years later, I'm still waiting.) But it didn't hurt, and my limp had
almost gone. At first, I did light tasks that didn't require much standing up. Working under the supervision of a Dutch corporal, I helped
to prepare the potatoes for the daily soup.

'*Dünn schälen,*' the corporal would say. 'Peel them thinly.'

As my leg grew stronger, I began to assist the orderlies who carried
the stretcher cases in for medical examination. This sometimes left
me waiting in one of the surgeries to carry the wounded back out.
Since there was little privacy I was able to observe what else was
going on. Once, I found myself watching a doctor insert a pointed
instrument into the penis of a Yugoslav patient.

'Does it hurt?' the doctor inquired innocently as the man let out a piteous groan. He was British, like Burton, but he managed to address his patient in a semblance of Serbo-Croat.

'And when you fuck – does it hurt then?'

'Next time, I'll use my hand,' gasped the Yugoslav. 'You meet a better class of person.'

I was baffled. How could a prisoner of war get a venereal disease?

There was a simple explanation. The men sent to the factories and the farms as part of an *Arbeitskommando* often met up with foreign female workers who had either been conscripted or voluntarily recruited from every corner of Nazi-occupied Europe. Some men even had affairs with German women whose husbands were away in the army – though, thanks to the *Rassenschande* laws on racial defilement, this was risky for both parties.

In the main, the Yugoslavs were handsome Serbs – tall, swarthy characters. They had been captured in the spring of 1941 as the Wehrmacht juggernaut rolled southwards through their country, on its way to more victories – this time against the Greeks and their British allies. The Serbs talked constantly of their sexual frustration in a way you never heard from the Old Poles and the French, whose enforced abstinence had lasted longer.

Every so often they would greet each other with the question: 'How long have you been without it?'

The correct response was to give a full reply that covered years and months; weeks, days and hours were optional.

The Yugoslavs' good humour made them popular in the hospital. Poles could usually converse with them quite easily in a mixture of German and those words and phrases our Slavic schisms had in common. They made each other laugh – and the other nationalities too – even though we didn't have all that much to laugh about. They were also admired for inventing the camp's most efficient cooking device. It was an ingenious machine whereby a fan (worked by turning a handle) was somehow attached to a brazier and dramatically flared its wood-fuelled flame.

One evening, one of the Yugoslavs allowed me to use his stove to heat up my soup. As I crouched beside him, he asked the inevitable question.

'How long have you been without it?'

I didn't think I could possibly equate my exposure to the voluptuous Nicole with what he was referring to. So, taking a deep breath, I decided to be honest.

'Sixteen years and two months.'

The Serb nearly fell over. Then, by the light of his stove, he examined my face.

'A virgin!' he cried. 'My God, a real virgin.'

This was certainly not a condition my contemporaries among the Warsaw wounded appeared to suffer from. At night, especially when the ward lights went off early because of air raids or to save power, their chat as we lay in our beds centred on two things: the Uprising and the sex lives that had mostly preceded it.

Some claimed to have killed as many as a dozen Germans, and there were fierce quarrels about the performance of their units and their sectors. Men who had been stuck in one place and had never had to go anywhere by sewer sometimes greeted my own story with some scepticism. They found it difficult to believe that, including my brief trip to the Old Town, I had been in every sector of the city except Żoliborz. They were mostly working-class boys who, since the beginning of the war, had rarely left the neighbourhoods in which they'd been brought up. Here they had apparently led lives of unbridled sexual freedom, losing their virginity to frustrated young war widows and then deflowering the younger sisters of their friends in communal lavatories and washrooms. Much of this congress seems to have been of a distinctly vertical nature. I felt my experiences with Lona, the blonde daughter of the 'captain in hiding' from the next-door apartment block, could hardly compete. After a kiss and a cuddle in a darkened doorway, she had sent my fourteen-year-old being into spasms of contrition by presenting me next day with a photograph of herself in her first communion dress. As for Nicole, I could hardly count her as a conquest.

A boy only slightly older than myself boasted of having made love to three women who worked in the same bakery as he did. By now I had discovered I was by no means the youngest there. In an adjacent ward lay a thirteen-year-old who had been machine-gunned in both legs while running a message across Jerozolimska Avenue before that wide thoroughfare was protected by a barricade. Everyone called him the 'General'.

All patients under the age of eighteen received two or three mugs of milk a week. No one had expected this degree of care. Nor did we expect a delegation of officers from General Franco's neutral but fervently anti-Communist Spain, who came to inspect the hospital. They were visibly impressed with German generosity towards their fellow Catholics. We suspected they were former members of the Spanish Blue Division, Falangist volunteers who were highly regarded by the Wehrmacht for their spirited performance against the Red Army. The division had been a repayment for the Nazis' military assistance during the Spanish Civil War and had been withdrawn towards the end of 1943 when Franco realized that, barring a miracle, Hitler was facing defeat and he needed to mend his fences with London and Washington.

That had been a year ago, and since then things had got much worse for Germany. Like all the prisoners in the hospital I was convinced the war would end in 1945. Night and day, we heard the Allied bombers heading for Berlin. The Russians were already at the Vistula and the Anglo-Americans were almost at the German frontier. Soon the British might even live up to the promise they made in their 1939 song about hanging out the washing on the Siegfried Line. Perhaps the western Allies would reach us before the Russians and then roll over the rest of Germany to liberate western Poland? When one of the Yugoslavs expressed the hope that the Red Army would beat them to it, I was appalled. We started shouting at each other, watched by some bemused Belgians who, once they realized the nature of our quarrel, probably thought we were being a little premature.

But things were moving fast. By 21 October, the Americans had captured Aachen on Germany's western border with Belgium, the Reich's first major city to fall to the Allies. We didn't hear about this until the middle of November, but it was impossible to keep any war news away from us for very long. Among 50,000 prisoners there might well have been one secret radio picking up the BBC. But even if there wasn't, we had other sources: some of our middle-aged

guards were practically bilingual German-Polish speakers from the
Silesian borderlands that the Nazis had declared part of the Reich,
considering its male inhabitants sufficiently German to be subject to
conscription. When I went for walks around the barbed wire that
surrounded the hospital, my right foot still falling without my total
control, some of these Polish speakers in the watchtowers above the
wire would try to engage me in conversation.

'How was the Uprising?' one asked me.

I told him how the people had supported us, and how the Russians
had let us down, but when I tried to sum up those sixty-three days I
found it impossible. All I could tell him was that I didn't think either
of us would be here next Christmas.

'Yes, perhaps the British and the Americans will make peace with
Germany, and we'll all be fighting the Russians,' he said.

It reminded me of General Rohr's quip about 'your Russian
friends' when the Soviet shells had landed near the Mokotów
wounded.

Now the Germans would like us to be friends with them, but it
was much too late. They had murdered too many of us.

As Christmas approached, the mood of most of the people in the
ward – both patients and staff – was subdued. Winter was setting in,
the front lines were frozen to the east and the west, and we were
resigned to the idea that there would be no major military developments before the spring. I recalled that other spring in Maków, in
1940, when my father and I had been so filled with hope for the
inevitable Anglo-French retribution in the Ruhr that would finish
off Hitler and end Poland's occupation. Instead, by the start of the
summer our captured church bells were pealing the fall of Paris and
the disintegration of France's huge army.

Then, for a few sickening days, it seemed that history might be
repeating itself. It turned out that the Germans had no intention of
waiting for the Anglo-Americans to mount a spring offensive. On
16 December, they managed to launch a brilliant surprise attack of
their own against weakly held American positions in the thickly
wooded hills of the Ardennes, on their border with Belgium and
north-eastern France. It was exactly the same place where they had

launched their blitzkrieg against the French in 1940. Photographs showing long columns of bewildered-looking GI prisoners appeared in the Goebbels propaganda sheet we were given, which informed us they had been captured during something called Operation '*Wacht am Rhein*', after the patriotic song. It was an attempt to drive a wedge between the US and British armies and to capture Antwerp, the Allies' main port. Four years earlier, regiments of defeated Frenchmen had trudged into captivity along these same roads. Now there was snow on the ground, and the helmets were different, but the lesson was clear: never underestimate the Wehrmacht. The Germans claimed 50,000 Americans had surrendered in the first forty-eight hours. We didn't believe it, but the chances were we wouldn't have believed the true figure either, which was only slightly under half that number.

Some of them turned up in our Stalag, but they had no idea of the total number of US troops taken prisoner in what was becoming known as the 'Battle of the Bulge' after the salient the Wehrmacht had fashioned for themselves. Then American paratroopers made their famous stand at Bastogne, an old fortress town built to thwart Germanic invasion, while their besiegers found their supply lines had been cut. By the end of January, the Germans were back behind their Siegfried Line, having been obliged to destroy a lot of irreplaceable tanks they had been unable to refuel. Even so, their initial success was hardly the kind of tidings of gladness and joy we expected for Christmas 1944.

I dare say Generals Eisenhower, Patton and Montgomery felt the same way about things.

A French padre celebrated midnight Mass with a small choir consisting of myself and five other Warsaw teenagers singing 'Christ Is Born' and other traditional carols. The service took place in one of the French wards where the beds, some still containing their patients, had been moved against the wall. It was preceded by a pale semblance of a traditional Christmas Eve supper. In Poland this is usually a vegetarian affair with almond soup, carp and pastries. The Stalag XI-A version was the usual mysterious soup and potatoes in their jackets, augmented by foods saved from Red Cross packages. Those of us lucky enough to still be receiving packages from the German-controlled territory west of the Vistula shared the contents around, while the British continued to marvel at their very existence and the pains our captors took to deliver them along railways subjected to constant air attack.

Two of the Polish wounded – a man without a leg and a seventeen-year-old who had lost an arm – began weeping in each other's arms, and that started us all off. Some masked French revellers did their best to cheer us up, as did Burton's friend the absurdist poet, Gałczyński, who recited a comic poem about a belly dancer and made various quips that went over most people's heads. It was the kind of material one might have heard in one of Warsaw's more avant-garde pre-war cabarets, but it was not the kind of sentimental and religious fare most of us craved.

Next day, Christmas Day itself, the food was the same but our mood was considerably lightened by a Polish puppet show making gentle versified fun of John Burton and all the hospital's leading lights. This was followed by a singalong of most of our favourites to the accompaniment of an accordion. But it was the French, who had been resident almost as long as the Old Poles, with over four years to polish their theatrical skills, who put on the highlight of the year end's festivities. Jaunty 'couples' – the female role attired courtesy of theatrical props supplied by the Red Cross – demonstrated the traditional costumes of all the major French provinces. While these actors paraded before them on a well-built stage, a choir sang regional songs to enthusiastic applause. I was delighted to discover how much French I could understand and realized I was learning how to live in an international community. All those lessons with Mateczka had paid off. I wished I could have written to tell her, but I didn't have her address.

'*Et maintenant,*' said the master of ceremonies, '*nous allons tous chanter "La Madelon".*'

And all sing '*La Madelon*' we did, in five languages. It was a popular First World War song about a girl who served sparkling wine in a tavern at the edge of a forest. It had been adopted and adapted, in translation, by armies on both sides of the conflict – rather like the way the British stole 'Lili Marleen' from the Afrika Korps.

Each national group sang in their own language and yet, amazingly, there was no dissonance.

> *La servante est jeune et gentille*
> *Légère comme un papillon . . .*

And the Polish version continued:

> *Oczy jej są iskier pełne*
> *Zwą ją wszyscy Madelon.*

The name remained unchanged in all languages. When we had reluctantly finished all possible encores we slowly dispersed, wishing each other, 'Next year in Paris!' None of us could bring ourselves to propose a rendezvous in a Warsaw that was in a heap of ruins, still in enemy hands and facing conquest by another enemy.

When it was over, some of us walked in the crisp air of the small compound outside, gazing at the stars and listening to the drone of Lancasters paying another of their night calls on Berlin. I didn't realize it at the time, but the Christmas decorations Burton had made for our ward contained some of the millions of strips of metal foil the RAF used to confuse the German radar. They must have landed in the camp.

On New Year's Eve, two British orderlies managed to acquire the key to the cupboard where the medicinal alcohol was stored and got roaring drunk. There were no repercussions, and this tolerance was regarded as proof of a new mood among the hospital's German administrators. For all the Wehrmacht's ability to lay on another spectacular in the Ardennes, it was hard to imagine that they were entirely confident of staying on their side of the barbed wire for much longer.

# 31. The Decision

In the early days of January 1945, I made what every adult in the hospital advised me was the stupidest decision of my young life – and had events not taken an unexpected turn, they would have been right. At the time, some of them thought I was clearly out of my mind.

What I did was volunteer to transfer to the main camp with two recently made friends, boys only slightly older than myself, who were being discharged from the hospital because the German doctor had declared them cured of whatever was ailing them and fit, if necessary, for work. We didn't have much in common by way of background or education. Nonetheless, the three of us had all participated in the sixty-three days of the Uprising, and that seemed quite enough. The little that had gone before it in our short lives counted for nought as our friendship grew on a diet of jokes and spontaneous bursts of song, as well as the camaraderie and mutual respect engendered by what we had seen and done.

Stubbornly ignoring warnings about the overcrowded conditions in the main camp, Dr Burton's spoilt melancholia patient was giving up his much-envied sinecure because having friends of his own age seemed more important than clean sheets and a hospital diet with its mugs of fresh milk. The authorities were confused. Nobody had ever volunteered to leave the hospital for the camp before. Dr Burton tried to talk me out of it. I think a lot of his concern had to do with the moral risks a blond and beardless youth might run in the company of grown men who had not known heterosexual sex for four or five years. He didn't say this. He simply pointed out that the chances were that I would be separated from my new friends.

But I wasn't listening. My mind was made up.

Our departure took place at dusk – an early and cold winter dusk. A group of about twenty prisoners in total gathered near the main entrance to the hospital grounds. Most of us carried what little we possessed in clumsy bundles and, as the reality of what we were leaving behind sank in, even my new friends and myself quietened down. Among us were several Frenchmen, a British sergeant, an elderly Polish lieutenant-colonel with an empty right sleeve and a tall, slim young man wearing an elegant civilian overcoat with a velvet collar. He introduced himself as a lieutenant from Warsaw's Żoliborz sector, which had eventually seen some heavy fighting when it became the last stretch of riverbank to be held by the insurgents. I guessed that, like my dinner suit, he had acquired the coat just before his surrender after he had divested himself of whatever bits of German uniform he had managed to acquire.

As we reached the complex of massive stables where the prisoners were housed, guards materialized and escorted the British sergeant and Frenchmen away. Then a lieutenant who stood ramrod straight and looked much too old for his rank courteously explained that the prisoners from Warsaw were still under quarantine and we would be joining them. I don't know what we were suspected of carrying – apart from a grudge. Our accommodation was to be a stable on the edge of the camp where, for the time being, we would have no contact with other nationalities. Officers would be in a partitioned part of the same stable, awaiting their transfer to an Oflag. The massive doors swung open and as we stepped inside the stench of body odour was overpowering.

A burly German soldier, apparently oblivious to it, clicked his heels and introduced himself as, '*Unteroffizier Jerke, Kompanie Führer.*' He then handed the new arrivals over to a Polish prisoner, mumbled some sort of farewell to him and disappeared.

'Don't worry about Jerke,' the Pole said once we were alone. 'He's a *Volksdeutsch* from Łódź, speaks good Polish and is working hard at securing a post-war future for himself. He even thinks he'll be able to go back to Łódź. He won't, of course.'

I thought this was very good news. In 1939, the Nazis had kicked my grandmother out of her home in Łódź, the house where I was born, in order to accommodate *Volksdeutsche* from elsewhere in Poland.

The Pole who had taken over from Jerke showed us to our sleeping places. I don't know what I had been expecting. The Polish section in the hospital had been crowded – there were about a hundred of us there – but it was nothing like this. The walls of the stable, dimly lit by three or four light bulbs dangling from the ceiling, were lined with triple-decker bunks that looked more like ambitious shelving. In the middle were three large tables, two of them occupied by noisy ping-pong players using balls and bats provided by the Red Cross. The constant background clacking of their games would become one of my abiding memories of the Stalag.

No one seemed to pay much attention to the new arrivals and, as Burton and others had predicted, the separation from my new friends was immediate. I was assigned a place in the least desired middle row, between two men I had never met before. After that, I was shown the bathroom facilities: two leaky taps and an open latrine outside.

One of my new bunkmates, a moody-looking man with a black beard, greeted me with, 'Don't jerk off here, or I'll knock your teeth out!'

During a somewhat mournful tour of my new accommodation I spotted one familiar face from the hospital, a man with whom I had shared some of Ada's food packages. At first his greeting was distinctly tepid but then, unable to ignore the history of our acquaintanceship any longer, he invited me to inspect his 'larder'. We climbed up to the top bunk where I was shown a well-organized wooden box filled with food.

'This is the compartment for bread, that one for tea and here for margarine and bacon,' he explained.

I politely feigned about as much admiration as seemed appropriate, and waited for the moment when I would be asked to sample these treasures. It never came. After a while, I told him I'd better be getting back to my own bunk.

Shortly afterwards, I heard a shout, 'Attention! Form up for the evening prayer.'

Well over a hundred of us lined up in two rows in front of a stocky, red-faced man who was standing on one of the tables. After a short prayer we sang the centuries-old traditional evensong, after which we were dismissed. I liked this ceremony – it was defiant and helped draw us together.

'Who is he?' I asked one of the prisoners.

'Sergeant Pawlak was a featherweight boxer before the war.'

'Is he the highest ranking man here?'

'No, but he's the hardest hitting. We elect our own leaders. He is on very good terms with Jerke, our German chief.'

As if on cue, the German suddenly reappeared.

'*Lichte aus in zehn Minuten,*' he announced, repeating in Polish, 'Lights out in ten minutes.'

I bedded down in the cold and smelly stable, covering myself with a blanket and a newly issued British greatcoat, compliments of the Red Cross. I noticed that some of the prisoners inspected their shirts, squeezing something between their fingernails.

'Shot down five tonight,' somebody said, followed by several other voices all announcing various scores.

It was the nightly lice kill, and I knew that I would have them soon – though after dark the temperature was so low, it was a wonder any parasites survived. My blanket and coat weren't enough to stop me trembling with the cold.

'You're wanking!' roared my bearded neighbour.

'Shut up! It's his prick,' said a voice that could have come from anywhere in the pitch dark.

Someone giggled.

The next day, I woke to find I had the kind of sore throat I knew could only get worse. Once I had collected the morning 'tea' I sought out the boys I had so loyally followed into this hellhole.

'My throat hurts,' I complained. Even as I was saying it, I knew I sounded like a child.

'Why don't you report it?' one asked, rather indifferently.

'You should have stayed in the hospital,' the other added.

Something snapped inside me then. I realized what a damn fool I'd been, and turned away.

One morning, we heard that our officers were leaving their separate accommodation en route to an Oflag.

We rushed out to give them a defiant send-off, shouting, 'Long live our officers!'

Then both groups – those of us crowding against the barbed wire inside the compound and the officers lined up in a column outside – started singing '*Siekiera, motyka*'. It was set to a familiar old folk tune that had carried many lyrics in its time, and had become one of the Uprising's most popular songs.

'Forward march!' ordered the German guard.

Still singing, off they went towards the station and their train to Bavaria.

Once I got used to the smell and the lice, and it was surprising how soon you did, I settled into the camp's routine. This mostly involved being bored, cold and hungry – though not always at the same time. There seemed to be a surfeit of labour, or perhaps we were not yet regarded as trustworthy enough to go out on an *Arbeitskommando* that might involve us working in a factory or unloading an ammunition train (the latter, strictly speaking, being against the Geneva Convention because it was aiding the enemy's war effort). A much-sought-after local work detail was peeling potatoes in the barracks of the German guards, because it gave you the opportunity to supplement your own rations by stealing a few.

We were all too aware that there were people worse off than ourselves. Our immediate neighbours, separated by a tall barbed-wire fence with its own watchtowers, were the penal company. This was the compound where you were sent if you had tried to escape or had misbehaved in some minor way on an outside work party. Most of the time they were locked in freezing cells, and their rations made ours look generous. But once a day, wearing the crude wooden clogs that had replaced their boots, they were permitted to shuffle around the perimeter wire. Sometimes we were able to speak to them. Once, I even attempted to trade cigarettes for a Russian prisoner's leather belt that I needed to keep my newly acquired American trousers in place.

'I'll throw the pack near the latrine,' I shouted to him, blithely disregarding the guard in a nearby tower who had obviously seen us talking but was doing nothing about it.

Then I heard the distinctive clicking sounds of a cartridge being fed into the firing chamber of a bolt-action rifle, and looked up to see a captured Lebel pointing at me.

'You son of a whore!' announced its owner in fluent Polish. 'Throw anything and I'll shoot.'

I walked back towards the stable, vowing vengeance on all *Volksdeutsche* who had betrayed their county. Most of the guards, Polish speaking or not, were easy-going and closed their eyes to petty violations.

When, at last, I got on to the potato-peeling detail a benevolent German cook allowed me to smuggle some out down my trouser legs, which were gathered at the ankle by cloth leggings. But while we were being marched back to camp, disaster struck. One of my leggings unravelled, leaving a trail of potatoes in my wake. I might have been charged with theft and ended up in the penal company. Instead, one of our Wehrmacht escort nonchalantly kicked the evidence into the gutter.

Even so, their loss was a blow. An extra potato with your evening meal was something to look forward to. As it happened, the following day several food packages arrived from Poland. I was one of the lucky ones: Kraków was still within range of the *Kriegsgefangenenpost* and Ada had not forgotten me. It turned out that this would be the last package I would receive from her.

Like the Germans in the Ardennes, the Soviets had also decided they would not wait for the spring thaw. Within days of the arrival of that package, Marshal Zhukov began a major offensive. In the space of three weeks the Red Army had not only liberated Kraków, the Auschwitz concentration camp and Warsaw, where a few survivors were discovered hiding out in its ruins, but had also established a bridgehead on the west bank of the River Oder. They were now only seventy kilometres from Berlin, and the roads into Germany were clogged with fleeing *Volksdeutsche*.

Prisoners of war from long-established camps in Poland were being herded westwards, through snow and slush, in what became dreadful death marches. Some of them were bound for Stalag XI-A, where a certain amount of reorganization would be required.

One morning, when Unteroffizier Jerke was reading out a list of Polish names, I heard my own among them. There were about sixty of us in all – just under half the number sleeping in our crowded stable.

'Nothing to worry about,' Jerke assured us. 'You're going to the camp annex, seven kilometres from here. Much better accommodation.'

Of course we did worry. Had their declining fortunes persuaded the Germans to change their minds? Were they going to take the troublesome *Banditen* in batches to some lonely wood and dispose of us with a shot in the back of the head?

It had snowed the day before we marched out of the camp, and much of it had turned into slush. There was a bitter wind and, since some of the smokers had traded their Red Cross greatcoats for cigarettes, several of the men were lucky if they still had the civilian overcoats they had been wearing when they left Warsaw. Our escort was composed of four tired-looking middle-aged soldiers who seemed to find the going as hard as we did.

At one point we passed some young women walking to work in a local factory. We usually referred to them as 'slave labour girls', but they were chattering away to each other and didn't seem particularly unhappy. The Nazis required them to wear identifying patches on their clothing, like Jews: Polish girls wore yellow and blue ones with the letter 'P'; the girls from the USSR, mostly blonde Ukrainians who had not been all that unwilling to go to Germany, wore patches that simply declared them to be 'OST'. East was where the *Untermenschen* lived. Some of our party shouted various ribald remarks at the girls, who either ignored them or answered in kind.

Once we were outside Altengrabow's town limits, we saw little else of interest as we trudged through a barren landscape of leafless trees set against a grey winter sky. At one point I thought of discarding some of the fairly useless objects, among them a leather map case, which I had acquired through my various bartering operations. But after nearly two hours, I arrived with my bundle intact at a collection of small wooden barracks on a windswept hill.

For some unknown reason the camp was called Heilbronn –

presumably after the town of that name in the Stuttgart region, over 400 kilometres to the south-west. As we entered its gates some prisoners shouted a welcome. French, Dutch and Russians predominated, but there was a contingent of Home Army Poles who appeared well ensconced and not unhappy with the conditions. Accommodation was arranged by nationality, but outside our barracks we could mix with each other as much as we liked.

Every morning a French bugler called reveille and we paraded in ranks of five for the ritual of the daily counting. The camp commander was a one-armed colonel wearing a coat with a fur collar. When he appeared, various national commands rang out.

*Garde-à-vous!*

*Smirno!*

*Baczność!*

The colonel then greeted each contingent with his left arm raised in the salute he was required to use to demonstrate his undying loyalty to the Führer. There were millions of enslaved people in the Reich, and half of Europe lay in ruins, but amidst this small cluster of wooden huts near a small town in Germany all military courtesies between captives and captors were punctiliously observed. It was as ludicrous as it was reassuring.

We had wood for our stove more frequently than in the converted stables of the main camp, and were considerably warmer. Even so, I had trouble with my throat again. I saw a French doctor who arranged that I would be excused the frosty air of the early-morning parades until my throat was better. Listening to the multilingual commands outside, I relished every second of those extra few minutes when I could remain in bed in the rare solitude of an empty barrack room. I had been brought up as an only child – my half-brother, Jerzy, was a very recent addition to my life – and so I was accustomed to a certain space and, I suppose, not always ideal material for communal living.

Once again, I did not have to look far to see people who were far worse off than myself. Without Red Cross packages, the Russians were periodically visited by officers of the collaborationist Vlasov Army trying to recruit them. Those who joined were given food, cigarettes and warm uniforms. Those who refused were sent back to their barracks to await a liberation overshadowed by the prospect of a forced labour camp as a punishment for having surrendered in the first place. Nonetheless, some of them remained remarkably cheerful. In exchange for cigarettes and food they performed a variety of chores for their better-off allies. They cleaned our latrines, washed our laundry and swept our barracks. And on the days when our Red Cross lifesavers arrived, Russian accordion players would turn up to entertain us. Normally they started with the cheerful, foot-stomping '*Katyusha*', probably the Red Army's best-known song about a girl dreaming of her soldier lover on the banks of a river. They almost always ended with '*Chubchik*', a plaintive refrain about having no dread of Siberia 'because it is also Russian soil'. And as they played, a cap would be passed around and we would temporarily forget about our old quarrel with their masters and drop some cigarettes in it.

I spent a lot of my time with the French prisoners, and there was no doubt that my French was getting better. In their barrack rooms I learned the songs they called *chansons de salle de garde*, a dirty but melodious repertoire. Soon I could join them when they broke into a ditty concerning *petite Amélie* who somehow lost all her pubic hair while making a carpet. One of my new French friends introduced me to one of his prized possessions: a book of coloured pornographic drawings. Hot with the memory of them, I took myself off behind the latrine to masturbate, anxiously glancing around me as I did so.

Out on a wood-gathering detail, picking up fallen branches for our stove, we met up with some American prisoners who were also scavenging for wood. They were from the main camp, dressed in waterproof jackets with zippers, and wearing the woollen hats they called 'beanies' or 'jeep caps'. Somehow they didn't look like other soldiers.

'Goddam Polacks,' one of them muttered as our two groups passed each other, each pushing a kind of pram for the wood.

I would learn that, for Americans, all other nationalities were 'goddam' whatever they were, and no great offence was intended.

We discovered that large numbers of captives from the Battle of the Bulge were arriving at Stalag XI-A. Some of them were hardly three months out of America, and the change in their circumstances had come as something of a shock. The French called them *hommes-machines* and gloated that, once these robots lost their creature comforts, they collapsed. But then the Americans were not all that admiring of the French either.

I thought about this and reflected on my own feelings about the various nationalities represented in the camp. My knowledge of their language made me feel most at ease with the French – no doubt about that – but I respected the British for their courtesy and neat appearance, exchanged friendly greetings with the Belgians and the Dutch, cracked jokes with the Yugoslavs and communicated easily with the Russians.

The GIs were a bit of an enigma. They frowned at the American uniforms supplied via the Red Cross and seemed to blame the lot of us for getting them into this goddam European mess in the first place.

And who could blame them?

Early in March, my number was posted on the bulletin board along with others who were scheduled to go back to the main camp. No reason was given. Our small group marched ankle deep in the melting snow, lifting our faces to catch the first shy rays of sun. When we reached the camp, we had to wait at the offices just inside the main gates before being taken to our various compounds.

'Two thousand Russians came in last night,' one of the French captives working in administration told me. 'The Red Army is moving fast. They're evacuating entire camps from the east – *à pied, mon petit!*'

As he spoke, Pawlak the boxer and elected chief of the Warsaw prisoners, turned up.

'You speak French?' he asked. 'What about German? How old are you? Sixteen? Don't worry, you'll be my interpreter. That'll keep you off ammunition train details.'

This time, the Warsaw contingent was housed in a different stable, in the centre of the camp, and was allowed to move everywhere. I was allotted a bunk in the top layer, one of the perks of my privileged position as the chief's official interpreter. Among my tasks was liaising with the French kitchen staff and, whenever Unteroffizier Jerke was not around, relaying various German demands. By then the prisoners looked almost prosperous; most wore American uniforms and khaki shirts that had recently arrived from the International Red Cross. Overcoats were stencilled on the back in thick white paint, impossible to remove, with the usual 'KG' for *Kriegsgefangener* (prisoner of war). In cold weather this was meant to deter escape – something most people didn't even consider, with the front line creeping nearer every day and the shrinking German territory packed with retreating troops and security services.

But when some British prisoners managed to get away, apparently before reaching the camp, all national groups were summoned on parade. Guards with fierce-looking dogs on short leashes walked along the ranks, counting the prisoners time and time again. The camp Kommandant himself turned up and made a fierce speech saying that the Wehrmacht was encircling the British and American armies and that he was ashamed to be in charge of a prisoner-of-war camp when he should be back at the front, ready to die for the Fatherland. Those few prisoners who understood what he was saying cheered.

More Russians arrived and were put under tents on the sports field. That same night, two were found trying to break into the kitchen stores. They were hanged from a makeshift gallows erected on the main parade ground.

Polish-speaking Americans started visiting our compound. In an antiquated, peasant Polish learned from their immigrant parents or grandparents they assured us that America was the best place on the planet: 'Verily thou shalt see how bountiful it is.'

We tried to keep a straight face. As for visiting America, that depended on the fortunes of war. If the Russians arrived at Stalag XI-A first, the Polish contingent was likely to be heading in an easterly direction, whether they wanted to or not. But my immediate future looked rosy enough. Prisoners sought my favour as Pawlak's interpreter and confidant.

'Stick with me,' said the former professional boxer. 'We'll get out of this shithouse yet.'

By camp standards I was affluent. A backlog of Red Cross packages had yielded 600 cigarettes, and I owned two uniforms – one British and the other American. And the Red Cross had delivered another present to me.

It had arrived at the hospital a week or so after I had left and been forwarded to the main camp, only to find I had moved to the Heil-bronn annex. It arrived there just after my recent return to Stalag XI-A, where it finally caught up with me. It was my first official notification that my mother, half-brother, grandmother and aunt were alive and well and staying in the convent at Pruszków. It was dated just a few days before Zhukov started the offensive that would take his forces across the Vistula, liberate the mostly empty ruins of Warsaw and pursue the Wehrmacht's transport, with all the bags of *Kriegsgefangenenpost* they could still be bothered to carry, up to the Prussian border.

Official communiqués spoke of 'strategic realignment' but the truth was obvious: German-controlled territory was shrinking by the day, and what was left of it was filled with the remnants of an army who had known almost nothing but retreat for over two years, mixed with civilian refugees and thousands of prisoners evacuated from Poland, East Prussia and Czechoslovakia.

Would the Germans surrender, or would they fight to the last man? And what would happen to us?

'They'll gas us,' predicted the pessimists. 'They won't have enough food to go round.'

Meanwhile, between ping-pong, card games and choir singing, camp life continued. A big man was accused of cheating at cards. High rollers might sometimes bet a whole pack of cigarettes on a single hand. A hastily formed tribunal heard the evidence against him and he was sentenced to twenty lashes. It took three men to remove his trousers and pin him down, and two others to flog him with alternate strokes of a leather belt.

'I beg you! I promise!' he pleaded.

But there was no mercy.

'Remember, never cheat at cards,' Pawlak told me as we watched the punishment. My mentor had joined the pessimists and was becoming increasingly concerned about our immediate future.

'These are the last weeks of the war,' he said. 'Do you think they will continue feeding us? What will happen to our Red Cross packages, if the Allies occupy the roads from Switzerland?'

It was shortly after this that he came up with a solution.

'I told you I would get you out alive. So listen to this.'

One of his contacts was a prisoner who worked in the *Kartei*, the records department, and through him Pawlak had learned of what sounded like the ultimate *Arbeitskommando*. A *Rittergut* – an aristocratic estate – needed fifteen prisoners as farmhands. It was run by an old countess and her two daughters, who were reputed to be very fair employers. Even better, it was situated a good 100 kilometres to the north-west of us, where we were much more likely to be liberated by the Americans or the British rather than the Russians.

'We'll have to work in the fields, but we will fake it,' said Pawlak. 'At least we won't starve. All we have to do is gather together a congenial group. Don't say anything about it; I will organize everything. Think about it: the smell of the countryside in spring, the flowers, the birds, the tinkling of the cowbells.'

For a moment I thought he might be joking, but he wasn't.

# 32.  Spring 1945

We assembled at dusk the following day. All of us had known each other from the camp and some of us had been together in the Uprising. I was the youngest and Pawlak, who was nearing forty, was the oldest. Most were in their early to mid-twenties. The only one of us who might have had any experience of agricultural labour was a forest partisan from the eastern part of Poland who had somehow survived capture. The rest of us were all from Warsaw, and I guessed that four of our number might come from my own kind of background.

The camp's *homme de confiance*, a burly old prisoner, carefully checked our names and numbers against his list, and then handed the fifteen of us our parting gifts: five large Red Cross packages, a football and two pairs of boxing gloves that had newly arrived from Geneva. The International Committee of the Red Cross obviously suspected that prisoners of war had a lot of pent-up energy to expend.

We were marched to the guard post near the main gate where prisoners assigned to other *Arbeitskommandos* awaited. There were a dozen Frenchmen and a small group of Russians. Our escort was made up of three of the usual old soldiers, carrying captured Lebels, commanded by a bespectacled lance corporal who seemed to have a bit of a limp. Our initial destination was a railway station near Dessau, some forty kilometres away, where we were to board trains to our various destinations. It was intended that we would walk there, an overnight trek expected to take us about ten hours.

Even with kitbags crammed with our latest Red Cross munificence, most of us were much more capable of making this march than were the soldiers in our escort. With twenty cigarettes to share among his small command and another pack for any driver willing to take us, the lance corporal agreed it made sense to try to hitchhike. We were lucky. The first approaching truck he stopped with a brief blackout-breaking wave of his torch was empty, big enough for all of us, and the driver was grateful for the fare. Like almost all German motor transport at this stage of the war, when fuel was reserved for aircraft and tanks, his vehicle was powered by a large Holzgas cylinder fitted behind the cab.

We passed through silent and blacked-out towns and villages. Sometimes, looming out of the darkness, the bobbing lights of a checkpoint indicated a chicane of east-facing concrete anti-tank obstacles that brought us to a halt. They were almost invariably manned by the home guard, known as the '*Volkssturm*' – old men whose ranks were often stiffened by aggressive Hitler Youth my own age or even younger. Some enjoyed shining their inquiring torches into our sleepy faces, but they always waved us on.

Not surprisingly, hours before schedule, we arrived at our rail point: a large marshalling yard near a sprawling station building. Somewhere nearby a locomotive could be heard building up steam and we noticed anti-aircraft guns in position. The guards spoke to some railway employees, then we were herded into an empty carriage standing on a siding. More cigarettes were exchanged and one of the railway men delivered an enamelled bucket filled with beer and several mugs. We sipped the tepid liquid with a sense of comparative well-being. This was the first time I remember thinking that perhaps leaving the hospital had not been such a bad idea after all.

I managed to find an empty corner in one compartment. But almost as soon as I had closed my eyes, an air-raid siren started up. I decided it was probably a general alert that enemy aircraft were passing overhead, bound for Berlin or some other major city, and did my best to get back to sleep. Then the anti-aircraft guns we had noticed on arrival started firing. Next, through the half-opened window of the compartment, we heard the massive roar of low-flying planes. A flash lit up the compartment followed by the noise of exploding bombs.

Had I really survived the Warsaw Uprising in order to be killed by the RAF?

I lay down on the dirty floor and put my head under the wooden bench. Flashes and bangs now came at regular intervals. The carriage quaked. From my prone position I noticed that four of the Russian prisoners were huddled together near the window, apparently oblivious to the air raid, muttering to each other. They had pulled out a small drinks table that was folded against the side of the carriage.

'Ace of spades,' I heard one of them say.

'Your deal.'

Cards were shuffled on the folding table. For the first time I realized what they were doing: the players were waiting for the light of another explosion to illuminate their hands. It was so incongruous that I lifted my head to watch, mesmerized by this weird scene.

One of them, a young man in a round peaked cap, noticed me. 'Well, little Pole,' he said cheerfully. 'Are you afraid to die?'

Just then another explosion ripped through the air and its brief light allowed the players to resume their game.

I sprang to my feet. I wasn't going to give a Russian any cause to accuse a Pole of cowardice. For the rest of the raid I remained glued to my corner, holding the bench with both hands (for all the good that would have done). Eventually, the explosions stopped and after a while the sirens sounded an all-clear. I breathed a sigh of relief.

But the Russians were unhappy. Deprived of illumination, their game had come to an abrupt end. One of them collected the pack, and soon all four of them were snoring their heads off, disregarding the distant noise of fire engines.

Before long, I was asleep myself.

'*Aufstehen! Aufstehen!*'

Most of us woke to the German command to get up. Parts of the grey dawn were still aglow after the night's raid. The guards straightened out the folds of their greatcoats and adjusted their *Gott mit uns* belt buckles. We followed them silently on to the platform, where we were divided into our national groups. The first commuters started appearing: women in headscarves, elderly men with battered briefcases, a uniformed figure or two. A chill breeze carried the smell of cinders. It reminded me of Warsaw.

The first train rolled in and we were told to sit in the same compartments as the civilians. The passengers paid little attention to the prisoners in their American and British greatcoats with 'KG' stamped on the back. Obviously we were a familiar sight. The commuter train seemed to stop every five minutes for more of the same shabby passengers, worn down by five years of war, to get on. There was little talk. Someone, almost casually, mentioned the previous night's air raid.

A man talked about his meat ration for a week. 'It wasn't even real sausage, it tasted like cardboard. *Ach, du lieber Gott.*'

We emerged from the train at a big station and were shocked by what we saw. All around us were skeletons of buildings, some smudged by recent fires. Blackened chimneys protruded from the wreckage. Nothing seemed to be intact.

'That's Hitler's Germany,' one of the prisoners said, carefully keeping his voice low.

'What is this town, Herr Wachmann?' I asked the bespectacled lance corporal in charge of us.

'Magdeburg,' he replied, adding the obvious, '*kaputt.*' This was followed by, '*Deutschland kaputt.*'

While he was saying this, he was smoking one of the American cigarettes we had given him. Magdeburg, an old city founded by Charlemagne, was a target for Allied bombing because it contained one of Nazi Germany's biggest synthetic fuel plants, extracting oil from lignite coal.

We were separated from the Russians and the French here and put on another crowded train, this time heading north-west. Most of Pawlak's group had to stand in the corridor among civilians wearing 'OST' or 'P' labels who were not inclined to fraternize with us. The Germans, mostly elderly, were also quiet – as were a few soldiers, presumably on leave. I had the feeling that the sight of ancient Magdeburg in ruins had depressed all of them.

The train stopped at every station, discharging passengers and picking up new ones. A little sunshine managed to pierce the clouds and the mood inside our car seemed to improve. A tall soldier wearing the ribbon of the Iron Cross and puffing at a pipe stood near an empty seat. I sat down and tried to get some more sleep.

'Why are you letting that prisoner sit while you're standing?' someone shouted to the soldier in a shrill, authoritative voice.

I looked up. A young man in a black SS uniform was glaring at me but was clearly addressing the soldier, who slowly removed his pipe.

'You fight your war,' he said, 'and I'll fight mine.'

The SS man didn't reply.

Obviously I had to do something. I couldn't remain seated while a decorated member of the master race was standing. At that point the train halted and a young woman got in, possibly pregnant. With a sigh of relief I jumped to my feet and offered her my seat. The soldier with the pipe looked at me and winked.

Soon the day became gloriously sunny. The train spent interminable hours waiting at sidings or simply idling in the middle of nowhere, amidst lush green fields dotted with early spring flowers. The passengers used these stops to leave the carriages and stretch their legs, or simply to enjoy the smells of spring. The guards didn't object to their charges doing the same. I found the whole thing incongruous. Here I was, in my khaki British battledress, sitting on a grassy knoll next to Hitler Youth and soldiers whom I would have shot on sight just six months earlier. Yet no one displayed the slightest curiosity about my background.

'Why are we waiting?' I asked one of their guards.

'Air raids,' he said.

I noticed that the first part of the train was a flatbed wagon transporting an anti-aircraft gun. Its crew did not descend to enjoy the spring grass. Behind the wagon was the locomotive itself, prominently displaying the slogan of the early war years: 'The wheels must roll towards victory.'

It was mid-afternoon when we disembarked at a country railway station with our Red Cross packages, football and boxing gloves. The lance corporal counted us all and then handed a piece of paper to a younger, taller soldier with a ruddy face and cold blue eyes.

'This is Corporal Meier, who will be your guard from now on,' he said. 'I'm leaving you here. Good luck. And don't try to escape – there's no point.'

Indeed, at the rate the western front was moving, the Americans or British were bound to reach us soon, I thought.

'You are in my charge now,' our new guard informed us, without

bothering to ask whether we understood German. He was a tall man
with the flushed features that often denote high blood pressure. 'If
you behave correctly, I will behave correctly. But I will not tolerate
any insolence. You are here to work and I'm going to make sure that
you work well. *Verstanden*?' Then, almost as an afterthought, he
added, 'I'm familiar with the Poles. I was your prisoner in 1939. Not
for very long, of course.'

'This is not going to be fun,' someone mumbled.

We filed out of the station building. A long horse-drawn cart on
rubber tires was waiting for us outside. The driver was a young man
with unruly flaxen-coloured hair and a 'P' badge on his sweater that
indicated he was a compatriot. He mumbled something that might
have been a greeting as we loaded our gear on board and climbed on.
The guard sat in the back of the carriage, facing us.

'*Wio!*' shouted the young driver, in the tradition of Polish peasants, and the horse jerked the carriage forward.

The town, which was called Falkenberg, was neat and clean with
little traffic of any kind. Beyond it, as far as the eye could see, stretched
brown and green fields as orderly as chessboards. Slave labourers,
both male and female, worked alongside the road. Some seemed to
recognize our uniforms and gave us a timid wave.

'Let's sing and show those slaves that we're not cowed,' ordered
Pawlak, suddenly asserting his leadership.

I noticed the expression of total dislike on the guard's face whenever Pawlak spoke. But the German did not object when we struck
up an old partisan anthem about delivering freedom at the points of
our bayonets.

If I say so myself, we had good voices and harmonized well. We
were still singing at the end of our half-hour ride, when we reached
a huge farmhouse surrounded by a thick wall and came to a halt in
the middle of its yard. Curious faces peered out at us from the barns
and the windows of the living quarters. As we got off the cart we saw
two attractive young women walking briskly in our direction. One
was blonde and the other dark.

'A perfect combination,' said an awed voice behind me.

We stood in a semi-circle, waiting while the guard reported to the women. By then a number of curious slave labourers – of both sexes and looking reasonably prosperous – had gathered in the rectangular courtyard. Several wore the remnants of Soviet uniforms, but there were also Frenchmen, some of whom wore the large berets of the *Chasseurs Alpins*.

We were objects of great curiosity. In our brand-new uniforms, carrying a football and boxing gloves, we looked more like some sort of sports club on a weekend outing than a prisoner-of-war working party reporting for hard labour.

'Do all of you understand German?'

It was the blonde woman who spoke. Like her sister she wore a simple dress and ordinary farm boots, but there was an air of elegance about both of the women.

'Try her in French,' Pawlak told me out of the corner of his mouth.

I did so, making sure I used the accent for which I had recently been complimented by many of my new French friends in the Stalag.

The woman smiled and replied in German that she used to speak French but had forgotten most of it.

Pawlak then nudged Preibisz, a young man with a delicate profile, who was the group's only English speaker. There were some embarrassed smiles from both women.

The dark-haired one said she spoke a little English, then demanded, 'Don't any of you speak any German at all?'

'*Natürlich. Wir sprechen Deutsch,*' some of us answered gallantly.

The two women – who were the daughters of the grand lady Pawlak had been told about by his friend in records, back at Stalag XI-A, and therefore countesses in their own right – eyed each other in apparent confusion. These polyglot prisoners, several of them younger than any the women had seen before, were unusual – to say the least.

The blonde countess explained in German that we were to be housed in a wooden barrack, and she pointed in its direction. Each of us would receive a blanket, food would be issued every other day, and one prisoner would be appointed as the cook and thus released from other work. The guard would count us twice a day and escort a detachment of five who would work at a neighbouring farm.

'And by the way,' she added, 'you will leave your boots in the kitchen every night. And the sleeping area will be locked. Any questions?'

'Will someone please tell her that, according to the Geneva Convention, we should be getting two blankets,' said Pawlak, who understood quite a lot of German but was shy about speaking it.

Seizing my chance, I translated his words – though my German was not as good as my French.

There was some hasty consultation between the two women. I saw one of them glance at the guard, who looked like he was longing to put this cocky crowd of barrack-room lawyers in their place, but he didn't say anything.

'A second blanket for each of you will be arranged,' said the dark-haired sister.

We had won our first round – and on a bluff. It seemed that nobody at the *Rittergut* had read the Geneva Convention. We certainly hadn't.

Next day, our first in Falkenberg, was a Sunday and a day off – even for slave labourers and prisoners of war. What seemed like a vast amount of food, including fresh vegetables, was delivered to us. The man who brought them revealed that the old countess herself – known to the French prisoners as the *Comtesse Noire*, because she always wore black – had referred to us as the '*Studenten aus Warschau*' and given orders that we were to be well fed. He also told us that both daughters were married but their husbands were away in the army, adding in a whisper, '*Ostfront.*'

It was odd to think that what, for years, had been the most terrifying prospect for the average adult German male was now only a couple of hours' drive away. The way things were going, the *Rittergut*'s missing menfolk would soon be able to commute to work.

Our prison hut consisted of two rooms: one was the sleeping quarters and the other a kitchen with a dining table. The tiny compound had a small area surrounded by barbed wire where we could stretch our legs after dinner before bedding down for the night – minus the boots that we left in the kitchen. Corporal Meier, the guard, then counted the prisoners, checked that the number of pairs of boots corresponded, and locked the door leading to the kitchen.

For those taken short there was a bucket to piss in. No separate provision was made for nocturnal attacks of diarrhoea, but on our improved diet this seemed unlikely.

Meier assembled us and explained how we were to organize ourselves. We would elect one man as our cook. That was easy. Marian was a tall young man with a flashing smile who had been training to be a chef in one of Warsaw's top hotels before the war interrupted his apprenticeship. The remaining fourteen would be divided into two groups. Nine would work at the *Rittergut* alongside Polish and Ukrainian civilians and French and Russian prisoners of war. The remaining five would labour on a neighbouring farm. Meier selected this smaller working party there and then. Among them were Pawlak and myself.

After Meier had left, one of the French prisoners commiserated with us. He explained that working on the farm of the kindly *Comtesse Noire* was the best *Arbeitskommando* you could possibly imagine. Even male Russian prisoners thrived there. Everybody was so happy, the Germans hardly bothered to guard them. The work was easy and there were enough Russian and Polish women around to make it unnecessary to '*se branler*'. I remember being rather proud that I understood the French for 'masturbate'.

But apparently the other farm was a very different proposition. The farmer was '*un salaud*'. He beat his slave labourers with a stick. The bastard even manhandled prisoners of war. One prisoner had died while working there. The Frenchman advised us to be very careful how we behaved there. It was obvious that Meier had selected Pawlak for this farm because he wanted to bring him down a peg or two – especially after the blankets business. I could only suppose that I had been included because I was perceived to be his right-hand man.

Next morning, we rose at 5.30. The day was cool and grey. Marian was already up and brewing the ersatz tea with which we would wash down our breakfast of bread and margarine. Then Pawlak assembled us in the small space where the barbed wire separated our compound from the rest of the farmyard, ready for the traditional Polish morning parade with prayers. Meier stood erect in freshly polished boots, with his rifle slung from his right shoulder, and waited until we had finished.

He announced that all those who were working at the *Rittergut* would be collected by the foreman. 'The other five follow me.'

With our solitary escort at the rear we went along the road in single file. I was the last, immediately in front of the German.

'Hey, Fifi,' I suddenly heard.

Fifi had become my nickname among Pawlak's group of late, based on my ability to speak French and on my youth. Now Meier was using it to attract my attention and whispering to me as we neared our destination.

'Watch out what you do here,' he was saying. 'If you work well, the man cannot harm you. If you don't work well, or try sabotage, no one will be able to help you, and you will end up in a Penal Company.'

'*Danke schön*,' I said, and I meant it. I was touched that this stiff and apparently humourless man was concerned for my welfare. I seemed to be discovering more and more 'good' Germans.

The notorious farmer awaited us in front of his main barn. His name was Holzer. He was a burly man with an apoplectic face, wearing a leather jacket and leather puttees, with a cloth cap on his head. True to the Frenchman's description, he clutched a walking stick of impressive proportions.

He glared at us. 'They look like a lazy bunch to me,' he snorted to Meier, '*Jawohl, eine faule Bande.*'

But Meier said nothing, simply clicked his heels and left without a word.

'Have any of you ever worked on a farm before?' Holzer rasped out. When we all admitted that none of us had had the pleasure, he nodded grimly to himself. 'I thought so, a lazy band.'

Holzer's foreman was a Pole – either conscripted for forced labour or a volunteer lured by the prospect of higher pay, and perhaps an easier life, than in occupied Poland. I remembered the German posters depicting smiling people waving from train windows and its caption: 'We're going to work in Germany!' We never missed an opportunity to tear them down. In Falkenberg you could sometimes distinguish the volunteers from the conscripts by what they were wearing and eating, but it wasn't always easy.

On Holzer's farm there were already a dozen workers. Most of them were Poles and Russians, among the latter a middle-aged couple said to be former schoolteachers. They kept to themselves, determined to survive the war with a minimum of fuss. According to gossip, they had volunteered for Germany and had no intention of going back to the Soviet Union. There were also two young German women and the newly arrived 'lazy band' from Warsaw.

The Poles were peasants who knew farm work and, above all, knew how to keep out of Holzer's way. But from the beginning there was friction between us and Holzer. No matter what we did, he screamed and hit the ground with his cane. When we invoked the Geneva Convention, he screamed louder.

'Stop fighting the old man,' one of the Poles advised us on the second day. 'It won't get you anywhere.'

Haughtily we replied that we weren't slaves but prisoners of war, and we weren't going to be cowed by any German. The peasant shrugged and went about his work.

We soon discovered that our work was hardly the bucolic idyll Pawlak had dreamed of in the Stalag. I planted potatoes, my back painfully bent – unlike the Polish females working alongside me, who somehow contrived to do it in a seemingly effortless rhythm. I helped clean the cow shed, gagging at a bovine odour that was so different from my childhood memories of the cavalry stables at Kielce barracks. Nothing came easy – and, above all, it was boring – but I was careful to avoid any reason to be accused of sabotage.

At noon we were collected by Meier. He marched us back to our compound for lunch, prepared by Marian. At 2 p.m. we were back at the farm for another four hours. At the end of the day we were exhausted and envious of our nine colleagues – who spoke of an undemanding routine, under a benevolent German supervisor, with occasional visits from one of the two countesses.

Meier continued to behave correctly, though he had a few verbal clashes with Pawlak. The antipathy between the two men was obvious.

'When the Americans come, I will personally hang that bastard from a tree,' our chief promised.

My own relationship with Meier was considerably enhanced by a trip I had to make to see a doctor in the nearby town of Seehausen. I had shown our guard an angry boil under my left armpit, and the following day he escorted me the seven kilometres to Seehausen to have it lanced.

The spring day was sunny and pleasant. Guard and prisoner chatted amiably as we walked along the side of the road, me the regulation two paces ahead of the rifle-carrying German.

'Not too fast, Fifi,' he admonished me on several occasions.

It was obvious that he wanted to take his time and enjoy the weather.

After the lancing – which was very painful because the elderly doctor had run out of local anaesthetic – Meier went to a butcher's shop to collect his week's meat ration. Instead of heading towards the farm, we sat on the grass near a bridge while he unwrapped various small bits and pieces: liverwurst, a chunk of pork and what looked and smelled like garlic sausage. Magnanimously he offered me a piece of the liver sausage on the point of his penknife.

'Eat,' he said to me in Polish.

I was surprised. 'I didn't know you spoke my language?'

'Old Meier is not so dumb, don't you worry,' he said, chewing and looking thoroughly pleased with himself.

I remembered my encounters back at the Stalag with the almost bilingual German- and Polish-speaking guards from the disputed Silesian borderlands. Had he been secretly privy to all our conversations, our fantasies about the looming post-war dismemberment of Germany? Pawlak's promises to hang him when the Americans came? But when he continued to demonstrate his Polish, it became obvious that it was very limited.

'Left, right, halt, advance . . . not bad, *nein*?'

It was no more than the few words he had picked up when he had been captured in the opening days of Germany's invasion of Poland, in 1939. 'I was not a prisoner for long, not even a week. Then our Panzers came and Poland was *kaputt*.'

For a moment I was tempted to say that now Germany was '*kaputt*', but I thought better of it. Anyway, it wasn't necessary.

'I know what you're thinking, Fifi. You're thinking, "Now Germany is *kaputt*." But you're wrong. Hitler and National Socialism will be defeated, *jawohl*. But Germany is too powerful to disappear from the map of Europe –'

'But look at your cities, all bombed out,' I interrupted, emboldened by his admission that Hitler was done for. 'Look at the destroyed factories and the number of dead you've suffered. And the damage you inflicted on your enemies. Do you think the Russians will leave Germany intact after this war?'

'The Russians don't matter,' he said. 'They're barbarians – I know, I spent two years on the *Ostfront* – and mark my words: sooner or later the Americans and the English will be at war with Russia. Then they will need Germany! And in a few years' time, the cities and factories that have been destroyed will be rebuilt by German genius and hard work. Never underestimate the Germans, Fifi! On the other hand, you belong to a small country squeezed between big powers. *Ein kleines Grenzland* – a small frontier country. Either the Russians will absorb you or a new, reborn Germany will. After this war, there will be no room for small nations. Only the big and strong will survive.'

'We're not small,' I protested. 'We had thirty-six million people before the war.'

'*Kwatsch*, Fifi,' said Meier calmly, wiping his penknife on the grass. 'Out of these thirty-six million, four million were Jews, one million were Germans and at least five million Ukrainians.'

We marched back to the farm, still in the amiable manner in which we had set out. I couldn't bring myself to believe his dire predictions of the new world order. Yet I felt a lot of what he said made sense – particularly the prospect of a conflict between the Soviets and the western powers. Poland was already under Communist control, and only the Americans and the British could change that.

Would the West refuse to tolerate the presence of the Soviet army in the heart of Europe? Was that our best hope for the resurrection of a free and truly democratic Poland? Or would London and Washington decide that, rather than risk another war as bad as this one, they would allow a new political map to be drawn? After all, that's what the big powers had done in 1919, after another terrible war. But that peace settlement had lasted only twenty years.

Over dinner that evening my conversation with Meier became the subject of considerable discussion, particularly his image of a Poland sandwiched between two great powers and unlikely to survive. Most of my fellow Poles did not see Germany as an ally of the West in any conflict with Russia. One of the few to agree with Meier was Katra, usually a rather silent young man, who was said to be an explosives specialist.

'That guard of yours, Fifi, is not so stupid,' he said in one of his rare pronouncements. 'Let's not forget that Germany is closer to the West than we are. And in the event of a new war, our country would be useless to them except, perhaps, for guerrilla actions against Soviet lines of communication.'

The discussion went on late into the night, even after Meier had locked us up – minus, of course, our boots. We soon regarded this as an utterly pointless routine. Who would try escaping now? Allied armoured columns were rumoured to be only a few days away. Excited by the prospect of liberation, we sang some of our favourite songs long into the night.

The Germans might imagine themselves rising from the ashes but the Polish phoenix was almost airborne – at least, that was the way it seemed to us then, and there wasn't a strong drink in the house.

Come the dawn and it was still April 1945. Pawlak's team were still prisoners in the village of Falkenberg, in what was left of Nazi Germany, apparently required to work until the bitter end. As our expected liberation approached so a clash with farmer Holzer seemed inevitable.

It came when Holzer heaped invectives on Pawlak and a man they called 'Sambo', accusing them of sabotage. I wasn't present but, according to the version repeated by slave labourers, Pawlak grabbed a stick that happened to be handy and aimed it at the farmer while Sambo, who spoke German, shouted something about the Geneva Convention.

Crimson with fury, Holzer telephoned Meier at the *Rittergut* and demanded that these miscreants be taken away and punished for threatening a German.

The following morning, the two packed their bags and prepared to march fifteen kilometres to a town where there was a prison for such culprits. I was sorry to see Pawlak go, but it was unlikely that whatever punishment was meted out would last very long. The front drew closer every day; the military traffic on our nearest main road, both motorized and horse-drawn, had greatly increased in both directions.

We elected a tall man by the name of Durski as our new chief. He was a pre-war officer cadet with a slight speech defect who told surprisingly few war stories and was courteous to everybody. When Meier had not returned by nightfall from escorting our two rebels to whatever dungeon awaited them, we were faced with a dilemma: was it time to escape? The gate to our barbed-wire enclosure had been left unlocked to allow us access to the water pump. Why didn't we simply sneak out into the night?

'Our duty is to escape at the first available opportunity,' two or three of the group argued. 'Has there ever been a better opportunity? There is no guard!'

'As your commander, I forbid you to escape!' Durski shouted, his impediment causing him to slur his words slightly, as if he was drunk. 'In those uniforms you would be picked up within hours. The area is crawling with retreating troops who would not be kind to escaping prisoners. I suggest you calm down and obey orders.'

The debate was ended by the appearance of the two young countesses. With embarrassed smiles they explained that, since Meier would not be returning that night, they had orders to count the prisoners and lock up our boots. The scene was grotesque: thirteen men trooping to leave their boots in the kitchen while two pretty young women waited patiently, keys in hand.

'*Gute Nacht*,' they said politely as they left.

'We're not soldiers, we're women,' someone said in the darkness.

'Shut up! I'm in charge here,' snapped Durski.

Meier was back in the morning, and in a sombre mood. There was no greeting for 'Fifi' when he escorted me and the other two remaining members of the Holzer working party back to the farm for our afternoon shift. He explained that he would be collecting us an hour earlier that evening.

That night, we heard a lot of traffic noise on the highway, including the sounds of heavy engines. Nowadays Allied air supremacy was such that, whenever possible, the Wehrmacht always moved under cover of darkness.

The April evening was warm and, through the open window with its criss-crossing of barbed wire, we smelled spring. I had no more doubts: this spring was going to bring us our freedom, at least from the Germans. It would happen in a matter of days, perhaps even hours.

Pawlak's stratagem had been brilliant. He had got us out of a camp that was near the Russian Front to a place that was going to be liberated by the Americans. I hoped the old boxer was safe and that, wherever he'd been taken, some fanatical Nazi hadn't put a bullet in his head. If only he had kept his temper, he might still have been with us.

The following morning was sunny and bright. Birds warbled in the small park adjacent to the manor, and I noticed that some of the women workers had donned bright kerchiefs. There were some German soldiers and women in uniform at the farm's water pump. They had spent the night in the barn and were brushing straw off their uniforms. They stopped chatting when the prisoners appeared. Two dusty trucks were parked in the yard.

In the kitchen our cook, Marian, tore a leaf off the calendar we had been given by a French prisoner. It was 12 April 1945.

'Eight days to Hitler's birthday,' someone said.

'*Holzer Kommando, heraus!*' shouted Meier.

The three remaining members of Holzer's farm detail filed out. As usual, we marched in single file, followed by our guard. Several trucks and ambulances passed us, heading east – towards the Elbe and the Russians, but away from the Americans. An exceptionally subdued Holzer handed us over to the foreman, a Polish slave labourer, who assigned work details.

'Did you hear the guns at night?' asked the foreman, after Meier had left. 'You must have heard the guns,' he insisted. 'And look at that,' he said, pointing towards the sky in the north. 'Balloons.'

Excitedly we counted them: a row of eight barrage balloons sway-ing gently against a blue sky. We wondered why anybody would bother to put up such an obstacle in the middle of nowhere?

That day, I worked in the field near the road. I was with the Rus-sian couple and a handsome, buxom German girl called Anna-Lisa. In bed at night I had frequently thought of Anna-Lisa, with her dark hair, her smooth cheeks and the breasts that even her loose work clothes failed to hide. I wondered if there was going to be a mad orgy of sex after the liberation. And, if so, whether Anna-Lisa might like to join in?

As the day progressed, we were given jobs closer to the main build-ing. The road outside the Holzer farm became more interesting: almost all the traffic was heading east, away from the Americans. At first, it was mostly obvious rear-echelon vehicles: officers in crowded Mercedes cars, hooting to get past overladen horse carts and trucks. Then the combat units also began to appear. First came tanks, covered in leafy branches, with their black-uniformed commanders glancing skywards from their open turrets. Then, much to my amazement, they were followed by a reconnaissance company mounted on bicycles – a remarkable anachronism in this sixth year of mid-twentieth-century warfare, and presumably yet another desperate measure to circumvent fuel shortages. Then an infantry unit virtu-ally took over the road. The soldiers were young – some may have been even younger than myself – and they had no helmets. Some car-ried *Panzerfaust* anti-tank rockets. They started blowing kisses at Anna-Lisa, who waved at them.

They answered this with whistles and shouts of, '*Komm mit uns, Schwarze.*'

'No, thank you,' she shouted back. 'I'm staying here.'

'She's waiting for the Americans,' said one of them amidst general laughter.

It was all light-hearted banter, and it was certainly not what I expected a defeated army to sound like.

But Meier was obviously not in a happy mood when he showed up, long before the noon break, to escort us back to our shack. We were told that for the rest of the day we would be working at the

farm of the *Comtesse Noire*. Some French prisoners also showed up
from the fields. We were all given brooms and told to sweep the yard.
Three stragglers turned up in dusty uniforms and held a whispered
consultation with Meier before disappearing into one of the barns.

The first shots rang out in mid-afternoon: machine-gun fire followed by some explosions. The Pawlak group rushed into their shack
and crowded around the small window.

One of the French prisoners unfurled a small tricolour before
another snatched it off him. 'Idiot!' he shouted. 'What if the Germans try to defend this place?'

'Look through the window, behind the park!'

Sure enough, through the new leaves on the park's trees, we could
make out one, two, three tanks heading east along the nearby highway. They had white stars painted on their sides and soldiers in big
helmets crouched around their turrets. Sporadic shooting accompanied them.

'Americans!' someone shouted, though this was hardly necessary.

We pushed open the door of our enclosure and rushed towards the
highway. Heading east was an endless column of tanks, wheeled
armoured vehicles of various types and small open-top cars with
their windscreens pushed down flat over their hoods. Somebody
identified them as jeeps. Tired-looking soldiers made 'V' for victory
signs at us with their fingers.

'We are Polish prisoners of war!' shouted Preibisz, our English
speaker, just to make sure we were not mistaken for Germans.

But the GIs acted like men who had seen all this before. Every
now and then someone hurled a pack of cigarettes or some cans of
Spam and corned beef in our direction.

'Long live America!' we shouted in unison.

Then, in almost all the languages we knew, the Warsaw Boys
started a new slogan.

'Give us arms!' we yelled in English, French and Polish. 'Give us
arms! We want to kill Nazis.'

But all we got from the victors was more canned meat and cigarettes.

★

A jeep with two US officers in it drove into the farmyard. They spoke briefly to Preibisz, then asked him to accompany them into the manor house as their interpreter. The old countess, in her usual black, was waiting at the front door flanked by her daughters. They made a dignified tableau and seemed to sense that they had nothing to fear from these Americans, who mainly wanted to tell them to put out a white flag. They were quick to comply. Before long the house and all its outbuildings were festooned with white sheets.

Meier appeared, without his rifle and belt, and carefully raised his hands. He looked pale but composed.

'I'll get that bastard!' shouted one of our number.

He rushed towards the German, but several of us pulled him back. 'Stop, you idiot,' said the cook, Marian. 'He didn't do us any harm.'

We escorted the hatless Meier to the road, where he was promptly showered with cigarettes from a passing column and paused to pick them up. For several minutes we watched him march along the road with his arms up, his hands full of American cigarettes. Then a truck came to a halt alongside him and an American soldier with a carbine motioned him to get in.

The road was now swarming with slave labourers who danced and embraced each other, savouring the moment they had dreamed of for years.

Then somebody screamed, 'Let's get Holzer!'

Others picked up the cry. Soon I was part of a crowd of about twenty or thirty people running towards his farm. On the way I noticed that every house I passed was decked out with white sheets of surrender. As we neared the Holzer farm I began to hear the sound of screaming and wailing. We got there to find a melee of people, mostly slave labourers, in a tight knot around something.

Holzer's wife was trying to claw her way through them. 'Leave him, I beseech you, leave him!' she pleaded.

As the crowd parted I saw Holzer's great bulk lying on the ground, his face badly bruised and blood trickling from the corner of his mouth. Some slave labourers were crouched around him. They were trying to put a noose around his neck while others – mainly women – were trying to stop them.

'That man killed prisoners!' someone roared. 'There are two graves in the garden.'

'Kill him!' I heard myself shout, then was almost immediately covered in shame. Was this why I'd been shouting for arms: to join a lynch mob?

The noose was now around Holzer's neck. Men in ragged Soviet uniforms were trying to lift his considerable bulk off the ground while one man was attempting to throw the end of the rope over the thick lower limbs of an ancient tree.

I thought: I'm about to witness a hanging.

In my short life I'd seen the dangling corpses of several innocents whom the Germans had strung up, but I'd never witnessed their final moments when the life was being choked out of them at the end of a rope. Nor was I going to start now. I turned and fled, running, tripping over stones, back towards the road along which I had watched the US Army driving east towards the Elbe. Behind me I heard what sounded like a triumphant roar followed by a piercing female shriek. I quickened my pace, walking along the now empty highway, heading back towards the estate of the *Comtesse Noire* and praying that, in the prevailing anarchy, no harm would come to her or her daughters.

I needn't have worried – no slave labourer or prisoner held a grudge against them. I arrived back to find the cows were being milked. Outside the stables one of the Polish grooms was busy with a curry comb. The only clue to the changed circumstances were the white sheets draped everywhere.

But suddenly it looked as if they might be premature.

Durski was trying to gather us around him for a war council when somebody rushed in shouting, 'The Americans are going back!'

We ran towards the road, staring with disbelief. Sure enough, tanks and armoured vehicles were now moving in the opposite direction. But was it all of them? Might it not just be some of them, and the rest were still heading towards the Elbe?

Then a civilian Pole, recognizable by his 'P' patch and a newly fashioned red and white cockade, pedalled frantically by on his bicycle. 'The Americans are pulling out!' he gasped. 'A whole SS division is coming.' And off he dashed, before we could make any further inquiries.

A whole SS division! And here we were in no-man's-land with Holzer's corpse dangling from a tree. I later learned that this wasn't the case: Holzer survived the lynching attempt, rescued at the last minute by the women, most of them Polish workers and loyal to his wife, who had treated them decently.

In any case, Durski had already decided that, whether an SS division was coming or not, it was crazy to risk recapture. 'We've got to follow the Americans,' he declared and assigned us various tasks. Some of us went to find a cart and two horses, others to procure bicycles. Meanwhile, dusk fell. The white sheets decking the farmhouse looked eerie in the darkness.

Two German soldiers, without belts or caps, turned up. They wanted to give themselves up to the Americans, and Durski agreed to take them with us. 'If we run into Americans, they'll be taken prisoner. And if we run into Germans, they'll tell them we treated them well.'

I was one of the four chosen to be point men. We were to cycle ahead of the remaining nine Warsaw Boys, who would be in the cart with the two Germans.

'Don't forget to leave my bike at the Gasthaus zum Hirsch,' shouted the elderly German whose machine I had stolen.

The whip cracked and the cart lurched forward behind the four cyclists. The French and Russian prisoners, as well as all the slave labourers, stayed behind.

We rode in silence – past houses draped in white flags, their shutters closed, past several burning vehicles of unknown provenance – all the way to Seehausen, where Meier had taken me to get my boil lanced. I don't think we saw a single living thing on our journey.

When we reached the outskirts of the town, a powerful searchlight came on. It revealed our own white flag, carried by a motley bunch wearing a mixture of American and British uniforms.

'Halt, who goes there?' demanded an American voice.

'Escaped Polish prisoners of war,' Preibisz replied in English.

We were allowed to approach the tanks blocking the entrance to the town. Dishevelled-looking soldiers gathered around us. American soldiers never seemed to bother to do up their buttons, or wear belts, but we could tell by the way they carried their weapons that they knew their business.

'Get those Krauts down,' one shouted, pointing to our two German deserters.

We spent the night sheltering from sporadic German shellfire under the massive oak tables at the guesthouse where our stay had started pleasantly enough, drinking tepid draught beer and eating sandwiches Marian had made.

Next morning, the shelling had stopped and Seehausen was basking in spring sunshine. Curious Germans were peering at their conquerors as they strolled around chewing gum and whistling at the girls. Hundreds of Polish women employed in a local factory were flirting with the Americans. Sometimes they disappeared into doorways together or headed for the bushes in the local park.

'When are you guys going home?'

The question came from a Polish American who was distributing chewing gum to anybody who wanted some. It was no more than average curiosity, but his question hit me like a thunderbolt. When indeed?

He obviously had a home somewhere in America and expected to return to it. But where was my home? My mother's Warsaw apartment had probably been destroyed and, when last heard of, she was living in a convent. I had no idea who was living in my father's old house in Maków. My country was now part of the Soviet Empire. And its capital, which I had learned to love, was a heap of ruins.

But how was I going to explain all this to a carefree Polish American who knew how to blow bubbles with his chewing gum?

Still wearing my prisoner-of-war uniform with the huge 'KG' stencilled on the back and clutching an unopened packet of gum, I walked along streets jammed with the vehicles of the most opulent army the world had ever seen. Polish girls munched American chocolate bars and looked right through me. Cheerful French and Belgian prisoners were holding up signs they had made for Paris and Brussels and trying to hitchhike.

After so many false hopes the spring that I had been promised since the autumn of 1939 had finally come.

But I couldn't go home.

I wasn't sure where home was.

# Afterwards

On the day we were told the war had ended, I was dating – if that's the right word for it – an eighteen-year-old German girl named Ute. She lived with her mother in a small half-timbered house in the wooded outskirts of a former prisoner-of-war camp. This had become our third resting place in the twenty-six days since we had reached the American lines at Seehausen, where we were joined by some other prisoners from the Warsaw Uprising who had managed to avoid being liberated by the Russians.

Unfortunately, I wasn't Ute's only suitor: a Soviet ex-prisoner not much older than myself also seemed to be there most of the time. I think Ute's mother encouraged our presence because not all the freed prisoners were so well behaved. Some vengeful survivors of a cruel captivity were busy terrorizing German civilians. Ute seemed quite happy to share her affections and so, in a comradely fashion, we took it in turns to indulge in what newspaper agony aunts used to call 'heavy petting'. This left me a very frustrated virgin indeed.

'Is your prick up yet?' my new Russian friend would amiably inquire, staring at my trousers.

It happened to be my turn with Ute when, on 8 May 1945, we all heard her mother's radio announce that Germany had unconditionally surrendered. I noticed the *hausfrau* wipe away a furtive tear, but her daughter showed little interest in the passing of the Third Reich.

Back at camp I joined in the singing of patriotic songs and we staged a victory parade for some visiting American officers. I think they were surprised to see that the Germans did not hold the monopoly on the goose-step, but they managed some polite applause.

Shortly afterwards, I was wishing Ute, '*Auf wiedersehen!*' We were on the move again. Our new billets were huts set up in the grounds of a disused factory where Polish officers who had been captured in 1939 were awaiting us. A military routine began with bugle calls,

morning calisthenics, foot drill and Sunday church parades. During
Mass we sang a hymn beseeching God to take us home 'weapons in
hand' but we all knew our chances of doing this were slim.

On 19 January 1945, with almost all of Poland occupied by the
Red Army, the Home Army had announced they were standing
down. Towards the end of March, Stalin responded to this by inviting sixteen army leaders to help organize the new Polish Government
of National Unity. Among them was Bór's successor, General Okulicki, who had made the daring train escape from his German escort.
When they presented themselves, they were all kidnapped by the
NKVD and secretly transported to Moscow's Lubyanka Prison
where its expert torturers got some of them to confess that they had
'collaborated with Nazi Germany'.

When the London Poles asked the British and Americans to stop
this obscenity the Russians first of all denied all knowledge of it, saying it was an invention of the 'Fascist Polish Government'. Then, on
5 May, the Kremlin admitted they were holding the men, but Stalin
assured US envoy Harry Hopkins that they would only receive light
sentences. Their three-day trial started on 18 June, with foreign press
and observers from the American and British embassies permitted to
attend. Three of the defendants were acquitted and eight received
sentences of eighteen months or less.

Having thrown this bone to the Anglo-Americans, Stalin did what
he had always intended to do. General Okulicki was sentenced to ten
years' imprisonment but never completed it. According to the
NKVD he died in Butyrka Prison on Christmas Eve 1946, as the
result of a hunger strike. Jan Jankowski, the government-in-exile's
deputy prime minister and its representative in Warsaw throughout
the Uprising, lasted longer. Sentenced to eight years, his unexplained
death came just two weeks before his release date, in 1953. Three
other ministers of the exiled government who had accepted Moscow's invitation to talks in good faith were sentenced to five years'
rigorous imprisonment – a sentence which, in one case, was extended
by another five years.

Western reaction to these sentences would later leave the Poles in no doubt where they stood. On 6 July 1945, the Anglo-Americans withdrew their recognition of the legitimate government-in-exile in London and recognized Moscow's puppet state in Warsaw. By this time, parts of Poland were on the verge of open insurrection.

The Home Army had been reborn as the WIN – the acronym for *Wolność i Niezawisłość* (Freedom and Independence). By no means all of the Home Army had given up their arms when Okulicki told them to stand down, and they still packed a punch. At about the time the Allies were celebrating Victory in Europe, WIN was ambushing the NKVD's 2nd Border Regiment in the Galician village of Kuryłówka, in south-east Poland. At least fifty soldiers were killed.

On 21 May came an even bigger success. A former Stalag at Rembertów, on Warsaw's eastern outskirts, was being used as a holding pen as part of the process that is estimated to have sent some 50,000 Poles, all of whom were deemed politically suspect, to Siberia. In a daring Saturday-night raid, timed to find some of the guards at their most inebriated, WIN stormed their way into the camp and, in just under half an hour, released at least 500 prisoners. These included about 100 sick and wounded from the camp's primitive hospital, who were evacuated in some hijacked trucks.

The émigré newspapers we received from London were full of these stories and declarations that Poland was once again on the verge of a national uprising. And yet, at the same time, we heard the beguiling voice of Radio Warsaw appealing for all Poles to come home and help rebuild the country. We knew, of course, that Radio Warsaw was really Radio Moscow. But after the West had recognized Poland's Communist government who was going to help us? What was the point of fighting on?

'What is the point? C'mon, boys, you disappoint me. If the British and Americans see the country is united – that it refuses to accept Communist rule – the Russians might just give up. Something is bound to happen. We still have a government in London, and we still have an army in the west armed to the teeth.'

The speaker was a Captain Lawina, a former Home Army officer now attached to the Arnhem veterans of the 1st Independent Polish

Parachute Brigade. Over beers in a German Gasthaus he succeeded in persuading me and five of my associates to join WIN. A few days later, we found ourselves at one of the brigade's camps in the British Zone undergoing an intensive course in basic infantry skills and sabotage.

For two weeks we practised keeping our heads down and crawling among piles of old rations tins while a sergeant fired a Bren gun over our heads; we panted over an assault course with Sten guns hanging from our necks; we were taught how to set the fuse on the strange-looking explosive-filled canvas bags the British called 'Gammon' grenades; and we were shown where to put the right amounts of plastique to blow up a bridge. At the end of the two weeks, I realized how inadequate my previous military training had been.

There were also lectures. We were shown a map of Stalin's new Poland – with gains from Prussia in the west partly compensating for its eastern concessions to the Ukraine – and, within these borders, the new administrative districts. We were taught to recognize different uniforms: Soviet NKVD border regiments; Polish People's Militia and the Berling units that had become the Polish People's Army.

'Remember, eighty per cent of the officers are Russians,' Lawina told us. 'They're your enemy. The troops are Poles. Some may have sold out, but others are waiting for their chance to act. It's fighters like yourselves who'll provide it.'

We learned by heart the names and addresses of two WIN contacts – obviously, we couldn't write them down – one of whom was a Dr Kryska in Kraków. We were supposed to report to him.

It was explained that we would undertake the journey by rail, mostly by hitching rides in goods wagons and freight cars. The whole of central Europe was awash with what, in that first anarchic summer of what passed for peace, had become known as 'displaced persons'. All of them were trying to get home, or find somewhere better.

Returning to Poland would involve crossing two frontiers. First, we had to go from the British Zone in West Germany to Soviet-controlled East Germany. Then we had to cross into Poland itself.

'You'll be doing nothing illegal,' Captain Lawina reminded us.

'You're simply responding to appeals to return and make your-self useful. You want to cooperate with the regime, help build a new Poland on top of the ruins of the old one. It's their favourite slogan.'

Before we left, he gave each of us two US five-dollar bills 'for emergencies'.

I was dreaming I was back in one of the cellars at Czerniaków and, as usual, somebody was trying to wake me up and get me back upstairs. I could feel his hand on my shoulder, gentle but insistent.

'Hey, you in the American uniform,' he was saying. 'We're getting close to Warsaw. Don't you want to see the city you helped burn down?'

It was one of Berling's soldiers, or their latest equivalent, who had boarded the train with me at Kraków. They weren't hostile, just curi-ous. They almost invariably gathered around me, feeling the texture of the American and British uniform I wore; it was almost as if I wasn't inside it.

'That's real quality.'

'Look at the soles on those boots.'

'How many uniforms does an American soldier have?'

Then, sooner or later, came their bewildered question, 'What made you come back? Did you believe the propaganda?'

My trip back to Poland was turning into an utter fiasco. Our initial reception, after crossing from the British to the Soviet Zone, had not been as entirely welcoming as Lawina predicted.

'*Armia Krajowa*, eh? So you've come back to sabotage,' said a patently hostile Russian major. 'Do you know what we do to sabo-teurs?'

We were held in a requisitioned apartment building, regularly fed and in comfortable conditions, but all too aware that we were locked in. One of the soldiers who had escorted us there was a member of one of Berling's Polish regiments who had been conscripted as the Red Army rolled through his village in eastern Poland. He didn't look much older than me but claimed he had fought all the way to Berlin. He seemed to miss the good old days. 'Things are really tightening up around here,' he told us. 'Nowadays, you can get five years for raping a German woman.'

Quartered nearby were some Soviet prisoner-of-war returnees waiting to explain why they had betrayed the Revolution by allowing themselves to be taken alive. They often sang the plaintive *'Chubchik'* song, its words a reminder of the Russians I had met in Stalag XI-A's satellite camp at the beginning of the year: 'I'm not afraid of Siberia / Siberia is also Russian soil.'

I was very much afraid of Siberia, or any other Russian soil. Too many Poles had ended up beneath it.

On the third day, after some basic questioning by a pleasant-enough lieutenant regarding our Home Army units and which Stalags we had been in, we were told we were free to continue our journey. After that, it was downhill all the way.

In Berlin, we boarded a freight train that was largely occupied by Russian labourers, mostly women, who were being repatriated. They were not very friendly and refused to let us share their cattle trucks. In desperation we split into two groups of three and squeezed into a couple of the old brakeman's cabooses, on the back of some rolling stock. I was with Długi and Godot, who had been with me at the farm of the *Comtesse Noire*. These shelters were not much bigger than the average telephone booth, and only one of us could sit down at a time. Compressed-air brakes had made them almost obsolete, except in the direst emergencies, and they were rarely occupied.

When we pulled into the new border town of Frankfurt-an-der-Oder, Soviet troops began to inspect the train. First of all we heard them teasing the women.

'So you worked for the Germans, eh?'

'We didn't volunteer, Comrade. They forced us to.'

'And what else did they force you to do?'

Then there was a commotion, with familiar voices shouting protests in a mixture of Polish and Russian. We froze.

'But we've been allowed by the Red Army to go back to Poland, Comrade,' one of our friends was saying.

'Don't you "Comrade" me. Since when are a pig and a goose Comrades?'

I peered through our caboose's narrow window. Beneath the station's pale lighting I could see them, slightly stooped under their shouldered kitbags, being led away by a couple of Russian soldiers. One of them was pointing his Pepesha tommy gun at them.

'Faster, mother-fuckers!' he shouted.

We stood in our caboose, hardly daring to breathe. Any moment now it would be our turn. But gradually the Russian voices faded, to be replaced by the ringing sound a railwayman's hammer makes when the wheels are being tested for cracks. Slowly the train edged forward, creaked over a bridge, then stopped at a small station where the locomotive was disconnected. Exhausted, we climbed on to the slightly curved roof of our wagon, spread out our blankets and fell instantly asleep. We awoke to find that the locomotive had been re-attached. We were rattling at breakneck speed into the rising sun, and were in imminent danger of being shaken off. Somehow, we got ourselves and our blankets down into the caboose area.

On either side of us the western Polish borderlands flashed past. This was the territory that had been annexed by Germany and filled with *Volksdeutsche*. We passed stations where the German place names, given by the Nazis, had been painted out and replaced by their old ones – but written in Russian Cyrillic letters, with our Latin script in much smaller letters underneath. The same went for the signs indicating waiting rooms and toilets. No one could doubt who was in charge.

Eventually, we halted at one of these small Polish stations. Next to us was a proper passenger train with people seated at the windows. We managed to board it unchallenged. As we had hoped, its next stop was Poznań – the rail hub where, ten months earlier, I had been among the Polish wounded exchanging good-natured banter with our recent German opponents in neighbouring ambulance trains. From here we could get a connection for Kraków, home of one of the WIN contacts Lawina had given us.

The train we wanted was at least two hours away. We were looking for the waiting room when we spotted a hut with a Red Cross symbol over its doorway and beneath it a sign: 'Returning Prisoners of War Report Here.' Inside, a friendly-looking woman seated behind a desk asked us for our identification papers. We handed over the ID cards issued to us by the US Army, which gave our names, ranks, birth dates and nationality. She wrote all this carefully down in a large ledger, then handed over three passes issued by the state-owned railways that were valid for three months' free travel anywhere in Poland. Apparently, all returnees from Germany were entitled to them – whether they were POWs, concentration-camp survivors or people who had found themselves working for the Reich. There were all these thousands of people wandering around a broken land, desperate to discover any traces of their previous lives. Before we left, she handed us some banknotes in a currency we didn't recognize.

'I hope you find your families,' she said.

It was the best thing that had happened to us since we left the British Zone.

On the same platform we found a food kiosk selling sausage, dark bread and a sweet soft drink. It cost about a third of the money we had just been given, but we hadn't eaten all day. We sat on our kitbags, on the platform, while we finished our snack.

Suddenly a voice above us inquired, 'And who are you boys?'

He was a short, stocky man. I can't recall what he was wearing, but for Poland in the summer of 1945 there was one thing that made him stand out: he was holding an expensive-looking leather briefcase. We told him we were newly arrived ex-prisoners of war on our way home. He must have already guessed this from our Red Cross-issue American uniforms – just as he knew that we must be Home Army, because we all looked too young to have been captured in 1939.

His hand shot into his case and emerged clutching a silver hip flask. He unscrewed the kind of top that also served as a tumbler, filled it and handed it to Długi.

'Have a nip of some real home-made Polish vodka,' he said. 'Believe me, you're going to need it.'

We each took a slug. It burned my throat a bit on the way down, but I found the after-effects soothing.

Then he squatted down beside us and started talking.

'If you think, because the Germans have gone, our country belongs to us, then you're in for a shock,' he said. 'And it's not going to get any better – not now, when they don't have any armed resistance to deal with.'

Up to that point I don't think any of us could decide whether he was merely a friendly drunk or an NKVD agent provocateur trying to get us to say something incriminating. Either way, all we wanted to do was get away from him. But now he had our complete attention.

'What do you mean?' asked Długi, innocence personified. 'What resistance?'

'You mean you haven't heard? The papers and the radio have been talking of nothing else. The Home Army, or whatever they call themselves lately, has packed it in. Entire regiments are coming out of the forests and lining up to surrender their arms. It's the biggest success for this government since the Americans and the British recognized it.'

He looked at us with his small, shrewd eyes.

'If you wanted to work with the government, the news should please you. If you had something else in mind, perhaps there's still time to go back.'

'We came home to finish our studies and lead a peaceful life,' said Godot evenly.

I thought he sounded unusually convincing. Perhaps he meant it? After all, we hadn't actually done anything yet.

'Well, whatever you do, I wish you luck, boys,' said this amiable dispenser of vodka and bad news. Before he left, he gave us a newspaper. 'It's all there.'

And so it was.

A photograph showed a long line of men at the edge of a forest laying their weapons on a trestle table. Alongside it was a list of local militia stations where members of WIN's urban units were required to report in order to demonstrate their loyalty to the new regime. Bolesław Bierut, a Polish Stalinist whose abject loyalty to Moscow had procured him the presidency of something called the 'People's Council', welcomed all those who wished to build a new system 'on the ruins of the old, corrupt one'. No surprises there. Much more shocking was an appeal from a certain WIN commander asking all those under his command to put aside their differences and join in this Marxist reconstruction of our country.

It was signed: Colonel Jan Mazurkiewicz.

Beneath his signature was the nom de guerre of the man who had commanded me as a very junior member of his headquarters' security platoon: Radosław.

I'd last seen him leaning on a cane with a heavily bandaged leg when I'd decided not to take my own wounded leg down that sewer in Mokotów and had elected, instead, to take my chances with the Germans. Radosław had refused to surrender: until now.

'The train for Kraków is approaching Platform Two,' announced a loudspeaker.

We looked down the track and saw that the train was already slowing to a halt. The locomotive was decked with red and white bunting, and it really did have a sign on the front pleading: 'Workers of the World Unite.'

'Well, we've still got Dr Kryska to see,' I reminded my companions, getting to my feet and picking up my kitbag.

'What for?' said Długi.

He and Godot just sat there looking up at me.

The doors on the Kraków train were being slammed shut.

I said a curt goodbye to Długi and Godot and heaved my kitbag up the steps of a carriage marked 'for soldiers'. After all, I *was* a soldier, I told myself, and – unlike my companions – I wasn't going to let Captain Lawina down.

It was a crowded train – in those days, all the trains were crowded – but I managed to wedge myself on to an overhead baggage rack and slept surprisingly well throughout my journey.

As I emerged from Kraków station, one of the first things I saw were two young men, perhaps only a few years older than myself, with closely shaven skulls, wearing striped prison garb and being escorted by an armed soldier. The trio walked carefully around a woman who was hosing down the dust on the pavement in front of the station.

'Must be from the Home Army,' she said when she saw me looking at them.

I noticed that people rarely said 'WIN'. I just nodded and asked her for directions to the address I had memorized for Dr Kryska.

She pointed to a tramcar and told me which stop to get off.

On the tram people were talking about a long convoy of Soviet trucks that had appeared alongside us, heading east. They were full of furniture, rolled-up carpets and household appliances.

'They're not leaving much behind,' the man standing next to me said.

'At least they're taking themselves away.'

'Yes, but how many are staying?'

My destination was a third-floor apartment, and there was no lift. I trudged up the stairs with my kitbag. But when I got to the doctor's front door, I didn't bother to knock. A typewritten notice with an official-looking stamp and signature had been pasted across the door-jamb. It read: 'This apartment has been sealed by the Citizens' Militia. Anyone who breaks the seal will be prosecuted by a military tribunal.'

I was back on a tramcar, then a train, heading back to the capital just as fast as I could go, burdened by my luggage and a strong desire not to draw undue attention to myself. Presumably, the local militia were either understrength or lacked the necessary dedication to keep the flat under the kind of observation that might have yielded more enemies of the people. Whatever the reason, I knew I had been very lucky. My attempt to visit Dr Kryska might easily have been my undoing.

Now here I was, on a train coming into Warsaw after a long ride from Kraków, dreaming I was back in one of the cellars beneath Czerniaków. Until I realized a member of the People's Army was sitting next to me, shaking me awake and asking if I wanted to see the city I'd helped burn down.

'We didn't do much burning,' I said, standing up and reaching for my kitbag in the luggage rack. 'We were too busy killing Germans. Where were you?'

'Careful, youngster,' he said, giving me a pat on the back. 'Not everybody's as harmless as I am.'

'I know,' I said.

As my train pulled into the makeshift platform (the main station was still far too damaged to reopen) I read the huge sign in red letters above the exit: 'Heroic Warsaw Greets Fighters for the Freedom of the Masses.'

Outside, in the bright August sunshine, some of the masses were raising a cloud of rubble-based dust. It came from thousands of feet and a variety of motor and horse-drawn transport. Drivers called out destinations for the trucks that served as buses; horse-drawn carriages were running on automobile tyres; the cycle-rickshaws that had so intrigued me when I first came to the capital were still thriving. But unlike Kraków, which had hardly been damaged by the war, there were no tramcars. Many of them had perished on our barricades and, in any case, the network of tracks had not yet been repaired. I looked down a roped-off side street and saw soldiers sorting bricks out of the rubble and tossing them into the backs of trucks. There were none of the bulldozers and other machinery the Americans and the British had deployed in Germany. These soldiers seemed to have little more than their bare hands.

I had heard so much talk of Warsaw being levelled that I was quite surprised to see so much of it still standing. I walked down Jerozo-limska Avenue. During the early part of the Uprising I had delivered mail by crossing the trench that had been dug to avoid snipers. Most of the southern side of the avenue appeared outwardly intact. True, its tall buildings were pockmarked by bullets and shrapnel, and the walls were stained black by smoke, but there was glass in the windows and the shops were open.

I entered an *owocarnia* and drank a glass of the fruit juice that is their speciality. The woman in charge of the café agreed to look after my kitbag for the day while I had a look around.

'Fought in the Uprising, did you?' she said, taking in the bits of

Anglo-American uniform the Red Cross had delivered to us in the Stalag.

Outside the café was a man who whispered, 'Dollars? I buy dollars.'

Standing in a doorway, we negotiated a rate for one of the five-dollar bills Lawina had given me. I pocketed the money and walked off, ignoring the importuning of the men with the cycle-rickshaws.

I was heading south, towards Mokotów and my mother's flat.

The first hopeful sign was that the corner grocery shop was open – coloured by Warsaw's ubiquitous smoke stains, certainly, but undeniably open. My heart was pounding as I turned the corner. Opoczynska Street was more or less as I had left it when I said good-bye to my mother, a couple of days before the Uprising started. Not a single building was in ruins – though, admittedly, they all looked gutted and empty – but I had steeled myself for the worst, and this wasn't the worst. At number 12 the gate was open. The stairs were intact, and I walked up to our first-floor apartment. The front door was missing and the place was empty, with not a scrap of furniture, just bare, burned walls. I crossed myself and walked back downstairs.

'How are you?'

The vaguely familiar voice made me jump out of my skin. It was the wife of the caretaker who lived in the basement flat. She was standing in the courtyard, her hands blackened from some clean-ing up.

'And how are your family?' she asked.

I told her, when last heard of, they were living in a convent at Pruszków. Having established that they had not returned to Mokotów, I was going to try to see them there that very afternoon.

'Almost everybody survived in this street,' she said. 'Those mad-men from the Uprising never managed to capture this place, so the Germans just kicked everybody out and tried to burn it down. It's all the fault of that General Bór, isn't it? All right for him. He's in England, and we're left with this.'

I decided it was pointless to remind her that she was speaking to one of the 'madmen' in question. Moscow's version of events was undoubtedly gaining ground. The old Polish officer corps who had led the Uprising were constantly being derided as a decadent – even corset-wearing – bunch with distinctly pro-German tendencies. A recurring theme was that the Home Army leadership were all enjoying the good life abroad, while ordinary Poles had to pick up the mess.

'They used kids like you to destroy this city,' a Polish lieutenant told me later. He and I got into conversation in a bar, and I told him how old I had been during the fighting.

By now I was in Pruszków, in search of my family, having arrived from Mokotów on the recently reopened electric suburban railway. I had convinced a wary Mother Superior of my identity – 'I'm sure you realize the delicate position the Church is in under this . . . ahem . . . system' – but all she could offer was some disappointing news. My mother, Jerzy, Aunt Olga and grandmother were no longer at the convent. They had all decamped to Łódź about a month ago.

This, of course, made perfect sense. My grandmother's house was there, and she was obviously anxious to reclaim it. Indeed, when I arrived in Łódź a few days later, I discovered they were staying with one of my grandmother's friends because squatters had occupied her home and a local People's Committee was 'considering her case'. Shortly after my arrival, they found in her favour and I helped her move back in.

'So much for their Communism,' said the squatter, who seemed to think I was some sort of hired help. 'Here I am, a working man with a family, and a general's widow is taking all this for herself.'

My mother greeted her teenaged son, just home from the war, in her usual restrained fashion. Grandmother and Aunt Olga made a great fuss of me, but my mother's main concerns seemed to be the date of my last bath and whether I was importing any Stalag lice. Should she have my clothes washed or incinerated? Unlike her mother and sister she seemed unimpressed by my war stories. When I wrote some of them down, she read them without comment. She made it plain that she considered the Uprising a shambles and, like the lieutenant in the bar, thought the Home Army had no business recruiting children.

This made me angry: I didn't regard myself as a child. And nor was I – except in the tedious matter of my virginity, something I intended to address at the earliest opportunity. Other mothers, I noticed, would talk endlessly of their sons' exploits, even if they were confined to distributing the *Biuletyn Informacyjny* and painting graffiti. My own never said a word – at least, not in front of me – though Aunt Olga assured me that when she'd heard enough inflated tales of minor derring-do, my mother enjoyed shutting her friends up with mention of a wounded son recently returned from Germany.

Schools were reopening, and by my seventeenth birthday I was studying for my matriculation – though history was not on the curriculum. Apparently, we were waiting for new textbooks that taught a view of Russo-Polish relations, and particularly the war of 1920, that had previously been denied to Polish students. My mother was waiting too. She was waiting for the husband she had not seen for six years to arrange passage for her and her two sons across Communist Poland's closed borders.

Colonel Władysław Michniewicz was ideally placed to do so. He was now based in Rome as deputy chief of intelligence at General Anders' 2nd Polish Corps. Polish military intelligence (*Dwójka*) was busy setting up a network within Soviet-occupied Poland. I don't know exactly how my mother and her husband managed to maintain contact, but I do know that by the early part of 1946 Michniewicz had begun to put in place our escape plan. False French laissez-passer permits were somehow provided for all three of us. My mother was also put in touch with a smuggler who liked to call himself 'Captain Piotrowski' and who owned a truck.

Shortly after Churchill had famously observed that 'an Iron Curtain' had descended on Europe, Piotrowski's truck crossed it at one of the few places where a chink of light remained. Poland's border with Czechoslovakia was two years away from the Communist putsch that would turn it into another Soviet satellite, and there was still unhindered passage via Austria to Italy.

For all three of us a lifetime's exile had begun in the growing Polish diaspora. My mother would eventually settle in Argentina with her husband and Jerzy. In Italy, I enlisted in Anders' 2nd Polish Corps and was stationed at their headquarters, at the Adriatic seaport of Ancona, where one of the enthusiastic amateurs that hung around its gates at last relieved me of my virginity.

Six months later, I moved to Britain as part of the Polish Resettlement Corps, a non-combatant unit. This was intended to give Poles under British command who wished to settle in Britain the chance to learn English and perhaps get some vocational training. The Labour government that had ousted Churchill had set it up despite considerable opposition from their trade union supporters, who were often great admirers of 'Uncle Joe' and took a dim view of those who spurned the Socialist Utopia he had so kindly arranged for us. During the Uprising, when people of similar views either refused to believe that Stalin wanted us dead – or thought we deserved it anyway – George Orwell, writing on 1 September 1944, had railed in the socialist weekly *Tribune* against Britain's 'boot-licking propagandists of the Soviet regime'. Two years on, the author of the newly published *Animal Farm* remained a lonely prophet.

About 114,000 of us volunteered for the Resettlement Corps. Some changed their minds and went home, or moved to other English-speaking countries. But the majority remained, and many managed to bring over their families. In 1951, the UK Census put Britain's Polish-born population at 162,339. I arrived in England speaking very little English – no more than the few sentences I'd picked up in the Stalag. Just under three years later, I was fluent enough to get into a respected American college.

For this I have to thank the intensive tuition I received from the Resettlement Corps' teachers, many of them recently discharged British officers. The teaching usually took place in the huts the British called 'Nissen' and the Americans 'Quonset' as we moved from one crumbling and often freezing wartime camp to another. We started near Liverpool then went to Dewsbury, in Yorkshire, where I was able to move into comfortable digs before being transferred to a former American airfield at Bodney, in Norfolk. Most of the time we remained in uniform and were paid British Army rates – in my case a lance corporal's, because the 2nd Polish Corps had accepted my last Home Army rank.

I ended up in London staying in a boarding house in Streatham, run by a Polish colonel, and working at the Peek Frean biscuit factory in Bermondsey. We were sometimes allowed to take home bags of broken biscuits – a welcome addition to our pay in a Britain impoverished by its long war, where food rationing was still tightly observed. Another bonus was the cheerful and flirtatious cockney girls working alongside me.

Having matriculated in Polish, with English as a secondary language (some of the papers I sat were in English), I just failed to get into the London School of Economics. Then I saw an advertisement in a Polish language newspaper. Alliance College in Cambridge Springs, Pennsylvania, had been founded in 1912 'to provide opportunities for Americans of Polish descent to learn about the Mother Country'. In the fall of 1949, I arrived there to read social sciences. It was, of course, accepted that as an incoming Pole who had never lived in America my own needs were exactly the opposite of those expressed in the charter laid down by its founding fathers.

A greater contrast to the Bermondsey biscuit factory and Austerity Britain would be hard to imagine. A campus of lawns and copper beeches surrounded neo-classical nineteenth-century red-brick buildings with a central clock tower and portico entrance. To supplement my scholarship I undertook various jobs, including mowing the college grass, washing the windows and writing speeches in Polish for its president, his own being a little rusty. In short, I acted exactly like any other ambitious kid who had never had to throw a grenade, crawl through a sewer, or lie wounded on a stretcher wondering whether he was about to be shot or saved.

By now the seed sown by my father back in Maków had firmly taken root; I had decided I wanted to become a foreign correspondent. Somebody advised me that, if I was serious about it, I should apply for a place at Columbia University's Graduate School of

Journalism, in Manhattan – the only Ivy League journalism school. I
followed up my letter there by going to New York and meeting the
admissions tutor, mostly to show him that, despite the funny foreign
name, I could speak reasonable English. He didn't make any promises, pointing out that they had only sixty-five places for prospective
students from home and abroad. But he was curious about my
background – though, like most people, he confused the Warsaw
Uprising with the much smaller affair in the ghetto the previous year,
when the Jews had at last fought back.

I graduated from Alliance in the summer of 1951 and started at
Columbia that September. At the end of the first semester, there was
a ritual culling of those deemed unlikely to succeed. The admissions
tutor thought I needed to improve my vernacular English and urged
me to watch more movies. Otherwise, I was considered promising
material and was reminded that Joseph Conrad was another Pole who
had spoken French before he spoke English. Would Columbia have
failed Conrad? Maybe they would have made him tighten things up
a bit.

In June 1952, I left Columbia with the Masters in Journalism that
got me my start as a reporter on the *Bethlehem Globe-Times*, the daily
newspaper for the steel-making city in eastern Pennsylvania. On
11 November 1954, Memorial Day, I was among 50,000 new US Citizens renouncing all fealty 'to any foreign prince, potentate or
sovereign' when we celebrated our Oath of Allegiance at New York's
Yankee Stadium. I was working in New York at the time, having
progressed from the local newspaper to the head office of the Associated Press, the global news agency.

Two years later, I had been posted to its bureau in Paris. I lived
there with my first wife, Tamara, who was originally from the
Ukraine. We had met at Columbia, where she was reading political
science. Our son, Andrew Junior, had just been born and four years
later his sister, Lisa, would arrive. I had been calling myself 'Andrew'
rather than 'Andrzej' since shortly after starting on the *Globe-Times*.
Most Americans, even second-generation immigrants, just couldn't
get their tongues around foreign names. And Andrew was a better
byline.

My arrival in Paris coincided with Eastern Europe's most turbu-
lent year since 1945. After Stalin died, in March 1953, there had been
vicious infighting in the Kremlin. Beria, the NKVD chief whose
long list of crimes included the Katyn massacre, had been shot. Then,
in February 1956, the 20th Congress of the Communist Party in
Moscow heard Nikita Khrushchev denouncing Stalin for the murderous despot everybody with an ounce of sense knew he was. So
began the Khrushchev Thaw.

The meltdown of the hated Stalinist clones the Soviets had
installed in its satellites was almost immediate. Poland's Bolesław
Bierut, who had been attending the congress, never even made it
home. A few days after Khrushchev's speech, this devout Stalinist
died in Moscow in unexplained circumstances. There were rumours
of suicide.

Bierut was eventually succeeded by Władysław Gomułka, who
had quarrelled with the Bierut faction and been kicked out of
the party for 'right-wing reactionary deviation'. This was a vile
calumny. Gomułka was a good Communist, but after Khrushchev's
revelations about Stalin he realized a more populist approach was
needed.

The liberalization that followed became known as Gomulka's
Thaw. One of the things he did was follow the Soviet leader's own
example and order the immediate release of political prisoners. He
made it easier for Poles to travel abroad too. Some of them came to
Paris where, as the Associated Press's only locally based Polish-speaking
reporter, I found I had a rich vein of stories. Some of the ex-prisoners
had been horribly tortured by Polish Stalinist interrogators in order
to extract meaningless confessions for kangaroo courts that were
going to convict them anyway. A favourite method was to inflict cigarette burns on the lips and eyelids.

One day, somebody told me that Radosław had been released. I
was rather shocked, as I didn't know he had been jailed. It appeared
that, in 1949, confident of his status as one of the men who had initi-
ated the ceasefire between WIN and the Communists, he had written
a letter to Stanisław Radkiewicz objecting to the continuing persecution of former Home Army soldiers. Radkiewicz's official title was

Minister of Public Security, but everybody knew he was head of the
Polish Secret Police (*Urząd Bezpieczeństwa*). He had been brought up
in Russia, fought in the Revolution and the civil war, and was personally acquainted with Stalin. In the 1930s, during the Great Purge,
he was said to have personally liquidated elements of the Polish
Communist Party considered disloyal, with his own gun. Perhaps
Radosław thought he knew Radkiewicz well enough by now to
write him a sharp note. Possibly he even assumed there might be a bit
of mutual respect. After all, how many wounds had the Nazis given
Radkiewicz?

During the two years of incarceration before his show trial began,
Radosław was regularly beaten and tortured. Some of his teeth were
pulled out. In court the prosecutor submitted the usual confession of
conspiratorial activities. At the end of the trial he was sentenced to
life imprisonment. By the time the Gomułka Thaw arrived, he had
been in jail for seven years – slightly longer than his service in the
Second World War.

I last saw Radosław a few months before I left Poland with my
mother and Jerzy, and he looked a broken man then. It was 2 November 1945, and the occasion was an All Souls' Day ceremony to
honour the growing number of the Home Army's fallen who
had been gathered at the Powązki Military Cemetery, in Warsaw.
(Masked search parties combing the city's rubble for makeshift
graves were rarely disappointed.) This kind of occasion made the
authorities jumpy, but they hadn't quite worked up the nerve to stop
them yet. I had heard about the ceremony and decided to come up
from Łódź for it – though it would mean missing a boxing match I
had been thinking of watching. There were posters all over town
announcing the return to the ring of the intrepid Sergeant Pawlak
whom I had last seen being marched off to jail for threatening farmer
Holzer.

I still had the valid rail pass the Red Cross woman had given me,
and I used it quite regularly. There had been a couple of trips to
Maków to pay my respects at my father's grave and, since I was in
uniform, to salute him soldier to soldier. After one of these visits

I returned with one of his fur coats that had been stored with a neighbour. My mother sold it at the local flea market. We needed the money. I also visited Ada, in Kraków. She was still working at the furniture factory, which went on producing goods as if nothing untoward had happened over the last six years. Herr Wimmer, the nice Nazi, had eloped with his Polish paramour.

It was still light when I arrived at the cemetery for the All Souls' Day ceremony. I could tell something unusual was afoot by the number of People's Army patrols pacing about with their Pepesha tommy guns. Hundreds of fresh graves were lined up in neat ranks. On the wooden crosses were their names, the pseudonyms they had fought under and their ages: I looked hard to find anyone over twenty-five. I had difficulty pushing my way through the crowd – though, once they had taken in the uniform, people usually moved aside for me. I saw a stack of wreaths and a pile of wood ready to be lit. There was a small group of men and women lined up in two ranks. Some of them wore the white-visored caps of university students; some, like myself, were wearing bits of uniform.

The two ranks were called to attention.

'On the soil of our liberated country, next to the graves of our comrades who have fallen to make it free, I am lighting this symbolic fire,' said Radosław.

I hardly recognized him at first in his civilian suit, the thinning hair almost completely white. Then, as the flames rose higher, I could make out the colonel I'd known in Czerniaków with the frustrated Russian radio operators in his headquarters, trying and failing to call in artillery support: '*Elektron, Elektron.* Why don't you answer me, *Elektron?*'

I felt the tears streaming down my cheeks, but I didn't care. The woman next to me was sobbing.

Radosław turned towards what was left of his unit. 'May God protect Poland,' he intoned.

We all started to sing the words of our national anthem (People's Army included). But what would the last line be?

Before the war it had been: 'Oh God, protect our Fatherland and

Freedom.' During the German occupation this was always amended
to: 'Oh God, *return* our Fatherland to Freedom.' But Radosław had
referred to 'the soil of our liberated country'.

Did he believe that? Had the Russians liberated us? Surely we were
still under occupation?

There was no hesitation. Voices swelled defiantly into the 'return'
version, and this included the sentinels clutching their Soviet
weaponry.

Years later, after his release from prison, Gomułka's regime made
my old commander vice-president of an umbrella organization that
looked after the interests of all the veterans who fought the Germans,
no matter which badge they had worn, and promoted him accordingly.

Brigadier General Jan Mazurkiewicz died, in May 1988, at the age
of ninety-five, having outlived the secret police chief Radkiewicz,
who was six years his junior, by about six months.

No charges were ever pressed against Radkiewicz who, for almost
ten years, had been one of the chief architects of Stalinist terror in
Poland, responsible for the execution of men who should have
received the highest honours in the land.

Heinz Reinefarth, the SS-Gruppenführer who complained that
he did not have enough ammunition to kill all the civilians on his
hands at Wola, also led a charmed life. Despite repeated Polish
requests that he be extradited to face charges of mass murder he
enjoyed a high-profile post-war career as a lawyer and local politician
in Schleswig-Holstein. When he died, aged seventy-five, he was
drawing a full general's pension.

Persistent reports that Oskar Dirlewanger joined the Foreign
Legion and fought in French Indo-China before finding employment
in President Nasser's Egypt were never proved. More likely, he was
the SS officer captured in June 1945 in the French-occupied part of
Germany who was beaten to death when he somehow fell into the
hands of recently released Polish prisoners.

If Mazurkiewicz had lived another couple of years, my commander at Czerniaków would have seen President Lech Wałęsa – our

first domiciled non-Communist head of state since 1945 – receive the presidential banner, sashes and state seals on 22 December 1990, in Warsaw, from Ryszard Kaczorowski, the last president of the Polish government-in-exile in London.

Thus for me, and thousands like me, the Second World War ended where it began: in Poland.

# Further Reading

Borowiec, Andrew. 2001. *Destroy Warsaw! Hitler's Punishment, Stalin's Revenge*. Westport, CT: Praeger.

Burton, John. 1986. *Mirador: My Term as Hitler's Guest*. London: Regency Press.

Davies, Norman. 2004. *Rising '44: 'The Battle for Warsaw'*. London: Penguin Books.

Forczyk, Robert. 2009. *Warsaw 1944: Poland's Bid for Freedom*. Oxford: Osprey Publishing.

Karski, Jan. 2012 (1944). *Story of a Secret State: My Report to the World*. London: Penguin Classics.

Krall, Hanna. 1986. *Shielding the Flame*. New York, NY: Henry Holt & Company.

Lukas, Richard. 2007. *Forgotten Holocaust: The Poles Under German Occupation 1939–1944*. New York, NY: Hippocrene Books.

Zamoyski, Adam. 2008. *Warsaw 1920: Lenin's Failed Conquest of Europe*. London: HarperCollins.